Flemming Hansen, Jeanette Rasmussen,
Anne Martensen and Birgitte Tufte (eds.)

CHILDREN

– CONSUMPTION, ADVERTISING AND MEDIA

Copenhagen Business School Press

Flemming Hansen, Jeanette Rasmussen,
Anne Martensen and Birgitte Tufte (eds.)

CHILDREN
– CONSUMPTION, ADVERTISING AND MEDIA

1. edition 2002

© Copenhagen Business School Press, 2002

Cover: Torben Lundsted
Typeset and print by Narayana Press, Gylling
Printed in Denmark
English revision: Nikki Lengkeek
ISBN 87-630-0100-4

Distribution:
Scandinavia

CBS Press/DBK Logistik Service, Mimersvej 4,
DK-4600 Koge, Denmark
Phone: +45 3269 7788, fax: +45 3269 7789

North America

Copenhagen Business School Press
Books International Inc.
P.O. Box 605
Herndon, VA 20172-0605, USA
Phone: +1 703 661 1500, fax: +1 703 661 1501

Rest of the world

Marston Book Services, P.O. Box 269
Abingdon, Oxfordshire, OX14 4YN, UK
Phone: +44 (0) 1235 465500, fax: +44 (0) 1235 465555

E-mail Direct Customers: direct.order@marston.co.uk
E-mail Booksellers: trade.order@marston.co.uk

TABLE OF CONTENTS

PREFACE

The idea behind the feature book, *Children – Consumption, Advertising and Media,* came from an international seminar on Children's Socialization as Consumers and their Perception of Advertising held by the Forum for Advertising Research, Department of Marketing, Copenhagen Business School in June 2001. At this seminar it was decided that it would be a valuable contribution to the field to gather together the newest international research on children and advertising.

We thank all the authors for their contributions and interest in being a part of this book. Furthermore, a special thank you to our research assistant, Lotte Yssing Hansen for her outstanding work in both reviewing the contributions and in the finalizing phase of the book. Thank you also to research assistant Lars Bech Christensen for his work in reviewing the contributions to the book.

Flemming Hansen and Jeanette Rasmussen
Frederiksberg, June 2002

1

CHILDREN

– CONSUMPTION, ADVERTISING AND MEDIA[1]

By Anne Martensen and Birgitte Tufte

INTRODUCTION

Research into *children and advertising* has been carried out internationally for many years. Until recently most of the research has taken place in the United States and Canada (Adler 1980, Dorr 1987, Seiter 1995, Pecora 1998, Ward, Wackman & Wartella 1997).

With increasing interest among politicians, parents, teachers and others all over the world due to globalization of the media – and the possible influence of advertising on children – the topic has gradually appeared on the agenda of European researchers as well (Bjurström 1994, Schultz Jørgensen (ed.) 1992, Borch 1996, Brembeck & Johansson 1996 (ed.), GfK 1997, Gunter & Furnham 1998, Sverdrup & Lunde 1995, Tufte 1993, 1999, Werner 1994).

A characteristic feature of research into advertising in general and in relation to children in particular is that it has taken place in the private as well as in the public sector. As early as in the 1920s and 1930s, private companies in the United States carried out large-scale market research. Public-sector research into advertising at universities and other institutions of education is more recent. Research into advertising has therefore always been characterized by different interests and resources.

Generally it can be said that the connecting thread in research has followed developments in media research, which means a shift from the effect of the content of media to an increasing interest in how media products are used in everyday life and how messages are decoded and understood. In other words, this represents a move from research into the effect of media to research into receptive and cultural studies. Whereas early media research focused on the sender perspective (the stimulus-response model), to an increasing extent modern-day research focuses on recipients, i.e. the ways in which recipients use the media in relation to their daily life and customs, their social relations and culture. A number of recently published studies on television, which focus on recipients, conclude with a new concept on »strong viewers« – that an active production of meaning takes place in the viewing situation, and that neither children nor adults are significantly affected. The concept of »the strong viewer« can be seen as analogous to the concept of the »competent child« and theories on children as constructive actors presented in recent child culture research (James et al. 1998, Qvortrup et al. 1994).

The American media researcher Ellen Wartella commented recently that a shift in paradigms has taken place in research, which focuses on children and media. While conclusions in the early phase promulgated that children were severely affected by the media, recent research has supported what she refers to as »the strong child« paradigm, since many studies suggest that children are able to distinguish between fact and fiction and adopt a critical attitude to media content. Ellen Wartella suggests more research is needed that focuses on children as persons who need protection, depending on their age, but who are also curious individuals capable of acting individually.

The idea of 'direct' effect preoccupied early media researchers many of whom argued that TV programming content was cognitively processed. Accordingly they tended to examine how children were influenced by and learned from TV by conducting simple experimental tests. Over the years, however, there has been a gradual shift from focusing on the effect of the media. Today theories from various disciplines are used when researchers are working with media, advertising and consumption. Interdisciplinary approach has become a key concept as will be seen from the collection of chapters in this book.

The aim of the book is to present recent studies made by researchers working in the field of consumption, advertising and media in relation to children, in order to shed light on the relationship between consumer behavior, advertising and communication in general and especially in relation to children and adolescents.

There seems to be no direct connection between the influence of advertising and consumer behavior. A range of variables play a role and the perspective should rather be from the recipient's point of view than from that of the sender (Katz & Liebes

1984, 1988, Höijer 1990). As mentioned earlier, mass communication theories are analogous to theories on »the competent child« and not least on the consumer as active and competent (Young 2002).

The discussion about children's understanding of television advertising and children as consumers has intensified recently in European countries, since advertising targeting children was banned in Sweden. With the Swedish presidency of the European Union (EU) during 2001 many people thought that the Swedish ban on advertising to children might be extended to all EU states. So far this has not been the case.

For many years it has been a central issue in public debates as to whether children are able to distinguish between commercials and the content of programmes.

Several studies show that most children are able to distinguish between the content of programmes and commercials when they are about seven years old. However, it is also emphasized that some children are able to make the distinction by the age of 3 or 4, while others are not able to do so until the age of 9 or 10. It has also been documented that the ability to distinguish between commercials and the content of programmes is closely related to children's ability to understand the purpose of advertising. If children understand the purpose of advertising they will to a greater extent be able to distinguish between programmes and commercials. The age at which children are able to understand the purpose of advertising and the extent to which they understand it depends very much on their family's attitude to advertising and the role played by their school in explaining and discussing the subject.

Many of the studies carried out on children and advertising and on children as consumers end up pointing to the necessity of what is called *advertising literacy* or *media literacy*. Nevertheless, media literacy is still lacking in educational curricula in the schools of most countries.

When it comes to studies regarding *children as consumers* there has recently been a growing interest in this field internationally. State of the art is given in one of the chapters in this book (Roedder John 2002), but even in the Nordic countries where the topic is new on the research agenda some research has been published (Frønes & Brusdal 2000, Feilitzen 1999, Drotner 2001, Halling & Tufte 2002). Most of the studies mentioned are qualitative with a cultural approach and are linked to children's role in relation to mass media. However, quantitative data and interesting new aspects on children as consumers are presented in a recent publication from the Forum for Advertising Research, Copenhagen Business School (Hansen et al. (ed.) 2002).

METHOD

Empirical studies can be categorized in several ways; however, the most important distinction is probably whether the study is of a qualitative or quantitative nature.

Qualitative studies, where relatively few unstructured exploratory interviews are carried out, e.g. in the form of in-depth interviews, focus groups, projective techniques and the like, has by far been the most commonly used data collection method for studies focusing on children, their socialization process and the factors that influence it. Rarely are quantitative studies carried out using a larger representative sample of children and a more or less structured questionnaire followed by certain statistical analyses.

The reason for this is that qualitative studies are often carried out when the knowledge of the studied area is limited. In this case, as a first step, a qualitative study may contribute to a greater understanding of the problem – this knowledge can then be used to develop hypotheses. However, in order to confirm or refuse the proposed hypotheses, it is necessary to carry out a quantitative study. The purpose of the quantitative study is precisely to discover whether the trends that appeared on a small scale will reappear on a larger scale. Thus, quantitative research is a form of conclusive research. During the last 25 years, researchers have been very interested in the research areas 'children's socialization process as consumers' and 'children and advertisements', however, the areas have been characterized by great heterogeneity with a great number of theoretical approaches. Further, the possibilities of proposing hypotheses that could subsequently be tested quantitatively have been limited.

Another important reason why studies have so far largely been of a qualitative nature is that the respondents are children. This relates to several issues, such as:

- Preschool children cannot read and so cannot complete a written questionnaire. Therefore, if the target group consists of children under the age of 7-8 years, the minimum requirement is that the parents participate in the study. In this case, the question becomes whose attitude is being measured, the children's or the parents'?
- Questionnaires of a certain length require great patience on the part of the child, so neither telephone interviews nor personal interviews are suitable. Only postal questionnaires that can be returned to several times seem workable.
- Depending on the child's age, her/his vocabulary clearly limits the type of questions that can be asked. Therefore, many studies have merely observed the children in more or less 'natural' surroundings to register their behavior.
- Small children, in particular, find it difficult to comprehend several different types of scales (Likert scale, Semantic scale, Paired comparison scale etc.) and more than a very few (measured 2-3) answering categories.

Even so, in relation to the studies described in the present book, it is interesting to note two aspects. First, it is worth noting that both qualitative and quantitative data collection methods are used in the described chapters. Secondly, the qualitative and quantitative results and conclusions correspond very well.

The last-mentioned fact prompts us to conclude that quantitative studies are also well suited as a method of data collection when dealing with children, and that the two methods of analysis should therefore be used in conjunction with each other in the future. The qualitative studies are used to gain preliminary insight into the problem and to develop a number of hypotheses, which may subsequently be tested quantitatively to elucidate the general application of the results. In certain situations, the quantitative results may also give rise to the identification of new problem areas where the existing knowledge is inadequate, and where further qualitative studies are needed.

STRUCTURE OF THE BOOK

This book consists of 10 chapters written by researchers from different countries.

The first section presents reviews of research in relation to consumption, advertising and media, the following section present new studies regarding the topic of the book; the ninth chapter focuses on the ethical implications of consumer behavior principles in relation to children, followed by the final chapter which discusses the commercialization of the classroom.

In CHAPTER 2, »Consumer Socialization of Children: A Retrospective Look at Twenty-Five Years of Research«, *Deborah Roedder John* provides an excellent literature review of the extensive research carried out over the last 25 years within the area of children's socialization process. The 'humble beginnings' for this area of research came in the shape of an article by Scott Ward in the *Journal of Consumer Research* in 1974, which defined children's socialization as »processes by which young people acquire skills, knowledge, and attitudes relevant to their functioning as consumers in the marketplace«. Since then, many different research directions and theoretical approaches have been adopted, which has made the area very heterogeneous.

Deborah Roedder John perceives the structuring of the most important contributions throughout the last 25 years as a challenge. She approached the task by developing a new conceptual framework to describe the stages of consumer socialization, which may be seen as a further development of theories on consumer socialization, for example Piaget (1957), Selman (1980) and Barenboim (1981)

Children's knowledge, skills, attitudes and values are largely a function of how old they are, which makes age the most important factor for children's development as consumers. Accordingly, Deborah Roedder John's frame of reference is developed around three age groups: 3-7 year olds are characterized as being at the conceptual stage; 7-11 year olds as being at the analytical stage; and 11-16 year olds as being at the reflective stage. For each of the three age groups, she explains what typically characterizes the children as to their cognitive and social development, that is, what knowledge do the children have, what are their motives and how do they think and behave as consumers in different situations as they get older?

The frame of reference for children's consumer socialization will henceforth be the point of departure for a discussion and literature review of five central areas that represent the outcomes of the socialization process and therefore to a lower or higher degree exerts influence on children's knowledge, skills, motives and values. The five areas are as follows:

1 Children's advertising knowledge
2 Transaction knowledge (including knowledge particularly related to products, brands, shopping and pricing)
3 Children's decision making skills and strategies
4 Purchase request and negotiation strategies
5 Children's consumption motives and values

The many empirical studies related to the three age groups once again support children's growing sophistication about products, brands, advertising, shopping, pricing, decision-making strategies and influence approaches.

The final part of the chapter provides a perspective of the area. Deborah Roedder John discusses the inadequacy and vagueness of the present theoretical as well as empirical studies, and also where future research, in particular, should be focusing its efforts. Each of the five areas mentioned earlier is addressed. Among the most significant questions that need to be answered, the following should be highlighted:

1 How does persuasion knowledge develop for children over the age of 12?
• Persuasive intent of advertisements?
• Specific advertising tactics and appeals?
• Type of bias or deception in advertisements, social context?

How can this insight be used for public policy concerns about adolescent response to advertisements for products such as cigarettes and alcoholic beverages?

2 How do children of different ages interpret and understand brands in relation to:
- Consumption symbolism at brand name level?
- What influences children's perception of brands, and how can they be changed?
- How does such an understanding relate to values in society (materialism etc.)?

3 Understanding of children's shopping skills:
- How do these skills develop over age?
- What factors initiate such changes?
- How do children compare different product attributes such as size, price, volumes and so on?
- How do children understand the concept 'value for money' (price contra quality)?

4 What decision strategies do children possess at different ages, and how do these strategies emerge over time (especially age 7–11)?

5 What goals do children of different ages have for consumer decision-making in relation to:
- Choosing a novel product, being surprised, having fun and so on?
- How do these goals differ from adult goals (making good decisions with least cognitive effort/rational input, buying the best product and so on)?
- How do children's goals compare to decision-making skills and behavior in different age groups?
- How do changes in goals during childhood influence the decision-making process?

6 How does the family influence the development of:
- Children's advertising, persuasion and transaction knowledge?
- The children's decision-making skills?
- The children's consumption motives and values?
- How does different family communication patterns influence these areas?
- How do other children and different institutions influence knowledge, skills and values?

7 What influence do technological changes have on children's socialization process?
- Internet, mobile phones, cable TV and the like

As you will see later, the present book's contributions will answer some of these questions.

The CHAPTER 3 by *Cecilia von Feilitzen,* »Times are Changing and Youth with Them. On Young People's Media Use in Sweden«, gives a description of the new global media landscape, which is changing rapidly with increasing access to more TV channels, national and international. She focuses on the changing media landscape and the generation factor, with Sweden as an example.

The increasing amount of media and the convergence of them provide the same media products to larger and larger parts of the world which means more and more advertising and more new advertising formats addressing not least children and young people.

The average media use of Swedish 15-24 year olds is 6 ½ hours per day, and – as she emphasizes – although the press says that the computer and the Internet have taken over TV viewing it is a fact that TV is the most important media for young people. She concludes by mentioning the five media that the 17 year-old young people in Sweden found most important in terms of entertainment/pleasure and knowledge/information. Boys as well as girls were of the opinion that television was the most important medium for entertainment/pleasure, whereas the boys gave priority to the Internet and the television when it came to knowledge and information. The girls would choose books first and television second. In relation to this, Cecilia von Feilitzen points to the need of conducting future in-depth studies with regard to what young people mean by more general expressions such as »facts and information«, »knowledge and information«, »news« and the like.

The CHAPTER 4 written by *Flemming Hansen, Jens Halling and Jens Carsten Nielsen,* »Danish Children's Upbringing as Consumers«, begins by describing the background of the research project »Danish Children as Consumers« in relation to the Forum for Advertising Research. The project dates back to 1999 and was inspired by Deborah Roedder John's chapter published in this book.

In 2000 Forum obtained access to large parts of a children's index database within Gallup/Taylor Nelson Sofres's annual children/youth media index. When the data became available there was a large amount of interesting information regarding children's behavior and upbringing as consumers that has now been collected in a book (Hansen et al. 2002). The chapter presents some of these data on children's economy and saving abilities, children and the emerging electronic world, brand awareness, transaction knowledge and shopping, media use and interest and activities in general. The chapter provides a picture of Danish children and young adolescents as active and busy with school, friends, sport, work, duties, entertainment and shopping. From an early age they have their own money and savings, and they become increasingly aware of money-related issues as they grow up. They exert influence in relation to the consumption of the family, and as they grow older they make their own purchases. They control their own media consumption and take part in electronic networks. The chapter argues that these Danish children and young adolescents are the first computer literate generation, a viewpoint which is not, however, shared with all of the other authors of this book, several of whom argue for media literacy as a necessity.

The authors emphasize that the findings are based on a collection of quantitative data, which means that it has not been possible to examine certain problems dealt with in the international research. However, the chapter gives an interesting summary of some of the findings and presents a varied picture of children's and young people's upbringing as consumers in a modern society.

Throughout modern history, many studies have focused on the effect of TV-advertisements on children, paying particular attention to the influence advertisements have on children's purchases of the advertised products or their pestering. The results have given rise to heated debates. One school of researchers and practitioners feel that advertisements have a damaging effect on children and that restrictions and limitations of the TV-advertisements should be employed for this age group. The other school of researchers, on the other hand, feels that the education of children should be emphasized to a higher degree, so that they learn to understand the purpose of advertisements more quickly and can see through their devices to finally be able to use advertisements as a natural part of their decision process.

In the CHAPTER 5, »Children and Advertising: Politics and Research in Consumer Socialization«, *Adrian Furnham* categorizes many contributions into 'opposite approaches', which he terms 'Educationalists' versus 'Protectionists' approaches and 'Academic' versus 'Public Policy' approaches. These two approaches perhaps simplify reality, nevertheless they provide a solid foundation for studying and understanding the development within the area of 'advertisements directed at children'. Adrian Furnham concludes that »the differences between educationalist and protectionist, and between researcher and public policy people means that this whole area is marked more by rhetoric than research«.

Adrian Furnham continues with a discussion of the role and influence parents exert over the wishes of their children to buy the products that are being advertised. Different empirical results show that advertisements directed at children have only one factor of influence, which is quite weak compared to the influence the parents hold. Findings show that parental styles in teaching consumption affect children's consumer knowledge, preferences and habits, and that children imitate their parents' behavior in shops.

Thus, Adrian Furnham believes that »we need to teach our children about advertising, what a commercial is and what it is trying to accomplish. You can't be coerced into doing something you don't want to do if you know and understand the process. Banning advertising of any sort shelters or at least delays a child's understanding and decision-making. It can be no substitute for parental guidance and influence. The responsibility for educating children into the economic world cannot be removed from their parents«.

The great majority of studies carried out to elucidate the area of children and advertising has so far been of a qualitative nature. *Anne Martensen* and *Flemming Hansen* have broken with this research tradition as their study is based on a large quantitative survey that was completed in the autumn of 2000 using 1600 children in the ages of 8-18 years. The survey was carried out using questionnaires; small children completed the questionnaire with the help of their parents. The results of this survey are based on approximately 50 questions.

With the CHAPTER 6 »Children's Knowledge and Interpretation of Commercial Advertising – Intentions, Truthfulness and Viewing Habits«, the authors examine four factors, namely: 1) Children's understanding of the intention of advertisements; 2) Children's perception of advertisements and different types of advertisements; 3) Children's perception of the credibility of advertisements; 4) Children's viewing of advertisements. Starting with a literature review, 17 specific hypotheses were proposed for the elucidation of these factors. The hypotheses were subsequently tested using the collected data from the quantitative survey. The most important results and implications of the survey are:

- Children understand the intention of advertising as early as 8 years of age. If advertisers want their messages to be taken seriously by the children, they must be designed in a way to make them appear credible and honest to children.
- Children perceive advertisements as lacking content – they want quality advertisements. They also develop a critical attitude to advertising at an early age, but despite their skepticism advertisements still influence their wishes and purchases. Such a clear result cannot be inferred from Adrian Furnham's study, which showed that advertisements only represent one among many factors that influence purchases, the most important factor, as mentioned earlier, being the parents.
- All this seems to indicate that the socialization process of children starts earlier as well as quicker than anticipated. Banning advertisements for children under the age of 8 is therefore more likely to result in children's socialization process being inhibited until the age of 8, as small children will not have the same opportunity of developing a critical attitude to advertising. Incidentally, this attitude clearly corresponds to Adrian Furnham's conclusion.

- Finally, the results show that children as young as 8 years watch many advertisements for children as well as advertisements for adults. Further restrictions and regulations of children's advertisements therefore seem meaningless. Following Adrian Furnham, the authors recommend that children should be taught to become more critical consumers and use advertisements more constructively.

Brian Young's CHAPTER 7 »The Child's Understanding of the Intent behind Advertising« gives a brief overview of his background (development psychologist oriented towards linguistics). He says he is looking for theories of communication and sees advertising as a form of communication with several functions. His theory of communication is suitable for explaining and predicting what children do with the different functions of advertising. Another aspect of Young's theoretical approach is the use of development theories. He focuses on the child's understanding of the intent of advertising and discusses its importance, partly based on psychological but mostly legal reasons. He comments on the history of banning with reference to the US and Sweden.

At the end of the chapter Young refers to some of his own research on the promotional aspect of advertising pointing at the ability of the children in relation to advertising literacy.

In the CHAPTER 8, »The Impact of Children's Affective Reactions Elicited by Commercials on Attitudes toward the Advertisement and the Brand«, *Christian Derbaix* and *Joël Bree* discuss a large empirical study they undertook on the impact of children's affective reactions elicited by TV-commercials on attitudes toward the advertisement (A_{ad}) and the brand (A_b).

They preceded the study with a literature review of the cognitive and affective reactions elicited by the advertisement, and, in accordance with the theory of the Elaboration Likelihood Model, they found that the attitude towards the advertisement may come from three main predictors, namely the central elements of the message, the peripheral elements of the message and the affective response elicited by the advertisement.

Second, they studied the literature on the affective responses of children as consumers, and concluded that children are far more susceptible to details such as the tone of voice, the presence of small animals, etc. than adults are. Furthermore, the affective response has a very positive influence on the attitude towards the brand

However, using theories on children's socialization process, it is also emphasized that children under the age of 9 years cannot distinguish between their attitude towards the brand itself, their attitude towards the brand depicted in the commercial and their attitude towards the advertisement itself. Thus, if there is a connection between their attitude toward the advertisement and the brand, this connection could be a natural consequence of reality or merely result from pure coincidence. The authors conclude that the link between A_{ad} and A_b for children remains hypothetical rather than validated by empirical research.

This led the authors to develop a conceptual model for the connection between a number of affective reactions in children caused by TV-advertisements and two effect variables, i.e. the children's attitude towards the advertisement as well as the brand, which they wished to test empirically.

Using the conceptual model as their point of departure, they propose four hypotheses to be tested empirically, i.e.: 1) A_{ad} has a direct and positive effect on A_b; 2) Judgment of the advertisement's characteristics has a direct effect on A_{ad}; 3) Verbal and non-verbal affective reactions elicited by the advertisement partly has a direct effect on A_b, but also an indirect effect via A_{ad}; 4) The effect of the verbal and non-verbal (facial expressions) affective reactions elicited by the advertisement is greater than the a priori attitude toward the brand as well as the judgment of the advertisement's characteristics.

The study, which used 770 children aged 7-10 years in as 'natural' surroundings as possible, confirmed that none of the affective reactions, with the exception of A_{ad}, mediate the impact of verbal affective reactions on A_b. In addition, the authors found that verbal affective reactions are important predictors of A_{ad} and A_b, whereas the contribution of facial expressions is limited. This result made the authors recommend that verbal measurement be used when measuring affective reactions elicited by advertisements.

Dan Freeman and Merrie Brucks' CHAPTER 9 »Drugs, Alcohol, and Tobacco Use Prevention Efforts: Benefits and Challenges of Targeting Young Children« discusses why a new prevention programme strategy will be necessary in the future, as well as the challenges that might eventuate from the operationalization of the programme.

The authors use the metaphor of a river to describe the socialization process leading from childhood naïveté to drug, alcohol and/or tobacco abuse or addiction. Traditionally, prevention efforts have been directed at teenagers, probably because of the view that it is possible to measure the effect of the efforts on the target group. However, the purpose of focusing on small children as well is to »create and maintain deeply held attitudes that will predispose the child against controlled substance use initiation«, which, according to the authors, requires that »early prevention programs focus directly on the promotion element of the marketing mix«.

The authors emphasize four reasons why the resources are put to much better use when the communication efforts are also directed at the small children: 1) It is easier to develop attitudes than to change existing ones, 2) Children are more susceptible to persuasion than teens; 3) Children are less likely to respond with psychological reactance than teens; and 4) Children have the potential (or – 'a high potentiality') to become cessation advocates.

When an early prevention programme is about to be initiated, four factors need to be considered: 1) Effective age-appropriate messages must be developed; 2) The children must understand the risk of drug, alcohol and tobacco use without their curiosity being aroused; 3) Unintended consequences for non-targeted groups of youths must be avoided; and 4) New prevention programmes without adverse effects on current substance users must be initiated.

According to the authors, carrying out an early prevention programme using these guidelines will create a synergy effect. As the children will have been acquainted with the negatives sides of drug, alcohol and tobacco use throughout their childhood, these will have a strong presence in their minds when they are confronted with the situation for the first time. This will decrease the probability of youths trying such drugs or, even worse, becoming addicted to them.

Whiton S. Paine in his CHAPTER 10, »Some Implications of Consumer Behavior Principles When Kids are Involved«, focuses on ethical issues in relation to two cases i.e. Barbie & Ritalin. The role of the doll Barbie has been enormous. Barbie has gradually become a cultural icon that both reflects and influences the culture, social values and family life. Over the years various groups have accused Barbie for socializing girls in ways that lead to poor body image, eating disorders, and materialism. Accordingly Barbie has undergone different changes, and is still selling well.

Ritalin is a drug made by Ciba-Geigy, which has had the approval of parents, experts, teachers and doctors as the main treatment of Attention Deficit Hyperactivity Disorder (ADHD). According to Paine the area of drugs for children creates serious and growing ethical challenges.

The case of Ritalin illustrates how a company (Ciba-Geigy) was able to create a community of parents, experts, teachers and doctors that were united in their approval of Ritalin as the main treatment of ADHD.

Using Barbie and Ritalin as examples Paine emphasizes that companies must constantly re-examine their role in the marketplace. The members of these brand-oriented communities have the potential to reinforce appropriate, or inappropriate, cultural values and marketers can influence this process.

Nancy Jennings begins in her CHAPTER 11 »Advertising, Branding and Consuming: The ABC's of Marketing in American Schools« by saying that marketers have realized that children are three markets in one i.e. they spend their own money, they influence their family's purchases and through their own consumer experiences as children, they can become brand loyal into adulthood. As a result there has been increasing interest in reaching young consumers. She describes different forms of commercialism in schools and comments that despite growing concerns regarding commercialism in the schools, public policy often falls behind public practice. And practice is often very different in different states; for instance, New Mexico law allows advertising in and on school buses whereas Virginia regulation prohibits such practices. Florida law permits school boards to establish policies regarding fundraising in schools, whereas New York regulations prohibiting commercial activities on school grounds.

Jennings concludes by saying that the commercialization of schools is a double-edged sword, providing materials and technology to schools while exposing them to more advertising and corporate sponsorship.

The only solution is that parents, teachers, administrators, legislators and the industry work together to address concerns and create a legitimate response to this growing phenomenon.

NOTE

1 Part of the chapter; English Translation. Tina J. Hindsbo, MA.

REFERENCES

Adler, R. et. al. (1980). *The Effect of Television Advertising on Children*. Lexington: Lexington books.

Barenboim, Carl (1981). »The Development of Person Perception in Childhood and Adolescence: From Behavioral Comparisons to Psychological Constructs to Psychological Comparisons«, *Child Development,* 52 (March), 129-144.

Bjurström, E. (1994). *Barn och TV-reklam [Child and TV-commercials]*. Stockholm. Konsumentverket. Rapport 1993/94;29.

Borch, A. (1996). *Barn og unge om tv-reklame*. En landsomfattende undersøkelse av 8-14 åringer. [Children and young ones about TV-commercials. A national survey of the 8-14 year-olds]. Rapport nr. 1. SIFO.

Brembeck, H. & B. Johansson (Red.) (1996). *Postmodern Barndom. [Postmodern childhood]*. Göteborg. Etnologiska föreningen i Västsverige.

Dorr, A. (1987). *Television and Children. A Special Medium for a Special Audience*. Beverly Hills. London & New Delhi. Sage Publications.

Drotner, K. (2001). *Medier for fremtiden: Børn, unge og det nye medielandskab. [Media in the future: Children, young ones and the new media landscape.]* Høst & Søn. København.

Feilitzen, von C. (1999). *Media Education, Children's Participation and Democracy* in C. von Feilitzen & U. Carlsson (eds.): *Children and Media,* The UNESCO International Clearing House on Children and Violence on the Screen at Nordicom, Göteborg.

Frønes, I. & R. Brusdal (2000). *På sporet av den nye tid.* [*On the track of the new times.*] Fagbok-forlaget, Bergen.

GfK Danmark A/S (1997). *Danske børns og deres forældres opfattelse af tv-reklamer for børneprodukter. En kvalitativ undersøgelse gennemført for:* Initiativgruppen vedr. tv-reklamer til børn. [*Danish children and their parents' perception of TV-commercials for children's products.* A qualitative survey conducted for: The initiative group concerning TV-commercials for children].

Gunter, B. & A. Furnham (1998). *Children as Consumers.* London and New York. Routledge.

Halling J. & B. Tufte (2002). Research paper No. 15: *The Gender Perspective – In Relation to Children as Consumers.* Department of Marketing. Copenhagen Business School. Frederiksberg.

Hansen et al. (ed.) (2002). *Børns opvækst som forbrugere [Children upgrowing as consumers].* Samfunds-litteratur. Frederiksberg.

Höijer, B. (1990). Studying Viewers' reception of Television Programmes: Theoretical and Method-ological Considerations, *European Journal of Communication,* 5:29-56.

James, A., Jenks, Chris & Prout, Alan (1998). *Theorizing Childhood.* London: Routledge.

Katz, E. & T. Liebes (1984). Once upon a Time in Dallas. *Intermedia,* vol. 12, no. 3.

Kline, S. (1993). *Out of the Garden. Toys, TV, and Children's Culture in the Age of Marketing.* London. New York. VERSO.

Mediekultur nr. 7, (1988). Tema: Receptionsforskning. Aalborg: SMID.

Pecora, Norma Odon (1998). *The Business of Children's Entertainment.* New York. The Tuildford Press.

Piaget, Jean (1957). The child and modern physics, *Scientific American,* 196, No. 3

Qvortrup, J. (1993). »Nine Theses about Childhood as a Social Phenomenon« in J. Qvortrup red. *Childhood as a social phenomenon: Lessons from an international project. Eurosocial Report no. 47, p. 11-18.* Vienna Austria: European Center for Social Welfare Policy and Research.

Schultz Jørgensen (ed.) (1992). *Børn og tv-reklame.* [Children and TV-commercials]. Nord-rapport 1992:4. København. Nordisk Ministerråd.

Selman, Robert L. (1980). *The Growth of Interpersonal Understanding.* New York: Academic Press.

Seiter, E. (1993). *Sold Separately: Children and Parents in Consumer Culture.* New Brunswick: Rut-gers UP.

Sverdrup, S. & T.K. Lunde (1995). *Reklame særlig rettet mot barn. En undersøkelse av påvirkning, lov-regulering og holdninger.* [*Advertisements directed at children. A survey on influences, law regulations and attitudes*]. Arbejdsrapport nr. 7-1995. SIFO.

Tufte, B. (1993). *14-16 åriges forståelse af »utraditionelle« markedsføringsmetoder i TV-reklame.* In: Otra-ditionelle marknadsföringsmetoder mot barn och unga. [14-16 year-olds' perception of »un-conventional« marketing strategies in TV-commercials]. Nord-rapport 1993:24. Copenhagen: Nordic Council of Ministers.

Tufte, B. (1999). *Children and TV-Commercials.* The Royal Danish School of Educational Studies. Copenhagen.

Ward, S. Wackman D.B. & Wartella, E. (1977). *How Children Learn to Buy.* London: Sage Publica-tions.

Werner, A. (1994). *Barn i fjernsynsalderen. Hva vet vi om medienes innflytelse?* [Children using TV. What do we know of the media's influence?]. Oslo: Ad Notam Gyldendal.

Young, B. (2002): »The Child's Understanding of the Intent Behind Advertising – A personal Story«. Children – Consumption, Advertising and Media. Copenhagen Business School Press.

2

CONSUMER SOCIALIZATION OF CHILDREN

– A RETROSPECTIVE LOOK AT TWENTY-FIVE YEARS OF RESEARCH

By Deborah Roedder John

INTRODUCTION[1]

Scholarly research examining children's consumer behavior dates back to the 1950's with the publication of a few isolated studies on topics such as brand loyalty (Guest 1955) and conspicuous consumption (Reisman and Roseborough 1955). Further recognition of children as a consumer market followed in the 1960's, as researchers expanded their scope of inquiry to understanding more about children's understanding of marketing and retail functions (McNeal 1964), influence on parents in purchasing decisions (Berey and Pollay 1968; Wells and LoSciuto 1966), and relative influence of parents and peers on consumption patterns (Cateora 1963). Though few in number, these papers were extremely important in terms of introducing the topic of children's consumer behavior to a marketing audience, presenting empirical methods and data pertaining to children, and communicating results in mainstream marketing journals.

Clearly, the pioneering work of researchers in the 1960's had set the stage for more widespread and programmatic research on children. But, it was not until the mid-1970's that research on children as consumers blossomed and gained visibility in the marketing community. This turn of events was based largely on public policy concerns about marketing and advertising to children, which emerged as consumer activist groups such as Action for Children's Television (ACT) and government bodies such as the Federal Trade Commission became vocal in their criticisms of advertising to young children.

About this time, a further impetus to development of the field occurred with the publication of a *Journal of Consumer Research* article entitled »Consumer Socialization,« which argued forcefully for studying children and their socialization into the consumer role. The author, Scott Ward, defined consumer socialization as »processes by which young people acquire skills, knowledge, and attitudes relevant to their functioning as consumers in the marketplace« (Ward 1974, p. 2). This definition gave focus to a new generation of researchers and an emerging field of study pertaining to children as consumers.

Twenty-five years later, an impressive body of research has accumulated on the topic of consumer socialization. Researchers have explored a wide range of topics reflecting children's growing sophistication as consumers, including their knowledge of products, brands, advertising, shopping, pricing, decision-making strategies, and parental influence and negotiation approaches. Also examined have been the »social« aspects of the consumer role, exploring the development of consumption symbolism, social motives for consumption, and materialism. Clearly, we have amassed a great deal of information regarding what children know about the marketplace and their roles as consumers.

The purpose of this paper is to merge findings from the last twenty-five years of research into a unified story of the way consumer socialization proceeds as children mature throughout childhood and adolescence. Integration of findings, both within and across topic areas, has been seldom attempted due to the vast body of heterogeneous literature that exists on children as consumers (for examples, see Moschis 1987; Young 1990). To provide an organizing theme, we focus on age-related developments in consumer socialization, with the objective of characterizing what children know and how they think as consumers at different ages. We develop a conceptual framework that identifies age-related patterns across areas, describes major characteristics of knowledge and reasoning at those ages, and identifies developmental mechanisms behind these changes.

In doing so, the review focuses on research reported by consumer researchers, published in marketing and communication journals, covering the period from 1974 to 1998. In effect, this excludes consideration of research by economists and psychologists pertaining to children's economic concepts (e.g., money values, saving, resource scarcity) and research by public health and medical researchers pertaining to children's consumption of products such as cigarettes, alcohol, and illegal drugs. Findings from research in other areas, or from studies prior to 1974, are included on occasion only to provide context or corroboration for more recent work by consumer researchers. We also exclude consideration of consumer research pertaining to children but outside the realm of consumer socialization. In effect, this excludes: (1) studies of the effects of advertising strategies, such as host selling or repetition, on children's responses to advertising (for a review, see Adler et al. 1980); (2) content analyses of television commercials aimed at children; (3) surveys of parental responses to children's purchase requests and parental views about advertising and marketing to children; and (4) discussions of specific public policy issues and regulatory debates.

This review is divided into three parts. First, we provide a conceptual overview of consumer socialization, summarizing important theoretical views on cognitive and social development and developing a conceptual framework that describes stages of consumer socialization. These stage descriptions identify general characteristics of children's knowledge, skills, and reasoning and specify ages at which these stages are likely to occur. In the second part, we present five sections that review research pertaining to the development of consumer knowledge, skills, and motives in children and tie these findings to our conceptual framework. Reviewed are findings about children's advertising knowledge, transaction knowledge (products, brands, shopping, and pricing), decision-making skills and strategies, purchase request and negotiation strategies, and consumption motives and values. In the final part, implications are drawn for future theoretical and empirical development in the field of consumer socialization.

A CONCEPTUAL FRAMEWORK FOR CONSUMER SOCIALIZATION

The period from birth to adolescence contains dramatic developments in cognitive functioning and social maturation. Children develop abilities to go beyond perceptual appearances to think more abstractly about their environment, acquire information processing skills to more readily organize and use what they learn about their environment, and develop a deeper understanding of interpersonal situations, which allows them to see their world through multiple perspectives.

Cognitive and social development during this period provides a backdrop for the growing sophistication children exhibit in understanding and performing in the consumer role. Age-related improvements in cognitive abilities contribute to the development of consumer knowledge and decision-making skills. For example, well-developed cognitive abilities facilitate the process of evaluating products, comparing them against other alternatives, and purchasing the chosen item from a store. Age-related improvements in social development are similarly helpful. Many consumer situations involve interpersonal understanding, from impressions children form about people who use certain products or brands to negotiation sessions with parents in an attempt to influence the purchase of desired items.

In this section, we describe several conceptual frameworks covering aspects of cognitive and social development. Selected for discussion are frameworks deemed most relevant for understanding aspects of consumer socialization and most important for understanding major changes that occur from preschool to adolescence. Common to these frameworks is a focus on successive stages of development, with each stage characterizing children's thinking, reasoning, and processing at particular ages. Next, we integrate these views to develop a conceptual framework for consumer socialization. Using the notion of stages, we propose that consumer socialization be viewed as progressing in a series of three stages, which capture major shifts from the preschool years through adolescence. We describe the characteristics of children's consumer knowledge, skills, and values at each stage and specify the approximate ages at which children move from one stage to the next.

STAGES OF COGNITIVE AND SOCIAL DEVELOPMENT

Cognitive Development. The most well-known framework for characterizing shifts in basic cognitive abilities is Piaget's theory of cognitive development, which proposes four main stages of cognitive development: sensorimotor (birth to two years), preoperational (two to seven years), concrete operational (seven to eleven years), and formal operational (eleven through adulthood) (Ginsburg and Opper 1988). Vast differences exist in the cognitive abilities and resources available to children at these stages, including the preoperational, concrete operational, and formal operational stages of most interest to consumer researchers. The preoperational stage features children who are developing symbolic thought but are still very focused on perceptual properties of stimuli. Preoperational children tend to be »perceptually-bound« to the readily-observable aspects of their environment, unlike concrete operational children, who do not accept perception as reality but can think about stimuli in their environment in a more thoughtful way. Preoperational children are also characterized by »centration,« the tendency to focus on a single dimension. In contrast, the concrete operational child can consider several dimensions of a stimulus at a time and relate the dimensions in a thoughtful and relatively abstract way. Finally, in the formal operational stage, children progress to more adult-like thought patterns, capable of even more complex thought about concrete and hypothetical objects and situations.

Beyond Piaget's approach, information processing theories of child development provide additional explanatory power for the types of cognitive abilities evidenced by children as they mature. Several formulations of information processing theory exist, but all share a focus on children's developing skills in the areas of acquisition, encoding, organization, and retrieval of information. In the consumer behavior literature, children have been characterized as belonging to one of three segments – strategic processors, cued processors, and limited processors – based on information processing skills they possess (Roedder 1981). Strategic processors (age 12 and older) use a variety of strategies for storing and retrieving information, such as verbal labeling, rehearsal, and use of retrieval cues to guide memory search. Cued processors, ranging in age from 7 to 11 years, are able to use a similar set of strategies to enhance information storage and retrieval, but typically need to be aided by explicit prompts or cues. Cued processors exhibit »production deficiencies,« referring to the fact that they have the ability to use processing strategies but do not spontaneously produce these strategies when needed. Finally, most children under the age of seven are limited processors, with processing skills that are not yet fully developed or successfully utilized in learning situations. These children are characterized as having »mediational deficiencies,« referring to the fact that they often have difficulty using storage and retrieval strategies even when prompted to do so.

The cognitive orientations described by these stages provide a basis for explaining the emergence of a variety of socialization outcomes, which will become evident as our review unfolds. To illustrate, consider for a moment the evidence about children's growing abilities to understand advertising as a persuasive medium distinct from television programming. As we will soon describe, younger children (preschoolers) distinguish commercials from programming on the basis of perceptual features (e.g., advertisements are shorter) instead of motive and intent (e.g., advertisements are intended to sell products). This result fits nicely with the notion of perceptual boundness in preoperational children. By the time children reach eight years of age (concrete operational stage), they possess quite a bit of knowledge about advertising's persuasive intent and bias. Yet, this knowledge is not necessarily accessed and used in evaluating advertising messages. Information processing views provide a ready explanation for this finding in terms of children's abilities at this age to retrieve and use information. Although 8 to 11-year-olds (cued processors) have a good deal of knowledge about advertising, their ability to retrieve and use this knowledge is still developing.

Social Development. The area of social development includes a wide variety of top-ics, such as moral development, altruism and prosocial development, impression for-mation, and social perspective taking. In terms of explaining aspects of consumer so-cialization, we consider social perspective taking and impression formation to be the most directly relevant for our consideration. Social perspective taking, involving the ability to see perspectives beyond one's own, is strongly related to purchase influence and negotiation skills, for example. Impression formation, involving the ability to make social comparisons, is strongly related to understanding the social aspects of products and consumption.

Developments in social perspective taking are addressed by Selman (1980), who provides a particularly apt description of how children's abilities to understand differ-ent perspectives progress through a series of stages. In the preschool and kindergarten years, the egocentric stage (ages 3-6), children are unaware of any perspective other than their own. As they enter the next phase, the social informational role taking stage (ages 6-8), children become aware that others may have different opinions or motives, but believe that this is due to having different information rather than a different per-spective on the situation. Thus, children in this stage do not exhibit the ability to ac-tually think from another person's perspective. This ability surfaces in the self-reflec-tive role taking stage (ages 8-10) as children not only understand that others may have different opinions or motives, even if they have the same information, but can actual-ly consider another person's viewpoint. However, the ability to simultaneously con-sider another person's viewpoint at the same time as one's own does not emerge until the fourth stage of mutual role taking (ages 10-12). This is a most important juncture as much social interaction, such as persuasion and negotiation, requires dual consider-ation of both parties' perspectives. The final stage, social and conventional system role taking (ages 12-15 and older), features an additional development, the ability to under-stand another person's perspective as it relates to the social group to which he (other person) belongs or the social system in which he (other person) operates.

Impression formation undergoes a similar transformation as children learn to make social comparisons on a more sophisticated level. Berenboim (1981) provides a cogent description of the developmental sequence that takes place from 6-12 years of age. Before the age of six, children describe other people in concrete or absolute terms, often mentioning physical appearances (»Nathaniel is tall«) or overt behaviors (»Eliza-beth likes to play softball«). However, these descriptions do not incorporate compar-isons with other people. In Barenboim's first stage, the behavioral comparisons phase (ages 6-8), children do incorporate comparisons as a basis of their impressions, but the comparisons continue to be based on concrete attributes or behaviors (»Matthew runs faster than Joey«). In the second stage, which Barenboim calls the psychological con-structs phase (ages 8-10), impressions are based on psychological or abstract attributes (»Christopher is friendly«), but do include comparisons to others. Comparisons based on psychological or abstract attributes do not emerge until the psychological compar-isons phase (11 or 12 years of age and older), which features more adult-like impres-sions of people (»Sara is more outgoing than Angela«).

The usefulness of these frameworks for understanding aspects of consumer social-ization can be illustrated by continuing our analysis of why younger children do not understand advertising's persuasive intent until they reach elementary school. The ability to discern persuasive intent requires one to view advertising from the advertiser's perspective. According to Selman's stages, this does not typically occur un-til children are 8-10 years of age. The ability to reason about advertisers' motives for specific advertising tactics and techniques, such as celebrity endorsers and humor, re-quires even more detailed thinking. Not only is there consideration of dual view-points (advertisers and viewers), but also reasoning about what techniques would be effective for what types of situations. Consistent with abilities characterized by Selman's last stage, we see knowledge of advertising tactics and appeals emerging in early adolescence and developing thereafter.

STAGES OF CONSUMER SOCIALIZATION

Consumer socialization occurs in the context of dramatic cognitive and social devel-opments, which are often viewed as taking place in a series of stages as children ma-ture throughout childhood. We propose that consumer socialization also be viewed as a developmental process that proceeds through a series of stages as children mature into adult consumers. Integrating the stage theories of cognitive and social develop-ment reviewed earlier, a clear picture emerges of the changes that take place as chil-dren become socialized into their roles as consumers. These changes occur as children move through three stages of consumer socialization – which we have named the per-ceptual stage, the analytical stage, and the reflective stage (see Table 1).

Characteristics	Perceptual stage, 3-7 years	Analytical stage, 7-11 years	Reflective stage, 11-16 years
Knowledge structures:			
Orientation	• Concrete	• Abstract	• Abstract
Focus	• Perceptual features	• Functional/underlying features	• Functional/underlying features
Complexity	• Unidimensional	• Two or more dimensions	• Mulitidimensional Contingent (»if-then«)
	• Simple	• Contingent (»if-then«)	
Perspective	• Egocentric (own perspectives)	• Dual perspectives (own + others)	• Dual perspectives in social context
Decision-making and influence strategies:			
Orientation	• Expedient	• Thoughtful	• Strategic
Focus	• Perceptual features	• Functional/underlying features	• Functional/underlying features
	• Salient features	• Relevant features	• Relevant features
Complexity	• Single attributes	• Two or more attributes	• Multiple attributes
	• Limited repertoire of strategies	• Expanded repertoire of strategies	• Complete repertoire of strategies
Adaptive	• Emerging	• Moderate	• Fully developed
Perspective	• Egocentric	• Dual perspectives	• Dual perspectives in social context

Table 1. Consumer socialization stages

These stages are characterized along a number of dimensions that capture important shifts in knowledge development, decision-making skills, and purchase influence strategies. In terms of knowledge development, the movement from the perceptual to the reflective stage is marked by shifts from concrete to abstract representations, from perceptual to underlying features of objects and events, from simple to more complex representations with multiple dimensions and contingencies, and from an egocentric to a socially-aware perspective. Changes in decision-making and influence strategies are characterized by similar dimensions, moving from an expedient to strategic orientation, from an emphasis on perceptually-salient features to more relevant underlying features, from a limited repertoire to a more complete repertoire of strategies capable of handling multiple attributes, and from limited to more fully-developed abilities to adapt strategies to tasks and situations.

Each stage is described in more detail below. The perceptual stage derives its name from the overwhelming emphasis that children in this stage place on perceptual as opposed to abstract or symbolic thought. The analytical stage is named for the vast improvements we see at this stage in children's abilities to approach matters in more detailed and analytical ways. Finally, the reflective stage derives its name from the emphasis that children in this stage place on understanding the complex social contexts and meanings related to consumption.

Perceptual Stage. The perceptual stage (ages 3-7) is characterized by a general orientation toward the immediate and readily observable perceptual features of the marketplace. Piaget's notion of »perceptual boundness« describes these children well, as does his idea of »centration« on single dimensions of objects and events. Children's consumer knowledge is characterized by perceptual features and distinctions, often based on a single dimension or attribute, and represented in terms of concrete details from their own observations. These children exhibit familiarity with concepts in the marketplace, such as brands or retail stores, but rarely understand them beyond a surface level. Due to constraints in encoding and organizing information, individual objects or experiences are rarely integrated into more generalized knowledge structures with multiple dimensions, perspectives, and contingencies (»if-then« rules).

Many of these same characteristics hold true for consumer decision-making skills and influence strategies at the perceptual stage. The orientation here can best be described as simple, expedient, and egocentric. Decisions are often made on the basis of very limited information, usually a single perceptual dimension. For example, children in this stage can be expected to make choices based on a single, perceptually salient attribute such as size. This type of strategy is rarely modified or adapted based on different choice tasks or situations. Limited adaptivity is also a feature of children's influence strategies. Children approach these situations with an egocentric perspective, unable to take into account the other person's perspective in modifying the strategy used to influence or negotiate for desired items. Although they may be aware that parents or friends have other views, children at this age have difficulty thinking about their own perspective and that of other person simultaneously.

Analytical Stage. Enormous changes take place, both cognitively and socially, as children move into the analytical stage (ages 7-11). This period contains some of the most important developments in terms of consumer knowledge and skills. The shift from perceptual thought to more symbolic thought noted by Piaget, along with dramatic increases in information processing abilities, results in a more sophisticated understanding of the marketplace, a more complex set of knowledge about concepts such as advertising and brands, and a new perspective that goes beyond their own feelings and motives. Concepts such as product categories or prices are thought of in terms of functional or underlying dimensions, products and brands are analyzed and discriminated on the basis of more than one dimension or attribute, and generalizations are drawn from one's experiences. Reasoning proceeds at a more abstract level, setting the stage for knowledge structures that include information about abstract concepts such as advertiser's motives as well as the notion of contingencies (e.g., sweetness is an appealing attribute for candy but not soup).

The ability to analyze stimuli on multiple dimensions and the acknowledgement of contingencies brings about vast changes in children's consumer decision-making skills and strategies. Now, children exhibit more thoughtfulness in their choices, considering more than just a single perceptually salient attribute and employing a decision strategy that seems to make sense given the task environment. As a result, children are more flexible in the approach they bring to making decisions, allowing them to be more adaptive and responsive. These tendencies also emerge in the way children try to influence and negotiate for desired items. The approach is more adaptive, based on their newfound ability to think from the perspective of a parent or friend and adapt their influence strategy accordingly.

Reflective Stage. The reflective stage (ages 11-16) is characterized by further development in several dimensions of cognitive and social development. Knowledge about marketplace concepts such as branding and pricing becomes even more nuanced and more complex as children develop more sophisticated information processing and social skills. Many of these changes are more a matter of degree than kind. More distinct is the shift in orientation to a more reflective way of thinking and reasoning, as children move into adolescence and become more focused on the social meanings and underpinnings of the consumer marketplace. A heightened awareness of other people's perspectives, along with a need to shape their own identity and conform to group expectations, results in more attention to the social aspects of being a consumer, making choices, and consuming brands. Consumer decisions are made in a more adaptive manner, depending on the situation and task. In a similar fashion, attempts to influence parents and friends reflect more social awareness as adolescents become more strategic, favoring strategies that they think will be better received than a simple direct approach.

Discussion. The consumer socialization stages being proposed here capture important changes in how children think, what they know, and how they express themselves as consumers. Consistent with our focus on age, we identify these stages with specific age ranges and describe the transition between stages as occurring primarily as a function of age. These stage descriptions, and the cognitive and social developments that support them, will be employed as explanatory devices in our review of empirical findings in consumer socialization, yet to come.

Before proceeding further, several observations regarding our stage descriptions are in order. First, the age ranges for each stage are approximations based on the general tendencies of children in that age group. To constrain the number of stages to a reasonable number, some degree of variance among children in an age range was tolerated. For example, children 7 to 11 years of age are identified with the analytical stage, even though differences in degree clearly exist between 8 year-olds and 10-11 year-olds. To deal with variations of this sort, we formulated our stage descriptions to be most representative of children in the middle to end of each age range and allowed the age ranges to overlap at transition points between stages. We also note that ages for each stage may be slightly different depending on the specific requirements of the consumer task or situation that children face. Tasks that are more complex, requiring consideration of more information or more in-depth knowledge, can be expected to increase the age at which children appear to have mastered a particular concept.

Second, we acknowledge that important developments in consumer socialization do not emerge in a vacuum, but take place in a social context including the family, peers, mass media, and marketing institutions. Parents create direct opportunities by interacting with their children about purchase requests, giving them allowances, and taking them on shopping excursions (Ward, Wackman, and Wartella 1977). Peers are an additional source of influence, affecting consumer beliefs starting early in life (see Hawkins and Coney 1974) and continuing through adolescence (e.g., Moschis and Moore 1980; Moschis and Churchill 1978). Finally, mass media and advertising provide information about consumption and the value of material goods (e.g., Atkin 1975b; Gorn and Florsheim 1985; Martin and Gentry 1997; Robertson, Rossiter, and Gleason 1979). These influences are not incorporated into our framework, due to our primary focus on age, but will be noted as we review each area of empirical research.

We turn now to a review of empirical findings pertaining to consumer socialization. We begin our review by examining evidence about what children know and understand about advertising, one of the most important and contentious topics in the history of consumer socialization.

ADVERTISING AND PERSUASION KNOWLEDGE

Early interest in the area of consumer socialization was ignited, in large part, by questions about children's knowledge and understanding of advertising. Beginning in the early 1970's, arguments emerged that advertising to children was inherently »unfair,« based on theories developed by child psychologists and exploratory research conducted by consumer researchers that revealed young children to have little understanding of the persuasive intent of advertising, viewing it as informative, truthful, and entertaining (e.g., Blatt, Spencer, and Ward 1972; Ward, Reale, and Levinson 1972). A rancorous public policy debate ensued, culminating in a 1978 Federal Trade Commission proposal to ban television advertising to young children under the age of eight. Although this proposal was ultimately defeated, concern over what children know about advertising and whether advertisers have an unfair advantage in persuading children continues to this day.

Here, we review what is known about children's knowledge and understanding of advertising. Our discussion is structured around major steps or building blocks of advertising knowledge, such as the ability to distinguish commercials from programs and the ability to understand advertising's persuasive intent. These steps are discussed in the order in which they emerge in the developmental sequence from preschool to adolescence.

DISTINGUISHING COMMERCIALS FROM PROGRAMS

As children move into the preschool years, they learn to identify television commercials and distinguish them from other forms of programming. By the age of five, almost all children have acquired the ability to pick out commercials from regular television programming (Blosser and Roberts 1985; Butter, et. al 1981; Levin, Petros, and Petrella 1982; Palmer and McDowell 1979; Stephens and Stutts 1982; Stutts, Vance, and Hudleson 1981). Even three and four-year-olds have been shown to discriminate commercials above chance levels (Butter, et. al 1981; Levin, Petros, and Petrella 1982).

A study by Eliot Butter and his colleagues illustrates findings in this area. Preschool children were shown videotapes of the »Captain Kangaroo« program, edited to include four 30-second commercials between program segments. Separators were placed between the commercial and program segments, consisting, for example, of a voice saying, »The Captain will return after this message.« While viewing the tape, children were instructed to tell the experimenter »when a commercial comes on.«

Children were also asked at approximately 10 to 15 seconds into each program segment, »Is this part of the 'Captain Kangaroo' show?« In addition to these direct assessments, children were also asked open-ended questions such as »Why do they put commercials on television?« and »What is the difference between a commercial and the »Captain Kangaroo« show?«

Using this methodology, Butter et. al (1981) found that 70% of the four-year-olds and 90% of the five-year-olds identified all four commercials. Older children identified significantly more commercials, yet even four-year-olds were able to distinguish commercials from programs at an above-chance level. However, the ability to identify commercials did not necessarily translate into an understanding of the »true« difference between commercials and programs (entertainment vs. selling intent). For example, 90% of the younger children could not explain the difference between commercials and programs, even though discriminating the two was relatively easy. Other studies have reported similar findings, noting that children of this age and slightly older usually describe the difference between commercials and programs using simple perceptual cues, such as »commercials are short« (Palmer and McDowell 1979; Ward 1972). Thus, as Butter et. al (p. 82) conclude, »young children may know they are watching something different than a program but do not know that the intent of what they are watching is to invite purchase of a product or service.«

UNDERSTANDING ADVERTISING INTENT

An understanding of advertising intent usually emerges by the time most children are seven to eight years old (Bever, Smith, Bengen, and Johnson 1975; Blosser and Roberts 1985; Robertson and Rossiter 1974; Rubin 1974; Ward, Wackman, and Wartella 1977). Prior to this, young children tend to view advertising as entertainment (e.g., »commercials are funny«) or as a form of unbiased information (e.g., »commercials tell you about things you can buy«). Around the age of 7 or 8, children begin to see the persuasive intent of commercials, coming to terms with the fact that advertisers are »trying to get people to buy something.«

These developmental patterns are well documented by Robertson and Rossiter (1974) in one of the earliest and most influential studies on the topic. First, third, and fifth grade boys were interviewed and asked a series of open-ended questions to assess whether they recognized the assistive (informational) intent and persuasive (selling) intent of advertising. For example, children were asked questions such as »Why are commercials shown on television?« and »What do commercials try to get you to do?« The findings reveal age differences in persuasive intent but not assistive intent.

Attributions of assistive intent remained constant across the three grade levels, with about half of the children mentioning the information function of advertising. Attributions of persuasive intent, however, increased dramatically from 52.7% of first graders (6-7 year-olds) to 87.1% of third graders (8-9 year-olds) to 99% of fifth graders (10-11 year-olds). These age trends parallel our description of children in the perceptual and analytical stages of consumer socialization. First graders, who are still in the perceptual stage, view the purpose of advertising from their own perspective as something that is informative or entertaining. Third and fifth graders, who are in the analytical stage, are now capable of viewing advertising from their own perspective (assistive intent) as well as from the advertiser's perspective (persuasive intent).

Similar age trends have been reported in much subsequent research, though additional factors have been identified that may moderate the specific age at which a child understands persuasive intent. Family environment, for example, plays a role. Children from black families exhibit lower levels of understanding of advertising's persuasive intent (Donohue, Meyer, and Henke 1978; Meyer, Donohue, and Henke 1978). Higher levels of understanding can be facilitated by parents with higher educational levels (Robertson and Rossiter 1974; Rossiter and Robertson 1976) and by parents who take a strong consumer education role with their children (Reid 1978). Common to both types of families is a greater degree of parent-child interaction about advertising, though the interaction must have an educational component to be effective.

In addition to background factors, features of the methodology used to measure children's understanding of persuasive intent have also come under scrutiny. Researchers have questioned whether measures of children's knowledge, using open-ended questions requiring abstract thinking and verbalization, result in an overly pessimistic view of what young children know about advertising intent. Employing nonverbal measures of advertising intent, Donohue, Henke, and Donohue (1980) reported high levels of understanding of commercial intent among two to six-year-olds. In this study, children were shown a television commercial for *Froot Loops* cereal featuring an animated character called Toucan Sam. After viewing the ad, children were shown two pictures and asked to indicate which picture best indicated, »What Toucan Sam wants you to do.« The correct picture was one of a mother and child in a supermarket cereal aisle, with the child sitting in a pushcart seat and the mother standing with a box of Froot Loops in her hand, ready to put it into the cart. The incorrect picture showed a child watching television. Children in the study selected the right picture 80% of the time, with even the youngest children (2-3 year-olds) selecting the right picture at above-chance levels (75%).

Replications of this study have produced results more in line with traditional verbal measures. Noting that the choice between the two pictures used in the Donohue et al. study was a rather easy one, which children could have successfully completed absent any knowledge of persuasive intent, Macklin (1985) replicated the Donohue et. al procedure using a set of four pictures. Two new pictures were added to the choice set, one depicting an activity portrayed by the characters in the commercial and another showing two children sharing the advertised product. The results were vastly different in this case, with 80% of the children (3-5 years of age) failing to select the correct picture. Further research by Macklin (1987), using similar nonverbal measures to assess children's understanding of the informational function of advertising, corroborates these findings. In sum, although nonverbal measures of persuasive intent may allow some children to express levels of understanding not uncovered with verbal measures, there is little reason to believe that the vast majority of children younger than seven or eight years of age have a command of advertising's persuasive intent.

RECOGNIZING BIAS AND DECEPTION IN ADVERTISING

By the time children reach their eighth birthday, they not only understand advertising's persuasive intent but also recognize the existence of bias and deception in advertising. Children aged eight and older no longer believe that »commercials always tell the truth« (Bever et al. 1975; Robertson and Rossiter 1974; Ward 1972; Ward, Wackman, and Wartella 1977), though children from black and lower income families are less discerning (Bearden, Teel, and Wright 1979; Meyer, Donohue, and Henke 1978). Beliefs about the truthfulness of advertising become even more negative as children move into adolescence (Bever et al. 1975; Robertson and Rossiter 1974; Rossiter and Robertson 1976; Ward 1972; Ward, Wackman, and Wartella 1977). For example, Ward, Wackman, and Wartella (1977) report that the percentage of kindergartners, third graders, and sixth graders believing that advertising never or only sometimes tells the truth increases from 50% to 88% to 97%, respectively. These percentage changes parallel those reported for understanding of persuasive intent for first, third, and fifth graders, illustrating once again the shifts that take place as children transition from the perceptual stage to the analytical stage.

Along with these more negative views comes a better understanding of why commercials are sometimes untruthful and how one can distinguish truthful from untruthful advertisements. For example, Ward, Wackman, and Wartella (1977) report that kindergartners often state no reason for »why commercials lie« (e.g., »they just lie«)

whereas older children (third and sixth graders) connect lying to persuasive intent (e.g., »they want to sell products to make money, so they have to make the product look better than it is«). The ability to detect specific instances of bias and deception also increases with age. Bever et. al (1975) report that most of the 7–10 year-olds in their study could not detect misleading advertising and admitted to their difficulties: »'[Advertisers] can fake well,' they said, and 'you don't really know what's true until you've tried the product'« (p. 114). Eleven to twelve-year-olds were more discriminating, using nuances of voice, manner, and language to detect misleading advertising. These children used clues such as »overstatements and the way they [the actors] talk,« »when they use visual tricks or fake things,« and when the commercial »goes on and on in too much detail« (p. 119). Clearly, developments in perspective taking that occur as children enter adolescence and the reflective stage facilitate the ability to associate such nuances in advertising executions with deception or exaggeration.

The ability to recognize bias and deception in advertisements, coupled with an understanding of advertising's persuasive intent, results in less trust and less liking of commercials overall (Robertson and Rossiter 1974; Rossiter and Robertson 1976). Robertson and Rossiter (1974) found, for example, that the percentage of children »liking all advertisements« decreased dramatically from 68.5% for first graders to 55.9% for third graders to 25.3% for fifth graders. Similar studies have replicated this general pattern, noting downward trends in liking or overall attitudes toward advertising in children from the early elementary school grades to high school (Lindquist 1978; Moore and Stephens 1975).

Family environment, peers, and television exposure also contribute to the development of skeptical attitudes toward advertising. For young children, critical attitudes seem to be furthered by parental control over television viewing (Soley and Reid 1984) and less television viewing in general (Atkin 1975; Rossiter and Robertson 1974). By the teenage years, skepticism towards advertising seems to be related more to the development of independent thinking and access to alternative information sources. For example, Mangleburg and Bristol (1998) report higher levels of advertising skepticism among high school students that have alternative sources of information (friends) and come from families that foster critical thinking (concept-oriented families), despite self-reports of heavier television viewing. Less skepticism was observed among students conforming to peer group norms, consistent with a pattern of less independent and critical thinking.

Using Cognitive Defenses Against Advertising

The evidence just reviewed points to a dramatic shift in how children see advertising as they move from the preschool years to early adolescence. The preschooler who believes that commercials are entertaining and informative turns into a skeptical adolescent who knows that commercials are meant to persuade and believes them to be untruthful in general. The knowledge and skepticism about advertising that is typical of children eight years of age or older is often viewed as a »cognitive defense« against advertising. Armed with knowledge about advertising's persuasive intent and skepticism about the truthfulness of advertising claims, children of this age and above are often viewed as having the abilities to respond to advertising in a mature and informed manner. Younger children (under 8 years) without these cognitive defenses are seen as an »at risk« population for being easily mislead by advertising.

Although this scenario seems straightforward, evidence regarding the extent to which children's general attitudes and beliefs about advertising function as cognitive defenses against advertising is quite mixed. Early survey research was successful in finding moderate links between children's knowledge of advertising's persuasive intent and their desire for advertised products (Robertson and Rossiter 1974) and children's negative attitudes toward advertising and their desire for advertised products (McNeal 1964). More recent experimental research, however, finds that children's cognitive defenses have little or no effect on evaluations and preferences for advertised products (Christenson 1982; Ross et. al 1984). For example, Christenson (1982) found that an educational segment on commercials was successful in increasing the awareness of advertising's persuasive intent and decreasing the perceived truthfulness of advertising, yet had little effect on younger (first-second graders) or older (fifth-sixth graders) children's evaluations of a subsequently-advertised product.

Several possibilities exist to explain why children's developing knowledge about advertising does not necessarily translate into more discerning responses to advertising. Perhaps the most obvious reason is that general knowledge and beliefs about advertising cannot be expected to dampen a child's enthusiasm for an enticing snack or toy. Clearly, adults with the same or higher level of cognitive defenses often want and purchase advertised products, even products with advertised claims that are »just too good to be true.« As Robertson and Rossiter (1974, p. 19) note: »Children's ability to recognize persuasive intent in commercials should not be taken as implying immunity to all commercials; clearly, individual commercials may be highly persuasive for children, just as for adults.«

A second possibility is that children's advertising knowledge can serve as a cognitive defense only when that knowledge is accessed during commercial viewing. Given the difficulty that children experience in retrieving stored information of all kinds, even through the analytical stage, access to and use of their advertising knowledge may be more restricted than previously thought. Brucks, Armstrong, and Goldberg (1988) present evidence to this effect in an experimental study with 9–10 year-olds, an age at which children typically understand the persuasive intent of advertising and are relatively skeptical of advertising claims. Brucks and her colleagues created a high level of advertising knowledge in one-half of the children by showing and discussing two educational films about the persuasive nature of advertising, including information about specific advertising techniques and tricks. An irrelevant film was shown to the remaining children. Three days later, students were shown actual commercials for children's products, completed cognitive response measures, and answered questions about the perceived deceptiveness of the commercials. Immediately prior to commercial viewing, one-half of the children were given a short quiz measuring children's attitudes about advertising, which served as a cue to help children access their advertising knowledge.

The most important, and interesting, findings relate to the number of counter-arguments children raised after viewing each commercial. Over 70% of the counter-arguments occurred in the high knowledge-cue present condition, in which children had been shown educational films and had received a cue encouraging them to access this knowledge prior to commercial viewing. Students in the high knowledge-cue absent condition generated advertising counterarguments for one commercial, which used techniques very similar to those critiqued in the educational films, but failed overall to use what they had learned about advertising at the time of commercial viewing. Children in the low knowledge condition failed to generate advertising counterarguments for any of the commercials, regardless of whether a cue for advertising knowledge was present or absent. These results support the idea that access to advertising knowledge is a bottleneck preventing children from using what they know as a cognitive defense against advertising. Equally important, however, the findings suggest that general advertising knowledge and beliefs are not sufficient defenses. As Brucks et. al (1988, p. 480-81) conclude: »… children (at least 9 to 10-year-olds) need more than just a skeptical or critical attitude toward advertising. They also need a more detailed knowledge about the nature of advertising and how it works …«

KNOWLEDGE OF ADVERTISING TACTICS AND APPEALS

What do children of different ages know about specific advertising tactics and appeals? Surprisingly, we have very few answers to this question, probably because most researchers have focused on advertising knowledge and beliefs possessed by children during their elementary school years (ages 5 to 11). Advertising knowledge of a more specific form, involving an understanding of what tactics and appeals are used by advertisers and why they are used, emerges much later in the developmental sequence as children approach early adolescence (11-14 years of age) (Boush, Friestad, and Rose 1994; Friestad and Wright 1994; Paget, Kritt, and Bergemann 1984). This developmental path is consistent with our characterization of children in the reflective stage, who possess substantial perspective-taking skills that allow them to reason about different perspectives (advertiser and viewer) across different contexts or situations.

An illustration of this developmental juncture is provided by Moore-Shay and Lutz (1997) in their research involving indepth interviews with second graders (ages 7-8) and fifth graders (ages 10-11). These researchers found that younger children related to advertisements primarily as a conduit of product information, evaluating specific commercials based upon their liking of the advertised product. In contrast, older children viewed advertisements in a more analytical nature, often focusing on creative content and execution, as illustrated in this commentary by a fifth-grade boy:

> »They show the shape of the cereal a lot of times. When they show the box a lot of times, they show the name a lot of times. Make sure you remember it. Or sometimes they have a song, and it's like when you get songs in your head and you can't get them out ...« (p. 35)

Knowledge of this nature continues to develop during adolescence, as documented by Boush, Friestad, and Rose (1994). Sixth through eighth graders were asked a series of questions about what advertisers are trying to accomplish when they use particular tactics, such as humor, celebrity endorsers, and product comparisons. Students were asked to rate eight possible effects (e.g., »grab your attention« and »help you learn about the product«) for each tactic, responding to the question »When TV advertisements [insert tactic], how hard is the advertiser trying to [insert list of effects]?« Ratings for each effect were obtained on a scale from »not trying hard at all« to »trying very hard.« These ratings were compared to those from an adult sample to derive an overall knowledge score. In addition, skepticism toward advertising was assessed by a series of questions relating to understanding of advertising intent and beliefs about the truthfulness of advertisement claims.

The results indicate that knowledge about specific advertising techniques increases during the period from sixth to eighth grade, consistent with what we would expect for young consumers moving into the reflective stage (ages 11-16). Interestingly, skepticism about advertising was high among all students and did not vary across grades. Boush and his colleagues conclude (p. 172): »... the current results suggest that negative or mistrustful predispositions toward advertising are well established as early as grade 6. This pattern of development, where skeptical attitudes precede more sophisticated knowledge structures, suggests that adolescent schemer schemas about advertisers' persuasive attempts start with general attitudes and then are filled in with more specific beliefs.«

A FINAL NOTE

As they mature, children transition from viewers that see advertising as purely informative, entertaining, and trustworthy to ones that view advertising in a more skeptical, analytical, and discerning fashion. In light of these trends, it might be tempting to conclude that the end result of this socialization process is a widespread skepticism and dislike of advertising by older children and adolescents.

Of course, this is hardly the case. Although older children and adolescents are quite savvy about advertising, and often voice negative attitudes about advertising in general, they also are discriminating consumers of advertising who find many commercials to be entertaining, interesting, and socially-relevant. By virtue of their growing sophistication, older children and adolescents find entertainment in analyzing the creative strategy of many commercials and constructing theories for why certain elements are persuasive (Moore-Shay and Lutz 1997). Advertisements are also valued as a device for social interaction, serving as a focus of conversations with peers, a means of belonging and group membership, and a conduit for transferring and conveying meaning in their daily lives (Ritson and Elliott 1998). Advertising serves important functions in the lives of adolescent consumers, as illustrated in this comment from a subject in Ritson and Elliott's study of high school students in England:

»If you're sitting here and someone starts talking about adverts (advertisements) and you haven't got a clue what they're going on about, you feel dead left out ... and you can't, you know ... You say, »Oh, I didn't see that« and then they just carry on talking around you. But if you've seen it, you can join in and you know what they're going on about so it makes you feel ... like ... more in line with the group ... part of it more.«

TRANSACTION KNOWLEDGE

Advertising plays an early role in the consumer socialization of children, but so do other consumer experiences such as shopping. For most children, their exposure to the marketplace comes as soon as they can be accommodated as a passenger in a shopping cart at the grocery store. From this vantage point, infants and toddlers are exposed to a variety of stimuli and experiences, including aisles of products, shoppers reading labels and making decisions, and the exchange of money and goods at the checkout counter. These experiences, aided by developing cognitive abilities that allow them to interpret and organize their experiences, result in an understanding of marketplace transactions. Children learn about the places where transactions take place (stores), the objects of transactions (products and brands), the procedures for enacting transactions (shopping scripts), and the value obtained in exchanging money for products (shopping skills and pricing). This set of knowledge and skills, which we refer to here as transaction knowledge, is explored in detail below.

PRODUCT AND BRAND KNOWLEDGE

To children, products and brands are probably the most salient aspects of the marketplace. Products and brands are advertised on television, displayed in stores, and found all around one's home. Even before they are able to read, children as young as two or three years of age can recognize familiar packages in the store and familiar characters on products such as toys and clothing (Derscheid, Kwon, and Fang 1996; Haynes, Burts, Dukes, and Cloud 1993). By preschool, children begin to recall brand names from seeing them advertised on television or featured on product packages, especially if the brand names are associated with salient visual cues such as colors, pictures, or cartoon characters (Macklin 1996). By kindergarten and first grade, children begin to read and spell brand names, which opens up even more opportunities for children to add to their knowledge base. By the time children reach middle childhood, they can name multiple brands in most child-oriented product categories such as cereal, snacks, and toys (McNeal 1992; Otnes, Kim, and Kim 1994; Rossiter 1976; Rubin 1972; Ward, Wackman, and Wartella 1977).

As they mature, several trends in children's brand awareness are evident. First, as suggested above, children's awareness and recall of brand names increases with age, from early to middle childhood (Rossiter 1976; Rubin 1972; Ward, Wackman, and Wartella 1977) and from middle childhood through adolescence (Keiser 1975). An illustrative set of findings is reported by Ward, Wackman, and Wartella (1977) who asked children from kindergarten to sixth grade to name as many brands as possible in four different product categories (soft drinks, gum, gasoline, and cameras). For soft drinks, for example, the average number of brands names increased from 1.2 to 2.4 to 3.3 brands for kindergartners, third graders, and sixth graders, respectively. Second, brand awareness develops first for child-oriented product categories, such as cereal, snacks, and toys. In a clever study analyzing children's letters to Santa, Otnes, Kim, and Kim (1994) found that about 50% of children's gift requests were for specific branded (toy and game) items, with the vast majority of children (85%) mentioning at least one brand name in their letter to Santa. Brand awareness for more adult-oriented product categories develops later as these products become more salient or more relevant to older children. In the Ward, Wackman, and Wartella (1977) study, for example, only the older children (third and sixth graders) were able to name at least one brand of gasoline and cameras, with sixth graders naming more brands on average than third graders.

These developments in brand awareness foster a greater understanding of brands and product categories. Children begin to discern similarities and differences among brands, learning the structural aspects of how brands are positioned within a product category. Children also learn about product categories themselves, developing a greater understanding of how product types are grouped together and distinguished from one another. We refer to this type of knowledge about product categories and brands as structural knowledge. Young consumers also begin to understand the symbolic meaning and status accorded to certain types of products and brand names. We refer to this type of knowledge as symbolic knowledge. Both types of knowledge development are reviewed below.

Structural Knowledge. Between early and middle childhood, children learn a great deal about the underlying structure of product categories. Although children learn to group or categorize items at a very early age, they shift from highly visible perceptual cues to more important underlying cues as a basis for categorizing and judging similarity among objects as they grow older (Denney 1974; Markman 1980; Markman and Callahan 1983; Whitney and Kunen 1983). By third or fourth grade, children are learning to group objects according to attributes that suggest taxonomic relationships (e.g., belts and socks share the same attribute of being items of clothing), attributes that indicate the relationship of categories to one another (e.g., fruit juices and soft drinks differ on the attribute of naturalness), and attributes inherent to the core concept of categories (e.g., taste, more than color, is central to the category of soft drinks). These are termed underlying, deep structure, or even functional attributes because they convey the true meaning of a category or the function a category might serve. Prior to the use of attributes such as these, young children typically rely on perceptual attributes that are visually dominant, such as shape, size, or color.

These tendencies are clearly in evidence with regard to the way children categorize products and discriminate brands (John and Sujan 1990a; John and Lakshmi-Ratan 1992; Klees, Olson, and Wilson 1988). A study by John and Sujan (1990a) illustrates this point. In this study, children from four to ten years of age were shown triads of products from the cereal or beverage category. One of the items was identified as a target, with the other two items in the triad sharing perceptual and/or underlying features with the target. For example, one beverage triad featured a can of 7-Up (target product), a can of Orange Crush that was similar to the target on the basis of a perceptual cue (both in cans), and a large liter bottle of Sprite soda that was similar to the target on the basis of an underlying cue (both lemon-lime taste). For all triads, children were asked to identify which of the two items was »most like« the target and why. In response, older children (ages 9–10) used underlying cues in a ratio of about 2:1, whereas the very youngest children (ages 4–5) used perceptual cues in a ratio of about 2:1 relative to underlying cues.

It would be a mistake, however, to label the use of perceptual cues as a totally ineffective strategy, devoid of any diagnostic value. Perceptual features and underlying attributes are correlated in many product categories, especially at the basic category level. Perceptual features that are highly correlated with underlying attributes can be quite diagnostic in determining category membership, leading even adults and older children to use perceptual cues to quickly and accurately categorize items. Younger children show emerging abilities to use perceptual cues in a similar fashion, favoring perceptual cues that are diagnostic over those that are undiagnostic of category membership (John and Sujan 1990b). What appears to develop over time is an appreciation for what perceptual cues are diagnostic, and therefore useful, and what perceptual cues are not diagnostic and should, therefore, be ignored in favor of underlying attributes or features.

These findings are consistent with our characterization of children in the perceptual and analytical stages of consumer socialization. The focus on perceptual categorization cues exhibited by 4-5 year-olds is a vivid illustration of the orientation of children in the perceptual stage. Similarly, the shift to functional or underlying categorization cues around 9-10 years of age is consistent with the movement toward symbolic thinking that characterizes children in the analytical stage.

Symbolic Knowledge. Early to middle childhood is also a time of greater understanding of the symbolic meanings and status accorded to certain types of products and brand names. During this time, children develop a preference for particular brands, even when the physical composition of the products is quite similar in nature. For example, children begin to express a preference for familiar branded items over generic offerings in the preschool years (Hite and Hite 1995), with preference for branded items escalating even further as children enter and move through elementary school (Ward, Wackman, and Wartella 1977). By the time they reach early adolescence, children are expressing strong preferences for some brand names over others, based on a relatively sophisticated understanding of their brand concepts and images (Achenreiner 1995).

Nowhere is children's increasing understanding of the social significance of goods more in evidence than in studies of consumption symbolism conducted by Belk and his colleagues (Belk, Bahn, and Mayer 1982; Belk, Mayer, and Driscoll 1984; Mayer and Belk 1982). To illustrate, in the Belk, Bahn, and Mayer (1992) study, children in preschool through elementary school and adults were shown pairs of pictures of automobiles or houses, which varied in size, age, or market value. For example, one pair included a Caprice (a large, traditional car) and a Chevette (a small economy car). Subjects were asked which of the cars would most likely be owned by different types of people (e.g., a doctor, a grandfather) to assess whether consumption stereotypes exist for each age group tested. Responses to these questions revealed that inferences based on ownership were minimal among preschoolers, emerging and evident among second graders, and almost fully developed by sixth grade. Thus, sometime between preschool and second grade, children begin to make inferences about people based on the *products* they use (Belk, Bahn, and Mayer 1982; Mayer and Belk 1982).

Inferences about people based on the *brands* they use also develop during childhood, albeit somewhat later than for the general types of products described above. A lag of this sort seems reasonable based on the fact that inferences about product types are often based on salient perceptual cues (e.g., small vs. large car), which are easily noticed by younger children in the perceptual stage, whereas inferences about brand names are based on more abstract conceptual notions about what is popular, new, more costly, or exclusive. Evidence to this effect is reported by Achenreiner (1995) in a study with children in second grade, sixth grade, and high school. Subjects were shown advertisements for jeans or athletic shoes, which included a picture of the product with a prominent brand name that was either a preferred (e.g., Nike) or nonpreferred (e.g., KMart) one. For example, one group of subjects saw an advertisement for athletic shoes with a Nike brand name; a different group of subjects saw the same advertisement for the same athletic shoes with a KMart brand name. Participants were asked to give their impressions of someone who would own the advertised product on several dimensions, such as »cool« or popular. Responses from second graders showed no difference in their impressions of owners of the preferred versus nonpreferred brand name. In contrast, impressions about the owners of the two brands were different for children in the sixth grade and for high schoolers. These findings are consistent with those of Belk, Mayer, and Driscoll (1984), who found stronger inferences about consumption-based stereo-types among sixth graders (versus fourth graders) for stimuli containing brand names.

Thus, by sixth grade, children have developed a very keen sense of the social meaning and prestige associated with certain types of products and brand names. Further, these items not only confer status to their owners, but also begin to symbolize group identity and a sense of belonging to certain groups. Product categories such as clothing are particularly notable in this regard, as reported by Jamison (1996) in a study with sixth graders. Sixth graders comment on clothes as a means of »fitting in« and as a way to identify membership in a particular subgroup, such as the »preppies,« »deadheads,« and »hip-hops.« A quote from an 11-year-old boy sums it up well:

> »I wear what I wear because it is in style … it also makes me feel real cool. Some of the kinds of clothes I like are Nike, Guess, Levi's and Reebok. When I wear my clothes it makes me feel real cool. I also blend in with all the other people at school and everywhere else I go.« (page 23)

These developments in symbolic knowledge are consistent with our stage framework for consumer socialization. Beginning in the analytical stage (ages 7-11), the seeds are sown by children's increasing abilities to think abstractly and reason about perspectives other than their own. By the time children reach the reflective stage (ages 11-16), they possess a more sophisticated approach to impression formation based on social comparisons of factors such as personality, social standing, and possessions. Perspective-taking skills also now incorporate group norms or points of view, consistent with findings of consumption symbolism related to group identity at this age.

SHOPPING KNOWLEDGE AND SKILLS

Early work in this area focused on children's knowledge of money as a medium of exchange (e.g., Marshall 1964; Marshall and MacGruder 1960; Strauss 1952). Research in this vein identified early childhood as a period of rapid development in abilities to understand where money comes from and its role in marketplace transactions, to identify specific coin and bill values, and to carry out transactions with money involving simple addition and subtraction. Significant jumps in knowledge were reported between preschool and first or second grade, with most second graders having acquired many of the basic concepts for understanding the exchange of money for goods and services.

Yet, a complete set of shopping knowledge and skills goes beyond understanding

money and its role in the exchange process. One must understand shopping procedures and scripts, learn how to compare prices and quantities, understand pricing as a
mechanism for relaying value, and become aware of the retail establishments where
most shopping activity takes place. Below, we summarize existing research on each of
these topics.

Retail Store Knowledge. Children are frequent visitors to retail stores at a young age.
Convenience stores, discount stores, and supermarkets are the favorites of younger
children (5-9 years), while specialty stores, such as toy or sporting good stores, are favorites with older children (10-12 years) (McNeal and McDaniel 1981). By the time
a child reaches middle childhood, s/he is visiting and making purchases in an average
of 5.2 stores per week, or over 270 shopping visits per year (McNeal 1992).

These shopping experiences, coupled with developments in cognitive and social
reasoning, lead to an understanding of retail institutions. In one of the few and earliest studies on this topic, McNeal (1964) reports interesting developments between the
ages of 5 and 9 years of age. At age 5, children see stores as a source for snack and
sweets, but are unsure of why stores exist except to fulfill their own needs for these
products. By the time children reach the age of 7, shopping is seen as »necessary and
exciting.« At age 9, shopping is seen as a »necessary part of life,« accompanied by a
much greater understanding that retail stores are owned by people to sell goods at a
profit. Thus, there is a considerable shift in understanding the purpose of retail establishments from the preschool years (an egocentric view of stores as fulfilling my
wants) to the early elementary school years (a dual view of stores as profit centers that
fulfill consumer wants). This shift is consistent with our view of the transition from
the perceptual stage, where children have an egocentric perspective, to the analytical
stage, where children have the ability to reason from another person's perspective, such
as retailers who have a profit motive.

Detailed knowledge about retail stores also expands during this age period. In a
recent study, McNeal (1992) asked children in second, third, and fourth grade to draw
pictures of »what comes to mind when you think about going shopping.« Findings
from a content analysis of the pictures supports the fact that older children understand
the process and purpose of shopping and include a variety of retailers (supermarkets,
specialty stores, discount and department stores) in their depictions. Children's drawings reveal that their shopping experiences have resulted in a good deal of knowledge
about aspects of store layouts, product offerings, brands, and the like. As McNeal concludes (p. 13): »By the time children are in the third and fourth grades, they can provide detailed descriptions of a KMart or Kroger store, including store layouts, product and brand offerings of items for children and their households, and names and
characteristics of some people who work in stores.«

Shopping Scripts. Understanding the sequence of events involved in shopping is clearly one of the most important aspects of transaction knowledge. As noted earlier, children acquire a vast amount of experience as an observer or participant in the shopping process at very early ages. But, exposure to the shopping process does not necessarily result in an understanding of the basic sequence of events involved in shopping until children reach the preschool or kindergarten years (Berti and Bombi 1988; Karsten 1996).

An illustration of this point is provided by Karsten (1996) in a study conducted with children in kindergarten through fourth grade who were asked to participate in a »shopping game.« Each child was shown a small toy with a price tag on it (e.g., a toy dinosaur for 17 cents) and told that they had been given money (e.g., a quarter) by their mother to buy the item at the store. A store area was set up nearby with a small cash register, containing visible amounts of coins and bills. Children were asked to show the interviewer/cashier how they would buy the toy in the store. Although the results reveal age differences in terms of understanding the need for change and calculating change amounts, the basic shopping script was enacted by even the youngest children in the study. As Karsten concludes (p. 109): »Even the youngest subjects in the study understood that one selected their item, checked their money, decided what to purchase and placed it on the cashier's counter, waited for the cashier to check and record the price and perhaps offer change – they even reminded the interviewer to hand them a pretend receipt.«

Shopping scripts undergo further development as children accumulate more experience and acquire the cognitive abilities needed to transform individual shopping experiences into more abstract and complex scripts. The role of experience and age-related cognitive abilities in script formation is illustrated by John and Whitney (1986) in a study with children from 4 to 10 years of age. The shopping script studied here was returning or exchanging an item at a store. The study was conducted in a rural area, where local stores were limited to gas stations and a small grocery store, with a larger retail area located about an hour away. Such a setting was chosen to minimize the amount of experience that children would have with returning items to the store, since the rural location made returns to the larger retail area quite inconvenient and infrequent. In order to study how scripts develop with experience, children in each of three age groups (4–5 years, 6–7 years, 9–10 years) were read different stories about a boy or girl exchanging or returning a faulty product to a store. The amount of experience was varied by the number of stories read, resulting in low (1 story), medium (3 stories), or high (5 stories) levels of experience about product exchanges and returns. After hearing the assigned number of stories, children were asked to describe, in their own words, how one would go about returning or exchanging a product.

The findings reveal that older children, with more substantial cognitive abilities, have an advantage in transforming individual episodic experiences into more abstract script representations. As more information became available via new stories, the 9-10 year-olds produced scripts that were generally more abstract and more complex in terms of conditional events (if »x« happens, then do »y«). For example, these children were able to pick up information about differences in return and exchange policies from the different stories and incorporate these contingencies into their scripts. The 6-7 year-olds also produced more sophisticated scripts as more information became available, although this effect was limited to differences between the low and moderate levels of experience (1 vs. 3 stories). In contrast, the scripts produced by 4-5 year-olds were similar across experience levels, with a relatively high percentage of episodic details and no conditional events.

Follow-up studies, utilizing a similar methodology, have provided further understanding of the specific types of age-related cognitive abilities that impact script acquisition (Peracchio 1992; 1993). One explanation examined in these studies is that younger children have more difficulty encoding the individual central events that eventually need to be represented in the script. In particular, it appears that young children have two different types of encoding problems, one involving elaboration of single central events and one involving the organization of multiple central events into a script-like format. For example, young children (5-6 years) are less able to recall or recognize central events than are older children (7-8 years) unless the presentation format facilitates encoding of these events, such as multiple exposures to the same set of events presented in an audio-visual format (Peracchio 1992, experiment 1) or massed repetitions of the same set of events presented in an audio format (Peracchio 1993, experiment 1). When young children are exposed to slightly different variations of a script enactment, additional problems with discerning the event structure of the script and organizing the individual events into a whole may surface. In this case, it may be necessary to provide cues about the structure and goals of the script to provide the internal organization that younger children are less able to generate on their own (Peracchio 1992, experiment 2).

A second explanation for age differences involves the existence of retrieval difficulties once central events are encoded in memory. In contrast to older children, younger children may need more external prompts and retrieval cues to access whatever script knowledge they possess. Evidence to this effect can be found in the Peracchio studies cited above. Children's script knowledge was assessed using several response formats, which varied in terms of how much contextual support and how many retrieval cues were provided. For example, the least retrieval support mirrored the response format used by John and Whitney (1986): »How do you return something from the store?« More retrieval support was incorporated into two alternative response formats, one asking the basic script question in a more concrete form (»What would you do if I gave you this [broken toy] for your birthday?«) and one assessing script knowledge by a recognition task rather than recall (children were given 12 pictures representing central events and asked to tell a story). Across studies, young children were able to access a greater number of central events in correct order with response formats featuring more retrieval support.

Overall, these findings are consistent with our stage view of consumer socialization. Children in the perceptual stage (3-7 years) understand the basic shopping script, which consists of a concrete set of events that unfold in a stable order. What develops as children move into the analytical stage (7-11 years) is an ability to transform concrete details into more abstract events and to formulate contingent events that may or may not happen in any particular shopping experience. These developments can be traced to the enhanced information processing skills that children in the analytical stage come to possess.

Shopping Skills. We use the term shopping skills to refer to wide array of abilities used for comparing product value prior to purchase. Although one might expect to see a considerable amount of research in this area, the only existing study is reported by Turner and Brandt (1978). Preschool (age 4) and elementary school (ages 10-11) children were given several shopping tasks, one involving a comparison of product packages and quantity and one involving a comparison of product prices and quantity. For the first, children were shown two packages containing the same product, with one containing many individually wrapped pieces of candy and the other containing the same candy in one large size. The child was asked to compare the two packages and determine which contained more of the product. The correct answer was identified by looking at net weight on the packages. For the second task, children were shown three different sizes and shapes of packages containing the same product and asked to determine which one would give the most product for the money. The correct answer was determined by comparing unit prices per package. Responses to both tasks revealed that older children were more accurate in their comparisons as were children who were given more opportunities at home to manage money and participate in consumer decision making with other members of the family.

Pricing Knowledge. Despite the fact that children have substantial shopping skills by middle childhood, they pay relatively little attention to prices as an aspect of the marketplace. By the time children are eight or nine years old, they know that products have prices, know where to look for price information, and know that there are price variations among products and stores (McNeal and McDaniel 1981). Despite this, very few children know the prices for frequently-purchased items (Stephens and

Moore 1975) and very few ask about price when listing the type of information they would want to know about a new product prior to purchase (Ward, Wackman, and Wartella 1977). Other cues, such as brand names, are far more salient and important to children. For example, in McNeal's (1992) study, in which children from the second, third, and fourth grades were asked to draw pictures about shopping, about 40% of the drawings pictured products with brand names whereas only 10% of the drawings showed actual price information (e.g., $3.99).

Perhaps part of the reason children pay little attention to pricing is that they have relatively undeveloped notions about how prices reflect the valuation of goods and services. Adults, for example, see prices as a reflection of the utility or function of the item to the consumer, the costs of inputs incurred by the manufacturer to make the item, and the relative scarcity of the item in the marketplace (Fox and Kehret-Ward 1985). Not until early adolescence do children perceive this full range of connections between price and value, with younger children viewing price simply in terms of concrete physical features of products (Berti and Bombi 1988; Fox and Kehret-Ward 1985; 1990).

A study by Fox and Kehret-Ward (1990) illustrates how notions of price and value develop from the preschool years to adolescence to adulthood. Subjects were told a story about a group of friends who decided to open a bicycle shop and needed to set a price for each bicycle; each of the friends had a different idea about how to price the bicycles, such as price based on physical size (larger bikes should cost more), amount of labor required for manufacturing, or preference (bikes people like best should cost more). After presenting these suggestions, children and adults were asked whether the pricing scheme was a good idea and why. The responses were informative in identifying what criterion the child sees as a basis for retail prices and the source of value connected to that criterion. Preschoolers pointed to a product's perceptual features, especially size, as the basis for pricing, but articulated no theory for why these features provide more value. Ten year-olds also linked price to perceptual features (size or fancy features), but reasoned that a higher price would be forthcoming due the amount of production inputs required. Thirteen year-olds exhibited a more abstract level of reasoning, viewing prices as a function of the quality of the product's inputs and the preferences of potential buyers. Adults voiced similar opinions, also adding notions about supply and demand to the mixture of factors contributing to value.

These age differences provide a vivid illustration of children's reasoning skills at different stages of consumer socialization. Children in the perceptual stage (ages 3-7) focus on perceptual features, but without abstract reasoning that connects these features to prices. Although children in the analytical stage (ages 7-11) also mentioned perceptual features, they related these features to functional reasons why the product should cost more. Adolescents in the reflective stage (ages 11-16) also considered the preferences of potential buyers, which reflects an enhanced understanding of other people's perspectives and opinions.

DECISION MAKING SKILLS AND ABILITIES

Children assume the role of consumer decision makers at a young age. Children as young as two years of age are commonly allowed to select treats at the grocery store, express desires for fast food, and indicate preferences for toys on visits to Santa. As they grow older, children develop more sophisticated decision-making skills and abilities. They become more aware of different information sources, seek out information about important functional aspects of products, utilize more attribute information in evaluating products, and adapt their decision strategies to the nature of the choice environment they face. These developments are reviewed in more detail below.

INFORMATION SEARCH

Awareness and Use of Information Sources. As children grow older, they develop a greater awareness of different information sources and deploy these sources in a more flexible manner depending on need (Moore and Stephens 1975; Moschis and Moore 1979; Stephens and Moore 1975; Ward, Wackman, and Wartella 1977). Much of the developing awareness of information sources takes place during early and middle childhood. To illustrate, Ward, Wackman, and Wartella (1977) asked kindergartners, third graders, and sixth graders where they could »find out about« three kinds of new products: toys, snack foods, and clothing. The average number of information sources increased with age, from a low of 3.66 sources for kindergartners to a high of 6.68 for sixth graders. Kindergartners relied most on in-store experiences, whereas third and sixth graders added mass media advertising and interpersonal sources to their lists.

During the adolescent years, further developments take place in the use and preference for information sources. Older adolescents seek out more sources of information as a prelude to purchasing (Moore and Stephens 1975; Moschis and Moore 1979; Stephens and Moore 1975). More importantly, adolescents develop preferences for specific information sources, favoring peers and friends over parents and mass media as they mature (Moore and Stephens 1975; Moschis and Moore 1979; Stephens and

Moore 1975; Tootelian and Gaedeke 1992). However, adolescents also become more flexible in using different sources, favoring peers and friends for some types of products and parents for others. For example, Moschis and Moore (1979) asked middle and high school students to identify the sources they would rely on most before buying eight different products. Friends were relied on most for products where peer acceptance is an important consideration (e.g., sunglasses), whereas parents were a favored source for products with a higher perceived risk in terms of price and performance (e.g., hair dryer). In addition, parents were more influential at the information gathering stage than at the product evaluation stage (see also Moschis and Moore 1983). Mass media appears to play a relatively small role as an information source, perhaps because adolescents have either learned to be skeptical of advertising or because adolescents watch less television than their younger counterparts (Moschis and Moore 1979).

Apart from aging, preferences for information sources can also be affected by family environment. Moschis and Moore (1978, cited in Moschis 1985) provide an example of how family communication patterns affect adolescent preferences for several sources of information, including parents, peers, and mass media. Four types of family communication patterns were studied: laissez-faire, protective, pluralistic, and consensual families. Laissez-faire families are characterized by little parent-child communication; protective families stress obedience and social harmony, with little consideration given to developing the child's own opinions; pluralistic families encourage the child to develop new ideas and promote open communication without requiring obedience to authority; consensual families combine the idea of children developing their own views with the need for social harmony and family cohesiveness (see Moschis 1985 for a more detailed description). Moschis and Moore found that adolescents from pluralistic families prefer information from a variety of sources, with a higher preference for parental advice than adolescents from other family types. In contrast, adolescents from protective families are highly receptive to peers, and to a lesser extent, television advertising. Laissez-faire children also rely less on parental advice, but are also less likely to rely on peers, implicating the use of fewer information sources overall.

Type of Information Sought. As children mature, they learn to rely on different types of information. Perhaps the most important development is a change from reliance on perceptual product attributes to a more detailed consideration of functional and product performance attributes. This trend is illustrated nicely by Ward, Wackman, and Wartella (1977) in their study with kindergartners, third graders, and sixth graders. Children were asked the following question: »Suppose you wanted to buy a new television set. What would you want to know about it?« Children of all ages inquired about perceptual attributes (e.g., color versus black & white), though mentions of this

sort were lower among sixth graders. With increasing age, however, mentions of performance attributes (e.g., easy to operate), functional attributes (e.g., quality), and
price became more common.

Similar findings have been reported with adolescents. In the Moschis and Moore
(1979) study described earlier, middle and high school students were asked to indicate
which of the following types of information could tell them the best product to buy:
»one that is on sale,« »one that is advertised a lot,« »one with a well-known brand
name,« »one that my parents like,« or »one sold by a well-known store.« Certain types
of information were more valued than others, with adolescents favoring products on
sale and with a well-known brand name. The focus on price and brand name (as a
surrogate for functional attributes) is consistent across product categories, as is the limited value placed on signals such as high levels of advertising or placement in a well-
known store.

Adapting to Search Costs and Benefits. One of the hallmarks of a mature decision
maker is the ability to adjust one's information search to the costs and benefits of
gathering information. More information is gathered in situations where the benefits
of doing so are greater; less information is gathered in situations where the costs of
doing so are greater. Mature decision makers consider the trade-off between cost and
benefits as they consider collecting more information about a product category, seeking more information about different brands in a product category, and making more
visits to different retail outlets.

Children learn to adjust their information search efforts in line with cost and
benefit considerations as they grow older. Many of the basic mechanisms develop during the period from preschool to the early elementary school years. Early in this developmental period, children show an ability to adjust their information search efforts
to at least one of the two cues. Davidson and Hudson (1988, experiment 1) report
that even preschoolers modify their search behavior in view of the benefits of searching more information prior to choice. Preschoolers in this study spent more time
searching through a set of alternatives when they were told that their final choice
would be irreversible rather than reversible at a later date.

The next step, adjusting information search in line with *both* costs and benefits,
emerges in the early elementary school years. An illustration of this development is
provided in a study by Gregan-Paxton and John (1995). Four to 7 year-olds were
asked to play a game called »house of prizes.« The game involved making a choice
between two cardboard boxes decorated to look like houses, with a prize hidden behind each of four windows of the house. Children were allowed to search windows
to uncover the prizes prior to making a choice, with differing costs and benefits of
doing so. In the low benefit condition, all four windows within a house contained the

same prize; in the high benefit condition, every window in each house had a different prize. In the low cost condition, children could uncover as many prizes as they wished prior to making a choice, with the only cost of doing so being minimal effort and additional time in making a choice; in the high cost condition, children were given several pieces of candy prior to the start of the game and had to give up one piece of candy for each prize they wanted to uncover. In all cases, the number of prizes uncovered was used as a measure of the amount of information search.

Older children modified their search behavior more in line with appropriate cost-benefit trade-offs than did the 4 to 5 year-olds. The 6 to 7 year-olds gathered the least information in the condition with the least favorable cost-benefit profile (high cost, low benefit) and the most information in the condition with the most favorable cost-benefit profile (low cost, high benefit). Younger children were less discerning, gathering the most information for one of the conditions warranting a very modest degree of search (low cost, low benefit) and much less information for one of the conditions warranting the most extensive information search (low cost, high benefit). These children exhibited a limited ability to adapt to cost-benefit trade-offs, reducing the extent of their information search in the low benefit condition when search costs were increased from low to high. The same abilities, however, were not in evidence in the high benefit condition when search costs were similarly increased. In contrast, older children modified their search behavior across all conditions, demonstrating a greater degree of differentiation in search activity and strategies.

These developments pertaining to information search are consistent with our description of consumer socialization stages. Young children in the perceptual stage (ages 3-7) tend to gather information from a small number of sources, focus on a small amount of information that is often perceptual in nature, and are just beginning to adapt their search strategy to the task at hand. Children in the analytical (ages 7-11) and reflective (ages 11-16) stages cast a wider net in searching for information, making use of additional information and information sources when needed. They approach the search process in a more strategic way, going beyond simple perceptual features of products as well as adapting their search strategies and sources to the situation they face.

PRODUCT EVALUATION AND COMPARISON

Children become more informed consumers with age, using the information they have gathered to evaluate and compare product offerings. With increasing age, children focus more on important and relevant attribute information (Davidson 1991b;

Wartella et. al 1979), use more attributes and dimensions in forming preferences (Bahn 1986; Capon and Kuhn 1980; Ward, Wackman, and Wartella 1977), more carefully consider these preferences in making choices (Roedder, Sternthal, and Calder 1983), and are more successful in comparing brands on dimensions such as price and quality (Turner and Brandt 1978). Several of these developments are described in more detail below.

Use of Attribute Information. The most consistent finding here is that younger children use fewer attributes or dimensions in forming preferences and comparing products. Researchers have demonstrated an increase in the use of attributes and dimensions as children move from preschool to early elementary school (Bahn 1986; Capon and Kuhn 1980; Ward, Wackman, and Wartella 1977) and from early elementary school to middle school and late adolescence (Capon and Kuhn 1980).

Capon and Kuhn (1980, experiment 1) provide a good example of this trend in a study with kindergartners, fourth graders, eighth graders, and college students. Subjects were shown notebooks that varied on four dimensions: color (red or green), surface (dull or shiny), shape (long/thin or short/wide), and fastening (side or top). Participants viewed each notebook individually and were asked to indicate how much they liked it on a 9-point scale. After rating all notebooks, subjects were asked to evaluate each notebook dimension, indicating how much more they liked one level than another (e.g., how much they preferred red over green notebooks or vice versa) on a similar 9-point scale. Comparing the dimension ratings with overall notebook preferences, the authors found that kindergartners had a difficult time incorporating preferences for even one dimension into their overall ratings, though more of these children were able to do so in a follow-up study with less complex stimuli (see experiment 2). Older children tended to use one single dimension, with integration of two or more dimensions becoming more common in late adolescence.

Use of Relevant Attribute Information. The ability to focus on relevant attribute information also emerges as children move through the early elementary school years. Kindergarten children are often attracted to perceptually salient information, which may or may not be relevant (Wartella et. al 1979). The ability to ignore irrelevant information, in favor of more relevant or important information, progresses as children move from kindergarten into the early elementary school grades (Wartella et. al 1979) and onward through early adolescence (Davidson 1991b).

An interesting example of this trend is offered by Wartella and her colleagues (1979) in a study conducted with kindergartners and third graders. Children were shown a series of cards, with each card containing a drawing of two or more hypothetical candies. These candies varied by the type of ingredient (chocolate, caramel, raisins, peanuts, and licorice) and the amount of each ingredient (five pieces or two pieces). For example, one card showed »Candy E« with lots of chocolate (5 pieces) and »Candy F« with a little chocolate (2 pieces), lots of raisins (5 pieces), and lots of peanuts (5 pieces). Children were told to imagine that they were choosing a present for a friend who likes some ingredients more than others (e.g., a friend who likes chocolate very much and raisins and peanuts less). The cards and attribute importance information were designed in such a way that the child's strategy for comparing and choosing items was revealed by the set of choices made.

Kindergartners focused their comparisons on the total amount of candy ingredients shown on the card, regardless of the attribute preferences of their friend. Over two-thirds of these children simply selected the candy with the most ingredients. In contrast, almost two-thirds of the third graders used the attribute importance information, comparing the different candies on the basis of at least one relevant ingredient. These data are consistent with our characterization of younger children in the perceptual stage (ages 3-7), where perceptual features are dominant in reasoning and information processing capabilities limit the amount of information that can be processed. As children move into the analytical stage (ages 7-11), one sees a shift in thinking from a perceptual to a more abstract (functional) orientation and the adoption of a more thoughtful evaluation process that results in a focus on relevant information and a broader consideration of more than one attribute.

DECISION MAKING STRATEGIES

Emergence of Decision-Making Strategies. Important developments in the emergence of decision-making strategies occur as children acquire the ability to selectively attend to and process more information prior to choice. Because many decision strategies require attention to multiple attributes, accompanied by a focus on the most important or relevant ones, these types of abilities must be in place before children can implement a number of compensatory and noncompensatory strategies.

Although research examining the emergence of specific strategies is sparse, the study by Wartella and her colleagues (1979) described earlier provides an interesting glimpse into this area of development. Recall that children were asked to make hypothetical choices among candies that varied in terms of the number of different ingredients (e.g., chocolate, raisins). Attribute importance information was supplied by describing the ingredient preferences of a friend who would receive the chosen candy as a gift. Given the particular set of choice alternatives and attribute (ingredient) preferences, the researchers were able to discern whether or not children were using a number of different strategies: best single attribute (choice based only on the amount of the single most important ingredient contained in the candy), variety of attributes (choice based on the number of different ingredients contained in the candy), lexico-graphic strategy (choice based on the amount of the most important ingredient and, in the case of a tie, on the amount of the second most important ingredient), and a weighted adding strategy (choice based on the sum of the products of the importance weights and amount of all ingredients contained in each candy).

The favorite strategy of kindergartners was to choose the option with the most ingredients, regardless of importance weights, consistent with what we would expect for children in the perceptual stage (ages 3-7). Third graders used a variety of strate-gies, split between the single best attribute, variety of attributes, and lexicographic strategies. The weighted adding strategy, which is compensatory in nature, was used by only a small percentage of the older children. These trends, especially the use of the single best attribute and lexicographic strategies by older children, signal the emergence of noncompensatory strategies in children by the time they reach middle childhood. Indeed, in subsequent studies described below, the use of noncompensa-tory strategies appears quite ingrained by the time children reach early adolescence (Klayman 1985; Nakajima and Hotta 1989).

Adaptive Use of Decision Making Strategies. With age, children not only develop a repertoire of decision strategies, but also learn how to use this repertoire in a flexible and effective manner. Perhaps the most important development is the ability to adapt strategies to the demands of the decision environment. Evidence to this effect is pro-vided by research that examines how children respond to increasingly complex deci-sion environments that are characterized by more choice alternatives and more infor-mation per choice alternative.

Mature decision makers adapt to more complex environments in several ways. As the number of alternatives and attributes increases, they restrict their search to a smaller proportion of the total information available, focus their search on more promising alternatives, and switch from using highly demanding compensatory choice strategies to less cognitively demanding noncompensatory ones (see Payne, Bettman, and Johnson 1993). Similar abilities to adapt develop in children as they move from middle childhood to early adolescence, being consistently exhibited by the time chil-dren reach 11 or 12 years of age (Davidson 1991a, 1991b; Gregan-Paxton and John 1997; Klayman 1985). Children's abilities undergo further refinement as they move into late adolescence, using a wider array of simplifying strategies in a more system-atic manner (Nakajima and Hotta 1989).

An illustration of these developments is provided by Davidson (1991a) in her study conducted with second, fifth, and eighth graders. Children made choices from sets of alternatives (such as bicycles) shown on information boards, which varied in terms of the number of alternatives and dimensions listed. Four information boards varying in complexity were shown: 3 (alternatives) x 3 (dimensions), 3 x 6, 6 x 3, and 6 x 6. For example, one of the 3 x 3 boards listed 3 alternatives on the left hand side (Bike S, Bike T, Bike W) and three dimensions across the top (size of bike, price of bike, number of friends that have bike). Information about each alternative on these dimensions was hidden from view by a card, but children were allowed to uncover as much information as they wanted prior to choice.

Age differences were apparent in the way children adapted to increasingly complex information boards. With increasing age, children were more efficient in gathering information prior to choice, searching less exhaustively and accessing a smaller proportion of available information as complexity increased. Related to this was the fact that older children (fifth and eighth graders) exhibited search patterns indicative of a greater use of noncompensatory strategies, eliminating some alternatives quickly and moving onto more promising ones. In particular, these children appeared to be using conjunctive decision rules, consistent with Klayman's (1985) findings. In contrast, younger children (second graders) responded to increasing complexity by making smaller adjustments in their search strategies without using a consistent simplifying strategy such as the conjunctive rule.

What accounts for these age differences? Although a full accounting is not yet available, there is evidence that two important skills contribute to children's growing abilities as adaptive decision makers. First, Davidson (1991b) notes that selective attention is an important component of many simplifying decision rules, as children must learn to focus their attention on more relevant information and ignore information about poor alternatives in the process of making a choice. As we have seen, selective attention to relevant choice information appears to be a stumbling block for younger children. Second, Gregan-Paxton and John (1997) suggest sensitivity to the costs of processing large amounts of information as an important component of adaptive decision making. In complex decision environments, children need to recognize that exhaustive decision-making strategies are very costly in terms of time and effort *and* that simplifying strategies yield a more effective balance of effort and accuracy. Young children pay less attention to these costs and, therefore, have less incentive to change their strategies, aside from a few minor adjustments that are relatively ineffective.

Both of these mechanisms relate to cognitive abilities and are consistent with our characterization of young children in the perceptual stage (ages 3–7). Older children in the analytical stage (ages 7–11) exhibit a more thoughtful and adaptive approach to decision making. However, our stage descriptions also suggest that social development may play a role, specifically the emergence of more mature perspective-taking skills. Children in the analytical stage begin to see their environment from multiple perspectives, understanding that a stimulus or situation can be viewed in different ways. This way of thinking may carry over to the decision making realm, as children become more accustomed to seeing more than one perspective or way of doing things, leading the way for adaptivity to occur.

PURCHASE INFLUENCE AND NEGOTIATION STRATEGIES

Children exert substantial influence on family purchases in several ways. Purchase requests are the most overt of all influence attempts, with children asking for a wide array of products such as toys, candy, clothing, sporting goods, and other products for their own use. Over time, children influence purchases for many of these items in a more passive way due to the fact that parents know what their children like and make purchases accordingly. But, the extent of influence does not stop with frequently purchased consumer package goods, toys, and athletic equipment. Children also exert some degree of influence in family decision making regarding items such as cars, vacations, computers, and home furnishings. In this role, they might initiate the purchase, collect information about alternatives, suggest retail outlets, and have a say in the final decision.

The extent to which children influence purchases within the family depends on several factors. Older children exert more influence than younger children, a pattern that holds true across a wide age range from kindergarten to high school (Atkin 1978a; Darley and Lim 1986; Jenkins 1979; Moschis and Mitchell 1986; Nelson 1978; Rust 1993; Ward and Wackman 1972; Swinyard and Sim 1987; Ward, Wackman, and Wartella 1977). Children have the most influence over purchases of child-relevant items (e.g., cereal, toys, clothes), a moderate degree of influence for family activities (e.g., vacations, restaurants), and the least influence for purchases of consumer durables and expensive items (Belch et al., 1985; Corfman and Harlam 1997; Foxman and Tansuhaj 1988; Foxman et al. 1989; Isler, Popper, and Ward 1987; Swinyard and Sim 1987). In these later categories, children's influence is greatest in the early stages of family decision making (e.g., problem recognition, information search) and declines as final decisions are made (Belch et. al 1985; Filiatraut and Ritchie 1980; Hempel 1974; Nelson 1978; Swinyard and Sim 1987; Szybillo and Sosanie 1977). And, finally, children tend to exert more influence in higher income families (Jenkins 1979; Nelson 1978), larger families (Jenkins 1979; Nelson 1978), and families with a less restrictive, less authoritarian, and more concept-oriented communication style (Burns and

63

Gillett 1987; Jenkins 1979; Moschis and Mitchell 1986; Szybillo, Sosanie, and Tenenbein 1977; Ward and Wackman 1972). These trends clearly point to purchase influence as an important part of children's developing role as a consumer.

More interesting, from a socialization perspective, is the fact that children learn ways to become successful as influence agents through the use of increasingly sophisticated influence and negotiation strategies. Toddlers and preschool children exert their influence in a very direct way, often pointing to products and occasionally grabbing them off store shelves for deposit inside their parent's shopping cart (Rust 1993). As children become more verbal in their requests, they ask for products by name, sometimes begging, screaming and whining to get what they want (McNeal 1992). For frequently-purchased items, such as snack food and cereal, children are often able to exert their influence simply by asking (Isler, Popper, and Ward 1987), due to parents who become more accepting of children's preferences for such items and more comfortable with the idea of occasionally yielding to those preferences.

Bargaining, compromise, and persuasion enter the picture as children make their way through elementary school. Instead of simple requests for products, which parents then accept or reject, interactions between parents and children of this age feature more mutual discussion and compromise (Rust 1993). Discussion of this sort is made possible by the fact that children are developing greater abilities to see situations from more than their own point of view, eventually being able to see multiple viewpoints, such as theirs as well as their parents, simultaneously. As we have noted, this dual perspective is characteristic of older children in the analytical stage (ages 7-11) of consumer socialization. Children are also primed to assume a more active role in purchase discussions after years of listening to their parents describe why certain requests can or cannot be honored (Palan and Wilkes 1997; Popper 1979), in effect learning to reason, persuade, and negotiate for what they want. Finally, it is also the case that extended discussions become more necessary as children shift purchase requests from inexpensive items such as candy and cereal to more expensive items, including sporting goods, clothes, and electronic goods (McNeal 1992).

By the time they reach early adolescence, and move into the reflective stage (ages 11-16), children have an entire repertoire of influence strategies available to them (Kim et al. 1991; Manchanda and Moore-Shay 1996; Palan and Wilkes 1997). These strategies are more sophisticated, appealing to parents in seemingly rational ways, and are used in a flexible manner to suit the situation or answer the objection of a parent. A good illustration of this sophistication is provided by Palan and Wilkes (1997) in a study of influence strategies conducted with 12-15 year-olds and their parents. Using depth interviews, the authors identified a large and diverse set of purchase influence strategies used by adolescents: (1) bargaining strategies, including reasoning and offers to pay for part of the purchase; (2) persuasion strategies, including expressions of opinions, persistent requesting, and begging; (3) request strategies, including straightforward requests and expressions of needs or wants; and (4) emotional strategies, including anger, pouting, guilt trips, and sweet talk.

Bargaining and persuasion were favorites among the group of adolescents, with emotional strategies favored least. Variations in frequency appear to be driven, in part, by which strategies adolescents perceive to be the most effective in obtaining desired items. Strategies such as reasoning and offers to pay for part of an item are seen as very effective; strategies such as begging and getting angry are seen as least effective. The sophistication of this group is revealed in the following excerpts from depth interviews, as the first subject (male, age 13) describes the use of a bargaining strategy and the second subject (male, age 15) describes the use of a persuasion strategy:

»When I got my Super Nintendo, at first it was really kind of hopeless. I said, »Dad, can I get a Super Nintendo?« even though I already had a Nintendo and a computer. He said it would depend on how I paid him back, so we have a bargain going on paying him back about $20 a month … Things that are pretty expensive that you can pay back over a period of time, those are things I negotiate deals for.« (p. 161)

»With my parents, if I just keep at it, I usually get it. Like with this computer … I dreamed up the idea and got my parents to agree to get the computer for a family Christmas gift. I've been at it for four months now, and it's come to the point where my dad is about to pick one out. Persistence. You have to keep at it.« (p. 163)

The growing sophistication of influence strategies among adolescents is consistent with our characterization of children as they move into the reflective stage. Also consistent are findings related to the way adolescents employ these influence techniques, adapting their strategies depending on what they view as most effective in influencing their parents. One way of doing so is by duplicating the strategies used by their parents for responding to their purchase requests. In the Palan and Wilkes' (1997) study, adolescents perceived reasoning as the most effective influence strategy when they came from families where parents reported the frequent use of reasoning strategies. Also perceived as effective were influence strategies that had a logical connection with the objections parents raised to a purchase request. For example, in families where parents often refused purchase requests by stating the family could not afford the item, adolescents knew it was effective to use strategies that reduced the monetary outlay, such as offers to pay for part of the item. Finally, some preliminary evidence suggests that adolescents also make adjustments in their use of influence strategies depending upon parental styles. For example, simple request strategies are used more frequently with authoritative and permissive fathers, who score high in warmth, and are used least with neglecting and authoritarian fathers, who score lower in warmth (Palan 1997).

CONSUMPTION MOTIVES AND VALUES

Consumer socialization involves more than the acquisition of knowledge and skills related to the consumer role. It also includes the learning and adoption of motives and values pertaining to consumption activities. Though a variety of motives and values might be transmitted, the focus of consumer researchers has been on »undesirable« outcomes of the socialization process, including orientations toward conspicuous consumption, materialism, and nonrational impulse-oriented consumption.

MATERIALISM

One of the most enduring concerns about consumer socialization is that our culture encourages children to focus on material goods as a means of achieving personal happiness, success, and self-fulfillment. Concerns of this nature have escalated as evidence has become available pointing to a heightened level of materialism among children. Direct expenditures and purchase influence for children 4-12 years of age have virtually doubled in the last ten years, as have marketing efforts to this age group (McNeal 1998). Media reports of assaults and thefts of items such as Nike athletic shoes and Starter athletic jackets have provided vivid portrayals of materialism among youth (Diaz 1992). Finally, longitudinal studies of materialistic values have shown a dramatic shift in focus toward materialistic life goals among high school seniors from the early 1970's through the 1980's (Easterlin and Crimmins 1991).

Understanding when and how such materialistic values form has been the central focus of consumer socialization research. Research suggests that children clearly value the possession of material goods from a very young age, sometimes favoring them above all else. A case in point is provided by Goldberg and Gorn (1978) in a study with 4-5 year-old boys. Children were divided into three groups. The first two groups saw an advertisement for a new toy (»Ruckus Raisers«), with the first group seeing the advertisement twice in one showing and the second group seeing the advertisement once each day for two days. A third group did not see any advertising for the new toy and served as a control group. After viewing the ad, children were given a choice between two hypothetical playmates: one described as »very nice« that did not own the new toy and one described as »not so nice« but owning the new toy. About a third of the control group selected the boy with the new toy, but 43%-65% of the group seeing the advertisement for the new toy selected this playmate. Children were also asked to choose between two hypothetical play situations: playing alone with the new toy or playing in a sandbox with friends (without the toy). Again, about a third of the control group selected the new toy; but, in both the experimental groups, a majority of children selected the play situation with the new toy.

Desires for material goods become more nuanced as children progress through elementary school, with material goods becoming aligned with social status, happiness, and personal fulfillment. Fueled by a greater understanding of the social significance of goods, consumption symbolism, and interpersonal relationships, materialistic values crystallize by the time children reach fifth or sixth grade (see Goldberg, Peracchio, Gorn, and Bamossy 1997). An interesting example of this development is reported by Baker and Gentry (1996) in their study of collecting as a hobby among first and fifth graders. Though children across grades collected similar types of items – such as sports cards, dolls, and rocks – they did so for different reasons. First graders often compared their possessions to those of others in terms of quantity. Collecting appeared to be simply a way of getting more than someone else. Among fifth graders, however, the motivations for collecting had more social connotations. For example, one boy appreciated collecting as a way of making himself unique: »you have stuff that maybe nobody else does« (Jeremy, p. 136). A second boy exhibited an even greater sense of personal achievement through his collecting: »it makes me feel good about myself that I got some baseball cards that some other people don't have« (Mark, p. 136).

These differences in motives between first and fifth graders illustrate the types of changes that occur as children move from the perceptual stage (ages 3-7) to the analytical stage (ages 7-11). First graders, who are in the perceptual stage, base the value of material goods on a perceptual dimension (quantity). Fifth graders, who have moved through the analytical stage, see things quite differently by virtue of their social comparison skills. At this age, children are beginning to place value on material possessions based on their ability to elevate one's status above others or to fit into the expectations of a social group. Shifts in social development, including impression formation and social perspective-taking, set the stage for the valuation of material goods in terms of personal fulfillment and social status.

Once the stage is set for the adoption of materialistic values, the extent to which adolescents exhibit these orientations depends on several factors in their environment,

67

such as family communication, peer communication, and television exposure. One of the most interesting set of findings links materialism and family communication structure. Children in families with a socio-oriented communication structure, which stresses deference and harmony among familiy members while avoiding controversy, exhibit higher levels of materialism (Moschis and Moore 1979b). This is even the case with consensual families who balance socio-oriented communication with concept-oriented communication, which encourages children to develop their own views and think through controversies (Moore and Moschis 1981). Families high in concept-orientation, such as pluralistics, produce children with much lower levels of materialism (Moore and Moschis 1981).

Exposure to communication outside the family is also influential. In particular, materialism is higher in children who more frequently communicate with peers (Churchill and Moschis 1979; Moschis and Churchill 1978) and are more susceptible to their influence (Achenreiner 1997). Exposure to television advertising and programming has a similar effect, with higher levels of materialism reported for adolescents who watch more television (Churchill and Moschis 1979; Moschis and Moore 1982) and watch television for social utility reasons to learn about lifestyles and behaviors associated with consumer goods (Moschis and Churchill 1978; Ward and Wackman 1971). The causal direction remains unclear, however, as exposure to peers and television might encourage materialism *or* materialism might encourage a search for information about valued goods from sources such as peers and television advertising. Whatever the case, correlations between the amount of television viewing and materialism become insignificant in the long-run when prior levels of materialism are partialled out (Moschis and Moore 1982). Correlations between television viewing and materialism are also insignificant in the long-run for families with high levels of communication about consumer matters (Moschis and Moore 1982).

In contrast to these findings, the search for demographic and socioeconomic influences on materialism has been less fruitful. Age, socio-economic status, birth order, among others, have been included as factors in several studies but have produced mixed results. Perhaps the only consistent findings are with regard to gender, with males reporting higher levels of materialism than females (Achenreiner 1997; Churchill and Moschis 1979).

SOCIAL AND ECONOMIC CONSUMPTION MOTIVES

Another facet of consumer socialization is the learning and subsequent adoption of motives for evaluating and selecting goods and services. In research to date, two contrasting motives have been examined, social motivations and economic motivations for consumption. Social motivations for consumption emphasize conspicuous consumption and social expression (e.g., peer approval), whereas economic motivations for consumption focus on functional and economic features of products (e.g., prices and guarantees). On a normative level, social motivations are often viewed as undesirable, with economic motivations typically viewed as more desirable socialization outcomes.

The findings regarding social consumption motives are virtually identical to those for materialism reviewed above. Stronger social motivations for consumption are positively associated with socio-oriented family communication (Moschis and Moore 1979c), higher levels of peer communication about consumption (Churchill and Moschis 1979; Moschis and Churchill 1978), greater exposure to television (Churchill and Moschis 1979; Moschis and Churchill 1978), and social utility reasons for watching television advertisements (Moschis and Churchill 1978). Social consumption motives are also reported to be higher in male than female adolescents (Churchill and Moschis 1979).

Economic motives for consumption are influenced by many of the same factors, albeit in an opposite direction. Stronger economic motivations are negatively associated with socio-oriented family communication (Moschis and Moore 1979c), greater exposure to television (Moschis and Churchill 1978), and social utility reasons for watching television advertisements (Moschis and Churchill 1978). In contrast, economic motivations are encouraged by more frequent family communication about consumption matters (Churchill and Moschis 1979; Moschis and Churchill 1978) as well as increasing age and maturity (Churchill and Moschis 1979).

GOING FORWARD: THOUGHTS FOR FUTURE SOCIALIZATION RESEARCH

We have proposed a framework for viewing consumer socialization as progressing in a series of three stages – perceptual, analytical, and reflective – capturing major shifts from preschool through adolescence. These stages have been characterized along a number of dimensions that characterize children's knowledge, skills, and values during childhood and adolescence (See Table 1). We have also reviewed empirical evidence consistent with these stages, documenting children's growing sophistication about products, brands, advertising, shopping, pricing, decision-making strategies, and influence approaches (See Table 2).

Topic	Perceptual stage 3-7 years
Advertising knowledge	• Can distinguish advertisements from programs based on perceptual features • Believe advertisements are truthful, funny and interesting • Positive attitudes towards advertisements
Transaction knowledge: **Product brand knowledge**	• Can recognize brand names and beginning to associate them with product categories • Perceptual cues used to identify product categories • Beginning to understand symbolic aspects of consumption based on perceptual features • Egocentric view of retail stores as a source of desired items
Shopping knowledge and skills	• Understand sequence of events in the basic shopping script • Value of products and prices based on perceptual-features
Decision making skills and abilities: **Information search**	• Limited awareness of information sources • Focus on perceptual attributes • Emerging ability to adapt to cost-benefit trade-offs
Product evaluation	• Use of perceptually salient attribute information • Use of single attributes
Decision strategies	• Limited repertoire of strategies • Emerging ability strategies to tasks – usually need cues to adapt
Purchase influence and **negotiation strategies**	• Use direct requests and emotional appeals • Limited ability to adapt strategy to person or situation
Consumption motives and values: **Materialism**	• Value of possessions based on surface features, such as »having more« of something

Table 2. Summary of findings by consumer socialization stage

Analytical stage 7-11 years	Reflective stage 1-16 years
• Can distinguish advertisements from programs based on persuasive intent • Believe advertisements lie and contain bias and deception-but do not use these »cognitive defenses« • Negative attitudes toward advertisements	• Understand persuasive intent of advertisements as well as specific advertisement tactics and appeals • Believe advertisements lie and know how to spot specific instances of bias or deception in advertisements • Skeptical attitudes toward advertisements
• Increasing brand awareness, especially for child-relevant product categories • Underlying or functional cues used to define product categories • Increased understanding of symbolic aspects of consumption • Understand retail stores are owned to sell goods and make a profit	• Substantial brand awareness for adult-oriented as well as child-relevant product categories • Underlying or functional cues used to define product categories • Sophisticated understanding of consumption symbolism for product categories and brand names • Understanding and enthusiasm for retail stores
• Shopping scripts more complex, abstract, and with contingencies • Prices based on theories of value	• Complex and contingent shopping scripts • Prices based on abstract reasoning, such as input variations and buyer preferences
• Increased awareness of personal and mass media sources • Gather information on functional as well as perceptual attributes • Able to adapt to cost-benefit trade-offs	• Contingent use of different information sources-depending on product or situation • Gather information on functional, perceptual, and social aspects • Able to adapt to cost-benefit trade-offs
• Focus on important attribute information – functional and perceptual attributes • Use of two or more attributes	• Focus on important attribute information – functional, perceptual and social aspects • Use of multiple attributes
• Increased repertoire of strategies, especially noncompensatory ones • Capable of adapting strategies to tasks	• Full repertoire of strategies • Capable of adapting strategies to tasks in adult-like manner
• Expanded repertoire of strategies, with bargaining and persuasion emerging • Developing abilities to adapt strategy to persons and situations	• Full repertoire of strategies, with bargaining and persuasion as favorites • Capable of adapting strategies based on perceived effectiveness for persons and situations
• Emerging understanding of value based on social meaning and significance	• Fully developed understanding of value based on social meaning, significance, and scarcity

Clearly, we have learned a great deal about how consumer knowledge, skills, and values develop as children mature. It is also the case, however, that significant gaps remain in our understanding of consumer socialization. Going forward, significant contributions can be made by focusing our efforts in several areas related to the outcomes and influences in the socialization process, which we describe in detail below.

SOCIALIZATION OUTCOMES

Our review of the consumer socialization literature covered five major topic areas – advertising and persuasion knowledge, transaction knowledge, decision-making skills and abilities, purchase influence and negotiation strategies, and consumption motives and values. These areas represent the outcomes of the socialization process, involving a variety of consumer knowledge, skills, and values. Going forward, opportunities exist in each area for expanding our knowledge of how consumer socialization progresses.

Advertising and Persuasion Knowledge. Despite the attention this topic has received to date, we still have much to learn about development in the period from early adolescence to adulthood. Most investigators have focused their inquiry on children under the age of twelve, capturing important developments in the understanding of persuasive intent, commercial bias and deception, and attitudes toward advertising in general. Yet, the few studies examining adolescents suggest that important developments occur during this period, including an enhanced understanding of specific advertising tactics, types of bias, and social context. Further examination of these topics would contribute to our understanding of how persuasion knowledge develops, as well as providing insight for public policy concerns about adolescent response to advertising for products such as cigarettes and alcoholic beverages.

Further research would also be welcome to explore how advertising and persuasion knowledge is utilized in children's responses to persuasive communications. Existing research focuses on what children know or believe about advertising, assuming that once advertising knowledge is acquired, it will be used as a cognitive filter or defense when children are exposed to persuasive messages. Yet, the few studies that examine how advertising knowledge is actually used by children in viewing situations suggests that more attention should be paid to understanding when such knowledge is accessed and used (see Linn, Benedictis, and Delucchi 1982). The evidence to date suggests that cognitive filters and defenses against advertising may emerge during early adolescence, providing yet another reason for more attention to developments during the adolescent years.

Transaction Knowledge. Our understanding of transaction knowledge could be enhanced by addressing several topics in more detail. First, more research on children's understanding of consumption symbolism would be useful, especially at the brand name level. Brands are a key aspect of the consumer landscape, yet little research exists on how children of different ages interpret and understand brands. Also of interest would be the relationship between developments in this area and those related to values such as materialism.

A second topic in need of further consideration is the development of shopping skills, involving comparisons between prices, volumes, sizes, and the like. We were able to locate only one study, conducted over twenty years ago, exploring these issues. Given the large body of research in child psychology on children's developing mathematical abilities and strategies (see Siegler and Jenkins 1989), it would appear to be an opportune time to revisit issues related to shopping skills. A related topic, children's understanding of pricing and value, would also be a natural candidate for further research.

Decision Making Skills and Abilities. Perhaps the most noticeable gap in this literature is a basic understanding of what decision strategies children possess at different ages. A substantial contribution could be made by exploring when children acquire different types of compensatory and noncompensatory strategies and how these strategies emerge over time. Existing research provides some clues, but empirical data is particularly limited for younger children.

Also important would be research exploring the goals children of different ages have for consumer decision making. To date, research has proceeded as if children shared the same decision-making goals as adults, such as buying the »best« product or making a good decision with the least cognitive effort. It may well be that young children have quite different goals in mind, such as choosing a novel product, being surprised, or having fun. This may, in fact, provide a richer explanation for some of the findings regarding age differences in decision-making skills and behavior. Evidence regarding children's goals as consumers would provide much needed insight into the decision-making process as children grow older.

Purchase Influence and Negotiation Strategies. Investigations using in-depth interviews have provided vivid examples of the growing sophistication of older children and adolescents. Observational research, often conducted in grocery stores, has provided a picture of influence attempts for very young children accompanying their parents to the store. What is missing is research focused on children between these age groups, primarily children between the ages of 6 and 11. As we have seen, much social development occurs during this period and it would be useful to track how changes in areas such as social perspective taking facilitate the development of purchase influence and negotiation strategies.

Also useful would be research looking at the connection between influence and negotiation strategies and other aspects of children's consumer knowledge and behavior. One example would be the relationship between purchase influence strategies and advertising knowledge. Although these areas have existed independently, it would appear that both deal with persuasion, either how to persuade someone else or how someone tries to persuade you. Another example would be the relationship between purchase influence and negotiation strategies and parent-child conflict, sometimes viewed as a negative effect of advertising to children (Atkin 1975a; Goldberg and Gorn 1978; Sheikh and Moleski 1977).

Consumption Motives and Values. The vast majority of work done in this area has been conducted with adolescents. Virtually no studies exist with younger children on the topic of social and economic motives for consumption, and only one or two studies with younger children directly address the issue of materialism. Unlike many of the other topics, the gap is in research with younger kids, not the other way around. As noted before, studies with younger children, especially those in the crucial 7-11 age period, would be useful in understanding the relationship between social and cognitive development and aspects of consumer socialization.

Also of note here is the finding of gender differences. This is perhaps the only area included in our review where consistent gender differences have been found, with males reporting more materialistic values than females. Little attention has been directed toward the issue of gender differences in consumer socialization, resulting in a lack of conceptualization about what the differences might be in related areas such as consumption symbolism, persuasion knowledge, and the like. These differences, whatever their form, are quite likely to be more salient as children enter adolescence and are likely to impact social consumption and norms more so than many of the basic types of consumer knowledge (e.g., understanding advertising intent, knowledge of multiple information sources) we have reviewed here.

SOCIALIZATION INFLUENCES

Our stage view of consumer socialization focuses on age as the primary factor driving the transition from one stage to the next. Considering the vast amount of research detailing the cognitive and social development that occurs with advancing age, as well as the dominant focus on age in the consumer socialization literature, there can be little argument that age is an important factor in the socialization of children into the consumer role.

However, there can also be little argument that other factors play an important role as well. Chief among them is the social environment in which children learn to become consumers, including family, peers, culture, and mass media. Most researchers acknowledge that these types of factors contribute to a child's socialization and, as we have seen, a number of studies include one or more of these factors. Despite this, we continue to have significant gaps in our conceptualization and understanding of exactly what role social environment and experiences play in consumer socialization.

Perhaps part of the problem is due to the accessibility of theories for understanding the role of social environment in child development. Theories certainly do exist, but are less accessible than those documenting age as a driver in cognitive and social development. Piaget, for example, included social influences as one of four major factors in cognitive development in his earlier writings, stressing the role that social interactions with peers and others had on transitions between stages. Vygotsky, a Soviet psychologist, represents an even stronger position, arguing that learning takes place only in the midst of social interaction with others within a culture (for a review, see Azmitia and Perlmutter 1989). These theoretical views, as well as newer research on contextual views of cognitive development, could provide a basis for understanding several important aspects of the social environment in which consumer socialization takes place.

In doing so, our review suggests several factors that would benefit from further examination. Going forward, we see significant opportunities to contribute to our understanding of the role that social environment plays by focusing more attention on family, peers, culture, and mass media. We consider each of these factors below.

Family. Family influences on consumer socialization seem to proceed more through subtle social interaction than purposive educational efforts by parents (Ward 1974). Parents appear to have few educational goals in mind and make limited attempts to teach consumer skills (Moschis, Moore, and Smith 1984; Ward, Wackman, and Wartella 1977). Given the more subtle nature of family influences, researchers have turned their attention to general patterns of family communication as a way to understand how the family influences the development of consumer knowledge, skills, and values. Most influential has been the typology of family communication patterns – including laissez-faire, protective, pluralistic, and consensual families – studied extensively by Moschis and his colleagues (e.g., Moore and Moschis 1981; Moschis and Moore 1979b; Moschis, Prahasto, and Mitchell 1979c). A similar typology of parental socialization types – including authoritarian, rigid controlling, organized effective, indulgent, and neglecting parents – has been identified by Carlson and his colleagues (Carlson and Grossbart 1988; Carlson, Grossbart, and Stuenkel 1992) and has just begun to be incorporated into empirical research (Palan 1997; Palan and Laczniak 1997).

Although these typologies have provided a useful overview of the family, it would also be useful to examine the family unit at a more disaggregate level. As we have seen, it is rare for consumer researchers to break down the family communication variable into more discrete units, such as father-son or father-daughter communication. There is every reason to believe that these individual relationships have as much, if not more, influence on consumer socialization than general family characteristics. Recent demographic trends toward one-parent families make this need to disaggregate family relationships even more important.

Additionally, there is a need to examine sibling relationships as an important context for consumer socialization. Although variables such as the number of siblings or birth order have been included in a few studies to date, significant findings have yet to emerge. Again, there is a need to look at these relationships at a more detailed level, perhaps incorporating the age differences and genders of siblings and the extent of their interaction. It may be that siblings that are far apart in age or of a different gender have little influence, or that siblings exert influence in some areas of socialization but not others. For example, it is unlikely that a 9 year-old child with an older sibling will exhibit any different understanding of advertising intent than a 9 year-old child without an older sibling. But, it seems highly likely that the presence of an older sibling would accelerate the 9 year-old's knowledge of popular brand names, understanding of consumption symbolism, and maybe even materialistic attitudes.

Efforts of this nature are important for at least two reasons. First, the role of the family in socialization across a variety of domains suggests that it is more important in the area of consumer socialization than the evidence to date would suggest. Much of the existing research on family communication structure focuses on adolescents, and one would expect the family influence to be even greater with younger children. Second, the limited evidence to date suggests that the family serves as an important buffer against undesirable media influences. For example, in the Moschis and Moore (1982) study of materialism, television exposure was positively related to materialistic values except in those families with strong communication patterns. Much of the criticism of advertising and marketing to children might be informed by a better understanding of how these influences operate and are mediated by the family environment.

Peers. Although it seems clear that peers are an important socializing influence, increasing with age as parental influence wanes (Moschis and Churchill 1978; Ward 1974), a surprisingly small amount of research exists on the topic. Most of the studies that include peer relationships have been conducted with adolescents by Moschis and his colleagues (e.g., Churchill and Moschis 1979; Moschis and Moore 1982). One of the main findings has been that peer influence operates most strongly in situations with weak family communication, socio-oriented family communication patterns, and unstable family environments.

More research on peer influence, especially with younger children, would be welcome. Both Piaget and Vygotsky, whose theories were mentioned earlier, place major emphasis on interaction with peers as an important facilitator of learning and socialization. In the consumer context, one can imagine that many aspects of socialization, including an understanding of consumption symbolism and materialism, arise from peer interaction. For example, in one of the few studies of peer group influence, Bachmann and her colleagues (Bachmann, John, and Rao 1993) found that such influence influences some types of products (public luxuries) but not others (private necessities), implicating a peer-driven influence on children's understanding of consumption symbolism. In further research, Achenreiner (1997) found that susceptibility to peer group influence was positively related to materialistic attitudes. Research along these lines could be furthered by breaking down peer relationships into factors such as frequency of interaction or age and gender parity.

Culture. A small body of literature is beginning to emerge on consumer socialization in other cultures and countries, such as China (McNeal and Yeh 1990; McNeal and Ji 1998; Williams and Veek 1998), India (Dholakia 1984; Misra 1990), Mexico (Kulen, Parker, and Schaefer 1996), and New Zealand (McNeal, Viswanathan, and Yeh 1993). Findings from these studies have been historically descriptive in nature, but are evolving into more general pictures of socialization as the number of studies steadily increases. Many of these studies concentrate on data from only one country, but cross-cultural research is also emerging and becoming more important.

Clearly, cross-cultural research affords an opportunity to better understand differences between cultures as they relate to the influence of certain factors, such as family structure or peer relationships, in the socialization process. For example, the influence of family structure might be investigated by comparing children from urban cities in China, where parents are allowed to have only one child, with children from countries without such restrictions or children from rural China, where the one-child policy in not as strictly enforced. Also interesting would be a comparison of only children from China, often referred to as »little emperors« due to the doting attention received from parents (Goll 1995), with only children from other countries such as the United States.

Mass Media and Marketing. No environmental factor has received more attention than advertising. The evidence to date provides strong support for the influence of television advertising on children's product preferences and choices (e.g., Atkin 1981; Galst and White 1976; Goldberg 1990; Goldberg and Gorn 1974; Goldberg, Gorn, and Gibson 1978; Gorn and Goldberg 1982; Roedder, Sternthal, and Calder 1983).

Less unequivocal are the findings pertaining to the cumulative effects of advertising on children's consumption behavior, although the data support at least some modest role for advertising in children's perceptions and usage of products such as cigarettes, alcohol, and heavily-sugared non-nutritious foods. Advertising fosters favorable perceptions of cigarette smoking and contributes (along with factors such as peer and family smoking behavior) to the initiation and use of cigarettes (Andrews and Franke 1991; Botvin et. al 1993; Sargent 1997; USDHHS 1994). Advertising has also been linked to demand for alcoholic beverages (Smart 1988) as well as to preferences and beliefs about heavily sugared foods (Atkin 1975b; Clancy-Hepburn, Hickey, and Neville 1974; Goldberg, Gorn, and Gibson 1978; Wiman and Newman 1989).

Despite the obvious importance of advertising as a socialization force, much could be learned by examining other aspects of mass media and marketing. In the realm of mass media, efforts to understand the influence of television program content, in addition to television advertising, would be welcome. Television programming portrays messages about the way products are used, the types of people who use them, and the social context of consumption (Wells, 1997). More attention could be devoted to these subtle messages that television delivers and the effects on young consumers. In the same vein, movies deserve more attention. Movie studios and executives have, in fact, come under much recent criticism regarding cigarette smoking portrayed in many popular movies aimed at teenage audiences.

Beyond mass media, socialization research should be broadened to include other aspects of marketing programs and promotions. Free t-shirts and backpacks offered by cigarette companies as part of their loyalty programs are but one example of marketing programs that support advertising efforts and carry their own potential for influencing consumption (Sargent 1997). Beach parties and contests sponsored by alcoholic beverage manufacturers are additional examples of such promotional efforts. Added to these potential influences are the products themselves, as product development efforts and launches in categories such as alcohol and tobacco would attest. For example, the introduction and success of wine coolers, with a sweeter taste that masks the bitter undertones of alcohol, has been argued as an important gateway for teenage consumption of alcoholic beverages (Goldberg, Gorn, Lavack 1994). Similar critiques could be leveled at new product entries such as flavored alcoholic drink mixes, flavored chewing tobacco, and light beer. The extent to which these types of products socialize adolescents into consumption of adult-oriented products has received little empirical scrutiny to date.

CONCLUSION

Twenty-five years of consumer socialization research have yielded an impressive set of findings. Based on our review of these findings, there can be no doubt that children are avid consumers and become socialized into this role from an early age. Throughout childhood, children develop the knowledge, skills, and values they will use in making and influencing purchases now and in the future.

Understanding consumer socialization will continue to be important for at least three reasons. From a theoretical perspective, it informs our ideas about consumer learning, development, and change. No other area of consumer behavior research is so focused on the process and outcomes of consumer learning that evolve over time. From a managerial perspective, consumer socialization research provides unique insight into the beliefs and behavior of an important consumer segment. Children 4–12 years of age spend over $24 billion in direct purchases and influence another $188 billion in family household purchases (McNeal 1998). Finally, from a public policy and societal perspective, there is probably no other topic in consumer research that holds more interest than socialization and the consumption of products such as alcohol, tobacco, and illegal drugs. Government agencies and consumer groups have had an uneven history of aggressively pursuing consumer protection for children and adolescents in these areas, but the current climate suggests that concerns and research in this area are not likely to abate anytime in near future.

Much has been learned about the antecedents, influences, and outcomes of the consumer socialization process. Yet, much remains to be learned and the field is ripe with opportunities to conduct meaningful theoretical and applied research. Cultural changes, such as the growth of single-parent families, and technological changes, such as the internet, suggest the need to revisit existing findings about socialization and address new concerns. It is our hope that the next twenty-five years of consumer socialization research are as productive as the past.

NOTE

1   The article is reprinted from Deborah Roedder John »Consumer Socialization of Children: A Retrospective Look at Twenty Five Years of Research«, in *Journal of Consumer Research*, Vol. 26, No 3, page 183-213, Copyright (1999), with permission from The University of Chicago Press. Comments on earlier versions of the paper made by JCR reviewers and the associate editor are gratefully acknowledged.

References

Achenreiner, Gwen Bachmann (1995). »Children's Reliance on Brand Name Heuristics: A Developmental Investigation«, unpublished dissertation, Department of Marketing and Logistics Management, University of Minnesota, Minneapolis, MN.

Achenreiner, Gwen Bachmann (1997). »Materialistic Values and Susceptibility to Influence in Children«, *Advances in Consumer Research,* Volume 24, ed. Merrie Brucks and Deborah J. MacInnis, Provo, UT: Association for Consumer Research, 82-88.

Adler, Richard P., Gerald S. Lesser, Lawrence Meringoff, Thomas S. Robertson, John R. Rossiter, and Scott Ward (1980). *Research on the Effects of Television Advertising on Children.* Lexington, MA: Lexington Books.

Andrews, Rick L. and George R. Franke (1991). »The Determinants of Cigarette Consumption: A Meta-Analysis«, *Journal of Public Policy & Marketing,* 10 (Spring), 81-100.

Atkin, Charles K. (1975a). *Effects of Television Advertising on Children: First Year Experimental Evidence, Report No. 1.* East Lansing, Michigan: Michigan State University, Department of Communication.

Atkin, Charles K. (1975b). *Effects of Television Advertising on Children's and Mothers' Responses to Television Commercials, Report No. 8.* East Lansing, Michigan: Michigan State University, Department of Communication.

Atkin, Charles K. (1978a). »Observation of Parent-Child Interaction in Supermarket Decision-Making«, *Journal of Marketing,* 42 (October), 41-45.

Atkin, Charles K. (1978b). »Effects of Drug Commercials on Young Viewers«, *Journal of Communication,* 28 (Autumn), 71-79.

Atkin, Charles K. (1981). »Effects of Television Advertising on Children«, *Children and the Faces of Television: Teaching, Violence, Selling.* Eds. Edward L. Palmer and Aimee Dorr, New York: Academic Press, 287-304.

Azmitia, Margarita and Marion Perlmutter (1989). »Social Influences on Children's Cognition: State of the Art and Future Directions«, *Advances in Child Development and Behavior,* Volume 22, ed. Hayne W. Reese, San Diego, CA: Academic Press, 89-144.

Bachmann, Gwen Rae, Deborah Roedder John, and Akshay R. Rao (1993). »Children's Susceptibility to Peer Group Purchase Influence: An Exploratory Investigation«, *Advances in Consumer Research,* Volume 20, eds. Leigh McAlister and Michael L. Rothschild, Provo, UT: Association for Consumer Research, 463-468.

Bahn, Kenneth D. (1986). »How and When Do Brand Perceptions and Preferences First Form? A Cognitive Developmental Investigation«, *Journal of Consumer Research,* 13 (December), 382-93.

Baker, Stacey Menzel and James W. Gentry (1996). »Kids as Collectors: A Phenomenological Study of First and Fifth Graders«, *Advances in Consumer Research,* Volume 23, ed. Kim P. Corfman and John G. Lynch, Jr., Provo, UT: Association for Consumer Research, 132-137.

Barenboim, Carl (1981). »The Development of Person Perception in Childhood and Adolescence: From Behavioral Comparisons to Psychological Constructs to Psychological Comparisons«, *Child Development,* 52 (March), 129-144.

Bearden, William O., Jesse E. Teel, and Robert R. Wright (1979). »Family Income Effects on Measurement of Children's Attitudes Toward Television Commercials«, *Journal of Consumer Research,* 6 (December), 308-311.

Belch, George, Michael A. Belch, and Gayle Ceresino (1985). »Parental and Teenage Influences in Family Decision Making«, *Journal of Business Research,* 13 (April), 163-176.

Belk, Russell W., Kenneth D. Bahn, and Robert N. Mayer (1982). »Developmental Recognition of Consumption Symbolism«, *Journal of Consumer Research,* 9 (June), 4-17.

Berey, Lewis A. and Richard W. Pollay (1968). »The Influencing Role of the Child in Family Decision Making«, *Journal of Marketing Research,* 5 (February), 70-72.

Berti, Anna and Anna Bombi (1988). *The Child's Construction of Economics.* New York: Cambridge University Press.

Bever, Thomas G., Martin L. Smith, Barbara Bengen, and Thomas G. Johnson (1975). »Young Viewers' Troubling Response to TV Advertisements«, *Harvard Business Review,* 53 (November-December), 109-120.

Blatt, Joan, Lyle Spencer, and Scott Ward (1982). »A Cognitive Developmental Study of Children's Reactions to Television Advertising«, *Television and Social Behavior, Vol. 4, Television in Day-to-Day Life: Patterns of Use.* Eds. Eli A. Rubinstein, George A. Comstock, and J.P. Murray, Washington, DC: U.S. Department of Health, Education, and Welfare, 452-67.

Blosser, Betsy J. and Donald F. Roberts (1985). »Age Differences in Children's Perceptions of Message Intent: Responses to TV News, Commercials, Educational Spots, and Public Service Announcements«, *Communication Research,* 12 (October), 455-484.

Botvin, Gilbert J., Catherine J. Goldberg, Elizabeth M. Botvin, and Linda Dusenbury (1993). »Smoking Behavior of Adolescents Exposed to Cigarette Advertising«, *Public Health Reports,* 108 (2), 217-24.

Boush, David M., Marian Friestad, and Gregory M. Rose (1994). »Adolescent Skepticism toward TV Advertising and Knowledge of Advertiser Tactics«, *Journal of Consumer Research,* 21 (June), 165-175.

Burns, Alvin C. and Peter L. Gillett (1987). »Antecedents and Outcomes of the Family Purchase Socialization Process for a Child's Toys and Games«, *1987 AMA Educators' Proceedings.* Eds. Susan P. Douglas, Michael R. Solomon, Vijay Mahajan, Mark I. Alpert, William M. Pride, Gary L. Frazier, Gary T. Ford, James C. Anderson, and Peter Doyle, Chicago: American Marketing Association, 15-20.

Butter, Eliot J., Paula M. Popovich, Robert H. Stackhouse, and Roger K. Garner (1981). »Discrimination of Television Programs and Commercials by Preschool Children«, *Journal of Advertising Research,* 21 (April), 53-56.

Brucks, Merrie, Gary M. Armstrong, and Marvin E. Goldberg (1988). »Children's Use of Cognitive Defenses Against Television Advertising: A Cognitive Response Approach«, *Journal of Consumer Research,* 14 (March), 471-482.

Capon, Noel and Deanna Kuhn (1980). »A Developmental Study of Consumer Information-Processing Strategies«, *Journal of Consumer Research,* 7 (December), 225-233.

Carlson, Les and Sanford Grossbart (1988). »Parental Style and Consumer Socialization of Children«, *Journal of Consumer Research,* 15 (June), 77-94.

Carlson, Les, Sanford Grossbart, and J. Kathleen Stuenkel (1992). »The Role of Parental Socialization Types on Differential Family Communication Patterns Regarding Consumption«, *Journal of Consumer Psychology,* 1 (1), 31-52.

Cateora, Phillip R. (1963). *An Analysis of the Teenage Market.* Austin, TX: University of Texas Bureau of Business Research.

Christenson, Peter Gilbert (1982). »Children's Perceptions of TV Commercials and Products: The Effects of PSAs«, *Communication Research,* 9 (October), 491-524.

Churchill, Gilbert A. and George P. Moschis (1979). »Television and Interpersonal Influences on Adolescent Consumer Learning«, *Journal of Consumer Research,* 6 (June), 23-35.

Clancy-Hepburn, Katherine, Anthony A. Hickey, and Gayle Nevill (1974), »Children's Behavior Responses to TV Food Advertisements«, *Journal of Nutrition Education,* 6 (July-September), 93-96.

Corfman, Kim and Bari Harlam (1997). »Relative Influence of Parent and Child in the Purchase of Products for Children«, working paper, Marketing Department, New York University, New York, NY.

Darley, William F. and Jeen-Su Lim (1986). »Family Decision Making in Leisure-Time Activities: An Exploratory Analysis of the Impact of Locus of Control, Child Age Influence Factor and Parental Type on Perceived Child Influence«, Advances in Consumer Research, Volume 13, ed. Richard J. Lutz, Provo, UT: Association for Consumer Research, 370-374.

Davidson, Denise (1991a). »Children's Decision-Making Examined with an Information-Board Procedure«, Cognitive Development, 6 (January/March), 77-90.

Davidson, Denise (1991b). »Developmental Differences in Children's Search of Predecisional Information«, Journal of Experimental Child Psychology, 52 (October), 239-255.

Davidson, Denise and Judith Hudson (1988). »The Effects of Decision Reversibility and Decision Importance on Children's Decision Making«, Journal of Experimental Child Psychology, 46 (August), 35-40.

Denney, Nancy Wadsworth (1974). »Evidence for Developmental Changes in Categorization Criteria for Children and Adults«, Human Development, 17 (1), 41-53.

Derscheid, Linda E., Yoon-Hee Kwon, and Shi-Ruei Fang (1996). »Preschoolers' Socialization as Consumers of Clothing and Recognition of Symbolism«, Perceptual and Motor Skills, 82 (June), 1171-1181.

Dholakia, Ruby Roy (1984). »Intergenerational Differences in Consumer Behavior: Some Evidence From a Developing Country«, Journal of Business Research, 12 (March), 19-34.

Diaz, Kevin (1992). »Symbol of Status, Target of Violence: Jackets May Put Teens in Danger«, Minneapolis Star and Tribune, April 22, 1992.

Donohue, Thomas R., Lucy L. Henke, and William A. Donohue (1980). »Do Kids Know What TV Commercials Intend?«, Journal of Advertising Research, 20 (October), 51-57.

Donohue, Thomas R., Timothy P. Meyer, and Lucy L. Henke (1978). »Black and White Children: Perceptions of TV Commercials«, Journal of Marketing, 42 (October), 34-40.

Easterlin, Richard and Eileen Crimmins (1991). »Private Materialism, Personal Self-Fulfillment, Family Life, and Public Interest: The Nature, Effects, and Causes of Recent Changes in the Values of American Youth«, Public Opinion Quarterly, 55 (Winter), 499-533.

Filiatrault, Pierre and J.R. Brent Ritchie (1980). »Joint Purchasing Decisions: A Comparison of Influence Structure in Family and Couple Decision-Making Units«, Journal of Consumer Research, 7 (September), 131-140.

Fox, Karen F.A. and Trudy Kehret-Ward (1990). »Naive Theories of Price: A Developmental Model«, Psychology & Marketing, 7 (Winter), 311-329.

Foxman, Ellen R. and Patriya S. Tansuhaj (1988). »Adolescents' and Mothers' Perceptions of Relative Influence in Family Purchase Decisions: Patterns of Agreement and Disagreement«, Advances in Consumer Research, Volume 15, ed. Michael J. Houston, Provo, UT: Association for Consumer Research, 449-453.

Foxman, Ellen R., Patriya S. Tansuhaj, and Karin Ekstrom (1989). »Family Members' Perceptions of Adolescents' Influence in Family Decision Making«, Journal of Consumer Research, 15 (March), 482-491.

Frideres, James S. (1973). »Advertising, Buying Patterns and Children«, Journal of Advertising Research, 13 (February), 34-36.

Friestad, Marian and Peter Wright (1994). »The Persuasion Knowledge Model: How People Cope with Persuasion Attempts«, Journal of Consumer Research, 21 (June), 1-31.

Galst, Joann Paley and Mary Alice White (1976). »The Unhealthy Persuader: The Reinforcing Value of Television and Children's Purchase-influencing Attempts at the Supermarket«, Child Development, 47 (December), 1089-1096.

Ginsburg, Herbert P. and Sylvia Opper (1988). *Piaget's Theory of Intellectual Development*. Englewood Cliffs, NJ: Prentice-Hall.

Goldberg, Marvin E. (1990). »A Quasi-Experiment Assessing the Effectiveness of TV Advertising Directed to Children«, *Journal of Marketing Research,* 27 (November), 445-454.

Goldberg, Marvin E. and Gerald J. Gorn (1974). »Children's Reactions to Television Advertising: An Experimental Approach«, *Journal of Consumer Research,* 1 (September), 69-75.

Goldberg, Marvin E. and Gerald J. Gorn (1978). »Some Unintended Consequences of TV Advertising to Children«, *Journal of Consumer Research,* 5 (June), 22-29.

Goldberg, Marvin E., Gerald J. Gorn, and Wendy Gibson (1978). »TV Messages for Snack and Breakfast Foods: Do They Influence Children's Preferences?«, *Journal of Consumer Research,* 5 (September), 73-81.

Goldberg, Marvin E., Gerald J. Gorn, and Anne M. Lavack (1994). »Product Innovation and Teenage Alcohol Consumption: The Case of Wine Coolers«, *Journal of Public Policy & Marketing,* 13 (Fall), 218-227.

Goldberg, Marvin E., Laura A. Peracchio, Gerald J. Gorn, and Gary J. Bamossy (1997). »A Scale to Measure Children's Materialism«, working paper.

Goll, Sally D. (1995). »China's (Only) Children Get the Royal Treatment«, *The Wall Street Journal,* February 8, B1 and B9.

Gorn, Gerald J. and Marvin E. Goldberg (1982). »Behavioral Evidence of the Effects of Televised Food Messages on Children«, *Journal of Consumer Research,* 9 (September), 200-205.

Gorn, Gerald J. and Renee Florsheim (1985). »The Effects of Commercials for Adult Products on Children«, *Journal of Consumer Research,* 11 (March), 962-967.

Gregan-Paxton, Jennifer and Deborah Roedder John (1995). »Are Young Children Adaptive Decision Makers? A Study of Age Differences in Information Search Behavior«, *Journal of Consumer Research,* 21 (March), 567-580.

Gregan-Paxton, Jennifer and Deborah Roedder John (1997). »The Emergence of Adaptive Decision Making in Children«, *Journal of Consumer Research,* 24 (June), 43-56.

Guest, Lester P. (1955). »Brand Loyalty – Twelve Years Later«, *Journal of Applied Psychology,* 39 (December), 405-408.

Hawkins, Del I. and Kenneth A. Coney (1974). »Peer Influences on Children's Product Preferences«, *Journal of the Academy of Marketing Science,* 2 (Spring), 322-331.

Haynes, Janice, Diane C. Burts, Alice Dukes, and Rinn Cloud (1993). »Consumer Socialization of Preschoolers and Kindergartners as Related to Clothing Consumption«, *Psychology & Marketing,* 10 (March/April), 151-166.

Hempel, Donald J. (1974). »Family Buying Decisions: A Cross Cultural Perspective«, *Journal of Marketing Research,* 11 (August), 295-302.

Hite, Cynthia Fraser and Robert E. Hite (1995). »Reliance on Brand by Young Children«, *Journal of the Market Research Society,* 37 (April), 185-193.

Isler, Leslie, Edward T. Popper, and Scott Ward (1987). »Children's Purchase Requests and Parental Responses: Results from a Diary Study«, *Journal of Advertising Research,* 27 (October/November), 28-39.

Jamison, David J. (1996). »Idols of the Tribe: Brand Veneration and Group Identity Among Pre-Adolescent Consumers«, working paper, Department of Marketing, University of Florida, Gainesville, FL.

Jenkins, Roger L. (1979). »The Influence of Children in Family Decision-Making: Parents' Perceptions«, *Advances in Consumer Research,* Volume 6, ed. William L. Wilkie, Ann Arbor, MI: Association for Consumer Research, 413-418.

John, Deborah Roedder and Ramnath Lakshmi-Ratan (1992). »Age Differences in Children's Choice Behavior: The Impact of Available Alternatives«, *Journal of Marketing Research,* 29 (May), 216-226.

John, Deborah Roedder and Mita Sujan (1990a). »Age Differences in Product Categorization«, *Journal of Consumer Research,* 16 (March), 452-460.

John, Deborah Roedder and Mita Sujan (1990b). »Children's Use of Perceptual Cues in Product Categorization«, *Psychology and Marketing,* 7 (Winter), 277-294.

John, Deborah Roedder and John C. Whitney, Jr. (1986). »The Development of Consumer Knowledge in Children: A Cognitive Structure Approach«, *Journal of Consumer Research,* 12 (March), 406-417.

Karsten, Yvonne Marie Cariveau (1996). »A Dynamic Systems Approach to the Development of Consumer Knowledge: Children's Understanding of Monetary Knowledge«, unpublished dissertation, Department of Marketing and Logistics Management, University of Minnesota, Minneapolis, MN.

Keillor, Bruce D., R. Stephen Parker, and Allen Schaefer (1996). »Influences on Adolescent Brand Preferences in the United States and Mexico«, *Journal of Advertising Research,* 36 (May/June), 47-56.

Keiser, Stephen K. (1975). »Awareness of Brands and Slogans«, *Journal of Advertising Research,* 15 (August), 37-43.

Kim, Chankon, Hanjoon Lee, and Katherine Hall (1991). »A Study of Adolescents' Power, Influence Strategy, and Influence on Family Purchase Decisions«, *1991 AMA Winter Educators' Conference Proceedings,* ed. Terry L. Childers, Chicago, IL: American Marketing Association, 37-45.

Klayman, Joshua (1985). »Children's Decision Strategies and Their Adaptation to Task Characteristics«, *Organizational Behavior and Human Decision Processes,* 35 (April), 179-201.

Klees, Donna M., Jerry Olson, and R. Dale Wilson (1988). »An Analysis of the Content and Organization of Children's Knowledge Structures«, *Advances in Consumer Research,* Volume 15, ed. Michael J. Houston, Provo, UT: Association for Consumer Research, 153-157.

Levin, Stephen R., Thomas V. Petros, and Florence W. Petrella (1982). »Preschoolers' Awareness of Television Advertising«, *Child Development,* 53 (August), 933-937.

Lindquist, Jay D. (1978). »Children's Attitudes Toward Advertising on Television and Radio and in Children's Magazines and Comic Books«, *Advances in Consumer Research,* Volume 6, ed. William L. Wilkie, Ann Arbor, MI: Association for Consumer Research, 407-412.

Linn, Marcia C., Tina de Benedictis, and Kevin Delucchi (1982). »Adolescent Reasoning about Advertisements: Preliminary Investigations«, *Child Development,* 53, 1599-1613.

Macklin, M. Carole (1985). »Do Young Children Understand the Selling Intent of Commercials?«, *Journal of Consumer Affairs,* 19 (Winter), 293-304.

Macklin, M. Carole (1987). »Preschoolers' Understanding of the Informational Function of Television Advertising«, *Journal of Consumer Research,* 14 (September), 229-239.

Macklin, M. Carole (1996). »Preschoolers' Learning of Brand Names From Visual Cues«, *Journal of Consumer Research,* 23 (December), 251-261.

Manchanda, Rajesh V. and Elizabeth S. Moore-Shay (1996). »Mom, I Want That! The Effects of Parental Style, Gender and Materialism on Children's Choice of Influence Strategy«, *1996 AMA Winter Educators' Conference Proceedings,* eds. Edward A. Blair and Wagner A. Kamakura, Chicago, IL: American Marketing Association, 81-90.

Mangleburg, Tamara F. and Terry Bristol (1998). »Socialization and Adolescents' Skepticism Toward Advertising«, working paper.

Markman, Ellen M. (1980). »The Acquisition and Hierarchical Organization of Categories by Children«, *Theoretical Issues in Reading Comprehension,* eds. Rand Spiro et al., Hillsdale, NJ: Lawrence Erlbaum, 371-406.

Markman, Ellen M. and Maureen A. Callahan (1983). »An Analysis of Hierarchical Classification«, *Advances in the Psychology of Human Intelligence,* Vol. 2, ed. Robert Sternberg, Hillsdale, NJ: Lawrence Erlbaum, 325-365.

Marshall, Helen R. (1964). »The Relation of Giving Children an Allowance to Children's Money Knowledge and Responsibility and to Other Practices of Parents«, *Journal of Genetic Psychology,* 104 (March), 35-51.

Marshall, Helen R. and Lucille MacGruder (1960). »Relations Between Parent Money Education Practices and Children's Knowledge and Use of Money«, *Child Development,* 31 (June), 253-284.

Martin, Mary C. and James W. Gentry (1997). »Stuck in the Model Trap: The Effects of Beautiful Models in Advertisements on Female Pre-Adolescents and Adolescents«, *Journal of Advertising,* 26 (Summer), 19-33.

Mayer, Robert N. and Russell Belk (1982). »Acquisition of Consumption Stereotypes by Children«, *The Journal of Consumer Affairs,* 16 (Winter), 307-321.

McNeal, James U. (1964). *Children as Consumers.* Austin, TX: Bureau of Business Research, University of Texas at Austin.

McNeal, James U. (1987). *Children as Consumers.* Lexington, MA: Lexington Books.

McNeal, James U. (1992). *Kids as Customers.* New York, NY: Lexington Books.

McNeal, James U. (1998). »Tapping the Three Kids' Markets«, *American Demographics,* 20 (April), 37-41.

McNeal, James U. and Mindy F. Ji (1998). »The Role of Mass Media in the Consumer Socialization of Chinese Children«, paper presented at the 1998 Association for Consumer Research Asia-Pacific Conference, Hong Kong, June.

McNeal, James U. and Stephen W. McDaniel (1981). »Children's Perceptions of Retail Stores: An Exploratory Study«, *Akron Business and Economics Review,* 12 (Fall), 39-42.

McNeal, James U., Vish R. Viswanathan, and Chyon-Hwa Yeh (1993). »A Cross-Cultural Study of Children's Consumer Socialization in Hong Kong, New Zealand, Taiwan, and the United States«, *Asia Pacific Journal of Marketing and Logistics,* 5 (3), 56-69.

McNeal, James U. and Chyon-Hwa Yeh (1990). »Taiwanese Children as Consumers«, *Asia-Pacific International Journal of Marketing,* 2 (2), 32-43.

Mehrotra, Sunil and Sandra Torges (1977). »Determinants of Children's Influence in Mothers' Buying Behavior«, *Advances in Consumer Research,* Volume 4, ed. William D. Perreault, Ann Arbor, MI: Association for Consumer Research, 56-60.

Meyer, Timothy P., Thomas R. Donohue, and Lucy L. Henke (1978). »How Black Kids See TV Commercials«, *Journal of Advertising Research,* 18 (October), 51-58.

Misra, Pranesh (1990). »Indian Children: An Emerging Consumer Segment«, *Journal of the Market Research Society,* 32 (2), 217-225.

Moore, Roy L. and George P. Moschis (1978). »Family Communication Patterns and Consumer Socialization«, paper presented to the Mass Communication and Society Division, Association for Education in Journalism Annual Convention, Seattle, WA, August.

Moore, Roy L. and George P. Moschis (1981), »The Role of Family Communication in Consumer Learning«, *Journal of Communications,* 31 (Autumn), 42-51.

Moore, Roy L. and Lowndes F. Stephens (1975). »Some Communication and Demographic Determinants of Adolescent Consumer Learning«, *Journal of Consumer Research,* 2 (September), 80-92.

Moore-Shay, Elizabeth S. and Richard J. Lutz (1997). »Kids' Consumption: How Do Children Perceive the Relationships Between Advertisements and Products?«, working paper, Office of Research, College of Commerce and Business Administration, University of Illinois, Urbana-Champaign, IL.

Moschis, George P. (1985). »The Role of Family Communication in Consumer Socialization of Children and Adolescents«, *Journal of Consumer Research,* 11 (March), 898-913.

Moschis, George P. (1987). *Consumer Socialization: A Life-Cycle Perspective.* Lexington, MA: Lexington Books.

Moschis, George P. and Gilbert A. Churchill, Jr. (1978). »Consumer Socialization: A Theoretical and Empirical Analysis«, *Journal of Marketing Research,* 15 (November), 599-609.

Moschis, George P. and Linda G. Mitchell (1986). »Television Advertising and Interpersonal Influences on Teenagers' Participation in Family Consumer Decisions«, *Advances in Consumer Research,* Volume 13, ed. Richard J. Lutz, Provo, UT: Association for Consumer Research, 181-86.

Moschis, George P. and Roy L. Moore (1979a). »Decision Making Among The Young: A Socialization Perspective«, *Journal of Consumer Research,* 6 (September), 101-112.

Moschis, George P. and Roy L. Moore (1979b). »Family Communication and Consumer Socialization«, *Advances in Consumer Research,* Volume 6, ed. William L. Wilkie, Ann Arbor, MI: Association for Consumer Research, 359-363.

Moschis, George P. and Roy L. Moore (1979c). »Family Communication Patterns and Consumer Socialization«, *1979 AMA Educators' Conference Proceedings,* eds. Neil Beckwith, Michael J. Houston, Robert Mittelstaedt, Kent B. Monroe, and Scott Ward, Chicago, IL: American Marketing Association, 226-230.

Moschis, George P. and Roy L. Moore (1982). »A Longitudinal Study of Television Advertising Effects«, *Journal of Consumer Research,* 9 (December), 279-286.

Moschis, George P. and Roy L. Moore (1983). »A Longitudinal Study of the Development of Purchasing Patterns«, *1983 AMA Educators' Proceedings,* eds. Patrick E. Murphy, Gene R. Laczniak, Paul F. Anderson, Russell W. Belk, O. C. Ferrell, Robert F. Lusch, Terence A. Shimp, and Charles B. Weinberg, Chicago: American Marketing Association, 114-117.

Moschis, George P., Roy L. Moore, and Ruth B. Smith (1984). »The Impact of Family Communication on Adolescent Consumer Socialization«, *Advances in Consumer Research,* Volume 11, ed. Thomas C. Kinnear, Provo, UT: Association for Consumer Research, 314-319.

Moschis, George P., Andjali E. Prahasto, and Linda G. Mitchell (1986). »Family Communication Influences on the Development of Consumer Behavior: Some Additional Findings«, *Advances in Consumer Research,* Volume 13, ed. Richard J. Lutz, Provo, UT: Association for Consumer Research, 365-69.

Nakajima, Yoshiaki and Miho Hotta (1989). »A Developmental Study of Cognitive Processes in Decision Making: Information Searching as a Function of Task Complexity«, *Psychological Reports,* 64 (February), 67-79.

Nelson, James E. (1979). »Children as Information Sources in Family Decision to Eat Out«, *Advances in Consumer Research,* Volume 6, ed. William L. Wilkie, Ann Arbor, MI: Association for Consumer Research, 419-423.

Otnes, Cele, Young Chan Kim, and Kyungseung Kim (1994). »All I Want for Christmas: An Analysis of Children's Brand Requests to Santa Claus«, *Journal of Popular Culture,* 27 (Spring), 183-194.

Otnes, Cele, Michelle Nelson, and Mary Ann McGrath (1995). »The Children's Birthday Party: A Study of Mothers as Socialization Agents«, *Advances in Consumer Research,* Volume 22, eds. Frank R. Kardes and Mita Sujan, Provo, UT: Association for Consumer Research, 622-627.

Paget, K. Frome, D. Kritt, and L. Bergemann (1984). »Understanding Strategic Interactions in Television Commercials: A Developmental Study«, *Journal of Applied Developmental Psychology,* 5 (April-June), 145-161.

Palan, Kay M. (1997). »The Role of Parental Style on Adolescent-Parent Interactions in Family Decision Making«, working paper, Marketing Department, Iowa State University.

Palan, Kay M. and Russell N. Laczniak (1997). »The Relationship Between Advertising Exposure and Children's Influence Strategies While Shopping: A Conceptualized Model«, working paper, Marketing Department, Iowa State University.

Palan, Kay M. and Robert E. Wilkes (1997). »Adolescent-Parent Interaction in Family Decision Making«, *Journal of Consumer Research,* 24 (September), 159-169.

Palmer, Edward L. and Cynthia N. McDowell (1979). »Program/Commercial Separators in Children's Television Programming«, *Journal of Communication,* 29 (Summer), 197-201.

Payne, John, James R. Bettman, and Eric J. Johnson (1993). *The Adaptive Decision Maker.* Cambridge: Cambridge University Press.

Peracchio, Laura A. (1992). »How Do Young Children Learn to Be Consumers? A Script-processing Approach«, *Journal of Consumer Research,* 18 (March), 425-440.

Peracchio, Laura A. (1993). »Young Children's Processing of a Televised Narrative: Is a Picture Really Worth a Thousand Words?«, *Journal of Consumer Research,* 20 (September), 281-293.

Popper, Edward T. (1979). »Mothers Mediation of Children's Purchase Requests«, *1979 AMA Educators' Proceedings,* eds. Neil Beckwith, Michael J. Houston, Robert Mittelstaedt, Kent B. Monroe, and Scott Ward, Chicago, IL: American Marketing Association, 645-648.

Reid, Leonard N. (1978). »The Impact of Family Group Interaction on Children's Understanding of Television Advertising«, *Journal of Advertising,* 8 (Summer), 13-19.

Reisman, David and Howard Roseborough (1955). »Careers and Consumer Behavior«, *Consumer Behavior Vol. II, The Life Cycle and Consumer Behavior,* ed. Lincoln Clark, New York: New York University Press, 1-18.

Ritson, Mark and Richard Elliott (1998). »The Social Contextualization of the Lonely Viewer: An Ethnographic Study of Advertising Interpretation«, working paper, Department of Marketing and Logistics Management, University of Minnesota, Minneapolis, MN.

Roberts, Mary Lou, Lawrence H. Wortzel, and Robert L. Berkeley (1981). »Mothers' Attitudes and Perceptions of Children's Influence and Their Effect on Family Consumption«, *Advances in Consumer Research,* Volume 8, ed. Jerry C. Olson, Ann Arbor, MI: Association for Consumer Research, 730-735.

Robertson, Thomas S. and John R. Rossiter (1974). »Children and Commercial Persuasion: An Attribution Theory Analysis«, *Journal of Consumer Research,* 1 (June), 13-20.

Robertson, Thomas S., John R. Rossiter, and Terry C. Gleason (1979). »Children's Receptivity to Proprietary Medicine Advertising«, *Journal of Consumer Research,* 6 (December), 247-255.

Roedder, Deborah L. (1981). »Age Differences in Children's Responses to Television Advertising: An Information Processing Approach«, *Journal of Consumer Research,* 8 (September), 144-53.

Roedder, Deborah L., Brian Sternthal, and Bobby J. Calder (1983). »Attitude-Behavior Consistency in Children's Responses to Television Advertising«, *Journal of Marketing Research,* 20 (November), 337-349.

Ross, Rhonda P., Toni Campbell, John C. Wright, Aletha C. Huston, Mabel L. Rice, and Peter Turk (1984). »When Celebrities Talk, Children Listen: An Experimental Analysis of Children's Responses to TV Advertisements with Celebrity Endorsement«, *Journal of Applied Developmental Psychology,* 5 (July-September), 185-202.

Rossiter, John R. (1976). »Visual and Verbal Memory in Children's Product Information Utilization«, *Advances in Consumer Research,* Volume 3, ed. Beverlee B. Anderson, Ann Arbor, MI: Association for Consumer Research, 572-576.

Rossiter, John R. and Thomas S. Robertson (1974). »Children's TV Commercials: Testing the Defenses«, *Journal of Communication,* 24 (Autumn), 137-144.

Rossiter, John R. and Thomas S. Robertson (1976). »Canonical Analysis of Developmental, Social, and Experiential Factors in Children's Comprehension of Television Advertising«, *The Journal of Genetic Psychology,* 129 (December), 317-327.

Rubin, Ronald S. (1974). »The Effects of Cognitive Development on Children's Responses to Television Advertising«, *Journal of Business Research,* 2 (October), 409-419.

Rust, Langbourne (1993). »Observations: Parents and Children Shopping Together«, *Journal of Advertising Research,* 33 (July/August), 65-70.

Sargent, J., M. A. Dalton, M. Beach, A. Bernhardt, D. Pullin, M. Stevens (1997). »Cigarette Promotional Items in Public Schools«, *Archives of Pediatric & Adolescent Medicine,* 151 (12), 1189-1196.

Selman, Robert L. (1980). *The Growth of Interpersonal Understanding.* New York: Academic Press.

Sheikh, Anees A. and Marvin L. Moleski (1977). »Conflict in the Family Over Commercials«, *Journal of Communication,* 27 (Winter), 152-157.

Siegler, Robert S. and Eric Jenkins (1989). *How Children Discover New Strategies.* Hillsdale, New Jersey: Lawrence Erlbaum.

Smart, Reginald G. (1988). »Does Alcohol Advertising Affect Overall Consumption? A Review of Empirical Studies«, *Journal of Studies on Alcohol,* 49 (4), 314-23.

Soley, Lawrence C. and Leonard N. Reid (1984). »When Parents Control Children's TV Viewing and Product Choice: Testing the Attitudinal Defenses«, *Marketing Comes of Age: Proceedings of the Annual Meeting of the Southern Marketing Association,* Boca Raton, FL: Southern Marketing Association, 10-13.

Stephens, Lowndes and Roy L. Moore (1975). »Price Accuracy as a Consumer Skill«, *Journal of Advertising Research,* 15 (August), 27-34.

Stephens, Nancy and Mary Ann Stutts (1982). »Preschoolers' Ability to Distinguish Between Television Programming and Commercials«, *Journal of Advertising,* 11 (2), 16-26.

Strauss, Anselm (1952). »The Development and Transformation of Monetary Meanings in the Child«, *American Sociological Review,* 17 (June), 275-286.

Stutts, Mary Ann, Donald Vance, and Sarah Hudleson (1981). »Program-Commercial Separators in Children's Television: Do They Help a Child Tell the Difference Between *Bugs Bunny* and the *Quick Rabbit?*«, *Journal of Advertising,* 10 (Spring), 16-25.

Swinyard, William R. and Cheng Peng Sim (1987). »Perception of Children's Influence on Family Decision Processes«, *Journal of Consumer Marketing,* 4 (Winter), 25-38.

Szybillo, George J. and Arlene K. Sosanie (1977). »Family Decision Making: Husband, Wife and Children«, *Advances in Consumer Research,* Volume 4, ed. William D. Perreault, Ann Arbor, MI: Association for Consumer Research, 46-49.

Szybillo, George J., Arlene K. Sosanie, and Aaron Tenenbein (1977). »Should Children Be Seen But Not Heard?«, *Journal of Advertising Research,* 17 (December), 7-13.

Tootelian, Dennis H. and Ralph M. Gaedeke (1992). »The Teen Market: An Exploratory Analysis of Income, Spending, and Shopping Patterns«, *The Journal of Consumer Marketing,* 9 (Fall), 35-44.

Turner, Josephine and Jeanette Brandt (1978). »Development and Validation of a Simulated Market to Test Children for Selected Consumer Skills«, *The Journal of Consumer Affairs,* 12 (Winter), 266-76.

U.S. Department of Health and Human Services (1994). *Preventing Tobacco Use Among Young People: A Report of the Surgeon General.* Atlanta, GA: U.S. Department of Health and Human Services, Public Health Service, Centers for Disease Control and Prevention, Office on Smoking and Health.

Ward, Scott (1972). »Children's Reactions to Commercials«, *Journal of Advertising Research,* 12 (April), 37-45.

Ward, Scott (1974). »Consumer Socialization«, *Journal of Consumer Research,* 1 (September), 1-14.

Ward, Scott, Greg Reale, and David Levinson (1972). »Children's Perceptions, Explanations, and Judgments of Television Advertising: A Further Explanation«, *Television and Social Behavior, Vol. 4, Television in Day-to-Day Life: Patterns of Use,* eds. Eli A. Rubinstein, George A. Comstock, and J.P. Murray, Washington, DC: U.S. Department of Health, Education, and Welfare, 468-490.

Ward, Scott and Daniel B. Wackman (1971). »Family and Media Influences on Adolescent Consumer Learning«, *American Behavioral Scientist,* 14 (January/February), 415-427.

Ward, Scott and Daniel B. Wackman (1972). »Children's Purchase Influence Attempts and Parental Yielding«, *Journal of Marketing Research,* 9 (November), 316-319.

Ward, Scott, Daniel B. Wackman, and Ellen Wartella (1977). *How Children Learn to Buy.* Beverly Hills, CA: Sage Publications.

Wartella, Ellen, Daniel B. Wackman, Scott Ward, Jacob Shamir, and Alison Alexander (1979). »The Young Child as Consumer«, *Children Communicating: Media and Development of Thought, Speech, Understanding,* ed. Ellen Wartella, Beverly Hills, CA: Sage Publications.

Wells, William D. (1997). »Narratives in Consumer Research«, working paper, School of Journalism and Mass Communication, University of Minnesota, Minneapolis, MN.

Wells, William D. and Leonard A. LoSciuto (1966). »Direct Observation of Purchasing Behavior«, *Journal of Marketing Research,* 3 (August), 227-233.

Whitney, Paul and Seth Kunen (1983). »Development of Hierarchical Conceptual Relationships in Children's Semantic Memories«, *Journal of Experimental Child Psychology,* 35 (April), 278-293.

Williams, Laura A. and Ann Veeck (1998). »An Exploratory Study of Children's Purchase Influence in Urban China«, paper presented at the 1998 Association for Consumer Research Asia-Pacific Conference, Hong Kong, June.

Wiman, Alan R. (1983). »Parental Influence and Children's Responses to Television Advertising«, *Journal of Advertising,* 12 (1), 12-18.

Wiman, Alan R. and Larry M. Newman (1989). »Television Advertising Exposure and Children's Nutritional Awareness«, *Journal of Academy of Marketing Science,* 17 (Spring), 179-188.

Young, Brian M. (1990). *Television Advertising and Children.* New York: Oxford University Press.

3

TIMES ARE CHANGING AND YOUTH WITH THEM
— ON YOUNG PEOPLE'S MEDIA USE IN SWEDEN

By Cecilia von Feilitzen

INTRODUCTION[1]

When talking about changes in people's media use it is necessary to consider if the changes are due to society and the media landscape, if they depend on the fact that different generations grow up and maintain their habits for life, or if the changes are expressions of different phases in the individual's life – is there, for example, a certain media use style characteristic? Research shows that all three factors play a role. When media and media outputs are changing, the habits of all of us change as well. At the same time children of today are born into and influenced by a different media situation than previous generations were. What is new for adults will also in the future be natural for the young – they will, partly continue to use the media and media contents they were used to in childhood and adolescence. With increasing age the role of music, for instance, is decreasing compared to how it was in youth, while interest in other media genres grows, genres that earlier were experienced as less interesting. In this chapter the focus is on the changing media landscape and the generation factor.

A CHANGING MEDIA LANDSCAPE

The media landscape is changing more and more rapidly. Since the mid 1980s we have in the Nordic Countries, as in many other countries access to more TV channels, both national and, above all, satellite channels. Digital television and radio offer an even more extensive output. Most people in the Nordic countries also have computers with an Internet connection at home. Still more people have mobile telephones, which until now have mostly been used for ordinary calls and SMS; however, this is also becoming an entry to the Internet. Another digital, interactive medium, are video games and computer games, an industry involving billions of dollars and which in the U.S.A. alone turns over more than the box-office receipts of Hollywood films, and ten times more than what is invested on the production of children's TV programmes there. Furthermore Japan is an even larger producer of software and hardware for video games (Kline 2000, Sakamoto 2000). Moreover, there is in the changing media landscape a convergence of the media, for example radio, music, newspapers, journals, books, television and electronic games are also available on the Internet.

The increasing amount of media and the convergence of them are not only dependent on technological development but also on an increasingly pronounced owner concentration – a few transnational conglomerates provide the same media products to larger and larger parts of the world. This »globalization« also means more and more advertising and new advertising formats addressing not least the young people. One example is the electronic games that are transformed into TV series and films (in themselves advertising new games in the same series) and are sold with an abundance of associated toys, clothes, food, sweets (so-called merchandising). Another example is the new kinds of advertising that are spreading on the Internet. A fan of a television soap may surf to the soap's web site in order to watch a particular scene again, for example where the boy gives the girl a necklace. Simultaneously, an advertisement of the necklace pops up on the site – it is only to click and buy (Montgomery 2001a, 2001b). The fact that children and young people to an ever greater extent are becoming target groups of advertising is partly due to the circumstance that they are regarded as a group with greater and greater purchase power, but also partly to the circumstance that competing media and trademarks want to make the young people their future, loyal consumers. In the U.S. alone, business enterprises now spend more than 12 billion dollars a year on sheer marketing to children, a doubling since 1992. It is estimated that U.S. children influence purchases of more than 500 billion dollars a year (Center for Media Education 2000).

YOUNG PEOPLE'S ACCESS TO MEDIA

Converted into concrete figures – Table 1 shows which media technology young people in Sweden have in the home:

Have in the home access to		%	%
TV set		94	
	only one TV set		27
	two TV sets		33
	three or more TV sets		34
Satellite television		63	
Set top box for digital television		8	
DVD player		11	
Video		89	
	only one video		58
	two or more		31
Personal computer		72	
	only one personal computer		47
	two or more		25
	with CD-ROM		61
	with Internet		62
Mobile phone		91	
	only one mobile phone		25
	two or more		66
n (number of interviewed persons) =		331	

Table 1. Media Technology at Home in 2000, proportions (%) of the population aged 15-24 in Sweden

Source: Nordicom-Sveriges Mediebarometer 2000

It is clear from Table 1 that most 15-24 year-olds have, according to the study *Mediebarometern 2000* [The Media Barometer in 2000],[2] television, satellite television, video, personal computer, Internet and mobile phone at home, and often there is more than one set of the medium. For example, two thirds of the young people stated that they have two or more TV sets at home. This also means that children and young people often have a TV set in their own room. An idea of how many young people this may be is given by another Swedish investigation from 1997/98,[3] according to which 64 per cent of the 15-16 year-olds declared that they had television in their own room. In the same study, 61 per cent confirmed having a video game at home (Livingstone, Holden & Bovill 1999). Information about possession of computer games is lacking, but the means for playing them in the home exist if there is a computer with CD-ROM. (Video games are instead played with the help of a special console connected to the TV set.) Besides, there is the possibility of playing other games via the computer – alone or with players from the whole world – through a connection to the Internet.

YOUNG PEOPLE'S TOTAL MEDIA USE

What does young people's media use look like? How much do they use different media and has media use changed over time? Has the spread of visual media influenced reading for example? Is the computer screen replacing television? And do the new so-called interactive media signify a more democratic participation in society?

LET US BEGIN WITH SOME ALL-EMBRACING FIGURES

During a day, the average 15-24 year-old devotes approximately 6 ½ hours to the media, according to *Mediebarometern 2000*. Of this, approximately 2 hours and 40 minutes is composed of listening – above all to music on the radio but also to a great deal on CDs (and gramophone records), as well as to some degree to audio cassettes. Two hours are, according to the interviewees, devoted to watching – mainly television but also video. Reading – books, daily press and different journals – takes slightly less than 1 hour. Slightly more than half an hour is, on average, dedicated to the Internet.[4] These figures are, as mentioned, averages – the individual differences are great.

Figure 1 presents the proportions of young people who have used the different media during an average day (so-called reach) – the time devoted to the medium is, therefore left out of the account here. These data, too, are from *Mediebarometern 2000*, as are the subsequent figures in the beginning of this chapter when nothing else is indicated.

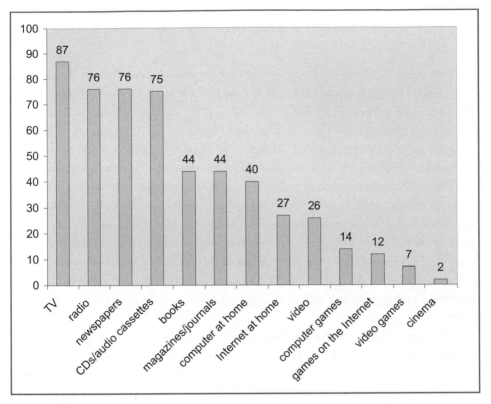

Figure 1. Proportions (%) of the population aged 15-24 who use different media on an average day, 2000

Source: Nordicom-Sveriges Mediebarometer 2000

Note: The information on computer games is estimated from the figures in the Media Barometer report and refers to playing computer games at home. The information on games via the Internet is estimated from the figures in the Media Barometer report and refers to »games/entertainment« on the Internet both at home and in other places. »Games/entertainment« on the Internet solely at home is about 5%. A joint figure on the proportion having played any electronic game (video game, computer game and/or game on the Internet) during a day is not available.

VIEWING MEDIA – TELEVISION, VIDEO, CINEMA

The proportion of young people aged 15-24 who watch *television* during a day is 87 per cent (Figure 1).The proportion is somewhat bigger among 15-19 year-olds than among 20-24 year-olds – this may be due to the fact that the younger still live at home with their parents whereas the older ones live by themselves and perhaps cannot afford a television set of their own. Gender differences are smaller (slightly more boys watch TV on an ordinary day). Several other studies show, however, that boys and girls partly prefer different TV programmes. For example, boys often watch more sports and action series, while programmes about relations such as soap operas, attract many girls. Research also indicates that children of parents with shorter education or lower societal position watch more television than children of parents with higher education/social position. However,TV viewing is also extensive among the latter children and young people (e.g., Livingstone, Holden & Bovill 1999). If comparing combinations of gender and socio-cultural background, for example working class boys vs. middle class girls, the differences are relatively conspicuous.

In the press, statements that the computer and Internet use is taking over TV viewing appear now and then. Even if this may be true for smaller groups, there is no support in Swedish research of such a general tendency. On the contrary, TV viewing among young people has increased with access to more channels and with a TV set in their own room. In the 1970s and 1980s when there were only two traditional public service channels in Sweden, SVT1 and SVT2, or in the 1950s and 1960s when there was only one such channel, TV viewing meant for young people to join the family around the only set, watching the same programme, something which is not always attractive during the liberation process of adolescence. Because of this, TV viewing among children and young people in earlier decades increased until about the age of 12, and was then successively levelling down in the teens. TV viewing increased again in adult age when someone was found who would share, live and watch television with (von Feilitzen et al. 1989). This decrease in TV viewing among young people has, more or less disappeared.

The TV channels young people choose to watch are above all commercial TV channels. Figure 2 shows the proportion of each age from 9 to 79 years who watched any of Swedish Television's (SVT) two channels (without advertising) and any commercial TV channel, respectively, on an average day in 1996 (von Feilitzen & Petrov 1998). (The curves are based on *Mediebarometern 1996* and the aggregated figures for different age groups are similar in *Mediebarometern 2000*.) While less than 40 per cent of young people aged 15 to 24 have watched something on SVT during a day, the corresponding figure for commercial television is 70-80 per cent.[5]

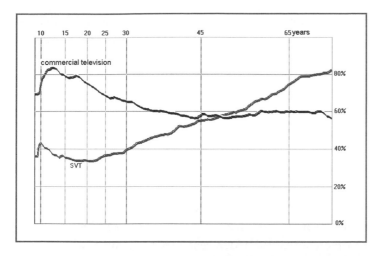

Figure 2. Proportions (%) of different ages from 9 to 79 who watch SVT and commercial TV, respectively, on an average day in 1996

Source: von Feilitzen & Petrov (1998)

The TV channel financed by advertising that most young people (and children and adults) watch in Sweden is the national TV4 launched in the beginning of the 1990s. After TV4, the Swedish-language satellite channels TV3 and TV5 are chosen. Relatively many young people also watch ZTV (a Swedish-language youth channel).

This signifies, as well, that young people more often watch the news on TV4 than the news on SVT, whereas adults more often watch SVT's news programmes. However, young people watch generally less news programmes than adults.

Even if young people is the age group that appreciates non-Swedish TV channels most, the proportion of 15-24 year-olds who has viewed any non-Swedish TV channel during a day is 27 per cent according to *Mediebarometern 2000,* and only 2 per cent has viewed *exclusively* some non-Swedish TV channel. Viewing non-Swedish channels is, thus, combined with the viewing of Swedish-language channels. All in all, young people clearly prefer Swedish channels to non-Swedish channels. The fact that roughly one quarter of 15-24 year-olds has viewed any non-Swedish TV channel should be contrasted to the figure that 85 per cent has viewed any Swedish channel on an average day.

Regarding the other visual media, 26 per cent of people aged 15-24 watch video on an average day. Video is generally not used every day but now and then, and most frequently used for watching either a rental, bought or TV-recorded film. Video viewing is also slightly more common among 15-19 year-olds than among 20-24 year-olds. Boys use video somewhat more than girls and children of parents in a lower socio-economic position somewhat more than children of parents in a higher social position (e.g., Livingstone, Holden & Bovill 1999).

Children in particular, but also young people, use the video much more than adults, something which is a consequence of, among other things, young people's interest in film. Going to the cinema is also an activity especially connected to youth (von Feilitzen & Petrov 1998). Few young people go to the cinema (2%) on an ordinary day but during a week 20 per cent of the 15-24 year-olds visit the cinema, and during a month this figure is 57 per cent (Mediebarometern 2000). As a whole, however, young people nowadays watch films on television and video much more than in the cinema.

Visits to the cinema are more prevalent among persons/young people of parents in a higher social position, which, among other things, is matched by expensive cinema tickets (compared to the costs of the video rent/video recording) and because there are more cinemas in bigger cities. Any clear gender differences among those going to the movies are hard to discover.

All together, regarding the viewing media they – apart from the cinema – to a somewhat greater extent attract boys and persons in a lower social position. Previous research also shows that several ethnic minorities watch television and video fairly much, something which may be connected with a worse economic/social situation, or for example greater efforts when reading written language.

In sum, a great change valid for the viewing media in the new media landscape is that television has become of greater significance for young people than during previous decades. Any general tendencies that young people are replacing television with computer screens cannot be gathered from existing research.

LISTENING MEDIA – RADIO, CDs/ RECORDS/AUDIO CASSETTES

In addition to television, *radio* and *CDs/records/audio cassettes* are important media to young people. As Figure 1 shows, 76 per cent listen to the radio on an average day and about as many (75%) to CDs/records/cassettes. Put together, young people declare that they spend more time on these *music media* than on the *viewing media*. Any clear age, gender or socio-cultural differences cannot be distinguished within the age span of 15 to 24 when it comes to radio. However, listening to CDs/records/cassettes is more common among 15-19 year-olds than among 20-24 year-olds. From other studies it is also known that music tastes vary greatly among young people.

The most interesting fact associated with radio listening in Sweden lately is perhaps its change as a consequence of the government's auctioning off of licencies to establish private local radio stations with advertising, something which started in 1993-94. Before that there were no commercial radiostations at all only Swedish Radio's public service channels P1, P2, P3 and P4, as well as local community stations (»neighbourhood radio«) owned by associations – the latter ones with proportionally very small audiences. The commercial radio stations of today are exclusively radio with popular music. In a similar way as young people prefer commercial television to traditional public service television, their radio listening is mainly focused on the commercial radio stations – see figure 3. (The figure refers to the situation in 1996 but the aggregated listening figures of different age groups are very similar in 2000 according to *Mediebarometern*.)

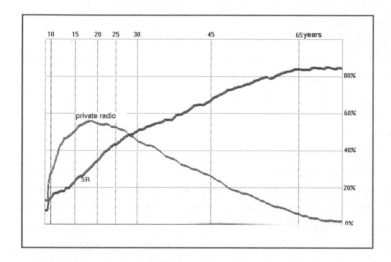

Figure 3. Proportions (%) of different ages from 9 to 79 who listen to public service radio (SR) and private radio, respectively, on an average day in 1996

Source: von Feilitzen & Petrov (1998)

PRINTED MEDIA – DAILY PRESS, MAGAZINES/ JOURNALS, BOOKS

Beside television, radio, and CDs/records/audio cassettes most (76%) young people at the age of 15 to 24 use *daily press* on an average day – see Figure 1. Here reference is given to any daily paper – ordinary morning papers, the free paper *Metro* and/or evening papers. Scrutinizing the interviewees' information on daily paper reading more in detail, it can be concluded that far more young people read morning papers (61% a day) than evening papers (27%) and that the proportion who *solely* reads *Metro* in a day is only a few per cent. Fewer young people than adults read newspapers during a day, something that is mainly true of morning papers, whereas the proportion of evening paper readers is roughly the same among young people as among adults. However, adult readers spend longer time on both morning and evening papers than the young readers.

Less than half – 44 per cent of 15-24 year-olds – has, according to *Mediebarometern* 2000, read a *magazine/journal* on an average day. Here all kinds of weekly and monthly magazines (for ladies, men, consumers, youth; comics, weekly, monthly and free show business papers) are referred to as well as all kinds of special and informative magazines or journals (for organizations or members; technical, professional, trade, scientific, cultural, political, etc.). Of these publications young people read mainly monthly magazines (21% during a week), special magazines (20% during a week), youth magazines (19% during a week), magazines for organizations or members (15% during a week) and ladies' magazines (10% during a week).

44 per cent of 15-24 year-olds have also read in a book on an average day. About the same amount has read course books/professional literature (36%) as well as fiction or youth literature (34%).

The most salient reading differences among different youth groups are on one hand that young people of parents with higher education/social position generally read more than young people of parents with lower education/social position (see also, e.g., Livingstone, Holden & Bovill 1999), something which, however, is valid for morning papers, special/professional journals, and books – but not for evening papers and weekly/monthly magazines. Partly there are gender differences; more boys read evening papers and special/professional journals than girls, while more girls read books and weekly/monthly magazines than boys.

With the spread of audiovisual media a frequent question has been whether reading is decreasing. The answer is affirmative regarding young people – but it is to a greater extent true of newspapers and certain magazines than books. Concerning newspapers the decrease is mainly true of evening papers – and adults read them nowadays less often, as well. However, there are also certain indications that book reading has declined somewhat among young people during the 1990s. A similar trend cannot be distinguished among adults but has been noticed for small children 3-8 years old (Filipson 1999).

DIGITAL MEDIA — COMPUTER, INTERNET, ELECTRONIC GAMES

Figure 1 also showed that 40 per cent of 15-24 year-olds use a *computer* at home on an average day, and 27 per cent *the Internet*. Figure 1 also presents the reach among young people regarding the use of different kinds of *electronic games*.

As to computer use at home it is as extensive among 15-19 year-olds as among 20-24 year-olds. Moreover, as many children of school age (9-14 years) as young people use a computer at home on an average day. Fewer adults use a computer at home.

When young people use a computer it is above all for the Internet and after that for games and school/work. For children games are the dominating computer activity.

This implies that Internet use at home is most common among young people. However, considering the Internet use at home and in school/at work all together, about the same proportion of young people as those of young adults (25-44 years) use the Internet in a day.

What are young people doing on the Internet? If they are at home, e-mail use is most common and, thereafter, »searching for facts/information«. But some young people also glance at newspapers, download music, play games, do business, chat, and so on. If the young people are in school/at work, however »searching for facts/information« is more frequent. The two Internet functions that are more common among children than among youth are to play games and to participate in discussions/chat.

Using computer and the Internet, including playing computer games, is more common among children and young people of parents with higher education than among children and young people of parents with shorter education, not least for the reason that highly educated families more often own computers, as well as more powerful computer equipment. However, playing video games is more usual among children and young people of parents with lower education (see, e.g., Livingstone, Holden & Bovill 1999).

In a study of 17 year-old young people in Stockholm in 1999 (Petrov 2000), in which practically all young people had access to the Internet at home except some girls of immigrant background it was obvious to how great an extent the use of Internet and computer games is a »male« activity. Of the fields of application for Internet that are included in Figure 4, for instance, it is only participation in chat groups that is more common among girls than among boys. Using e-mail is similar for both sexes. For the other fields of application boys dominate.

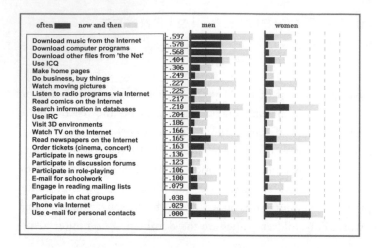

Figure 4. When you use the Internet, how often do you usually do the following things? (%)
The vertical lines indicate every 20th percent of the respective group

Source: Petrov (2000)

More boys also possess video and computer games. Figure 5 illustrates the boys' and girls' preferences for different kinds of electronic games according to the same study.

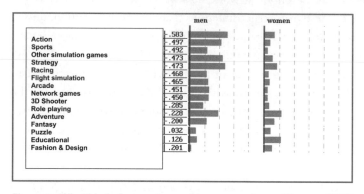

Figure 5. What kind of computer or video games do you like most? (%)
The vertical lines indicate every 20th percent of the respective group

Source: Petrov (2000)

The study also clearly showed that boys' and girls' preferences for different contents in the digital media were strongly related to the young people's interests in different contents in the traditional media, as well as to their different leisure activities.

It was evident that young people who took great interest in societal information, defined as history, politics, literature, natural sciences, education, theatre, and to some extent economy and news, that is, fields of knowledge related to what the French sociologist Pierre Bourdieu calls economic and cultural capital in society, or in other words »legitimate« or societally more accepted knowledge, searched for such information om the Internet than young people who were less interested in societal information according to this information. Young people with great interest in societal information also more often generally searched for such information in the traditional media, and they more often performed »socially more legitimate« cultural activities, such as listening to classical music, discussing politics, going to the theatre, visiting art exhibitions and museums, and so on. Likewise they used printed media more than young people with a small societal interest.

On the other hand, the groups were very similar as far as popular culture is concerned – young people with either a great or a small societal interest appreciated, for instance, comedies, thrillers, horror films, soap operas, to an equally high degree.

The Internet is often optimistically regarded as a medium that can contribute to increased participation in society and to democracy. No doubt every one with access to the Internet can for example chat, play, make websites, something that is both social and interactive activities and perhaps in a way can be said to involve participation in the media on more equal conditions than the traditional media offer. The above-mentioned research results show, however, that only a small group of the young people used the Internet as a source of societal information in the traditional sense, in spite of the fact that practically all had access to the Internet. This does, naturally, not prove that the Internet is unsuitable as a platform for enlightenment and debate in a democratic societal sense of the word. But the study indicates that the large differences in the youth groups' use of the Internet in the first place are due to other factors than access to IT equipment, namely to the focus of their other media use, to leisure activities, and to the cultural and other values that young people have – factors that in their turn appeared to be strongly correlated with young people's socio-cultural background (the parents' social position, type of school and study programme at college), the socially constructed genders included. Thus, far more basic factors and social conditions are influencing young people's disposition to actively partake via the media in the decision processes of society than solely access to media (Petrov 2000).

INCREASED DIFFERENTIATION IN MEDIA USE

Even if media use mainly depends on for example, the individual's socio-cultural background, fundamental values and dispositions, there also exists with the increasing media output a tendency for individual preferences playing a more important role for media choices.

Naturally, media use has always been individual. One must, for example, bear in mind that the information presented so far, valid for today or as tendencies over time, are averages for young people or for different youth groups (according to age, gender, social background, etc.). Of course, great differences are hidden behind such statistical abstractions. Many young people listen to music more or less all day long, others watch a lot of television, some do not care at all about books, and so on.

However, in addition to these individual differences, much indicate that the media use is becoming more and more individualized over time because of new television and radio channels, digital media, etc.

An analysis of children and young teens in ten European countries (Johnsson-Smaragdi 2001) showed that their media use could be categorized into eight different styles. Figure 6 presents estimates of the proportions of children and young people with the different styles (see the percentages under the columns) and the total amount of time that the different groups spent on the media (see the columns, which indicate minutes per day) – however, listening media excepted.

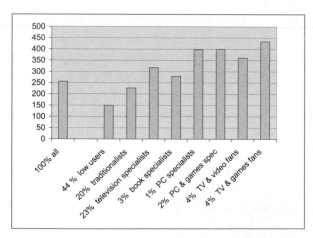

Figure 6. Average media use among 9-16 year-olds in ten European countries in 1997/98, minutes per day

Source: Johnsson-Smaragdi (2001)

The first column indicates that on average 9–16 year-olds in 1997/98 devoted about 4 ¼ hours a day to all mass media (apart from the listening media that, as mentioned, were excluded from the analysis). Considering the eight media styles, they had the following – and other – specific characteristics:

- *Low media users* were most common. They constituted approximately 44 per cent of all children and spent much less time, about 2 ½ hours a day on the media, than the average. Low media users were primarily distinguished by their relatively low use of television, though they watched more television than anything else. On the whole they tended to have a diversified pattern of media use.
- *Traditional media users* made up about 20 per cent of all children and spent less than 4 hours a day on the media. The traditionalists were low on digital media and about average on other media.
- *Television specialists* constituted nearly one quarter of all children. They focused heavily on television, on average spending over 3 ½ hours a day on it, thereby being the group devoting most time to this medium. Their total media use was above average, approx. 5 ¼ hours a day.

The three media use styles mentioned above were, as evident, extensive. The following five groups were in 1997/98 each composed of less than five per cent of the children in the analysis.

- *Book specialists* spent about 1 ½ hour a day on books. They also spent more than average amounts of time on other print media. Despite this, they spent more time on television than on books, so their total media time was slightly above average.
- *PC specialists* were keen on computers and the Internet. They were also very interested in, for example, electronic games, but fairly low on television. Their total media time was high, well over 6 ½ hours a day.
- *PC & games specialists* were also strongly focused on computers and the Internet but even more on electronic games than the above-mentioned group. Their total media use was about the same as that of the PC specialists.
- *Television & video fans* spent a large amount of time on both television and video, but were low on games, computers and books. Their total media use amounted to 6 hours a day, much above average but less than that of the PC and PC and games specialists.
- *Television & games fans* spent on average 2 ½ hours a day on electronic games and about as much on television. These children were also relatively high on video and computer games. The group had the highest total media use of all eight groups, about 7 ½ hours a day.

As mentioned, the Figure presents an aggregated profile of the media styles in ten countries – there are, naturally, country specific differences. In Sweden, for example, the low media users and the television specialists were somewhat fewer, while the PC & games specialists, television & video fans and television & games fans were slightly more. Since more children and young people in the Nordic countries have access to digital media than children in the rest of Europe, this could, among other things, indicate that particularly the groups who use digital media much may increase over time.

However, at the same time the analysis showed that – in spite of individualization – television was still the dominant medium for *all* media style groups, both in terms of the number of users and the amount of time spent. Everyone watched television and television viewing made up the main part of his or her media time.

CLOSING WORDS

For those who want to address young people via the media (apart from direct advertising that has not been dealt with here), similar analyses are thus required. Analyses that, in addition, take young people's great interest in music and their different music tastes into consideration, as well as their preferences for different media contents, their different interests, leisure activities, values, gender, ethnic belonging, study programme in school, their parents' social position, etc. …

Let me conclude with some information regarding which of five given media – television, radio, newspapers/magazines, books and the Internet – the 17 year-old young people in Stockholm found most important in terms of entertainment/pleasure and knowledge/information, respectively (Petrov 2000): Both boys and girls were of the opinion that television was the most important medium for entertainment/pleasure. As to knowledge and information the boys gave priority to the Internet in the first place and television in the second. The girls chose books first and television second.

However, there is also reason to conduct future in-depth studies with regard to what young people mean by more general expressions such as »facts and information«, »knowledge and information«, »news«, and the like. It appeared from the same study that the Internet's most popular fields of application for these young people without doubt had to do with entertainment and pleasure. And when the youth searched on the Internet it was often to get news or information on, for instance, travels, show business, film, and the like, as well as – more on part of the boys – information on computers, sports, cars, motors, shares, prices of products and services, etc. At the same time, especially boys who seldom used the Internet for searching societal information (according to the previously mentioned more »socially legitimate« definition) more often than other young people were of the opinion that the Internet was their main source of knowledge.

NOTES

1 A Swedish version of this chapter was presented at a Nordic research seminar on young people, media and consumption, arranged by Forbrugerinformationen, the Danish national consumer agency, in cooperation with corresponding national agencies in the Nordic countries, on November 9, 2001, in Copenhagen, Denmark.

2 The Media Barometer is conducted yearly since 1979, nowadays by Nordicom, Göteborg University, and gives average information for an average day based on telephone interviews during 28 days spread throughout the year with a simple random sample of the population aged 9-79. The interviews refer in the first place to media use yesterday; the interviewees are asked if they used the medium and, if so, to estimate how long they spent on it. In 2000, a total of 2,316 persons of a sample of 4,374 persons were interviewed. Non-response was, thus, 40 per cent.

3 In this study 6-16 year-olds in southern Sweden were included. The replies of the school-aged children were collected via group questionnaires in school classes. The number of answering 15-16 year-olds was approx. 425. The Swedish study, headed by Ulla Johnsson-Smaragdi, Lund University, was part of a larger European comparative project.

4 Time spent on electronic games was not measured.

5 It should be added that Swedish Television with its many children's programmes attracts a larger audience among 3-8 year-olds (see, e.g., Sveriges Television 1999).

REFERENCES

Center for Media Education, USA, http://www.cme.org (November 2000).

von Feilitzen, Cecilia, Filipson, Leni, Rydin, Ingegerd & Schyller, Ingela (1989). *Barn och unga i medieåldern. Fakta i ord och siffror* [Children and Young People in the Media Age. Facts in Words and Figures]. Stockholm, Rabén & Sjögrens Förlag.

von Feilitzen, Cecilia & Petrov, Peter (1998). »Barns och ungdomars medieanvändning 1996 [Children's and Young People's Media Use in 1996]«, *MedieNotiser, nr 2: Barn och ungdomar i det nya medielandskapet. Statistik och analys.* Göteborgs universitet, NORDICOM-Sverige, 25-39.

Filipson, Leni (1999) *Barnbarometern 98/99. 3-8 åringars kultur - och medievanor* [The Child Barometer in 98/99. 3-8 Year-Olds' Cultural and Media Habits]. Stockholm, Mediamätning i Skandinavien.

Johnsson-Smaragdi, Ulla (2001). »Media Use Styles Among the Young«, in Sonia Livingstone & Moira Bovill (Eds.) *Children and Their Changing Media Environment. A European Comparative Study.* Mahwah, NJ, Lawrence Erlbaum, 113-139.

Kline, Stephen (2000). »Killing Time? A Canadian Meditation on Video Game Culture«, in Cecilia von Feilitzen & Ulla Carlsson (Eds.) *Children in the New Media Landscape. Games, Pornography, Perceptions.* Göteborg University, The UNESCO International Clearinghouse on Children and Violence on the Screen at Nordicom, 35-59.

Livingstone, Sonia, Holden, Katherine J. & Bovill, Moira (1999). »Children's Changing Media Environment. Overview of a European Comparative Study«, in Cecilia von Feilitzen & Ulla Carlsson (Eds.) *Children and Media. Image, Education, Participation.* Göteborg University, The UNESCO International Clearinghouse on Children and Violence on the Screen at Nordicom, 39-63.

Montgomery, Kathryn C. (2001a). »Digital Kids. The New On-Line Children's Consumer Culture«, in Dorothy G. Singer & Jerome L. Singer (Eds.) *Handbook of Children and the Media.* Thousand Oaks, Sage Publications, 635-650.

Montgomery, Kathryn C. (2001b). Speech at the 3rd World Summit on Media for Children, March 23-26, 2001, Thessaloniki, Greece.

Nordicom-Sveriges Mediebarometer 1996 [The Media Barometer in 1996] (1997). Göteborgs universitet, Nordicom-Sverige, MedieNotiser nr 1.

Nordicom-Sveriges Mediebarometer 2000 [The Media Barometer in 2000] (2001). Göteborgs universitet, Nordicom-Sverige, MedieNotiser nr 1.

Petrov, Peter (2000). *Stockholmsungdomars Internetanvändning* [Stockholm Youth's Internet Use]. Stockholm, Kungliga Tekniska Högskolan, CID. There is also an abridged version of the report: »New Media and Young People in Sweden«, in Cecilia von Feilitzen & Ulla Carlsson (Eds.) *Children in the New Media Landscape. Games, Pornography, Perceptions.* Göteborg University, The UNESCO International Clearinghouse on Children and Violence on the Screen at Nordicom, 103-117

Sakamoto, Akira (2000). »Video Games and Violence. Controversy and Research in Japan«, in Cecilia von Feilitzen & Ulla Carlsson (Eds.) *Children in the New Media Landscape. Games, Pornography, Perceptions.* Göteborg University, The UNESCO International Clearinghouse on Children and Violence on the Screen at Nordicom, 61-77

Sveriges Television (1999). *Publik & Utbud. Barnens tittande* [Audience & Output. Children's Viewing]

4

Danish Children's Upbringing

– as Consumers

By Flemming Hansen, Jens Halling and Jens Carsten Nielsen

Background[1]

The project, »Danish Children as Consumers,« has a complicated but brief history. As early as 1999, Forum for Advertising Research, FAR, Department of Marketing, Copenhagen Business School, has been concerned with children, especially children and advertising. In 1999, Deborah Roedder John's »Consumer Socialization of Children: A Retrospective Look at Twenty-Five Years of Research« (*Journal of Consumer Research*, April 1999) also appeared. The article convincingly documents 25 years of accumulated international experience with research on children, particularly their role as consumers. The results are based primarily on qualitative interviews, but quantitative studies with children were also included. Naturally, one of the research questions for FAR was whether these observations were still valid, and whether they were valid in other cultural settings besides the USA, where the data originates.

During the summer of 2000, FAR became aware of the updating and reorganization taking place within Gallup/TNS' annual children/youth media index. As it turned out, it was possible to buy a share in this index and thereby incorporate a number of questions directly linked to hypotheses formulated in accordance with the international research results. In addition, FAR were given access to large parts of the children's index database. With the exception of certain specific, customer-related questions, we were able to use most of the questions.

As these data became available in the autumn of 2000, it quickly became evident that, in addition to FAR's own questions about advertising, there was an exceptional amount of unutilized information for the elucidation of children's behavior and up-bringing as consumers. This information could be processed using Deborah Roedder John's theoretical formulations. The completion of the project involved several re-searchers, including the authors: Flemming Hansen and Anne Martensen. Berit Pug-gaard from Gallup TNS, as well as Jens Halling, Gitte Bach Lauritsen, Trine Gammel-gaard and Jens Carsten Nielsen from FAR.

It is necessary to emphasize that the project is characterized by the fact that a unique collection of data was available for the elucidation of a highly topical problem. How-ever, it is important to remember that the nature of this material is quantitative. There-fore we have been unable to examine certain problems dealt with in the international research. It is also worth emphasizing that, it was only possible to formulate specific questions relating to the international research within the area »children and advertis-ing«. As for other topics within the problem area, such as children's values, transaction knowledge and decision power, the work is based on the available information. As this was varied and detailed, the following account presents a varied and valuable examina-tion of children and youth's upbringing as consumers in a modern, economic society.

INTRODUCTION

The interest in children as consumers has been rapidly increasing within Europe, the USA and Australia/New Zealand for many years. The increasing interest can be found among politicians, child carers and others who, using public funds, are concerned with children and consumption. The interest has yielded some research, which has been dis-cussed elsewhere (Tufte 2001, von Feilitzen 1999, and Drotner 2001). The research has largely been linked to children's role in relation to mass media. It has been character-ized by a low degree of integration with research regarding other aspects of children's development.

Furthermore, from a business point of view, children have sparked interest as con-sumers. A number of, often corporately funded, projects have been reported such as Guber and Berry (1993), ESOMAR (1997) and Furnham (2001). Here, the focus was on how to communicate with children, what children prefer and how they make decisions and use information. These results have often been presented with a view to increase the knowledge about the best way to market products to children. Both research traditions have been characterized by an unwillingness to integrate the results found in international research about children's development as consumers. This is the motivation behind this attempt to elucidate Danish children's situation in the year 2000.

EXAMINATION METHOD

Commercial and scientific research about children has been undertaken using quantitative, as well as qualitative methods. The qualitative methods include observation and intensive interviews. The latter is conducted either as focus groups or single interviews. The quantitative data collection methods include, not least, studies conducted in school environments and interviews with parents to learn about their attitudes and perceptions, but also studies conducted in the homes of children and young people (ESOMAR 1997). Regardless of the method, the rule is that the younger the child is, the higher the demands on guidance and instruction will be when it comes to answering the questions.

The data collection method used in the present report was questionnaires to be completed at home. The method is rather unconventional in form and as far as we know, it has not been employed in any other study. The parent's consent was obtained for questionnaires to the younger children (12 years and under). In connection with the younger children, the parents accepted the role of supervisors to complete the questionnaires. The questionnaires for the children were prepared in four different versions to suit the age groups, 5-7, 8-12, 13-18 and 19-29 years. The survey aimed to have 125 respondents per year. A reward was offered for the completion of the questionnaire.

The selection of respondents was conducted as follows: The respondents who agreed to be interviewed again were pooled as a representative quota selection. Within this selection, the households were contacted. If contact was not made after eight attempts, further contact was abandoned. Using this procedure, contacts were established with an adequate number of households with a qualified respondent who agreed to complete the questionnaire. If there was more than one child in the household, only one questionnaire was distributed.

2830 non-balanced interviews were carried out among the 5-30 year olds. The results reveal that the children are remarkably similar. The data, therefore, can be said to fulfill all reasonable requirements for being representative across the selected population.

The children's ability to answer all of the questions posed could, however, be questioned. This is not least true for the more complex questions about attitudes and interests. The analyses of the answers for these questions, however, show that the answers make sense.

The accumulated database comprises 40-44 pages of questions, a little different in form and extent for children of different ages. In the present study, data is available for each year/age. For the sake of clarity, however, in the main, we have chosen to report findings within the following age groups: 5-7, 8-10, 11-12, 13-15 and 16-18 years.

STRUCTURE OF THE PRESENTATION

We have chosen to focus on the following topics.

- Children's economy and saving abilities
- Children and the emerging electronic world
- Brand awareness, transaction knowledge and shopping
- Media use
- Interests and activities

CHILDREN AND YOUNG ADOLESCENTS' ECONOMY

Children receive pocket money, they receive gifts from family and others on birthdays, as well as on other occasions, and they make their own money at a very early age.

The monthly available income for children of different ages is shown in Table 1.

Dkr.	age 5-7	age 8-10	age 11-12	age 13-15	age 16-18
Avr.	N/A	134	273	1386	2884

Table 1. Average monthly allowance Danish kroner (1 eur. equals 7.5 Dkr. May 2002)

The monthly allowance is doubled from ages 8-10 and 11-12 years, while at age 13 the available income explodes. The income increase comes mostly from part time jobs.

The children take jobs as babysitters, shop assistants, paperboys/girls and the like. The dramatic jump in the available income around 13-14 years is because Danish employers are not allowed to employ persons below 13 years of age.

This is also reflected in Table 2.

%	age 8-10	age 11-12	age 13-15	age 16-18
works 1-3 times or more a week	4,9	16,5	47,7	57,2

Table 2. Percentage who works 1-3 times or more a week

In Table 2 it is shown that the major step happens around the age of 13. It should also be noted that the children work a lot – that almost half of the 13-15 year-olds work 1-3 times or more a week is a remarkable finding.

The youngsters mostly spend their money on CD's, clothing, sports, gifts, videos and fast food. In other areas, their spending decreases as they mature.

ELECTRONICS

In some areas consumption increases at first, then decreases: this is true for things such as computer games and cartoons.

The children are very good at saving money. This is especially the case with the youngest age groups as they may be saving for special occasions such as computer equipment, a television, a stereo, PC equipment, etc. This is reflected in the coverage of these products in the child's own room as well (Table 3).

Coverage own room (%)	age 5 7	age 8-10	age 11-12	age 13-15	age 16-18
TV	37,6	50,5	64,0	72,4	76,1
PC	7,5	17,0	20,0	27,9	34,1
PC-games	7,4	16,4	17,0	23,7	24,4
Playstation	13,5	24,7	25,4	18,8	10,1
Gameboy	18,9	38,0	42,9	28,5	13,1
Video	13,8	19,3	25,5	44,0	47,3
Camera	7,8	14,3	33,4	44,3	51,6
Stereo	17,9	38,8	53,5	69,2	79,5
Ghettoblaster	36,4	38,9	33,2	23,2	18,2
CD	20,6	27,5	26,9	35,3	37,8
MP3	0,4	0,2	1,4	2,3	3,1
Walkman	25,4	32,5	46,0	50,4	52,8
Discman	5,9	19,7	39,9	51,8	52,1
CDs	40,1	53,8	69,7	72,2	75,6
Telephone	1,8	3,9	9,2	18,4	35,3
Mobile phone	1,2	3,6	23,4	36,7	29,7

Table 3. Electronics in own room

Furthermore, the children report that they have significant influence on purchases such as television sets, PC's, printers, game–boxes and other durables. This varies with age as well (Table 4).

Influence on household purchases (%)	age 5-7	age 8-10	age 11-12	age 13-15	age 16-18
TV	20,2	34,1	45,6	45,4	44,6
PC	12,2	22,7	47,0	43,8	46,1
PC-games	65,4	66,0	59,7	40,7	29,7
Playstation	50,9	54,0	43,2	31,0	20,6
Gameboy	66,7	56,6	46,8	33,5	23,3
Video	17,0	19,4	38,0	41,2	37,0
Camera	10,7	19,7	36,2	35,8	36,1
Stereo	51,6	30,0	43,1	39,1	32,4
Ghettoblaster	35,0	48,4	43,1	37,2	27,7
CD	25,0	33,2	41,9	34,5	15,1
MP3	21,4	13,3	27,5	16,4	17,7
Walkman	35,0	43,1	44,9	31,4	29,2
Discman	26,5	35,8	45,1	36,7	25,5
CDs	76,8	63,3	41,7	88,4	9,4
Telephone	5,5	9,1	30,3	33,6	34,0
Mobile phone	3,0	8,5	27,8	28,8	22,0

Table 4. Percentage who claim to have influence on household purchases

The children and youngsters may even influence their family's purchase of, for example, houses, cars and vacations. Here, influence comes partly from the children's need to be taken into consideration when purchases are made, and partly from the children participating in the decision-making process prior to purchases being made.

As mentioned earlier, children and adolescents live in an electronic world. The extent to which they have access to electronic equipment of different kinds in their own room across different ages is exceptional. Table 3 shows that approximately 75% of the 16 to 18 year-olds have their own television and stereo in their rooms. Half of them also have a video by the time they reach the age of 16 to 18 years.

Even the young children, aged 5-7, frequently have electronic hardware in their own room, walkmans and televisions, in particular, are found in more than one-third of children's playrooms.

They also use their access to electronic media to keep in contact with the world outside. This increases dramatically with age, and both mobile phones and the Internet are frequently used among teenagers in Denmark. This development is shown in Table 5.

%	age 5-7	age 8-10	age 11-12	age 13-15	age 16-18
Mobile phone coverage		7	33	63	72
Uses the Internet 2 or more times a week	2	10	42	52	59

Table 5. Contact with the world

Toys, of course, play an important, practical role in the lives of a young child. However, this role decreases rapidly with age. This phenomenon is shown in Table 6.

%	age 5-7	age 8-10	age 11-12
Interested in toys	85	60	17
Plays with toys alone	83	45	9
Plays with toys with others	83	44	8

Table 6. Toys

The percentage of children who play with toys once or more times a week drops from 85% among the 5-7 year-olds to 17% among the 11-12 year-olds. The data also shows that the more interested the child is in computer games, the faster the interest in toys will decrease.

BRAND AWARENESS, TRANSACTION KNOWLEDGE AND SHOPPING

Children and young people learn about brands through personal use, from observing use among parents and friends, from participating in shopping situations and from mass media.

In the study, aided recall of brand names are measured for more than 300 brands in twenty different product categories.

Collectively, children know between 6 and 20+ different brands from different product areas. The way in which brand awareness develops for selected product areas is shown in Table 7.

	age 5-7	age 8-10	age 16-18	age 19-30	Number of Brands
Cereals	10	11	13	14	19
Soft drinks	8	11	12	12	13
Sports clothes	3	5	6	6	6
Mobile phones	1	6	8	7	12

Table 7. Brand Awareness (number of brands known)

From these and similar figures for other product categories, it can be estimated that 5-7 year-old children know of 300+ different brands.

Among the 16–18 year-olds, the number of known brands is twice as high and the increasing brand awareness occurs in very different areas.

The fact that brand awareness is established at a very early age is remarkable. To illustrate how brand awareness develops with age, selected brands are shown in Table 8.

%	age 5-7	age 8-10	age 11-12	age 13-15	age 16-18
Coca Cola	97	97	98	97	98
Fanta	93	95	97	97	98
Pepsi	81	91	96	97	98
Kellogg's Cornflakes	95	96	98	97	97
Kellogg's Frosties	87	91	95	94	96
Adidas	74	94	97	95	97
Nike	60	81	95	95	97
Hummel	45	68	85	89	95
Ericsson	21	50	86	92	94
Nokia	18	67	89	94	96
Motorola	8	32	65	79	84

Table 8. Brand Awareness

For some product areas, where use of the product does not become important until the child matures, brand awareness develops with age.

This clearly applies to mobile phones and, less prolifically, to sport brands. For soft drinks and breakfast products, however, brand awareness is high as early as ages 5-7. Not only do children and youngsters possess exceptional brand awareness. For many products, their specific knowledge may be as great as, or greater than, their parents'.

This clearly applies to many electronic products, but is also the case with many fashion related products.

Children visit many different stores. From the age of 13-15, they frequently visit clothes shops and other chain stores. With age, they also frequently make their own purchases. This is illustrated in Table 9 for selected product areas.

%	age 5-7	age 8-10	age 11-12	age 13-15	age 16-18
Soft drinks	2	3	12	27	45
Beer	..	..	..	27	66
Chips	4	7	16	29	34
Chocolate bars	6	16	2	49	67
Fastfood	0	1	10	37	72
Toothpaste	0	0	1	2	6
Deodorants	0	3	19	43	60
Perfume	0	2	9	31	58

Table 9. Children's Personal Purchases

Personal purchases begin to be important from age 11 onwards. Naturally, this increases with age and reaches a level at age 16-18 that is not very different from what can be observed among the 19-30 year-olds. It is certainly interesting that the most frequently purchased items are fast food, chocolate bars and beer. It is also interesting that the youngsters themselves largely purchase deodorants and perfume. With regard to toothpaste, they rely on purchases made for the household. Even when children do not make the purchase themselves, they have considerable influence on purchases made by the family. See Table 10.

%	age 5-7	age 8-10	age 11-12	age 13-15	age 16-18
Cornflakes	62	62	53	52	58
Yoghurt	62	56	52	49	55
Chips	61	61	54	41	37
Soft drinks	62	65	65	49	43
Fastfood	72	68	56	36	12
Toothpaste	37	57	56	58	66
Shampoo	30	35	50	61	77

Table 10. Purchase Influence

For example, it is reported that, among the 5-7 year olds, 62% have a say in cereal purchases. This influence, however, does not increase with age.

Conversely, influence on toothpaste and hair shampoo purchases dramatically increases with age. The decrease in influence on fast food purchases, reported in Table 10, is ascribable to the fact that children increasingly make their own purchases in this product category.

MEDIA USE

Children are heavy users of media. The data for this factor is shown in Table 11.

Avr. Min. a day	age 5-7	age 8-10	age 11-12	age 13-15	age 16-18
Radio	21	22	36	62	80
TV	73	90	124	139	131
Video	60	59	93	87	65
Internet	16	17	25	33	32
Computer games	53	75	90	73	63
Comics	20	45	53	55	47
Books	0	33	37	37	33

Table 11. Media Use

Media use increases from a daily consumption of 3.7 hours among the 5-7 year-olds to more than 8 hours among 13-15 year-olds where media consumption peaks. Even though children sleep less as they grow older, mass media takes up an increasing part of their time from age 5 to around age 11.

The percentage of children's total hours (awake) taken up by mass media increases dramatically. Radio use increases fourfold from age 5 to 18. Television and video watching increases from 2.25 to 3.6 hours among the 13-15 year-olds per day. Internet or computer activities take up just over an hour among the 5-7 year-olds and increases to almost 2½ hrs. among the 11-15 year-olds, finally decreasing to just over 1½ hours among the 16-18 year-olds.

Reading increases up to about age 10, from then on the activity remains relatively stabile throughout childhood.

Differences between boys and girls are minor until 12 years of age (apart from computer games – boys are more active in this area). Girls from age 12, however, use radio, books and magazines much more than boys. The data is shown in Table 12.

avr. min a day	girls	boys
Radio	72	49
TV	138	139
Video	82	92
Internet	31	35
Computer games	43	109
Comics	64	44
Books	41	33

Table 12. Media use (gender specific)

INTERESTS AND ACTIVITIES

In addition to the areas investigated above the data material comprises of three large batteries, which describe the young people' interests (32 questions) and activities (37 questions). The results for those sets of questions are very interesting and show consistency in the overall patterns between the groups.

The young people were asked how interested they were in 32 different topics. The answers were given according to a 5-point scale ranging from »interested« to »not interested at all« and according to a 7-point scale ranging from »daily« to »never« – There are minor differences in the 32 »interest« questions + 37 »activities« questions depending on the age group.

Apparently, there is a connection between a number of different interests and activities. If you like watching cartoons on TV, you are likely to enjoy watching children's programs as well. If you are interested in computers and PCs, chances are that you will also be interested in IT games. If you are interested in watching TV, you will undoubtedly also be interested in renting videos.

There are several ways in which you can examine the grouping of such interests. The object is to group together those interests that attract the same respondents. We have opted to work with a factor analysis and, subsequently, based on the results from the overall analysis, we have opted to work with eight factors. As an illustration, the results for the 13-18 year-olds are shown in Table 13. (Only the four highest loading questions in each factor are shown).

Factor	Question	
Playing	BR(A)	0,76
	Games dept. In BR(A)	0,73
	Toys´R´us(A)	0,72
	Toy dept. in dept. Store(A)	0,70
	...	...
Computer/games	Computer & games(I)	0,79
	Playing on the PC(A)	0,73
	Computer / PC(I)	0,73
	Games dept. in Electronics store(A)	0,65
	...	...
Teenage stuff/Gossip	Reading tabloid magazines(I)	0,69
	Reading about celebrities(I)	0,66
	Secrets and gossip(I)	0,64
	Youth programs on TV(I)	0,61
	...	...
Out-going	Rent a videofilm(A)	0,63
	Going out to cafees(A)	0,63
	Going to concerts(A)	0,61
	Going to the cinema(A)	0,60
	...	...
Sport	Practice sports(A)	0,80
	Like sports(I)	0,77
	Spectator at sport events(A)	0,75
	Sports shop(I)	0,72
	...	...
Friends	Visit friends(A)	0,70
	Have friends over(A)	0,66
	Be with friends(I)	0,59
	Listen to music(I)	0,49
	...	...
Culture	Experiences in the nature(I)	0,62
	Pollution- and environmental issues(I)	0,55
	Board games(I)	0,53
	Jokes and satire(I)	0,39
	...	...
Books and comics	Borrow books at libraries(A)	0,73
	Read books(A)	0,71
	Attend libraries(I)	0,63
	Borrow comics at libraries(A)	0,51
	...	...

Table 13. Interest (I)/Activity (A) Factors for the 13-18 year-olds

The included numbers indicate the connection between the questions and the individual factors (factor loading). The numbers may be interpreted in such a way that the answers to for example, the question »interested in reading magazines« is correlated with 0,69 using the otherwise unknown factor 3. »Reading about celebrities« is similarly correlated with 0,66 using the same factor. By looking at which questions are first and foremost closely related to the factor, it is possible to infer what it represents. The eight factors explain 47% of the variation, which may be characterized as follows:

- Playing/Toy shopping
- Computer/Games
- Teenager stuff/Gossip
- Out-going
- Sport
- Friends
- Culture
- Books and Comics

It is remarkable that analyses performed for each of the age groups, 5-7, 8-12, 13-18 and 19-30 only show slight variation compared to the overall result. The way in which the children and young people's interests and activities are grouped together only varies slightly with age and between boys and girls. As an example, the 8-factor solutions for the four age groups are compared below in Table 14.

8 factors - age 5-7	8 factors - age 8-12	8 factors - age 13-18	8 factors - age 19-30
Computer/games	Computer Games	Computer/games	Computer/games
Culture	Culture	Culture	Culture
Sport	Sport	Sport	Sport
Shops and shopping			Shops and shopping
Comics	Comics	Comics /Books	Comics
Playing/Toy shopping	Playing/Toys	Playing/Toy shopping	Playing/Toy shopping
Out-going	Friends /Out-going	Out-going	Out-going
Friends		Friends	
	Teenage stuff/Gossip	Teenage stuff/Gossip	Teenage stuff/Gossip

Table 14. Outline of the interest/activity factor for the 4 age groups

A different matter all together is, of course, that the different age groups assess the eight dimensions very differently; this is analyzed in Table 15.

Factor	Question	boy	girl	age 8-12	age 13-15	age 16-18	age 19-30
Playing/ toy shopping	Visit BR (A)	0,27%	0,62%	2,89%	0,33%(1)	0,78%	0,60%
	Visit game dpt. In BR (A)	0,82%	0,62%	2,13%	0,90%	0,83%	0,20%
	Visit Toys´R´us (A)	0,00%	0,21%	0,37%	0,08%	0,23%	4,3%(1)
Computer/ games	Gamebox & games (I)	65,75%	19,83%(1)	73,09%	38,72%(1)	32,94%	30,30%
	Playing games on PC (A)	63,56%	17,97%(1)	57,43%	37,54%(1)	29,48%(1)	26,20%
	Computer /PC (I)	66,30%	26,23%(1)	64,09%	43,21%(1)	38,49%	45,9%(1)
Teenage stuff/Gossip	Read tabloid magazines (I)	13,97%	37,39%(1)	14,41%	30,73%(1)	27,09%	24,20%
	Read about celebrities (I)	20,00%	47,52%(1)	16,59%	37,83%(1)	32,04%	19,6%(1)
	Secrets and gossip (I)	28,49%	62,60%(1)	–	49,22%	46,09%	28,3%(1)
Out-going	Visit café (A)	4,93%	7,64%	–	5,06%	10,63%(1)	11,90%
	Concerts (A)	2,19%	1,45%	–	1,59%	2,19%	0,90%
	Visit movie theaters (A)	2,47%	3,72%	1,05%	3,54%(1)	2,83%	3,30%
Sport	Practice sport (A)	63,29%	60,33%	72,17%	61,37%(1)	56,02%	50,60%
	Practice sport (I)	70,14%	69,21%	73,73%	69,78%	68,55%	60,1%(1)
	Spectator at sport events (A)	11,78%	8,26%	10,04%	9,76%	9,21%	8,10%
Friends	Visit friends (A)	76,99%	76,24%	77,83%	76,58%	78,03%	57,2%(1)
	Have friends visiting (A)	72,33%	69,21%	77,02%	70,08%(1)	69,49%	54,6%(1)
	Being with friends (I)	90,68%	96,69%(1)	94,36%	93,88%	95,31%	91,5%(1)
Culture	Experiences in nature (I)	32,33%	34,09%	55,69%	32,17%(1)	36,59%	55,2%(1)
	Polution & environmental issues (I)	25,21%	24,59%	15,74%	23,52%(1)	32,37%(1)	40,5%(1)
	Board games (I)	12,05%	5,78%(1)	40,10%	8,43%(1)	7,19%	21%(1)
Books/ comic books	Borrowing books at libraries (A)	6,85%	7,64%	33,64%	7,83%(1)	3,37%(1)	4,70%
	Reading books (A)	20,82%	33,88%(1)	67,92%	27,99%(1)	23,27%	34,3%(1)
	Visit libraries (I)	12,05%	23,34%(1)	35,66%	18,20%(1)	21,70%	26,9%(1)
	(1) Significant difference between this and the previous						

Table 15. The 13-18 year-olds interests and activities across each of the eight interest and activity factors. The numbers show the percentage of respondents who either answered very interested or rather interested (I), daily, almost daily or 1-3 times a week (A).

In Table 15, the interests and activities are shown in accordance with the answers to the three questions that were most characteristic for each of the eight interest/activity factors for the 13-18 year-olds. It is clear that interest in toys, computers and games is decreasing. Contact with friends is still very important and the youngsters have become a bit more out-going. The cultural interests, not least, are increasing. The differences between the younger age groups of 13-18 years reflect the same tendency.

The difference between boys and girls is more pronounced among the 13-18 year olds than within the younger age groups. The girls' interest in computers and games is almost non-existent; their interest in »teenager stuff/Gossip« on the other hand is dramatically increasing and greater than the boys'. The girls also read more, and are slightly more out-going (cafes and cinemas). In contrast, the boys are more active in sports. Overall, there are far more significant differences between the boys' and girls' answers to individual questions than among the younger age groups.

In summary, whereas children hold onto their early perception of activities and interests, with only a few slight adjustments, until they are young adults, the degree to which they commit themselves to the activities and interests in question varies greatly. Naturally, interest in toys decreases, while interest in reading, cultural and social activities among other things increases.

The 5-7 year-olds are surprisingly homogenous, but the difference between boys and girls becomes far greater as they grow older. The differences increase across other dimensions too. In our segmentation analysis performed for each of the three age groups, we could observe increasingly greater heterogeneity among the children as they grew older.

SUMMARY OF FINDINGS

The enormous amount of information in this survey makes it difficult to summarize what we have learned. However, some general points can be made.

- In brief, children are active in contemporary Denmark; they are busy with school, friends, sport, work, duties, entertainment and shopping.
- From an early age, they have their own money and savings, and they become more and more aware of money-related issues as they mature.
- They exert considerable influence in all aspects of family consumption.
- As they grow older, they make their own purchases, influence shopping, and develop preferences for fast moving consumer goods and durables, especially when it comes to electronic hardware.
- They control their own media consumption more or less independent of their parents, and early on, participate in open networks where information flows freely 24 hours a day.
- They are the first computer literate generation with access to global information and entertainment – 24 hours a day.

NOTE

1   English translation Tina J. Hindsbo, MA

REFERENCES

Drotner, Kirsten (2001). *Medier for fremtiden: Børn, unge og det nye medielandskab.* [Media in the future: Children, young ones and the new media landscape.] København, Høst & Søn.

ESOMAR Seminar on youth research (1997). *»How to be number one in the youth market«*, København, 22-24 oktober 1997.

Feilitzen, Cecilia v.& Ulla Carlsson (eds) (1999). *»Children and Media (Image Education Participation)«*, The UNESCO International Clearinghouse on children and violence on the screen at Nordicom

Furnham, Adrian (2001). »Parental attitudes to pocket money/allowances for children«, *Journal of Economic Psychology,* Vol. 22, No. 3, June 2001, 397-422.

Guber, Selina & Jon Berry (1993). Marketing to and through kids. McGraw-Hill, New York.

John, Deborah Roedder (1999). »Consumer socialization of children: A retrospective look at twenty-five years of research«, *Journal of consumer research,* vol. 26, December, 183-216.

Tufte, Birgitte et. al. (2001). »Børnekultur, Hvilke børn? Og hvis kultur?«. [Children's culture, What Children? And whose culture?] Akademisk forlag.

5

CHILDREN AND ADVERTISING
– POLITICS AND RESEARCH IN CONSUMER SOCIALIZATION

By Adrian Furnham

INTRODUCTION

It is often surprising to find that ideas from a popular book whose theories have long been discredited still holds sway over the opinions of lay people. Myths so easily and unscientifically created seem so difficult to destroy. For over fifty years the effect of Vance Packard's (1957) *Hidden Persuaders* has led people to believe that manufacturers and marketeers somehow know how to, and do, persuade people to buy against their will: to be, somehow, unconsciously persuaded to buy products they do not ever »see« advertised. Careful research showed the whole subliminal issue to be preposterous, absurd, ludicrous and laughable. However the hidden persuader myth has convinced people that advertisers, sales staff and shop planners are able to ensure rational customers to do things they probably would not otherwise do … that is, to buy particular products. It is an attractive idea and one that has become a self-perpetuating myth … despite the evidence against it. Furthermore it is assumed that if rational adults can be so easily hoodwinked to buy things against their better judgement this is all-the-more the case with naive children who therefore need protection.

This chapter looks at the science and politics of advertising to children where equivalent myths exist: the myth of the naïve and gullible child; the myth of the devious and avaricious manufacturer; the myth of the effectiveness of protectionism.

Research in this area is difficult but it seems many pressure groups have turned their back on the scientific evidence preferring political techniques of persuasion and social engineering to disinterested scientific inquiry.

TWO APPROACHES

It is possible to detect both in popular debate and the media two quite different groups interested in this area those in favour of banning/regulating television advertising to children and those more interested, in educating children in the modern consumer world.

Protectionists	Educationalists
Legislate	Educate
Left Wing	Right Wing
Anti Business	Pro Business
Infantalise Children	Adultise Children
Appeal from surveys	Appeal from experiments
Collectivistic	Individualistic
Stress certainty	Stress equivocation

Table 1. Two opposite approaches

Table 1 compares and contrasts the two approaches. This maybe criticised for being simplistic and stereotypic and not based on evidence. Indeed this may well be true but it serves initially to clearly distinguish between two approaches to deal with the central issue of advertising to children.

Protectionists argue that advertising needs strict control through legislation. They argue that there is data, usually privately commissioned surveys, to suggest that children do not understand advertising and are gullible to devious techniques. They stress that all parents are of like mind on this issue and that advertisers particularly of toys and fast-foods are unfair to children exploiting their naivity. To the other group, ie the Educationist they appear to be anti-business, left wing, anti-empirical, infantalisers of children. Protectionists have been successful in certain European countries in ensuring government legislation, as opposed to industry regulation, of particular advertisements particularly on television. Frequently various pressure groups combined together to find and proselytise on behalf of a protectionist banner. However it probably remains true to say there is little or no evidence that this strategy works in dissuading children from wanting particular goods or »protecting« them from advertisers.

Educationists, on the other hand, argue that it is both unwise and unethical to ban advertising for two reasons. First children need education and banning advertisements simply puts back their consumer education. It renders them more naïve and unable to understand and effectively deal with the new consumer society. Second they argue from experimental data both that advertisements are clearly not exclusive in determining preferences and sales, and that children are sophisticated consumers of the media even by the age of eight. Educationalists also argue that strict voluntary codes that advertisers have to follow are more than sufficient to protect young children from unfair advertising. Opponents see them as right-wing, pro-business, apologists who are »in the pocket« of advertisers. They are often to be found in think tanks and maybe supported by manufacturers. They often commission academic research in the certain knowledge that it will show the complexity of the factors and processes leading to child product requests.

Academic research conclusions	Public policy recommendations
Descriptive	Pro-pre-scriptive
Cautious	Certain
Aimed at knowledge, insight, understanding	Aimed at action, operation, control
Derived from empirical data	Second-hand, selective database
Frequently complex	Frequently simple
Uncertainty dealt with statistically	Uncertainty dealt with by experts
Low urgency	High urgency
Academic journals/books	Press release, conference, public policy documents

Table 2. Academic vs public policy approaches

Another distinction can be made between academic researchers in the area and public policy people who are eager to apply academic research (see Table 2). Again it may be thought that this table is too simple. However it tries to highlight the epistemology and practice of those interested in the area. Essentially academic researchers like to think of themselves as disinterested and impartial researchers who try to understand processes. Empiricists derive theories, collect data, analyse the data to test hypotheses. In this area they admit the number of factors that have to be considered when trying to understand answers to seemingly simple questions like »when do children understand the purpose of advertisements?« or »what determines children's preference for a particular product?« The research is often painstaking and gets published in journals and books for the benefit of other academics. Not all the research is good however and researchers are most eager to criticise peers if they believe they warrant it.

Public policy people are in the business of changing behaviour by persuasion and legislation. They see themselves as applied researchers trying to ensure there are guidelines, laws, and policies that help and protect people in society. Inevitably they try to understand essence of issues which may, to the academic eye, too frequently look like simplification. They read and may commission academic research though they may not act on the recommendation of the researchers.

The two groups can have different values, different preferences and different temperaments which can easily lead to distrust and dislike. This is all the more the case when large sums of money are involved.

The differences between educationalists and protectionists, and between academic researchers and public policy people mean that this whole area is marked more by rhetoric than research (Bas 1996, 1998, Boyfield 1999, Furnham, 1993, 2000, Goldstein 1994, 1999).

HISTORY OF RESEARCH

It is now over 30 years since the first serious qualitative original research was done exploring the effects of television advertising on children and adolescents (Ward 1971). However over the years, particularly since the mid 1980s there has been considerable research in the whole topic of children as consumers (Beatty & Talpade 1994, Gunter & Furnham 1998, John 1999, Keillor et al 1996, McNeal 1987, 1992, Moore & Lutz, 2000). Early research was, and still is, largely in response to concerns about exploitation. The four factors that were thought to have a major effect on the issue were:

1 Stage of cognitive development indicated by age; that is what they can understand when they watch television.
2 Amount of media exposure, that is how much they get exposed to different media.
3 Parental mediation of media behaviour, that is the rules imposed by parents in such things as television watching.
4 Parental mediation of purchasing behaviour, that is rules, examples and practices of parents when shopping.

The results have always been mixed regarding development but much clearer findings about the role of parents who were thought to be critical. Early models had three sorts of components.

Antecedent Factors	Independent Variables	Dependent Outcome measure
Sex	Exposure to TV	Attitude to Advertisements
Age	Parental TV rules	Advertisement preferences
Nationality	Shopping/purchasing practices	Purchasing due to Advertisements

Figure 1. The factors involved

This model informs research today (Sherry, Greenberg & Tokinoya 1999). It is a causal model that emphasises the role of demographic, home and parental variables on all aspects of responses to television advertisements. There are also cultural and economic factors that play a part making the research very difficult.

There are many early simple minded ideas that assume parenting is made more difficult solely because of the media. Somehow television commercials (and maybe even programmes), it is assumed, turn children into irrational, demanding, uncontrollable »beasts«. Diagrammatically the theory is shown in figure 2. Television advertising, according to this model, creates (false, dangerous and expensive) wants in the child; not needs. This makes the (poorly socialized) child pester parents remorselessly with constant demands. Parents try to resist but this causes conflict so they give in and buy something they cannot afford, that the child both does not need and may even come to cause harm. Television advertising is thus accorded a primary motivational role and hence the problem can be solved by banning it. To believe that advertising *alone* can create wants is very naïve – advertising helps companies satisfy demand at best. Even to the most gullible viewer advertising cannot persuade people to buy brands they really do not want.

TV COMMERCIAL ➤ WANTS ➤ DEMANDS ➤ CHILD-PARENT CONFLICT ➤ PURCHASE BY PARENT

Figure 2. The standard argument

There are many interesting paradoxes in this approach. Protectionists who adhere to this model argue both that children do not understand the commercial; but blandly want everything equally on commercials. Children are too young to understand television advertising yet they are powerfully influenced by it presumably because they do not understand the role of advertising.

PEER INFLUENCE ➤ WANTS ➤ SELECTIVE VIEWING OF COMMERCIALS ➤ REQUESTS ➤ PARENTAL DECISION

Figure 3. An alternative approach

Goldstein (1999) has proposed an alternative model. Peer and parental influences are known to play a far more important role in purchasing decisions than advertising. Parental responsibility and decision making influence the highly selective nature of attending to the media and to advertising. The multiple meanings and uses of advertising by young people, particularly adolescents, means that television adverts are just one factor. Note that the first model (Figure 2) both ignores the child's peer group and renders the parent reactive rather than proactive. Even the second model (Figure 3) does not place parental values and socializing processes as primary factors.

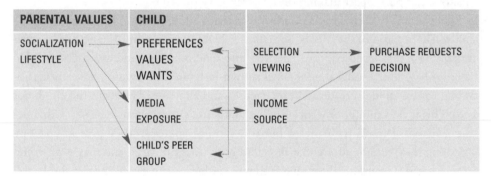

Figure 4. Another alternative approach

Furnham (2000) has proposed a yet more complex model. This model (Figure 4) suggests that the way parents bring up their children is the central and most powerful causative issue. This determines the child's values, his or her allowed (and later preferred) media consumption habits (including television) and friendship network. These in turn determine which television programmes are watched which maybe one factor that influences purchasing wants.

All of these models are testable. Certainly the latter two (Figure 3 and 4) have received most support and one (Figure 2) least. The key to understanding the problem lies in the consumer socialization literature of how young people learn about the commercial world and begin to show clear preferences. What these models do indicate is the self-evident point that children's understandings and preferences are multi-determined.

CONSUMER SOCIALISATION

Goldstein (1999) reviewed seventeen salient papers in the area and found that the literature is equivocal and that there is little substantial evidence that children are especially vulnerable to advertising and that »youth fads« often precede rather than follow, advertising. In a review of four other European reviews he concludes: »There is no convincing evidence that advertising affects children's values and materialism, eating habits, the use of tobacco and alcohol gender and ethnic stereotypical, violence, socialization or has any long-term effects« (p. 113). Goldstein (1999) points out the recent research tends to suggest that children's ability to understand »the grammar of television« (the meaning and purpose of advertising) has been underestimated.

Partly because of the politicisation of the debate there has been an increasing amount of research on children and advertising. This literature is called »the consumer socialization of children«. Recently John (1999) has done an excellent and comprehensive review of a quarter century of research in the area. The focus was particularly on the growth of understanding of children over time as they react to advertising and persuasion. One consistent theme is the sophistication of children. Thus she notes that older children »are discriminating consumers of advertising who find many commercials to be entertaining, interesting, and socially relevant. By virtue of their growing sophistication, older children and adolescents find entertainment in analysing the creative strategy of many commercials and constructing theories for why certain elements are persuasive. Advertisements are also valued as a device for social interaction, serving as a focus of conversations with peers, a means of belonging and group membership, and a conduit for transferring and conveying meaning in their daily lives« (p 191-192).

This excellent review has a most useful table showing developmental changes in children from 3-16 years. It illustrates both the complicated nature of the whole issue and how passionate debates over simplify careful research findings often to attempt to infantilising children. Secondly it illustrates how sophisticated most seven year olds are about the whole world of consumption.

Topic	Perceptual stage, 3-7 years
Advertising knowledge	• Can distinguish advertisements from programs based on perceptual features • Believe advertisements are truthful, funny and interesting • Positive attitudes towards advertisements
Transaction knowledge: Product brand knowledge	• Can recognize brand names and beginning to associate them with product categories • Perceptual cues used to identify product categories • Beginning to understand symbolic aspects of consumption based on perceptual features • Egocentric view of retail stores as a source of desired items
Shopping knowledge and skills	• Understand sequence of events in the basic shopping script • Value of products and prices based on perceptual features
Decision making skills and abilities: information search	• Limited awareness of information sources • Focus on perceptual attributes • Emerging ability to adapt to cost-benefit trade-offs
Product evaluation	• Use of perceptually salient attribute information • Use of single attributes
Decision strategies	• Limited repertoire of strategies • Emerging ability strategies to tasks – usually need cues to adap
Purchase influence and negotiation strategies	• Use direct requests and emotional appeals • Limited ability to adapt strategy to person or situation
Consumption motives and values: Materialism	• Value of possessions based on surface features, such as »having more« of something

Table 3. Summary of findings by consumer socialisation stage

Analytical stage, 7-11 years	Reflective stage, 11-16 years
Can distinguish advertisements from programs based on persuasive intent Believe advertisements lie and contain bias and deception-but do not use these »cognitive defences« Negative attitudes toward advertisements	• Understand persuasive intent of advertisements as well as specific advertisement tactics and appeals • Believe advertisements lie and know how to spot specific instances of bias or deception in advertisements • Sceptical attitudes toward advertisements
Increasing brand awareness, especially for child-relevant product categories Underlying or functional cues used to define product categories Increased understanding of symbolic aspects of consumption Understand retail stores are owned to sell goods and make a profit	• Substantial brand awareness for adult-oriented as well as child-relevant product categories • Underlying or functional cues used to define product categories • Sophisticated understanding of consumption symbolism for product categories and brand names • Understanding and enthusiasm for retail stores
Shopping scripts more complex, abstract, and with contingencies Prices based on theories of value	• Complex and contingent shopping scripts • Prices based on abstract reasoning, such as input variations and buyer preferences
Increased awareness of personal and mass media sources Gather information on functional as well as perceptual attributes Able to adapt to cost-benefit trade-offs	• Contingent use of different information sources depending on product or situation • Gather information on functional, perceptual, and social aspects • Able to adapt to cost-benefit trade-offs
Focus on important attribute information – functional and perceptual attributes Use of two or more attributes	• Focus on important attribute information – functional, perceptual and social aspects • Use of multiple attributes
Increased repertoire of strategies, especially noncompensatory ones Capable of adapting strategies to tasks	• Full repertoire of strategies • Capable of adapting strategies to tasks in adult-like manner
Expanded repertoire of strategies, with bargaining and persuasion emerging Developing abilities to adapt strategy to persons and situations	• Full repertoire of strategies, with bargaining and persuasion as favourites • Capable of adapting strategies based on perceived effectiveness for persons and situations
Emerging understanding of value based on social meaning and significance	• Fully developed understanding of value based on social meaning, significance, and scarcity

There is some doubt, in academic circles, of the virtue of stage-wise theories as set out in table 3. However the table is faithful to the extant academic literature and interpretable by policy makers. It should be made apparent however that this is based exclusively on American data. It is quite likely the results would be quite different if dealing with third-world children who are less exposed both to television and many commercial goods.

There are relatively few recent published empirical studies on children and advertising (Moore & Lutz, 2000). One reason for this is that this research is difficult. Another is that academics all acknowledge that advertising alone cannot and does not influence children's understanding and preferences. For instance Moore and Lutz (2000) showed that product usage and advertising together and interactively influence children's product impressions and that these differ in 7-8 and 10-11 year olds.

Yet many people see advertising as able to profoundly influence behaviour. It is ubiquitous and difficult to evade. Advertisements contain, it is said, emotionally charged, deceptive messages therefore it persuades. But as Bergler (1999) points out there is a dramatic difference between the conclusions of scientific and layman psychology. He notes: »The love of a »no risk« society results increasingly in substituting scapegoats outside one's own sphere of influence for self responsibility. Due to its universal presence, advertising is one of those scapegoats; also because – fitting in with the naïve theory of the effects on advertising – it is attributed to having a direct effect on behaviour, it provides psychological relief from the strain on self-responsibility« (p 413).

From the extensive German data available Bergler (1999) sets out to examine six hypotheses about children and advertising:

1 Children are intensive consumers of television and are therefore intensively exposed to advertising. German data show that children between 3 and 13 years spend only 1.4 percent of their waking time watching television advertisements.
2 Children are gullible to advertising because they are not yet able to differentiate between adverts and programmes. Data from various sources show nearly two-thirds of six year olds can even distinguish the intention of advertising while a third even question the credibility of advertising at this age.
3 Advertising leads to a constant increase in children's desires »after which, they then get their own way if necessary with weeks of 'psycho terror' despite great opposition from their parents« (p 417). Children, especially adolescents, influence parental purchasing decisions with respect to clothes and goods. Yet the data say the influence on parental purchasing decision is overestimated.
4 Children are not critical of advertising because of poor powers of judgement or evaluation of risk. There is now abundant evidence that for socio-economic rea-

sons children lose their positive naivety much earlier than was the case for the previous generation. Indeed young people are particularly aware of health and related risks.

5 Parents are powerless toward the influence of advertising on their children. Bergler (1999) summarizes the extensive literature to refute this assumption thus: »Parents are only helpless toward external influences on their children if they themselves are helpless in the way they handle their children« (p 401).

6 Politicians accept the assumption that there is a naïve causal link between advertising and negative health behaviours in young people. Smoking is a classic example yet research shows at least a dozen other, as powerful, predictive factors such as parental cigarette consumption, leisure time activities and negative attitudes to school and teachers.

Bergler (1999) concludes »when examining the available scientific literature systematically and critically, as well as taking into consideration the high number of empirical studies on prevention research carried out by the Institute of Psychology at the University of Bonn, the conclusion must be drawn that up to now no serious study has been able to prove a direct and exclusive causative link between advertising and child or juvenile purchasing behaviour« (p 423).

Some advertisements are designed by Government Health Bodies to attempt to dissuade particular forms of behaviour like smoking. Those too, have been the object of research (Pechmann & Ratneshwar 1994). What is surprising perhaps is the relative paucity of research showing they have any immediate or long term benefits.

Thus we have a curious but not uncommon paradox. Those in favour of legislation talk of the power of advertisements and the naivety of children. So why do certain anti-product advertisements and campaigns work? Were the advertisements not as attractive or the message as clear? It is easy enough to anticipate the responses of the legislation lobby:

• They do not have enough money to »throw at« advertising and had they »the millions« of the (wicked) industry their adverts too would be persuasive.

• Children are already »addicted« to the product either pharmacologically or behaviourally. Hence the weakness of the health advertisements.

Certainly most health researchers know of the complex number of factors that come to play when examining children and adolescents behaviour. For instance, we know that personality factors play less of a role in explaining why children begin to smoke but more of a role in deciding whether they keep smoking. Equally social factors (peer group norms and pressure) are much more effective, in determining when and whether a child begins to smoke than whether they continue.

The advertising to children debate is also often marked by oversimplification and naivety. It becomes a political debate uninformed by the important and relevant available.

It is received wisdom that people dislike, even hate advertising. But like all received wisdom it is inaccurate and uninformed. American studies on attitudes to advertising date back to the 1950s. At that time the public liked advertisements which they found informative, but believed they increased the cost of products. However, small scale studies tended to indicate that people began to dislike and distrust advertising though a sizeable number said they were entertained by advertisements.

Yet better and more recent studies show the public to be more favourable than assumed. Shavitt, Lowrey & Haefner (1998) found most Americans reported that they enjoyed advertisements they saw, tended to find advertising generally informative and useful in their purchasing decisions. Thus:

- 44 percent reported to liking advertising with 30 percent having no opinion
- 61 percent agreed that advertising was informative
- 65 percent said they were confident in using information they see in an advert to make a decision
- 19 percent said there was too much government regulation on advertising
- 56 percent said the industry itself should regulate advertising
- 68 percent reported that they used advertisement information to make purchasing decision

They note: »Most Americans (71 percent) feel that the current amount of government regulation is either too much or just right (with 29 percent believing it is too little). And more feel that regulation should be done by the advertising industry (57 percent) than feel it should be done by the government (31 percent). When asked about regulating the content of advertisements that they themselves see, responses again appeared somewhat more moderate although still not supportive of regulation. Specifically, 40 percent support more government effort to regulate advertisements that they see (compare this to the 29 percent who believe the current amount of government regulation is too little, as reported above), whereas 47 percent support less government effort« (p 17-18). They believe that television advertisements may elicit more negative forms of advertising than other forms (radio, print, billboards).

Children as young as 5 have clear preferences for certain television programmes. They quite clearly purposely select and expose themselves to particular programmes as a function of their personality, their age (and cognitive development) and their gender (Valkenberg & Janssen 1999). As with adults children are not passive recipients of television programming and advertisements they seek them out. Further even 10 year olds are sceptical towards TV advertising (Boush, Friestad & Rose 1994).

Advertisements however clever or creative have a commercial strategy and an intended effect. It can also have unintended effects. That is specific advertisements aim to inform and persuade about a particular product or service but they also inform in other ways as well. Preston (1999) has described advertising – literate children who, like adults, are active creators of meaning.

PARENTING STYLE

There is considerable evidence that parents adopt styles of parenting which are a function of their personality and values. Developmental psychologists have tried to clearly categorize these various types. Inevitably there exist somewhat different categorical schemes though it is not difficult to see that they contain significant overlap.

Two dimensions of parental rearing styles emerge consistently from the various methods employed to study parenting patterns: the first, separates parents that are *controlling* and *demanding* from those that are not demanding; the second, differentiates between parents that are *child-centred, accepting* and *responsive* and those that are parent-centred, rejecting and unresponsive (Parker, Tupling & Brown 1979). Baumrind (1971) did a large scale study on the different patterns of parental authority employed in raising children. She conducted extensive analyses of these dimensions and revealed three types of parenting (authoritative, authoritarian and permissive) behaviours that have empirically been associated with different outcomes for the children. Based on Baumrind's definitions authoritative parents are viewed as optimum for child development. These parents combine control and acceptance with child-centred involvement. They are strict and expect appropriate levels of discipline and behaviour, but are willing to explain the reasons behind rules and punishments, and will often value the child's point of view. These parents are perceived by their children as warm and nurturant. The children in turn tend to be: independent, assertive, co-operative with adults, friendly with peers, intellectually successful; enjoy life and posses a strong motivation to achieve.

Authoritarian parents are typically more dictatorial in their dealings with their children. They have an absolute set of standards to which children must conform. They are perceived to be not particularly warm or affectionate. This style of parenting supposedly tends to produce children low on self-reliance, responsibility, and achievement motivation. Permissive parenting is characterised by accepting, responsive, child-centred, nonpunitive parents who place few demands on their children, leaving them to exercise as much control as possible over their own activities. Children of this parenting style tend to be very positive in their moods and possess more vitality than those of authoritarian parents. Their behaviour however is less mature due to low impulse control, responsibility and self-reliance. Having defined these characteristic parenting patterns one should note that most parents use a combination of all three styles, calling on a particular style as and when it is appropriate.

Baumrind (1971) suggested that permissive parents tended to make fewer demands on their children than do other parents, allowing them to regulate their own activities as much as possible. Thus permissive parents are generally less controlling, and tend to use a minimum of punishment with their children. Authoritarian parents tend to be highly directive with their children and expect unquestioning obedience in their exercise of authority over their children. She argues that authoritarian parents discouraged verbal give-and-take with their children, instead favouring punitive measures to control their behaviour. Baumrind saw parental style as a spectrum with permissive and authoritarian parents at either end and authoritarian parents falling somewhere in between these extremes. She saw authoritative parents as providing clear and firm direction for their children, but also warmth, reason and verbal exchange. Measurements by Baumrind (1971) and Baumrind and Brown (1976) of permissive, authoritarian and authoritative parenting have been based on interviews with parents and their children, as well as parents interacting with their children.

Baumrind (1971, 1982) reported authoritative parenting as more likely to result in self-reliant, independent, achievement oriented and self-controlled children than are either permissive parenting or authoritarian parenting. She went further to suggest that authoritarian parenting was deleterious to the development of personality and behavioural correlates of self-esteem. Buri et al. (1988) concluded that parental authority may have either a negative or positive effect upon self-esteem, depending upon the type of authority exercised. They found a strong positive relationship between parental authoritativeness and adolescent self-esteem, and a strong inverse relationship between parental permissiveness and self-esteem consistent with Baumrind's (1971, 1984) findings.

In another study Klein, O'Bryant and Hopkins (1996) found authoritative parental styles were generally correlated to positive (late adolescent) self-perceptions and authoritarian style to negative self-perceptions. Authoritarian parental styles in the mother seemed particularly associated with low self-worth while authoritative styles seemed particularly related to children feeling good about themselves. Herz and Gullone (1999) argued that the quality of the parent-child relationship has a significant impact on the confidence, resilience and well-being of individuals. They believe the literature highlights two orthogonal but salient dimensions: parental warmth, nuturance, acceptance/responsivity and secondly the amount of control, structure, involvement or demandingness.

The issue for researchers is whether parents with a particular style feel more pressurized by advertising than others. The theory would suggest that the authoritative parent would have the least, and the permissive parent the most, »pester power problems«. Indeed it may be predicted that the very parenting style of certain parents inevitably leads to pester power conflict irrespective of what is advertised on television. The ideas in figure 3 suggest that parental style determines such things as the amount of television watched (and under what conditions), the amount of pocket money available and a clear understanding of what it is for, as well as careful monitoring of the child's peer group. Together these factors are likely to have a profound influence on their children's economic understanding and material wants.

Various studies done in different countries have demonstrated the fairly obvious observation that parental reactions to advertising are indeed related to parental style. In one study 151 mothers of children aged 9-12 years were categorized in terms of their preferred parenting style e.g. authoritative, indulgent, neglecting etc. (Walsh, Laczmake & Carlson 1998). They were then tested for their preferences for regulating children's television. They found that authoritative mothers preferred to rely on themselves to teach their children about consumption. Further indulgent mothers assumed some personal responsibility for education but consistently looked to others for mediation of children's television. Results indicated that authoritarian mothers favoured more government legislation and self-regulation of independent bodies. Finally, neglecting mothers favoured the idea of personal responsibility for educating their children about consumer affairs the least.

Another cross national study compares Japanese and American parents reactions to advertising (Rose, Bush & Kahla 1998). Based on previous research they were able to place parents into one of four categories. These are related to, but slightly different from, the three categories mentioned above. They found Laissez-faire (low socio-, low concept-orientation) mothers had the most positive attitudes toward and the lowest mediation of their children's exposure to television advertising. Pluralistic (low socio-, high concept orientation) and consensual (high on both dimensions) mothers had the highest mediation of and most negative attitudes toward advertising. The responses of protective mothers (high, socio-, low concept-orientation) were between those extremes. Overall, American mothers were distributed relatively equally across categories, whereas Japanese mothers were classified primarily as either laissez-faire or protective.

		Socio-Orientation	
		Low	**High**
Concept-Orientation	**Low**	**Laissez-Faire** • Little communication with children • Little parental impact on consumption	**Protective** • Stress vertical relationships • Obedience and social harmony • Children's exposure to outside information is limited
	High	**Pluralistic** • Stress horizontal relationships • Issue-oriented communication • Children are encouraged to explore ideas and express opinions	**Consensual** • Maintain control over children's behaviour • Stress both issue-oriented communication and the consideration of others

Table 4. Family communications patterns

They note »Information gained from examining family communication types could be used to segment markets internationally and formulate effective positioning strategies. For example, advertising managers and media planners could use such categorization to target international advertising campaigns. Our results show four distinct profiles of families with different television viewing habits. Because protective and consensual mothers limit outside influences and control viewing, perhaps television may not be the most efficient medium to reach children in those family types. Further the question of who should be the target of an advertisement could be addressed by such categorization. Parents could be a particularly important target for advertisers trying to reach consensual families whereas children could be a particularly important target in laissez-faire families. Overall, the family communication typology applied in our study is useful in predicting parental mediation of the media both within and across countries. Family communication patterns could also predict the type of programs children are allowed to view and the type of products they are allowed to use. For example, consensual families may be particularly receptive to educational programs and developmental products, such as educational software. Future research could investigate the specific types of products and programs that families in each communication category allow their children to purchase and watch« (p 82).

Other factors associated with parental reactions to children's purchasing requests have been shown to include:

1   The age of the child: The older the child the more successful his/her requests will be but the link is very weak.
2   Parental attitudes to the product: Cereals are top, pet food bottom. Certainly parents are more likely to yield in requests for cereals and snacks (and other foods) compared to requests for toys.
3   Perceived origin of the request: Parents feel better if they think the requests are not based on TV commercials alone because they feel more secure that the child has made a definite choice.
4   Way of asking: Polite requests usually (and obviously) do better than impolite demands.

Curiously the social class and the sex of the parent seem to show no consistent effects. Further it has been pointed out that a child's request could just as easily be seen as an educational opportunity as to the realities of the consumer market place than yet more pestering. Reviews have also shown it is quite exaggerated to claim that parents' refusal to buy something usually leads to conflict. Some researchers report that in only 5 percent of all cases, children actually react in a truly negative way. Further even if a parent's refusal to yield to a request leads to a situation of conflict, it is highly questionable whether advertising can be held responsible for this. Many other factors that brought a child to purchase behaviour, including parenting style, peers, or the real-life confrontation with the products in shops or supermarkets and the impact of the package of the product.

PESTER POWER

Given the research it seems wiser to concentrate the emphasis on the power of parents rather than that of children. When examining issues of children's responses to television advertising Bas (1996, 1998) have written two pamphlets to help parents. The first, subtitled »Raising children in a commercial world« argues quite rightly that somewhat surprisingly even best selling parenting manuals say almost nothing about how to introduce the topic of advertising to children. She argues that nothing can substitute for an adult's actively interest in what a child is thinking and doing. Parents set examples of how to become »adwise«. They offer opinions about products and advertisements while watching television, in the movies, in the supermarket and in the home. The home and family environment is a crucial source of knowledge and values about everything including the commercial world.

Bas (1998) argues from her evidence that most parents generally feel confident that their children become progressively more able to make good commercial decisions about goods and services of relevance to them. She recommends family television viewing with discussion about programmes and advertisements. All children learn to negotiate and compromise for things they want and that tantrums and nagging are counter productive. Shopping tantrums and displays of pester power are not universal. Some parents report it never happening … others say it did occur only when children were under five. Most parents take food to give them or try to divert their attention. Children like and request foods they have at home; not things they have seen for the first time.

Interesting studies on adults have found that most lament the fact that their parents did not educate them and talk about money issues. Table 5 shows some typical data.

Question	Yes %	No %
When I was growing up, I knew how much my father made per year	23	77
I knew how much my family's mortgage/rent payments were	30	70
I knew what kind of insurance coverage my family had	23	77
I knew how much it cost to outfit me for grade school	26	74
I would like my children to understand more about financial realities	91	9
I would like to understand better how to educate my children about money	73	27

Table 5. Attitudes to children and money in America

What factors come into play when various family members (including children and adolescents) jointly make purchasing decisions. As in most areas of life there are multiple factors that play a part. Researchers in the area have distinguished at least three salient factors (Beatty & Talpade 1994).

- Child/teenager characteristics: Not only sex and age but financial resources of the child, their product knowledge and the product importance and usage in the family as a whole.
- Parental and household characteristics: Demographics (dual-income, class), values, communication style, stage in family life cycle and modern vs traditional orientation of parents.
- Decision characteristics: where the decision is made, about what and the history of the family

Beatty and Talpade (1994) in their research found the product usage and parental employment status powerful predictors in children/teenagers influence. It remains debatable who has most influence on adolescent consumers: i.e. parents, siblings or peer group but nearly all agreed advertising (and other promotional factors) are never the most influential (Keillor, Parker & Schafter 1996). Certainly studies that examine how individuals and families together make consumer decisions also point to a large number of factors in addition to simple television advertising.

POCKET MONEY

Parental beliefs and behaviours with respect to pocket money is a very important feature in a child's understanding of the economic world. Parents use pocket money/allowances to encourage economic understanding and values in their children. Some hope to teach postponement of gratification, others the costs of goods or more simply the limitations of resources. However many adults admit that although they did not receive very good monetary education from their parents they would like to give it to their children. The topic has been studied since the beginning of the century (Furnham 2000, Furnham & Kirkcaldy 2000). We know there are class differences – working class people start pocket money later, give more and are more lax about rules than middle class parents. We also know that rules about pocket money are most important in teaching young children how the world of money works.

In a recent study Furnham (1979) found parents agreed with the following rules:

1	Parents should discuss television adverts to make their children »ad-wise«.	7.0
2	Children take as a role model their parents' buying habits	7.1
3	While shopping parents should discuss purchasing decisions	6.9
4	Parents should exercise strong control over the frequency and content of the television programmes their children watch	7.6
5	Parents should distinguish between needs and wants	8.3
6	Parents' buying habits are important examples to their children of how to spend money	7.5
7	Children should be made aware of the family budget	6.6
8	Books on parenthood should give advice on shopping and spending	6.2
9	Children over 16 should be told about parental incomings and outgoings	5.7
10	I believe that it is important to talk to children about the value of money	8.9

Table 6. Parental beliefs. The number refers to the mean rating
on a 1 (Disagree) to 10 (Agree) rating scale

The imposition and fair maintenance of these rules has been shown to be an excellent way to ensure monetary literacy in children.

Survey Results		Yes
Do you think that pocket money should be increased annually (say on a child's birthday?)		63.2%
Do you think that children should receive their pocket money:	Weekly:	82.6%
	Monthly:	6.3%
	When they need it:	11.1%
Do you believe that all children should be expected to do household chores?		86.1%
Do you believe that children's pocket money should be dependent on this?		51.9%
Should household chores be an opportunity to earn extra money?		71.8%
Do you think parents and children should agree, in advance, what items pocket money should cover?		54.7%
Do you think that children should be forbidden to purchase certain items?		75.3%
Do you think that children should be encouraged to tell parents how they spend their pocket money?		86.8%
Do you think that children (under 10 years old) should be encouraged to save some of their pocket money?		73.4%
If yes, should it be a fixed percentage of their pocket money?		35.4%
At what age should saving begin?		6.63 yrs (2.63)
Do you think that children should be encouraged to save some of the money they receive as gifts?		71.8%
Where do you think that children should be encouraged to save some of their money? Rank the following from 1-4, with 1 as the most important:		Mean
	Moneybox:	1.92
	Bank account (their own)/savings account:	1.58
	Parents look after it:	3.03
	Other (please specify):	3.54
Do you think children, 10 years and over, should be encouraged to investigate the different accounts available for savings, e.g. bank account interest rates, the free gifts on offer, and other incentives offered in exchange for opening an account?		76.1%
Do you think that children, 10 years and over, should be encouraged to make donations from their own money?		43.0%
Do you think that it is a good idea to give children, 5 years and over, money as a gift on special occasions?		86.6%
Do you think that other adults should be discouraged from giving cash gifts to a child (5-16 years)?		7.5%
Do you think that school success should be financially rewarded? (i.e. money given for exam success). If yes, at what age should this start?		49.5% 8.48 yrs
Do you think that children should be encouraged to have a part-time job?		54.0%
Do you think that children should be encouraged to save part of their wages from a part-time job?		61.8%

Survey Results	Yes
Do you think that children, 11 years and over, should be encouraged to go shopping for you, on their own?	49.3%
Do you think that children, age 16 and over, should be allowed to have their own credit cards?	13.7%
At what age would you allow a child to have their own bank debit card (percent selecting each category):	
14 years of age:	2.3%
15 years of age:	2.7%
16 years of age:	24.7%
17 years of age:	15.4%
18 years of age:	45.5%
Other:	8.4%
Do you think that children (6-16 years) should be encouraged to do the following:	
Borrow money from other children:	1.4%
Lend money to other children:	3.3%
At what age should one stop giving children an allowance?	
16 to 17 years of age:	17.2%
18 years of age:	12.3%
When they finish full-time education (at whatever age):	28.7%
When they start a full-time job (at whatever age):	30.6%
Only when they are economically independent (at whatever age):	10.8%

Table 7. Parental attitudes to pocket money/allowances

Table 7 shows then results from a large British study. Along with pocket money attitudes Furnham (2001) obtained a measure of parental allowance style scored on an adaptive-maladaptive dimension. He found that this was a predictive variable in understanding parental involvement and education of their children.

The literature in this area appears to indicate that parents have clear attitudes and beliefs, and attendant-behaviours with respect to the economic socialization of their children. Thus their belief about money, spending, television watching and work are inter-related. Presumably their attitudes to television advertising are related to those beliefs though not directly investigated in these studies. Furnham (2001) however found a representative group of British adults by-and-large in favour of economic socialization.

Godfrey (1994) has noted how pocket-money systems can be used to install values of responsibility, sharing, charity and honesty. It can be used to teach all-important rules about deferment of gratification and how to become a good citizen of the household.

Pocket money systems help to teach children financial literacy and money management. She also points out how parents can educate their children using television. »Commercials try to sell children everything from cereals to toys to tennis shoes, and there is a growing sentiment among both parents and educators against advertisers and their methods of sending conscious and subconscious buying messages to kids. Some people even feel that commercials on children's programming should be banned. My solution is a little different. I maintain that we need to teach our children about advertising, what a commercial is and what it is trying to accomplish. You can't be coerced into doing something you don't want to do if you know and understand the process« (p 108).

CONCLUSION

Very few people would deny that many factors influence children's consumer good preferences and choices. These include how much advertising they are exposed to as well as pocket money requirements. They include a range of socio-demographic factors associated with both parents and children (parents' social class, parenting styles, school chosen for children) which manufacturers can target but not change and also product specific issues (quality, price, availability and advertising) over which they have some control.

Many new products fail irrespective of the quality and quantity of advertising. Equally some of the most successful products ever introduced for children have succeeded despite having never been advertised on television.

All advertising, especially that aimed at children is already carefully regulated and regulatory bodies receive relatively few formal complaints. Children grow up in a world full of products and need help, guidance and education to make informed choices. Banning advertising of any sort delays a child's understanding and decision-making. It can be no substitute for parental guidance and influence. The responsibility for educating children into the economic world cannot, and indeed should not, be removed from their parents.

Some more important findings suggest for instance that children imitate their parents' behaviour in shops. Parents are more effective consumer educators than schools or businesses. Children's sophistication in the consumer world is frequently underestimated, particularly in the West. Interesting various research studies have shown third-world, developing children to be more economically sophisticated than first-world developed country children because they get actively involved in the economic world earlier, for instance, running fruit stalls while their parents are taking a break.

Parental styles in teaching consumption do affect children's consumer knowledge, preferences and habits. To deny, downplay or underestimate the role of parents in children's general and economic understanding and development is to fly in the face of considerable academic evidence.

A number of groups are potentially interested in educating young consumers. These include: parents and families; schools; manufacturers and retailers. Advertising to children is a source of influence, information and choice. The evidence that consumer protection works is fairly limited though there are a few good studies in the area. Because research is difficult, expensive and politically charged public policy decisions are often made on the basis of political ideology rather than research findings. This, for any academic is a lamentable situation that can only be rectified by an increased research effort.

REFERENCES

Bas, J.(1996). *Parent Power: Raising children in a commercial world*. London: Advertising Association

Bas, J. (1998). *Parent Power 2: A practical guide to children, shopping and advertisements*. London: Advertising Association.

Baumrind, D. (1971). »Current patterns of parental authority«, *Developmental Psychology Monographs*, 4, Part 1.

Baumrind, D. (1982). »Reciprocal rights and responsibilities in parent-child relations«, in J. Rubusters & B. Slife (Eds). *Talking Sides: Clashing views on controversial issues*, 237-244. Guildford, Co: Dushkin.

Baumrind, D., & Brown, A. (1967). »Socialization practices associated with dimensions of competence in preschool boys and girls«, *Child Development*, 38, 291-327.

Beatty, S. & Talpade, S. (1994). Adolescent influence in family decision making. *Journal of Consumer Research*, 21, 332-341.

Bergler, R. (1999). »The effects of commercial advertising on children«, *International Journal of Advertising*, 18, 411-425.

Boush, D., Friestad, M., & Rose, G. (1994). »Adolescent scepticism toward TV advertising and knowledge of advertiser tactics«, *Journal of Consumer Research*, 21, 165-175.

Boyfield, K. (1999). *The Effects of Advertising on Innovation, Quality and Consumer Choice*. London: AAEC.

Buri, J., Louiselle, P., Misukanis, T. & Mueller, R. (1988). »Effects of parental authoritarianism and authoritativeness on self-esteem«, *Personality and Social Psychology Bulletin*, 14(2), 271-282.

Furnham, A. (1993). *Reaching for the Counter. The New Child Consumers: Regulation and Education*. London: Social Affairs Unit.

Furnham, A. (1999). »Economic Socialization«, *British Journal of Developmental Psychology*, 17, 585-604.

Furnham, A. (2000). *Children and Advertising: The allegations and the evidence.* London: Social Affairs Unit.

Furnham, A. (2001). »Parental attitudes to pocket money/allowance for children«, *Journal of Economic Psychology*, 22, 397–422.

Furnham, A., & Kirkcaldy, B. (2000). »Economic socialization«, *European Psychologist*, 5, 202–215.

Galst, J. & White, M. (1976). »The unhealthy persuader: The reinforcing value of television and children's purchase – influencing attempts at the supermarket«, *Child Development*, 47, 1086–1096.

Goldstein, J. (1994). *Children and Advertising: Policy Implications of Scholarly Research.* London: Advertising Association.

Goldstein, J. (1999). *Children and Advertising: The Research, Advertising and Marketing to Children.*

Godfrey, N. (1994). *Money doesn't grow on trees.* New York: Fireside.

Gunter, B., & Furnham, A. (1998). *Children as Consumers.* London: Routledge

John, D. (1999). »Consumer socialization of children: A retrospective look at twenty-five years of research«, *Journal of Consumer Research*, 26, 183–213.

Herz, L. & Gullone, E. (1999). »The relationship between self-esteem and the parenting style«, *Journal of Cross-Cultural Psychology*, 30, 742–761.

Keillor, B., Parker, R., & Schaefer, A. (1996). »Influence on adolescent brand preferences in the United States and Mexico«, *Journal of Advertising Research*, 36, 47–56.

Klein, H., O'Bryant, K., & Hopkins, H. (1996). »Recalled parental authority style and self-perception in College women and men«, *Journal of Genetic Psychology*, 157, 5–17.

McNeal, J. (1987) *Children as Consumers.* Lexington, MA: Lexington books.

McNeal, J. (1992). *Kids as consumers: A handbook of marketing to children.* New York: Lexington Books.

Moore, E., & Lutz, R. (2000). »Children, advertising and product experiences. A multi-method inquiry«, *Journal of Consumer Research.* 27, 31–48.

O'Donohoe, S. (1995). »Attitudes to advertising: A review of British and American Research«, *International Journal of Advertising*, 14, 245–261.

Packard, V. (1957). *Hidden Persuaders.* New York: D. McKay.

Parker, G., Tupling, H., & Brown, L. (1979). »A parental bonding instrument«, *British Journal of Medical Psychology.* 52, 1–10.

Preston, C. (1999). »The unintended effects of advertising upon children«, *International Journal of Advertising*, 18, 363–376.

Pechmann, C., & Ratneshwar, S. (1994). »The effect of anti-smoking and cigarette advertising on young adolescents' perceptions of peers who smoke«, *Journal of Consumer Research*, 21, 236–251.

Rose, G., Bush, V., & Kahle, L. (1998). »The influence of family communication patterns of parental reactions toward advertising. A cross national examination«, *Journal of Advertising*, 27, 71–85.

Shavitt, S., Lowrey, P., & Haefner, J. (1998). »Public attitudes to advertising. More favourable than you might think«, *Journal of Advertising Research*, 7, 7–27.

Sherry, J., Greenberg, B., & Tokinoya, H. (1999). »Orientation to TV advertising among adolescents and children in the US and Japan«, *International Journal of Advertising*, 18, 233–250.

Valkenburg, P., Janssen, S. (1999). »What do children value in entertainment programmes«, *Journal of Communication*, 49, 3–21.

Walsh, A., Laczniak, R., & Carlson, L. (1998). »Mothers' preferences for regulating children's television«, *Journal of Advertising*, 27, 23–26.

Ward, S. (1971). *Effects of Television Advertising on Children and Adolescents: An Overview (No 1).* Boston, MA: Marketing Science Institute.

6

CHILDREN'S KNOWLEDGE AND INTERPRETATION OF COMMERCIAL ADVERTISING

– INTENTIONS, TRUTHFULNESS AND VIEWING HABITS

By Anne Martensen and Flemming Hansen

INTRODUCTION

Children's ability to understand and interpret advertisements greatly depends upon their age. The cognitive potential and resources of children, including their ability to remember and recall information from their memory, vary considerably for children of different ages. In discussing how advertisements affect children, you have to consider the age group in question.

Previous studies (Piaget 1957, Bahn 1986, John 1981, McNeal & Chyon-Hwa 1993, Selman 1980, Barenboim 1981, Peracchio 1992) have emphasized age as the most important discriminating factor for children's ability to understand the intention of advertisements and their ability to interpret them. The literature deals with several different age groups, but the most common are 2-7 year-olds, 7-11 year-olds and 11-16 year-olds. The most significant arguments in favor of the importance of age when studying children and advertisements may be summarized as follows:

Small children between the ages 2-7 generally perceive things in concrete terms. They focus on a single dimension of an object, which is often based on their own observation; they are very self-centered and only see things from their own perspective.

They process information fast and simply as a result of their limited ability to decode and organize information. The decision process is also simple and consists of a limited set of strategies that uses little information.

Children aged 7–11 approach things in a far more detailed and analytical manner. They understand that others may have opposing views and motives, and are capable of seeing things from somebody else's point of view. The children start to get a far more detailed perception of markets and brands, perceptions that go beyond their own emotions and motives. The children look at the functional and motivational conditions of the advertisements, they are concerned with relevant features, compare products and brands across more than one dimension, and include their own experiences as well as the advertiser's motives for advertising. The children use various storing and recalling strategies, and begin to consider decisions they have to make more carefully. Their choices are based on several abilities, therefore the children are more flexible when making their decisions, and may adapt and react to a given situation.

The oldest children, aged 11–16, are capable of seeing things from their own as well as somebody else's perspective simultaneously. They can process information in an abstract manner and use a number of different strategies to store and recall information (which will help them when they need to search their memories). These include verbal labeling, rehearsal, use of mnemonics, and finally they can manage many relevant features of the alternatives they are weighing. The children adapt their decisions to the situation and circumstances. Social interaction, such as persuasion and negotiation with mutual consideration on both sides, also begins to come into play. The children become more focused on social relations and the need to create an identity for themselves, which in one way or another fits in with the expectations of the group. In this way, children focus on understanding complex social relations and meanings related to consumption.

PURPOSE

The purpose of the chapter is to examine children's:

➤ Understanding of the intention of advertisements
➤ Perception of advertisements and different types of advertisements
➤ Perception of the credibility of advertisements
➤ Viewing of advertisements

The study focuses on children and youngsters between the ages of 8-18 years. This gives the opportunity to study the effect of the development of knowledge and interpretation of advertisements in relation to age. Children of 7 years or less have not been included in the study, since children's ability to understand the intention of the advertisement requires them to be able to see the advertisement from the advertiser's point of view. According to Selman's phases (1980), this does not typically occur until the ages of 8-10. Furthermore, it requires an even more detailed and abstract way of thinking to be able to understand why the advertisers use different agents and tactics such as well-known people, humor and product comparison in the advertisement. The children need to be able to see things from both the advertisers' and their own perspective, they also need to be able to discern which agents and techniques are the most effective in a given situation. This requires even older children.

A number of international studies exist on this subject. However, the question is whether these results are still accurate and whether they can be transferred to the Danish mentality and media situation. Many of the existing studies date back to the 1970s and 1980s when the media situation was quite different to what it is today. Moreover, most of the studies originate from USA and, naturally, the question is whether the results from these studies can be transferred to the European arena.

It is also worth mentioning that children's socialization process has undergone significant changes in the last two decades. The question is, therefore, how this influences the areas examined here.

It is worth noting that a great majority of the studies have so far been qualitative, i.e. various observation methods, focus groups and experiments have formed the basis of the results. In contrast, this study is quantitative; we have conducted thousands of interviews with children of different age groups. The children were asked to judge a number of statements according to what degree they agreed or disagreed. Consequently, the design of the study is distinctively different from previous.

RESEARCH HYPOTHESIS

Specifically, the purpose of the study is to examine the following four themes and their underlying hypotheses:

Understanding the Intention of Advertising

Children's understanding of the many purposes of advertising, such as to provide information about the product, or to persuade somebody to buy, varies with age. The study aims to scrutinize how this insight changes with age.

Several studies (see e.g. Levin et al. 1982, Butter et al. 1981) show children as young as 3-4 years old are able to distinguish between TV-advertisements and programmes. However, a deeper understanding of the intention of advertising is not developed until the ages of 7-11 and then only gradually. Robertson & Rossiter's (1974) study shows that 50 percent of children aged 7 understand the intention of advertising, whereas the percentage rises to 100 percent for 11 year olds. Against this background, the following hypothesis is interesting:

➤ **HYPOTHESIS 1:**
**CHILDREN FROM THE AGE OF 8 CLEARLY UNDERSTAND THE GENERAL
INTENTION OF ADVERTISING.**

Perception of Advertising

In the above, the hypothesis was proposed that children from the age of 8 understand the intention of advertising, albeit a deeper understanding is not developed until later years. This is further supported by for example, Blosser & Roberts (1985), Robertson & Rossiter (1974) and Ward et al (1977) who, in general, found that children under the age of 7 classify advertisements as 'funny' or as 'something that tells me what I can buy' without understanding that advertisements may distort the truth. Not until age 7 do children realize that 'advertisements attempt to make people buy something'. However, children in this age group find it difficult to discern advertisements that provide information about a product; they only pick up on the persuasive effect. From age 8 children are able to see the advertisements from their own point of view, that is, advertisements as information, as well as from the advertiser's point of view, that is, advertisements as persuasion.

Consequently, it is interesting to note how children's perception of advertisements varies as they grow older. How do children of different ages experience features such as entertaining, creating attention, informative, persuasive, etc? The second hypothesis is:

➤ **HYPOTHESIS 2:**
**CHILDREN BECOME MORE AND MORE CRITICAL TOWARDS ADVERTISEMENTS
WITH AGE — THAT IS, THE PERCENTAGE OF CHILDREN WHO VIEW ADVER-
TISEMENTS AS ENTERTAINING, INFORMATIVE OR CREATING ATTENTION
DECREASES WITH AGE.**

A Danish qualitative study (GFK 1997) of children and their parents shows that the plot of the advertisement is very important for children under the age of 9-10 years old, and that even complex plots are understood and remembered. From ages 9-10 and older, the focus is moved to 'special effects'. The unexpected is the capturing element. However, the extreme action must be 'real' to catch the attention of the children.

Children under the age of 8-9 years do not understand ambiguity, subtle remarks and irony– they perceive things literally. This is concurrent with the cognitive development of children of this age. GFK's (1997) study also lends support to the idea that children need to be able to identify with the 'actors' and/or the plot, albeit the identification process is different for small and big children as well as for boys and girls.

Based on the above discussion, it is worthy of note to examine what form of advertising children of different ages like the best. Do children like entertaining, childish or informative advertisements the best? In this connection, the following hypotheses emerge:

➤ HYPOTHESIS 3:
CHILDREN THINK THAT IT IS IMPORTANT FOR ADVERTISEMENTS TO BE ENTERTAINING.

➤ HYPOTHESIS 4:
THE OLDER THE CHILDREN ARE, THE MORE IMPORTANT IT IS THAT THE ADVERTISEMENTS APPEAR 'ADULT' (RATHER THAN CHILDISH).

➤ HYPOTHESIS 5:
CHILDREN THINK THAT IT IS IMPORTANT THAT ADVERTISEMENTS ARE INNOVATIVE AND EXTREME.

➤ HYPOTHESIS 6:
THE OLDER THE CHILDREN ARE, THE MORE IMPORTANT IT IS THAT THE MESSAGE OF THE ADVERTISEMENT IS INFORMATIVE.

The two latter hypotheses should, of course, be regarded as part of children's socialization process, that is, the process of getting closer to an adult mindset and need for information.

Perception of the Credibility of Advertisements

Do children perceive advertisements as credible? How does this perception of credibility vary with age? To what extent can children discern whether an advertisement is trying to bend the truth and is clearly exaggerating the message? To what extent do children perceive the objects in advertisements as looking better than they do in reality? To what extent do they understand that the product does not always live up to the promise of the advertisement?

Previous studies (see for example, Ward et al. 1977, Robertson & Rossiter 1974 and Bever et al. 1975) have shown that children from around the age of 8 can discern that advertisements do not always tell the truth, and the older the children get the more skeptical they become towards advertisements. The Ward et al. (1977) study concluded that the percentage of children who believe that advertisements are not always truthful, increases from 50 percent in kindergarten (6-7 years) to 88 percent in the third grade (9-10 years) to 97 percent in the sixth and seven grades (13-15 years). This is concurrent with children's cognitive and social abilities of the mentioned age groups.

When Ward et al. (1977) posed the question of why advertisements cannot be trusted, children under the age of 7 answered 'the advertisements just lie', while the 9-10 year olds mentioned that 'the advertisers wish to sell the products to make money, and therefore they need to make the products look better than they do in reality'. However, many children have difficulties pinpointing, when the advertisers are cheating. In Bever et al.'s (1975) studies, 7-10 year old children mention, that 'it's hard to say what's true and untrue until you have tried the product'. The 11-12 year olds are subtler when they mention credibility. These children mention factors such as voice, choice of words, exaggeration, visual tricks, etc. On the basis of the above discussion, we believe that it is relevant to state the following hypotheses:

➤ HYPOTHESIS 7:
THE OLDER THE CHILDREN ARE, THE LESS THEY EXPERIENCE ADVERTISEMENTS AS CREDIBLE.

➤ HYPOTHESIS 8:
THE OLDER THE CHILDREN ARE, THE BETTER THEY WILL BE ABLE TO DISCERN WHETHER AN ADVERTISEMENT IS CREDIBLE, BASED ON THE WAY THINGS ARE SAID (VOICE).

Another question worth examining is: What effect children's perception of the credibility of advertisements has on whether they will want to have the advertised products, and/or whether they want to buy the advertised products? A priori it is expected that:

➤ HYPOTHESIS 9:
AMONG THE CHILDREN WHO PERCEIVE ADVERTISEMENTS AS UNTRUST-
WORTHY, THE YOUNGER CHILDREN WILL BE INFLUENCED BY THE ADVER-
TISEMENTS TO WANT THE ADVERTISED PRODUCTS TO A GREATER DE-
GREE THAN THE OLDER CHILDREN WILL.

➤ HYPOTHESIS 10:
AMONG THE CHILDREN WHO PERCEIVE ADVERTISEMENTS AS UNTRUST-
WORTHY, YOUNG CHILDREN ARE MORE LIKELY TO WANT THE ADVERTISED
PRODUCTS THAN THE OLDER CHILDREN ARE.

Children's ability to see through the exaggerated and untrustworthy content of advertisements, compared with their ability to see through the intention (equal to persuasion to buy) of advertisements, influences the children in the following way: the
older they get, the less they will like advertisements and the more negative their attitude towards advertisements will be. The Robertson & Rossiter (1974) study found
that the percentage of children who like advertisements decreases from 69 percent at
age 7 to 56 percent at ages 8-9 and to 25 percent at ages 10-11. This leads us to state
the following hypothesis:

➤ HYPOTHESIS 11:
THE YOUNGER CHILDREN ARE, THE BETTER THEY LIKE ADVERTISE-
MENTS.

Viewing of Advertisements
How often do children watch advertisements for children and adults? If children
watch many adult advertisements, does it then make sense to ban children's advertisements? Swedish experience shows that it may not be such a good idea to ban
children's advertisements, as it is very difficult to distinguish between advertisements
for big and smaller children, teenagers and adults.

Do children watch advertisements with their family and/or with friends? How does
the fact that children watch advertisements with others affect them? Do children talk
about the advertisements they watch with others? How does the fact that children
watch advertisements with others influence their understanding of the intention of the
advertisement, how they feel about advertisements in general and their ability to assess
the credibility of the advertisement in particular? Previous studies (see e.g. Reid 1978,
Carlson et. al. 1992 and Moschis 1985) show that if parents discuss advertisements with

their children, it has a significant effect on their knowledge and interpretation of advertisements. The more the parents discuss the matter with their children, the better the children will become at viewing the advertisements critically, regarding the influencing intention of advertisements. The above questions and results make it fascinating to study the following hypotheses:

➤ HYPOTHESIS 12:
BOTH SMALL AND BIG CHILDREN OFTEN WATCH ADVERTISEMENTS DIRECTED AT CHILDREN.

➤ HYPOTHESIS 13:
BOTH SMALL AND BIG CHILDREN OFTEN WATCH ADULT ADVERTISEMENTS.

➤ HYPOTHESIS 14:
IT IS PRIMARILY THE SMALL CHILDREN WHO DISCUSS ADVERTISEMENTS THEY HAVE WATCHED WITH THEIR FAMILY.

➤ HYPOTHESIS 15:
CHILDREN, WHO TALK TO OTHERS ABOUT ADVERTISEMENTS THEY HAVE WATCHED, UNDERSTAND THE INTENTION OF THE ADVERTISEMENT MUCH BETTER.

Is there a connection between how often children watch advertisements and their understanding of the advertisements' intention of influencing? Are children, who often watch advertisements, influenced to want the advertised products more than children who rarely watch advertisements? In relation to this, it would be interesting to examine the following hypotheses:

➤ HYPOTHESIS 16:
CHILDREN WHO OFTEN WATCH ADVERTISEMENTS UNDERSTAND THE INTENTION OF ADVERTISEMENTS BETTER.

➤ HYPOTHESIS 17:
CHILDREN WHO OFTEN WATCH ADVERTISEMENTS ARE MORE LIKELY TO WANT THE ADVERTISED PRODUCTS THAN CHILDREN WHO RARELY WATCH ADVERTISEMENTS.

METHODOLOGY FOR THE EMPIRICAL STUDY

During the autumn of 2000, data was collected. The study was part of a larger survey about children and youth that Gallup TNS carried out: 'Children Index/Gallup 2000'. Questionnaires were sent by mail to a representative segment of children and their parents, who agreed in advance to be a part of the study.

The data collection for this study is a part of the Gallup 'Children Index'. This means that our study has been limited by the age grouping of the Index: 8-12 year-olds and 13-18 year-olds.

Children of ages 8-12 received help from their parents to complete the question-naire, while children of age 13 and above completed their questionnaires.

In both age groups, 800 interviews were completed. The subsequent results are based on a total of 1600 interviews.

Our part of the questionnaire was composed partly on the basis of literature studies, and was partly inspired by practical experience. The subsequent results are based on a total of 46 questions for the 8-12 year olds, and 51 questions for the 13-18 year olds, which capture specific dimensions of the topics discussed above.

A 3-point scale was used to assess the degree to which the 8-12 year olds agreed or disagreed with the 46 questions, and a 5-point scale was used to assess the degree to which the 13-18 year olds agreed or disagreed with the 51 questions.

RESULTS

Understanding the Intention of Advertisements
If we look at Figure 1, it is clear that the proposed hypothesis 1 is verified.

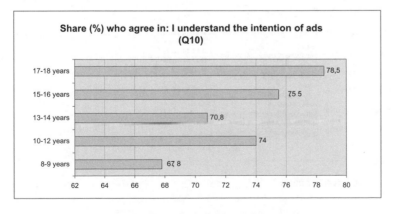

Figure 1. Understanding the intention of advertising

Even children from age 8 generally understand the intention of advertisements; 68% of the 8-9 year olds agree with question 10: 'I understand what the advertisements are trying to accomplish'. This percentage increases to 74 percent for the 10-12 year olds and to 79 percent for the 17-18 year olds. These percentages are markedly different from Robertson & Rossiter's (1974) previously referenced study, but the difference should perhaps be viewed as an effect of different test designs, rather than as an actual difference in the children's comprehension.

Two significant consequences emerge from the information that seven out of ten 8-9 year olds are able to discern the intention of advertising, and that this percentage increases with age.

Firstly, the advertisers should, to a higher degree, design their advertisements in such a fashion that children perceive them as more credible and honest. Credibility is a significant factor in children's decision to take advertisers' message seriously or not, as well as in shaping their perception of a product's ability to persuade them to buy, thus obtaining a more long-term positive effect.

Secondly, the evidence that 70 percent of the 8-9 year olds understand the intention of advertising could indicate that children's socialization process both starts earlier and develops quicker than just ten years ago. To ban advertisements targeting children under the age of 8 could thus inhibit this socialization process, and result in it not really evolving till after age 8. In this way, small children will not have the same opportunity to learn to be critical of advertisements.

Perception of Advertisements
Figure 2 depicts children's perception of selected statements about advertisements, according to their age group.

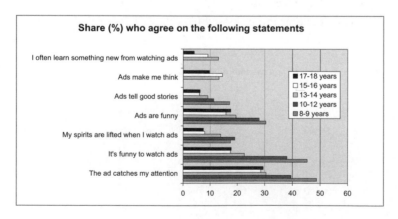

Figure 2. Perception of the advertisement

It is very clear that the older children are, the more critical they are towards the statements about advertisements, which confirms the proposed hypothesis 2. The 8–12 year-olds feel that it is fun to watch advertisements, that their spirits are lifted, and that advertisements are funny, more so than children in the other age groups. This result is in accordance with the theoretical view that children of that age are only able to see things from their own point of view, i.e. the entertaining aspect is the dominant one; not until they are 8 do they start to develop the ability to see things from the advertiser's point of view, i.e. the informative and persuasive aspect. Our study shows a significant decrease in children's perception of advertisements as entertaining from the age of 13.

Furthermore, it is evident that from the age of 15 there is no change in young people's perception of advertisements, which, compared to the 8–12 year olds' perception, is very significant.

Another feature worth noticing is that, in general, the degree of agreement is very low for all of the statements; for the 8-9 year olds, the level of agreement for the seven statements is between 17 percent and 48 percent and it decreases with age to between 4-30 percent for the 17-18 year olds. Clearly, the message for the advertisers is that the advertisements lack content. Only one in every ten children, on average, thinks that advertisements tell good stories, that they learn something new from the advertisement, or that the advertisement provides food for thought.

It is also interesting to note that advertisements catch the attention of every second child in the age group of 8-9 year olds, whereas this is only the case for every third child in the older age groups.

But what determines whether the advertisement catches the attention of children? For the purpose of answering this question, a number of regression analyses were completed where the dependent variable was defined as:

➤ 'The advertisement catches my attention' (Q1).

To further explicate the variable, the following nine questions were included:

➤ It's fun to watch advertisements (Q2).
➤ My spirits are lifted when I watch advertisements (Q3).
➤ Advertisements are funny (Q4).
➤ Advertisements tell good stories (Q5).
➤ Advertisements are honest and credible (Q6).
➤ Advertisements make me think (Q7).
➤ I often learn something new from watching advertisements (Q8).
➤ In general, I like advertisements (Q13).
➤ In general, I like to watch advertisements (Q14).

AND FLEMMING HANSEN

regression analyses for each of the five age groups is reproduced in
he significant variables have been marked.

ble	8-9 years	10-12 years	13-14 years	15-16 years	17-18 years
It is funny to watch TV advertisements	*	*	*	*	*
My spirits are lifted when watching TV advertisements	*				
TV advertisements are funny	*		**	*	*
TV advertisements tell good stories		*			
TV advertisements are honest and credible		*			
TV advertisements make me think			**		
I often learn something new from watching TV advertisements			**		
In general, I like TV advertisements		*	**	*	*
In general, I like to watch TV advertisements		*			
R^2	0,518	0,512	0,452	0,432	0,502

Table 1. Factors explaining advertisement awareness:
Results of regression analysis with advertisement awareness (Q1) as the dependent variable

* = *Significant on 5% level (two-tailed test)*
** = *Significant on 10% level (two-tailed test)*

The following conclusions may be drawn:

➤ It is important for all children that it is fun to watch advertisements – an aspect
that can be said to permeate children's perception of all aspects of life!
➤ In order to capture the attention of the children, advertisements must be funny. All
the children, except the 10–12 year olds, agreed to this statement.

These two results clearly confirm hypothesis 3: that children want advertisements to
be entertaining.

➤ For the 8–9 year olds, the entertainment aspect is the only aspect that determines
whether the advertisement creates attention. This corresponds to the well known
previous conclusion.
➤ For the 10–12 year olds, the credibility of the advertisement determines whether
the advertisement captures their attention. Interestingly, the question of credibility
in advertisements is only important to this age group. Credibility does not play a

significant role for the younger children or for the teenagers when th
are trying to draw attention to their advertisements.

➤ For the 13-14 year olds, it is important that the advertisements have
so that they feel that they are learning something new and that the advertisement
provides 'food for thought'.

➤ Just like the youngest, the 17-18 year olds want to be entertained, but they also
emphasize a message – that the advertisement tells a good story.

The last two points must be said to confirm hypothesis 6; that the older the children
are, the more important it is that the message of the advertisement is informative.

On the basis of the above listed results, we can conclude that children become
more critical towards advertisements with age; they feel that advertisements should
have substance and message, albeit presented in a funny way. Even the children emphasize quality in advertisements. If the advertisers want to draw attention and interest to advertising, they must fulfill children's expectations to form and content.

This led us to pose the question: What design and substance should advertisers
choose if they wish to not only capture the attention of the children, but also draw
their attention to the advertisement and persuade them to buy? Hypotheses 3-6 reflect this design problem in advertising, and has already been confirmed. To test the
remaining hypotheses, the children were asked to assess which kind(s) of creative executions they liked best. Three statements relate to the information value of the advertisement, namely: 'I like it when the advertisement tells me something new and
unexpected' (Q51), 'the best advertisements are the ones that show which people use
the products' (Q50) and 'I like advertisements that emphasize the product the best'
(Q46). The next three statements reflect the entertainment value of advertisements: 'I
like advertisements that are funny the best' (Q48), I like advertisements that tell a good
story the best' (Q47) and 'I like the music in most TV and radio advertisements'
(Q49). Finally, two aspects were included that examined the more childish advertisement designs: 'I like advertisements that have children in them the best' (Q44) and 'I
like advertisements that have cartoon characters in them the best' (Q45).

The result of the children's assessments of these three dimensions is shown in Figure 3, 4 and 5.

Here, too, it is confirmed that children want to be entertained; children want funny advertisements, regardless of whether they are 8 or 18. Only 1-2 children out of
10 do not agree with this.

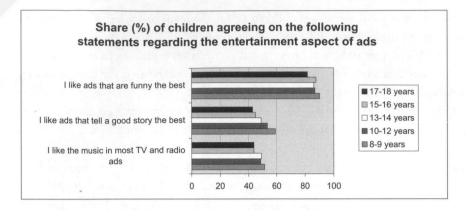

Figure 3. Advertising form: How amusing is the advertisement?

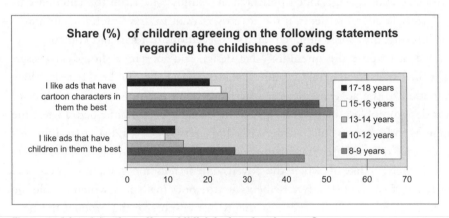

Figure 4. Advertising form: How childish is the advertisement?

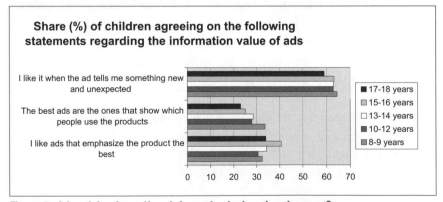

Figure 5. Advertising form: How informative is the advertisement?

It is interesting to compare this result with Figure 2. Children like fun ments, but because of the way advertisements are designed today only 2 of the children feel that this is the case. Subsequently, a funny advertisem the areas where the potential for improvement is greatest. All in all, we must conclude that hypothesis 3, 'advertisements need to be entertaining', is confirmed.

The advertisement also needs to tell a good story – yet another aspect of the entertainment dimension. Children do not feel that this condition is fulfilled either, see for example Figure 2, where only 1 out of 10 children agrees that this is the case. Since good stories are important to children, there is potential for improvement by the advertisers too. However, this potential is not fulfilled by today's advertisements.

Every second child also feels that the music in connection to the advertisements is important.

It comes as no surprise that the childish aspect of the advertisements does not appeal to the older children. They do not think that children or cartoon characters make for a good creative execution. Fortyfive percent of the 8-9 year olds feel that it is okay for children to play a part in advertisements, while this percentage is almost halved for the 10-12 year olds; the percentage is halved yet again for the older age groups. Incidentally, this result is in accordance with GFK's (1997) study, which concluded it is important for children to be able to identify with the actors in advertisements. Even 10 year old children no longer identify to a significant degree with other children as actors in the advertisements; from age ten, there are other more important aspects besides other children to include in the advertisements. The results clearly confirms hypothesis 4, which states that the older the children are, the more important it is that the advertisements are designed in an 'adult' (non-childish) way.

This result lead to the recommendation that children's advertisements should not be designed with childish elements, and that advertisers should aim to design their advertisements in a more adult and entertaining way for children as young as 9-10 years. This result corresponds nicely with the conclusion in the previous section concerning the understanding of advertising. Here we found that children's socialization process develops quicker today than it did ten years ago, and that children approach adulthood faster. The period of time that children 'remain children' has been shortened – for example children find it embarrassing to play with dolls or cars at the age of ten.

The third dimension regarding the information value of advertising supports the compressed socialization process that children go through today. In assessing the statement 'I like advertisements that emphasize the product the best', there is a small, but significant difference between the youngest age groups (8-12 years) and the oldest (13-18 years). The older children would like more information about the advertised products – a wish that also appears among adults. Once again, hypothesis 6 is confirmed: 'The older the children are, the more important it is that the message is informative'.

'Whether the children get to see which type of people use the products becomes less and less significant the older the children get'. Only 1 in 5 older children agreed to this. Children look for extreme elements of action, but they have to be 'real' to have an effect. This was one of the conclusions from the study by GFK (1997). This is confirmed here where all age groups clearly express that they want advertisements to relate to something new and unexpected – 60 percent or more agreed to this statement. Consequently, hypothesis 5, that the innovative and extreme elements are fascinating for all children, is also confirmed.

PERCEPTIONS OF THE CREDIBILITY OF ADVERTISEMENTS

Children's perception of different aspects of the credibility of advertisements is shown in Figure 6. More interesting results may be drawn from this Figure.

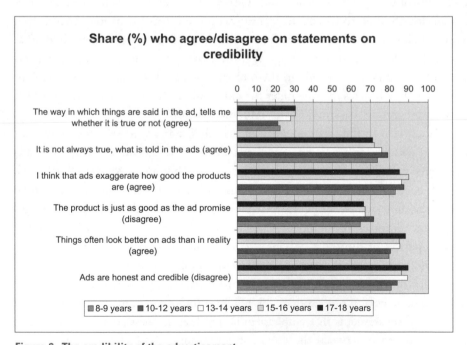

Figure 6. The credibility of the advertisement

First, it is remarkable that children as young as 8 have learned to see through advertisements; 8 out of 10 children at the ages 8-9 do not think that advertisements are honest and believable, and this percentage increases to 9 out of 10 children in the three oldest age groups. Clearly, with age, there is a growing mistrust in the credibility of advertisements. Once again, the conclusion can be reached that you cannot 'cheat' even young children, and that the frequent exposure to advertisements wherever children go has resulted in rapidly developing healthy and critical attitude towards advertising. As such we have confirmed hypothesis 7: The older children get, the less credible they find the advertisements. Actually, children as young as 8 can see that advertisements are dishonest and untrustworthy. The above result thereby supports Ward's (1977) empirical study where the percentage of 8-9 year old children who are able to discern the lack of credibility in advertisements reaches 88 percent.

Even though Ward (1977) found that children find it hard to explain how advertisements 'cheat', this study shows that 65 percent of the 8-9 year olds disagreed with the statement that 'the product lives up to the promise of the advertisement', 80 percent agree that 'things in advertisements often look better than in real life' and 74 percent agree that 'often you can't trust what they say in advertisements'. This indicates that children are not easily fooled by advertisements – they are able to discern the exaggerated message and the attempt of certain advertisements to bend the truth.

The very detailed and subtle description of the credibility of advertisements on the basis of the voice in the advertisement is only discernible for the three oldest age groups, which perfectly corresponds to Ward's (1977) results. This shows hypothesis 8 is clearly confirmed.

Are children, who are able to discern that advertisements are not always credible, still influenced by advertisements to wish for or buy the advertised products? Figure 7 examines hypotheses 9 and 10. It is obvious, here, that age plays a decisive role in how advertisements influence children. The 8-9 year olds let themselves be manipulated by the advertisements to wish for the advertised products to a far greater degree (41 percent and 47 percent) than the 10-12 year olds (29 percent and 39 percent), the 13-14 year olds (21 percent and 34 percent) and the 15-18 year olds (17 percent and 25 percent). This clearly confirms hypotheses 9 and 10.

Since young children do not have the same opportunity to buy the advertised products themselves, the direct effect on the purchase has only been examined for the older children of the ages 13-18.

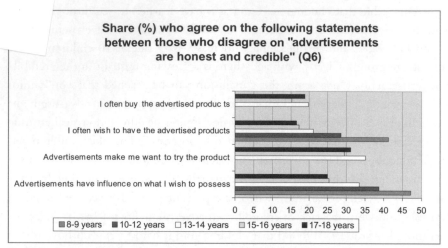

Figure 7. Relation between the credibility of the advertisement and desire to buy the advertised products

The result was that every fifth teenager agreed that they often buy products they have seen advertisements for, despite that they perceive advertisements as untrustworthy. Perhaps the high number should be viewed in the light of it being important for teenagers not to differ too much from their friends. Perhaps the result is a function of peer pressure that teenagers subject each other to, rather than a function of an advertising effect.

Figure 8 shows the effect of advertisements *without considering* the children's perception of the credibility of the advertisement. It is interesting to note that there is *no significant* difference in the children's level of agreement with the four statements that examine the effect of advertising (Q11, Q12, Q22 and Q23), regardless of whether they find advertisements untrustworthy or not. The same pattern can be observed for Figures 7 and 8, that is even though children have learned to be critical towards advertising, the study still shows there is no significant influence that determines how impressionable children are to advertising.

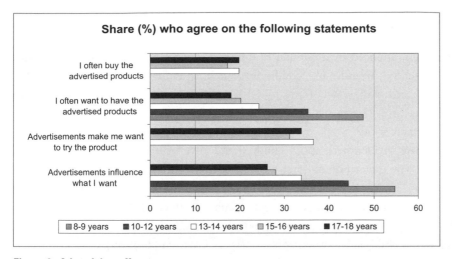

Figure 8. Advertising effects

Figure 9 shows children's assessment of how well they like advertisements. Here, it is clear that hypothesis 11, 'the younger the children are, the better they like advertisements', is confirmed. Also, the results are in accordance with those of Robert-son & Rossiter (1974), who studied the number of children of different ages who like advertisements. However, in this study it was found that fewer 8-9 year olds (34 percent and 39 percent) agreed they like advertisements compared with Robertson & Rossiter (1974) percentage of 56 percent. Once again, it is confirmed that children today learn to have a more critical attitude towards advertisements than they did 10-20 years ago.

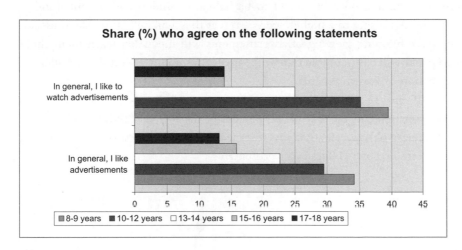

Figure 9. Total judgment of the advertisement

VIEWING OF ADVERTISEMENTS

Children are influenced by a number of different sources such as the Internet, youth magazines, school, friends, and children's own independent choice of media takes place earlier and earlier. According to GFK's (1997) qualitative study, this happens round the age of 8-9 years, which is also a consequence of many children having their own TV in their room.

The debate in Denmark about children and advertising is very concerned with whether the law governing children's advertisements should be tightened. The basis for the debate in Denmark is that children are heavily influenced by the media and advertising, and that this may have a negative effect on the children's socialization process. The results of this study, however, indicate that advertisements are instrumental in accelerating children's socialization process, and that children today are critical towards advertisements at a very young age, but they also indicate that advertisements do influence what children wish for and what they buy.

Therefore, the question is whether the debate should deal with regulation in the area of children's advertisements, or whether it should focus on how to raise children to be consumers instead. As consumers, children need to learn to make choices, they need to be able to collect relevant information, assess and compare products and employ different decision strategies and so on.

Advertisements will inevitably be an element in the consumer's decision process, and the question is whether it would not be better for children to learn how to see advertisements for what they are, and ultimately be more critical of the quality of advertisements. Children probably ought to be helped to understand the intention of and means in advertising to a higher degree, so that they will be better able to use advertisements. Children's viewing of advertisements will inevitably teach them about advertising and will – in conjunction with discussions about advertising – influence their perception of advertisements.

Figure 10 and 11 clearly show that 50 percent of the 8-12 year olds watch children's advertisements daily, while 60 percent of the 8-9 year olds and 68 percent of the 10-12 year olds watch adult advertisements daily. It is questionable whether it even makes sense to ban children's advertisements.

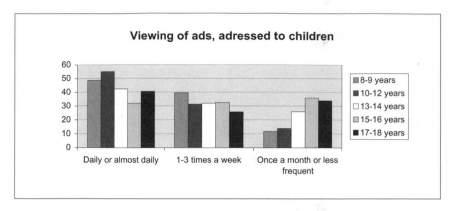

Figure 10. Children's viewing of TV advertisements, addressed to children

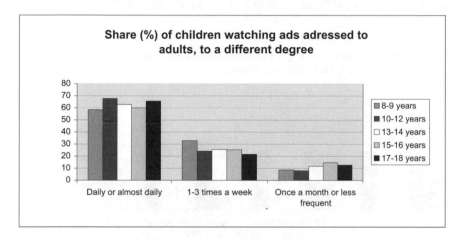

Figure 11. Children's viewing of TV advertisements, addressed to adults

Another issue worth noticing is the relatively large percentage of teenagers who watch children's advertisements (30-40 percent), and that the percentage of teenagers who watch adult advertisements is the same as for the two younger age groups.

The above confirms both hypothesis 12 and 13: That both small and big children often watch advertisements for children and adults.

How often children watch TV-advertisements with others is shown in Figure 12 and 13.

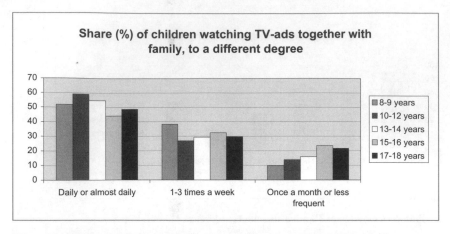

Figure 12. Children's viewing of TV-advertisements, together with their family

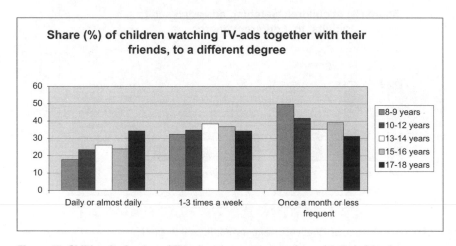

Figure 13. Children's viewing of TV-advertisements, together with their friends

To watch TV-advertisements with your family is more common than to watch them with friends among small children. Approximately 50% of the small children watch TV-advertisements with their family daily. It is worth noticing that the 15–16 year olds watch significantly fewer TV-advertisements with their family. This age group, in particular, has a strong desire to break free from their parents, and therefore the significantly lower percentage can be interpreted as a special teenage-effect as well as a result of having their own TV.

Another interesting aspect emerges among those children who often watch advertisements with their friends. The older the children are, the more time they spend with friends, and the more often they watch TV-advertisements with friends.

The children's conversations with their family about the advertisements they watch are reproduced in Figures 14 and 15 for the children who watch children's advertisements (Figure 14) and adult advertisements (Figure 15) daily or almost daily. It seems that only the 8-9 year olds have a meaningful dialogue with their parents about the advertisements they watch, and this goes primarily for the children's advertisements (43 percent in agreement and 34 percent in agreement). Again, a teenage-effect for the 13-16 year olds is found; those who agree that they discuss the advertisements with their family represent a significantly smaller percentage (19-20 percent). It is quite understandable and positive that the small children in particular discuss advertisements with their family; after all, they are the ones who have the greatest need for understanding the advertisements. Hypothesis 14 has therefore also been confirmed.

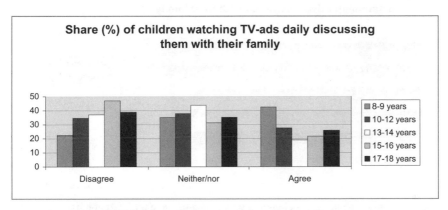

Figure 14. Children's conversation with their family about TV-advertisements addressed to children

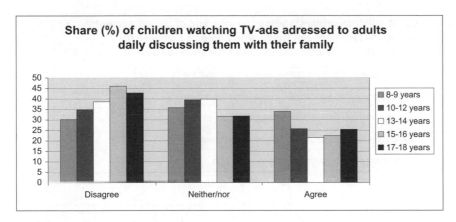

Figure 15. Children's conversation with their family about TV-advertisements addressed to adults

Figure 16 and 17 demonstrate how children's viewing and discussion of advertisements with others influence their understanding of advertising intentions. When the advertisements are debated, with family or friends, there is a tendency towards an increase in the children's understanding of the intention of advertisements. However, there is only a statistically significant difference between the disagreement–agreement percentage among the 10–12 year olds who talk to their family about the advertisements and among the 17–18 year olds who discuss the advertisements with their friends.

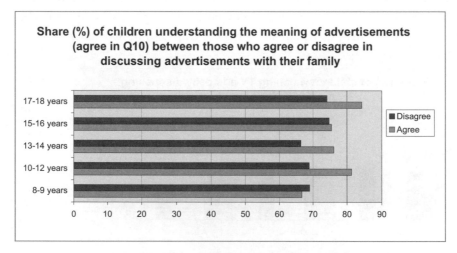

Figure 16. Relation between dialogue about the advertisements and understanding of the advertisements' purpose

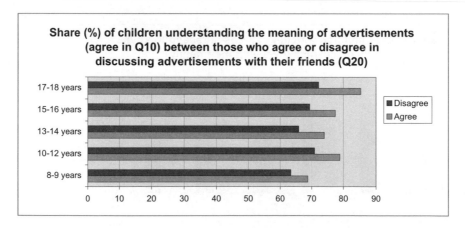

Figure 17. Relation between dialogue about the advertisements and understanding the meaning of advertisements

All in all, hypothesis 15 can only be confirmed for those two age groups when they talk to their family or friends. However, it cannot be argued that when parents discuss advertisements with their children, it has a significant effect on children's interpretation of the advertisements.

Hypothesis 16 that a priori assumes there is a positive connection between the frequency of watching advertisements and the understanding of the intention of advertising cannot be verified. Thus, neither the quantity of advertisements nor the subsequent debating of advertisements is crucial for understanding the intention of advertising; it is the children's age.

Are children who often watch advertisements manipulated to want the advertised products to a higher degree than children who rarely watch advertisements? The answer can be found in Figure 18.

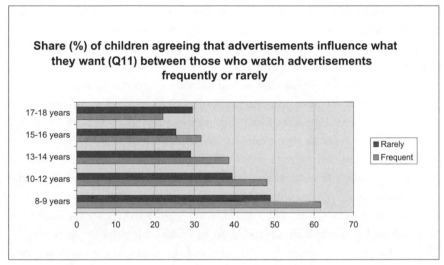

Figure 18. The advertisements' influence on what children wish to possess

The frequency of teenagers who watch advertisements is not the determining factor in whether they want the advertised products or not, as they have learned to see through the advertisements. In contrast, for the 8-12 year olds there is a significant difference between how often they watch children's advertisements and whether the advertisements influence what they want. The more often children watch advertisements; the more they want the advertised products. Therefore hypothesis 17 is verified for children of aged 8-12, but not for children aged 13-18.

IMPLICATIONS

The results show that children develop the skills to understand the intention of advertising as young as 8 years; 68 percent of the 8-9 year olds stated they agreed that they understand what the advertisements are trying to do. We believe that if advertisers want their messages to be taken seriously by children they will have to design advertisements in such a way that children perceive them as credible and honest. Furthermore, we strongly believe that children's socialization process not only starts earlier, but also develops quicker than before. To ban advertisements for children under the age of 8 is more likely to result in children's socialization process being inhibited until the age of 8, as small children will not have the same opportunity to develop a critical attitude towards advertising.

Advertisers' lack of credibility with children may also be because children perceive advertisements as lacking substance. On average, only one in ten children thought that advertisements tell good stories, that they learn something new from the advertisement, or that they provide food for thought.

Therefore, the question is what design and substance advertisements should aim for in order to maintain the attention and interest of children as they grow older.

First, children want to be entertained; they want funny advertisements whether they are children of 8 years or youngsters of 18 years. However, the way advertisements are designed today, very few of them (20-30 percent of the children) perceive this to be the case. Thus 'funny advertisements' is an area where there is great potential for improvement.

Second, advertisements should tell a good story – good stories are an important aspect for children, but advertisements today do not fulfill this need satisfactorily.

Third, advertisements for children of 10 years and above should contain fewer cartoons, and children as actors are no longer important. In conclusion, the older the children are, the more important it is for advertisements to have an 'adult' design.

Finally, 60 percent or more agree that the plot of the advertisements should preferably be innovative. All ages clearly want advertisements to impart something new and unexpected.

All in all, children want quality advertisements, just like the adult audience!

This study shows that children's ability to discern advertisements as more or less credible is great. Eight out of 10 children aged 8-9 did not find advertisements to be honest or believable, and this percentage increases to 9 out of 10 for the three older age groups. Even 8-9 year old children are not easily fooled by advertisements – they are perfectly able to see through exaggerated messages. Even though many children from age 8 are able to discern the intention of advertisements, as well as the fact that advertisements are not always truthful, they still let themselves be influenced by advertisements and to want the advertised products. The more often they watch advertisements, the more pronounced the wants created by advertising are. Even though this tendency is very clear for the younger children, we also find it among older children. Just as advertisements influence adults, they also influence children and youngsters. Thus, we conclude that advertisements help to accelerate children's socialization process: Today children develop a critical attitude to advertising at an early stage, but despite their skepticism advertisements still influence children's wishes and purchases.

The study also shows that children of the ages 8-9 debate children's advertisements with adults. However, only for the 10-12 year olds is it true that the percentage of children who understand the intention of advertising is significantly larger for those who discuss advertisements with their family than for those who do not talk to their family about advertisements; i.e. talking to your family has an impact on the understanding of the intention of advertising. When you look at all age groups there is no significant difference. It is not possible to statistically prove that the volume of watched advertisements either increases or decreases children's ability to discern the intention of advertising.

Even the 8-9 year olds watch many advertisements for children as well as for adults. In this light, a further tightening and regulation of children's advertisements that is the focus of the debate in Denmark seem less important for the future. Instead, the debate should focus on the way children are taught to be more critical consumers and to use advertisements more constructively.

As consumers, children need to learn how to make choices, to collect relevant information and assess and compare products, or to use different decision strategies. Advertising will inevitably be an element of this decision process, and the goal is to teach children to be critical users of advertisements. Children should learn to understand the intention and means of advertising as early as their stage of development allows it, so they can become better at using the advertisements constructively.

In order to prevent any political interventions towards children's TV-advertisements, the Danish public service channel TV2, since the fall of 2000, has tried to limit the broadcasting of children's advertisements that are immediately before programmes for children under the age of 8. Other channels have followed the guidelines laid down by TV2. In this way, the television broadcasters are beginning to succumb to the public demand to live up to ethically acceptable norms regarding children.

However, we do not feel that a further ban on advertising would be a good solution. Advertisements have become part of children's lives; they are influenced by many different sources – such as the Internet, youth magazines, school, friends. This is why we believe that advertisements should be debated as much as possible, and in the process, children should be taught to be critical users of advertisements in order to better understand the intention and agents of advertising at an earlier stage.

In conclusion, we would like to emphasize that several of our results correspond with the results and conclusions of previous studies. This makes it possible for us to conclude that the collected data is valid, and that it is possible to use a quantitative research design of this nature to examine the issue of children and media.

APPENDIX: QUESTIONNAIRE

THE INTENTION OF ADVERTISEMENTS

Q1.	The advertisement catch my attention
Q2.	It's fun to watch advertisements
Q3.	My spirits are lifted when I watch advertisements
Q4.	Advertisements are funny
Q5.	Advertisements tell good stories
Q6.	Advertisements are honest and credible
Q7.	Advertisements make me think
Q8.	I often learn something new from watching advertisements
Q 9.	Advertisements are convincing
Q10.	I understand the meaning behind the advertisements
Q11.	Advertisements influence what I want
Q12.	Advertisements make me want to try the product
Q13.	In general, I like advertisements
Q14.	In general, I like to watch advertisements

UNDERSTANDING OF ADVERTISEMENTS

Q 15.	How often do you watch advertisements addressed to children?
Q 16.	How often do you watch advertisements addressed to adults?
Q 17.	How often do you watch advertisements together with your family?
Q 18.	How often do you watch advertisements together with your friends?
Q 19.	When I watch TV advertisements together with my family, we discuss them afterwards
Q 20.	When I watch TV advertisements together with my friends, we discuss them afterwards
Q 21.	I watch TV-advertisements, so that I can discuss them with my friends afterwards

ADVERTISING EFFECTS

Q 22.	I often want to have the advertised products
Q 23.	I often buy the advertised products

CREDIBILITY

Q 24.	Things often look better in advertisements than in reality
Q 25.	The product is just as good as the advertisement promises
Q 26.	I think that advertisements exaggerate how good the products are
Q 27.	It is not always true, what is told in the advertisement
Q 28.	The way in which things are said in the advertisement, tells me whether it is true or not

MEANS

When advertisements are funny, the purpose is:

Q 29.	To catch my attention
Q 30.	To make me remember the advertisement
Q 31.	To make me believe in the advertisement
Q 32.	To make me interested in the product
Q 33.	To make me try the product

When famous persons appear in advertisements, the purpose is:

Q 34.	To catch my attention
Q 35.	To make me remember the advertisement
Q 36.	To make me believe in the advertisement
Q 37.	To make me interested in the product
Q 38.	To make me try the product

When advertisements compare products, the purpose is:

Q 39.	To catch my attention
Q 40.	To make me remember the advertisement
Q 41.	To make me believe in the advertisement
Q 42.	To make me interested in the product
Q 43.	To make me try the product

EXECUTION

Q44.	I like advertisements that have children in them the best
Q45.	I like advertisements that have cartoon characters in them the best
Q46.	I like advertisements that emphasize the product the best
Q47.	I like advertisements that tell a good story the best
Q48.	I like advertisements that are funny the best
Q49.	I like the music in most TV and radio advertisements
Q50.	The best advertisements are the ones that show which people use the products
Q51.	I like it when the advertisement tells me something new and unexpected

Comments to questionnaire:

- For children 8–12 years, a 3-point scale is used.
- For children 13–18 years, a 5-point scale is used.
- Question 7,8,12,21, and 23 are left out for children 8–12 years
- For children 8–12 years, the text in question 33, 38 and 43 is changed to: »To make me wish to have the product«
- All the remaining questions are identical for the two age-groups

REFERENCES

Bahn, Kenneth D. (1986). »How and when do brand perceptions and preferences first form? A cognitive developmental investigation«, Journal of consumer research, 13, (December), 382–393.

Barenboim, Carl (1981). »The development of person perception in childhood and adolescence: From behavioural comparisons to psychological constructs to psychological comparisons«, *Child development*, 52, (March), 129-144.

Bever, Thomas G., Martin L. Smith, Barbara Bengen & Thomas G Johnson (1975). »Young viewers' troubling response to TV advertisements«, *Harvard Business Review*, 53 (November-December), 109-120.

Blosser, Betsy J. & Donald F. Roberts (1985). »Age differences in children's perception of message intent: Response to TV news, commercials, educational spots, and public service announcements«, *Communication research*, 12, (October), 455-484.

Butter, Eliot, Paula M. Popvich, Robert H Stackhouse & Roger K. Garner (1981). »Discrimination of television programs and commercials by pre-school children«, *Journal of advertising research*, 21 (April), 53-56.

Carlson, Les, Sanford Grossbart & Kathleen Struenkel (1992). »The role of parental socialisation types on differential family communication patterns regarding consumption«, *Journal of consumer psychology*, vol. 1, no. 1, 31-52.

GfK Denmark A/S (1997). *Danske børns og deres forældres opfattelse af tv-reklamer for børneprodukter.* [Danish children and their parents perception of advertisement for children's products] Report no. 612 746.

John, Deborah Roedder (1981). »Age differences in children's responses to television advertising: An information processing approach«, *Journal of consumer research*, vol. 8, no. 1 (September), 44-53.

John, Deborah Roedder (1999). »Consumer socialisation of children: A retrospective look at twenty-five years of research«, *Journal of consumer research*, vol. 26, (December), 183-213.

Levin, Stephen R., Thomas V. Petros & Florence W. Petrella (1982). »Pre-schoolers' awareness of television advertising«, *Child development*, 53, (August), 933-937.

McNeal, James U. & Chyon-Hwa Yeh (1993). »Born to shop«, *American demographics*, (June), 34-39.

Moschis, George P. (1985). »The role of family communication in consumer socialisation of children and adolescents«, *Journal of consumer research*, 11 (March), 898-913.

Peracchio, Laura A. (1992). »How do young children learn to be consumers? A script-processing approach«, *Journal of consumer research*, 18, (March), no. 4, 25-40.

Piaget, Jean (1957). »The child and modern physics«, *Scientific American*, 196, No 3, 46-51.

Reid, Leonard N. (1978). »The impact of family group interaction on children's understanding of television advertising«, *Journal of advertising*, 8 (Summer), 13-19.

Robertson, Thomas S. & John R. Rossiter (1974). »Children and commercial persuasion: An attribution theory analysis«, *Journal of consumer research*, 1, (June), 13-20.

Selman, Robert (1980). *The growth of interpersonal understanding*, New York: Academic Press.

Ward, Scott, Daniel B. Wackman & Ellen Wartella (1977): *How children learn to buy*, Beverly Hills, CA:Sage.

7

THE CHILD'S UNDERSTANDING OF THE INTENT BEHIND ADVERTISING
— »A PERSONAL STORY«

By Brian Young

INTRODUCTION[1]

The purpose of this chapter is to introduce the interested reader to some of the main issues and some of the findings on the subject on how children understand the intent behind advertising. In order to provide structure to the subject I shall approach this issue historically. But the history is my own history and if you are looking for a chronology of research in children and advertising then you have come to the wrong place. I make no apologies for telling this story and I assume readers are not that interested in me and my attempts to explore the field. It is just that the odyssey is an easier story to tell. Like all narratives, however, it has its own demand characteristics and I am probably guilty of making the story a little bit more coherent than it really was and putting myself at the centre. One of the pleasures of being human is that I am flawed like all of us.

IN THE BEGINNING ...

In the 1980s I was fortunate to be asked by the Health Education Council (HEC; now known as the Health Education Authority or HEA) in the UK to look at a particular research issue. Fortunate in a couple of ways. At the time I was working as a psychologist in a Department of Sociology and Anthropology in a University in the North of England and I needed a focus and a change in my own research plans. And more importantly, the universities at that time were suffering under a political regime that was determined to cut back on public services and radically change the whole climate of public funding in the UK. It is now known as 'Thatcherism' after the Prime Minister of that time. Cuts and redundancies were looming on the horizon and the HEC had offered to pay my salary for 18 months so I could concentrate on this one task. The research problem as defined in the title of the final report to the HEC was *The Incidence and Content of Television Advertising of Sugared Products to Children: A British Study* and the report itself ran to almost 600 pages. But not all of these pages provided an account of what is on TV and how much is there and in fact most of the report reviewed the literature on the subject and, more importantly I think, defined the context or framework within which much of this research had been conducted.

Being a psychologist working in a Department of both Sociology and Anthropology I was able to take into account the interests and questions that I would ask and also those that my colleagues asked when I talked about and discussed the research with them. Psychologists are not just interested in showing to the world a fact that is well-known to any casual viewer of commercial television – that a lot if not most of television advertising to children consists of foods that, taken together, would constitute a diet high in added sugar, salt and fat.[2] But psychologists are interested in how viewers interpret, understand, and generally make sense of the world of television advertising.

So we should be interested in the developmental psychology of the child and the various psychological processes that are involved in 'reading advertisements'. We should explore the stimulus i.e. advertising itself and try and define and describe what it is and what aspects of it the child has to master if understanding is to be achieved. We need to look at advertising within the natural history of children – children growing up as collectives, as cliques, groups, gangs and friends. How is advertising consumed? What role does it occupy in the life of the playground, the mall or the coffee bar? We shall see that psychologists have done this and have given answers although a lot of work still remains to be done.

The second point is the context or framework within which the research was conducted. Here I can put on the sociologist's hat or maybe try and be an anthropologist. It was quite obvious that the research I had been asked to do was not politically neutral and that the models of children and childhood and how advertising actually worked were also not neutral.[3] And at this point I had better explain in more detail just what I mean.

POLITICS AND IMAGES OF HOW THINGS WORK IN THIS FIELD

Dentists are concerned about public health and in particular about kids and bad teeth. Dental caries is an expensive problem in contemporary society. It is also a multi-factorial research problem. Adding fluoride to the water supply or toothpaste is one factor that can make things better but there are also inherited factors and behavioural factors. So for example, how much sugar you eat and more importantly how you eat it (e.g. snacking) and what dental health precautions you take (e.g. rinsing and cleaning before bed) will also influence the likelihood you will get caries. How do we stop it or more realistically try and reduce it? Some things are difficult to change. Perhaps there are political problems in fluoridation and you can't do very much about the teeth a child brings into the world and whether they are going to be susceptible to the disease or not. But dentists can educate children in dental health and teach them how to brush and when to brush.

The metaphor of 'attack and defence' is appropriate[4] where dentists are defending and protecting children. Who's attacking them? Who can *we* attack? Why advertising of course! Advertising is on the front line as the communicative arm of the world of goods and services and is the most visible and salient part of that world. In addition advertising has several characteristics that, I would argue, evoke concern in average members of the public. Consumers like to see themselves as in charge and responsible for their actions and feel threatened when faced with the 'hidden persuaders'.[5] The consumer as victim is one of the dominant images of the consumer (Gabriel and Lang 1995). The peculiar mix of information and rhetoric that makes up advertising reflects the relationship between reason and emotion in many consumers, especially when the two are sitting side by side in one communicative act. In addition, consumers have now elevated shopping to a ritual with sacred overtones (Belk et al. 1989) and everyone comes to the high altar of consumption.

So advertising is there; it is vulnerable, it is visible and it is scapegoated. Advertising is regulated in many countries in Europe and the rest of the world. If this regulatory framework is part of a democratic society then it can be changed and people can be elected to change things and the media can be managed so that one's own point of view gets a fair hearing. In other words – we have a means, a motive (or rather plenty of them) and an opportunity[6] which are not only the essential ingredients for any crime but are also the prerequisites for social action.

I spent many months in the winter of 1983–84 reading general and popular books and magazine articles and vague polemical pieces about advertising and children to get a general feel of the area and what the lay assumptions were. Not that myths and misunderstandings were a monopoly of lay people. Quasi-experts and experts themselves seemed to assume and presume so much about the images, concepts and metaphors underlying advertising and children, and about the way advertising worked.

The academic literature was mixed. Partly that was due I suspect to the various people working in the field from backgrounds in marketing, market research, semiotics, consumer research, developmental psychology and communication studies all pitching for publication in a disparate collection of journals. I wanted a copy of each of the articles so I could see the evidence for myself and my library bill (on loans from other libraries and photocopies) was large for a provincial University in England and stretched my HEC grant. I was glad I did go back to original sources, though[7] because it was clear that there were dubious methodologies and dangerous assumptions in so many of the articles. Eventually the original work done in the context of the HEC work and other research and theorising about advertising that I worked on for several years afterwards was all put together and published in 1990 (Young 1990).

So – Where is the Theory?

There are two sets of theories here. My original education and training was as a developmental psychologist and indeed my first job was as a research assistant on a project looking at cognitive and linguistic development in pre-school children. So I was interested in establishing just what children knew about advertising at different ages and seeing if the theories of that time could predict what children should know and then testing to see if they did or did not know. These theories were largely based on the work of Jean Piaget who was popular in the late 1960s and early 1970s in Scotland (where I was working).

There were two other developments however at that time that proved to be influential. One was psycholinguistics that had emerged as part of psychology intimately related to linguistics as exemplified in the writings of Noam Chomsky. The other was a growing tendency in developmental psychology to emphasise the role of culture and social experience in the life of the child. Vygotsky's work had already been translated and published in English (Vygotsky 1962) and Bruner's research at the Center for Cognitive Studies at Harvard (Bruner 1966) was very much 'in' in developmental research. In the UK, the publication of *Children's Minds* by Margaret Donadson in 1978 symbolised the synthesis between the grand generalities of the master, Piaget and the more contextualised and culturally sensitive experiments and theories that were emerging at that time.

The two sets of theories that drove my own work in the 1990s were anchored in interests in psycholinguistics and theories of child development. These had emerged well before children and television advertising happened to come into view as a serendipitous opportunity to survive the austerity and change of the early 80s in England. But psycholinguistics, when I first learnt about it, was a rather formal and academic pursuit. When I read about 'how to read advertising' I recognised this same formality and attempts to apply general theories of structure in the work of the writers in semiotics such as Leymore (1975). What I wanted was a general theory of communication that could then be applied to advertising with plenty of local rules and contextual caveats. Maybe I was sacrificing parsimony and generality for a 'model with patches'[8] as current models are sometimes called. But at this stage in the research I needed a model to guide any empirical work.

PRAGMATICS AND BEYOND

Advertising as a form of communication has several functions. None of these are unique to advertising and one way of functionally identifying the nature of advertising is to see most advertising[9] as the intersection or conjunction of all the following characteristics that advertising shares with other communicative forms.

A Advertising is involving and attracts the child's attention. There are many communicative forms that have this quality such as telling ghost stories or listening to a good teacher.

B Advertising provides information. So do encyclopaedias, or instructions on how to install and programme a digital television.

C Advertising is about goods and services. The area of discourse is commercial. Holiday programmes on TV or consumer reports are also about goods and services.

D Advertising is promotional. That is, it only tells you about the positive aspects of the brand that is advertised, never the negative qualities. People are promotional when they present at interview or show off.

E Advertising is rhetorical. Advertising uses visual and verbal rhetoric in order to communicate propositions about brands. Poetry is similar and so is the rhetoric of politics and the court (although the topics are not brands).

Now, this is not an analytic system of categorisation that I have constructed so that a formal and exhaustive 'anatomy of advertising' will eventually emerge. Rather, it is a useful working model that can inform the real stuff – what children have to do to achieve an understanding of advertising. They will have to understand the promotional function of advertising for example and later on I will describe an experiment we did to assess just that. Another advantage of framing the theory in terms of a general theory of communication is that an immediate parallel emerges with other non-institutional forms of communication. How do kids cope with the interpersonal forms of communication like sarcasm and irony in speech (*e* above) or showing off by peers (*d* above)? Questions like these emerge naturally from the general theory, and answers in the developmental literature on the children's understanding of different aspects of talk and conversation can inform the research.

As I was reviewing the literature on different theoretical approaches to advertising there was one candidate that looked promising. The great American philosopher of language, John Searle (1976), had classified speech acts into five functional groups. This sort of approach has a strong resonance for a psychologist as it clearly and simply poses a question of functionality, i.e. what is language for? And he answers it.[10] Directives – speech acts that try and get someone to do something – are one such functional group. They would include questions (e.g. 'what's your name?') and requests such as 'pass the salt'. We are getting closer to advertising with this analysis and that is the sort of approach that is attractive to me where one approaches the target, gradually adding more refinements.

Pateman (1980) was one of the few people to see a resemblance between advertising and speech act theory and classified advertising as a directive. If we replace speech act with communicative act then we would take into account not just the implicit language in the advertisement but other aspects of the communication such as the sounds, the music, and most importantly the images that constitute the visual message. This communicative act is not found in isolation as a 'text' that needs to be unwrapped, decoded, analysed or dug for meaning (to use but a few metaphors employed in different forms of textual analysis). Instead we must consider it as part of a natural communicative process within a setting and with an audience, either real or assumed. In that sense we adopt a pragmatic[11] approach to the analysis of the communicative acts known as advertising and consider the setting within which the events occurred and the interpretation provided by the audience or interpreter of the advertisements and how all of these interact.

Part of the pragmatic approach to communication involves attempts to specify the various rules of communicative conduct that guide and govern our normal adult use of the various communicative systems at our disposal. The work of Grice (1975, 1978) is relevant here. Grice laid out what he called a cooperative principle that describes a basic tenet of cooperative conversation. This requires one to »make your contribution such as is required, at the stage at which it occurs, by the accepted purpose or direction of the talk exchange in which you are engaged.« (cited in Levinson 1983, p.101). What does this mean? Grice put forward several maxims that derived from this principle and they can be summarised by saying that participants in a co-operative exchange should communicate with sincerity, being relevant and clear while providing sufficient information. People, of course, often do not do this. So the power of Grice's approach lies in his prediction of what would happen if one of these rules was not obeyed.

Imagine I asked you (what I thought was) a straight, sensible, pertinent question and got (what I thought was) an evasive, irrelevant reply back. At this apparent breach of rules of canonical communicative conduct I can make one of several inferences. One could be that you are deliberately being un-cooperative and do not wish to talk. Or, I could assume that the principle of cooperative communication is not being abandoned and that you are breaching the rule to some purpose. I then have to do some mental work in order to re-establish your communicative intent. Perhaps you are signalling to me that the topic is a sensitive one and should not be discussed now. Or you are trying to be sarcastic or humorous. The details of the inferences made, the extent to which these inferences are drawn and the conditions limiting them are not important in this context. What is important is that there are two stages in the process. One is the recognition of rule-breaking and the other consists of the details of the mental work done to reconstruct communicative intent.

Although Grice talked about the general principles of communication, there is no reason to suppose that all communication should adhere to this simple rule.[12]

There are different communicative genres and many more being invented. Perhaps we can identify some local rules and claim that they apply to certain genres only?[13] At the time there was very little work in this area of identifying Gricean rules that were appropriate for the genre of advertising and I only found about three authors (Young 1990, chapter 5) that provided some examples adopting ideas based on Grice.[14] What was needed was a principled Gricean description of a category of communication that is similar to advertising. Then my attention was drawn[15] to a paper by May (1981).

May (1981) was concerned with a particular communicative situation where one of the participants is Interested (as opposed to Disinterested) in that s/he wished to generate a preferred response in the other. This would certainly include advertisers but would include many other people who would be concerned with changing other people and were intentionally doing this.[16] Advertisers would come into this category as advertisers persuade people to buy brands, but other sources would also be included (such as advocates, exhorters, seducers, pleaders, and evangelists in various guises).

May presents certain maxims for interpreting the messages of Interested participants, one of these being the so-called maxim of Best Face. The maxim of Best Face requires the reader to treat the case that is put as the strongest case that can be made. The type of approach exemplified by May is valuable as it places advertising with other kinds of communicative activities and establishes a firm characteristic of advertising. It should be possible to lay out various maxims on the lines of May (op. cit.) to account for the characteristics of communication by Interested parties. Advertising would then be placed in this category. If the maxim of Best Face is recognised more in the breach than in the observance, and that seems to be characteristic of Gricean rules, then other forms of inference occur. I am assuming now that the maxim of Best Face has some psychological validity. So, if the maxim of Best Face is violated this is recognised implicitly by the reader to the extent other forms of inference toward an interpretation are brought into play. If an advertisement is expected and the maxim of Best Face is brought to bear on the situation so that the case that is put is treated as the strongest case that can be made and it is apparent that the advertiser is understating the case, then the reader has some mental work to do.

If advertising is framed as a special case of the genre of communication known as 'interested' within the definition provided by May, then it is less easy to simply demonise advertising. Psychological approaches to advertising have traditionally located it in the context of persuasion in social psychology. So advertising is seen as persuasion in action. This immediately drags in the debate about the ethics of persuasion, whether the communicator is fully informed, whether one is trying to subvert reason and so on. I recognise that these criticisms are legitimate and people are anxious about the rhetoric and maybe buying goods that they really did not want in the first place but there is a danger of ignoring other aspects of advertising just because the frame of understanding – persuasion – does not place them on the agenda. 'Interested' communications are the stuff of 21st century communications.

The rise of Talk TV and Talk Radio means that, for many people, the only conversations they hear are between journalists and broadcasters and members of the public, politicians, business people and so on. The agenda here is one of keeping the viewers and listeners involved so they do not switch off or switch over and the ratings look good. This agenda is the same for public service media, state subsidised media and commercial media as for all of them success is measured by ratings irrespective of whether the service appeals to a general or a mass audience. To maintain attention it is necessary to stimulate and entertain and the easiest way to do this is to encourage short, pertinent and rhetorically powerful contributions ('sound bites') and emphasise the conflicting nature of the discussion. Consequently all parties are '-interested' in presenting their own views and, if they have been trained in media encounters (and most politicians are), they will get these across irrespective of the other side's views.[17]

In addition, there has been an upsurge of interest in 'ways of talk' that would have been assumed, 30 or 40 years ago, to be parasitic on the canonical mode as defined by Grice.[18] The traditional view as espoused by Grice is that there is an assumed model of canonical communicative conduct and forms as used in poetry, persuasion and the like are defined relative to that the standard model – they are 'marked' (in linguistic terminology) against the unmarked version. Keenan (1976) has claimed that everyday discourse in a language called Malagasy does not adhere to all Grice's maxims thereby challenging the universality of these maxims. Feminist writers such as Tannen (1984) have argued that women's talk has different conversational goals than men's talk. This does seem to threaten the presumption by Grice that it is natural to start one's enquiry by assuming certain universal rules of conduct in conversation when they are probably rules for certain kinds of talk.

In summary there is a theory of communication, based on pragmatics, that is a suitable candidate to explain and predict what children do with the different functions of advertising. Although based on linguistics there is no reason why it cannot be extended to images and signs in general.[19]

THEORIES OF DEVELOPMENT

Grand theories of development á la Piaget or Vygotsky can inform our understanding of what to expect from children at different ages. If, however, we are to establish a theory of the child's understanding of advertising we need to appeal to local or micro-theories that are specific to particular areas of development. For example, one of the main findings in Piaget's account of the pre-operational period of development from about 2 to 6 years is that young children can only infer on the basis of perceptual information. After this time they are able to reason based on inferred properties of objects. So the classic example is that young children think there is actually more in a ball of clay if it is rolled into a long sausage because it *looks* like more than it did before as it is longer. They focus on one perceptual dimension and judge on that basis.

Older children can understand that 'the amount of stuff' is a quality that is inferred, it is not actually there in what you see. So changes in shape does not change amount – it's only more or less than before if you add more stuff or take some away. We can use this well-known property of children's thinking to predict[20] that young pre-school children will sometimes say that advertisements are different from programmes but can only use reasons like 'advertisements are short and programmes are long'. Or that children before about 5 or 6 years of age will usually say that 'advertisements are there for fun – to make you laugh' when asked about the intention behind advertising – just because the advertisements they see and notice *are* funny and amusing. They can't go further than that at that age.

The alternative and better way to approach a specific research question (and we are now getting nearer after a lengthy preamble to the research question given in the title to this chapter) is to ensure that theory and experiment mutually inform each other. Ideally the experiment will force some change, or strengthen a hypothesis within the theory, and the theory will generate the experiment and future experiments. It is this transactional approach between theory and experiment that enables science to totter forward. Often however, a research area in an applied field (like advertising to children) will rarely if ever reach this goal simply because the agenda is set by others and not completely generated by the interplay of experiment and theory. The others, who often determine where grants and funding go, are concerned that research is applicable and will help those in positions of power and influence make up their minds better.

So the dilemma I felt (and I am sure I am not alone here) was that I was now working in this area, and it did feel right in that my own background and experience was appropriate, but I also had to develop some intellectually respectable approach to the whole issue that brought together new developments. The answer that I found at the time lay in the concept of advertising literacy. As a psychologist I saw the task as one where one identifies different strands of development that are appropriate as resources for understanding and interpreting advertising at different stages of development.

Advertising Literacy

In 1984 I had the pleasure of attending a conference in Provence, France, on television advertising and children. I gave a paper on advertising to children called as I remember 'new approaches to old problems: the growth of advertising literacy'. The conference papers were published later as a book edited by Ward and Brown and my (revised) paper appeared there (Young 1986). At the time I was using the term as a suitable turn of phrase to hang ideas on and had not really explored the implications. For example, I had assumed that this kind of literacy would be a set of skills that children acquire[21] and, as a psychologist, I would be interested in identifying these skills and tracking their development as the child grows up. Others (Ritson and Elliott 1995, Ritson and Elliott, forthcoming)[22] have developed the idea of 'advertising literacy' using theories of literacy that emphasise the importance of 'interpretive communities' creating their own meaning out of the cultural stock of advertising as a resource using various narratives that are shared within the group. So the initial conception of advertising literacy can be extended to cover a lot of different observations of children and young people consuming advertising as well being able to establish how they understand it. There is a behavioural aspect to advertising literacy (what people do) as well as a cognitive and affective component (what they think and feel).

The title of this chapter is the child's understanding of the intent behind advertising. This would suggest that all the other issues in advertising literacy such as the child's understanding of brands, the world of goods and services, how children understand money and other ways of getting what they want (such as negotiation strategies within the family) and in general all that children bring to bear when they understand why advertisements are there and what they are for, is relegated to the position of extra or ancillary information. Most readers will know that a line has to be drawn in any focussed study between what is relevant and vital to know and what must be put to one side because chapter length imposed by editors and the attention span of readers are both necessarily limited. And yet we must recognise that discussion of any issue eventually will and should embrace many other matters that are, in some sense, relevant. Answers to the question of children's understanding of advertising and why advertising is there have to be restricted although the general question of 'advertising literacy' is an open one.[23]

Why is the Child's Understanding of Intent Important?

The reason is partly psychological, but mostly legal. The history of regulating advertising to children can be traced back to the US federal government proceedings of the 1970s and in particular the Federal Trade Commission (FTC) and Federal Communication Commission (FCC) submissions (for references and history, see Young 1990; chapter 2). At one point in the late 1970s it looked possible that the FTC would be able to ban television advertising to children on the grounds that such advertising is *unfair* [emphasise added] to children. 'Unfair' in this context suggested that there is a generic category of communications, called advertisements, and that there is a case that certain people are not in a position to understand the point or intention behind these communications. So young children below a certain age could fall into this category. Psychologists could have a role here if they were in a position to provide expert evidence on the age when children can understand advertising intent. In fact, after much pressure from commercial lobbies the FTC was effectively emasculated in that they were only permitted to consider *deceptive* [emphasise added] advertising which consisted of communications from sellers to buyers which are false or misleading and which induce purchases.

Although the political climate was such that a ban was impossible in the US at that time, the issue has not gone away and resurfaced in 2001 with Sweden's attempts to ban advertising to children in Europe. The argument was similar – that children do not really understand the point of advertising and therefore it is unfair to allow them to be exposed to this kind of communication.

Psychologically, there are problems with making claims that children before a certain age do not understand something and after that age they do. Firstly, understanding advertising as I have argued above is part of advertising literacy that consists of several streams of development. So, the one I am describing in this chapter is concerned with the child's understanding of the promotional nature of advertising framed in the pragmatic theories I have mentioned previously. Secondly, although legislation wants to establish exact ages of transition,[24] psychologists are unable or unwilling to stake claims on ages which – even with stage developmental theories – are meaningless. So for example does one assume a mean age[25] as marking the transition? Or should one look for a majority? Are percentages important anyway when they are translated into number of children who *do not* understand? And finally, being able to understand does not necessarily mean that one is able to utilise that understanding in practice.[26] So for example, John (1999) reviewed the literature on consumer socialization of children over the last quarter of the 20th century. John's model of child development, although recognising the validity of much of Piaget's stage-developmental theories, assumes three stages in the processing of information. Children under seven years of age are seen as limited processors. In the language of information processing they have mediational deficiencies where storage and retrieval are difficult even when they are prompted and cued to do so. Children over 12 years of age on the other hand are able to use various strategies for storing, retrieving and utilising information and that can be done in the absence of prompting and cueing. Between the ages of 7 and 11 however, although children might be able to deploy strategies to enhance information storage and retrieval that are similar to those used by older children, they need to be aided by explicit prompts and cues. Consequently, although children might be able to understand a lot about the intention behind advertising by 8 years of age, they still have a problem with advertising until 12 years of age. This problem is to do with the access and utilisation of that knowledge. In a sense although the understanding is there and can be used to critically cope with advertising, it may not necessarily be accessed and used in evaluating advertising messages.

John also makes a case that there is a skill concerning the child's ability to take the perspective of other people (Selman 1980) that develops from early childhood to adolescence and that these developmental stages should be taken into account when considering the child's understanding of advertising. Children before the age of six years are unable to take the perspective of other people and view the world from their own point of view. Between 6 and 8 years of age children realise that others have different opinions or motives, but believe that this comes from the other person having different information rather than adopting a different perspective on a situation. Between 8 and 10 years children acquire an understanding that people with the same information can have different opinions or motives and can take this into account and consider another person's point of view. Development does not stop at 10 years of age, however, and being able to simultaneously consider the other person's point of view emerges from 10-12 years. This skill is vital in interpersonal negotiation and persuasion when people interact socially. Finally the young adolescent can take the mature detached position of seeing another person's perspective as relating to social group membership or the social system within which they operate.

Both of these developmental sequences – information processing and perspective taking – are important when considering how literate children are when coping with advertising in all its multifunctional aspects. Being able to acquire and, importantly, utilise understandings about advertising and being able to understand the advertiser's point of view seem to be important elements of advertising literacy. Does this mean then that advertising to children under 12 is unfair and that this evidence should be used when regulating and controlling what, if any, advertising should be shown to children? Certainly the evidence should be considered and it is not surprising that understanding such a complex genre like advertising has a developmental trajectory at least to adolescence.[27]

Bjurström (1994) was suggesting this when he concluded the relevant section of his Report with the words »... it is only around or after the age of 12 that we can be more certain that most children have developed a fuller understanding of the purpose or objective of advertising« (*op. cit.*; p. 42). This answer in my opinion is very different from the answer to the question 'when do most children have an *adequate* or 'good enough' knowledge of the intent and purpose of advertising. Most of the evidence (in cultures with an experience of advertising) points to 8 years of age as the time when this emerges. It may be that children older than 8 years but younger than 12 apply this knowledge erratically but that could apply to many people of different ages. The minimal requirements for understanding that advertising has intent to persuade people to buy goods and services, that it informs and entertains but presents promotional material, are in place in most children by eight years of age.

THE EXPERIMENT

In the final part of this chapter I want to report on some research I did with my students[28] recently on the child's understanding of the promotional aspect of advertising. Although this is published elsewhere (Young 2000), and I refer the reader to that paper for a more detailed account, it is worthwhile describing it as a consequence of the theoretical work outlined above.

The rationale behind the research was to investigate the child's understanding of promotional communication as discussed above. One of the advantages of framing the research problem in terms of May's maxim of Best Face is that it assumes that although children will eventually understand this principle of interested or promotional communication, it is an empirical issue of whether they understand the principle in the context of interpersonal communication at the same time as they understand it as part of advertising. At least one can use evidence from what we know about children's understanding of how people self-promote in order to set up a hypothesis of what they know about the principle in advertising. There is little literature on children's abilities to self-promote (Aloise-Young 1993) and their understanding of self-promotion in others (Bennett and Yeeles 1990). Six to seven-year-olds seem to be unable to self-promote – to show themselves to others only in a positive light to gain an advantage. This would suggest that it is only later, maybe after seven years of age, that children will understand promotion in advertising. The difficulty is how to assess this and we spent some considerable time on this problem.

The procedure we used was as follows. It was decided early on in the research to use a non-verbal methodology to investigate the child's understanding of the promotional principle in advertising. Interview techniques rely for their effectiveness on the expressive abilities of children with language and as such are limited in their applicability with young children. A non-verbal research procedure where the response measure consists of choice (by pointing or picking up) from a range of alternatives is preferable. It is rarely if ever possible to bypass the use of language in conducting an experiment in psychology and this procedure is best described as one where the use of language is minimised especially at the dependent variable response stage. The logic behind the design of the experiment was as follows.

From a review of the literature on the child's understanding of advertising intent we know that the majority consensus is that there is a developmental sequence where advertising is first understood by pre-school children as being there just for fun or entertainment. At some point in the primary school period children will realise that advertising obeys a promotional principle. At this stage of development some advertisements are still seen as funny and amusing but the child sees the fact that they only say positive things about the brand as a more important and fundamental defining principle of advertising. If the child can be shown an advertisement with different endings that reflect the child's understanding at different stages of development then we can ask the child to choose the 'best' ending and see if there are differences between older and younger children.

The version that was produced in this study emerged as follows. Many advertisements have a narrative structure that is based on what has been described as the 'pain, pill, pleasure' model (Berger 1974). A problem is posed in the first part. Perhaps body odour is present, washing is not clean or the character has a cough. The brand is then introduced as the solution to this problem. The final brief sequence shows the consequence of consuming the brand. Happiness reigns or one is immediately attractive to members of the opposite sex and the possibilities are only limited by the imagination of creative department of the agency. Unfortunately these sequences are usually present in advertising for products that are consumed by adults such as OTC drugs, detergents or toothpaste. Advertising to children is designed to attract and present the brand in an exciting way with much surreal imagery and rapid pacing and rarely has this structure. On the other hand, children do watch advertising that is not directed to them and, if the child has a generic concept of advertising, they should be able to draw appropriate inferences.

We decided then to sample a set of pain-pill-pleasure television commercials from a stock accumulated by the author over many years and chose those that were old (over 10 years old in many cases) so that it was very unlikely that the child had seen them. We stopped the commercial before the final 'pleasure' sequence. Seven television commercials were selected according to the criteria described above. The 'pleasure' sequence was edited out and three alternative versions of the end were prepared. This was done grabbing a still from the pleasure sequence that typified this sequence and subjecting it to three transformations using computer graphics.

The first was called 'promotional' and used either the naturally occurring still or, in some cases, this still was deliberately enhanced to emphasise the pleasurable aspect. The second was labelled 'neutral' where the still was modified to look as neutral in affect as possible. Finally the third alternative, called the 'entertaining' alternative, was constructed. In this the still was deliberately modified to produce a picture which was entertaining but where the principle of promotional communication was deliberately flouted so that the product was shown in a negative way. In both the promotional and entertaining alternatives a shot and/or logo of the brand was present whereas this was deliberately left out in the neutral alternative. This was done to force a choice between entertaining and promotional alternatives for those participants who might only have the limited understanding that advertisements talk about brands. All three alternatives for each of the seven commercials were printed out from the electronically modified files on a colour printer and presented on laminated cards.

We interviewed 133 children with approximately an equal number of children in each year band ranging from 4-5 years of age to 8-9 years. The critical question in the interview schedule was asked after showing the three alternatives:

> »As you can see the end is missing. But we think we can use one of these pictures for a possible ending. Which one do you think should be used when the advert's shown on TV? Which one is the best to use?«

We recorded the choice and the children were then asked to justify their choice for each commercial (»Why do you think this one is best? Why did you not choose the others?«) and the next commercial was shown and the same procedure was followed. At the end of the task each child was then asked to choose the funniest of the three alternative endings for each of the seven commercials. This was to provide an independent check that the ending we thought was the most amusing (the entertaining one) was in fact the one that the children chose as the funniest.

The results are given in Table 1.

Age band	Entertaining	Neutral	Promotional
4-5 years	49.6	35.3	15.1
5-6 years	29.1	33.3	37.6
6-7 years	14.2	33.0	52.8
7-8 years	9.2	36.4	54.4
8-9 years	2.6	20.6	76.7

Table 1. Row percentages of responses across seven trials in the three categories of promotional, neutral and entertaining for each child categorised into five age bands.

Table 1 shows that almost half the 4-5-year-olds chose the entertaining alternative as the one that '… should be used when the advert's shown on TV' and a small minority chose the promotional, i.e. the correct adult response. About a third of the children up to the age of 7-8 years chose the neutral response and this dropped to a fifth by 8-9 years of age. By 5-6 years of age the promotional ending was selected by a majority of children and this steadily became the dominant response with increasing age.

These results provide a strong indication that early in the primary school years there is a growing understanding that a promotional ending, rather than an ending that although funny breaks the promotional rule, is appropriate for television advertising.

So how can we explain these results?[29] The results certainly showed a clear trend for children to change with age from choosing an entertaining ending that breaches the promotional rule as a suitable ending for a commercial to selecting an alternative that they do not think is the funniest but one that promotes the product. What might be the processes involved in the choice patterns shown in Table 1 for older children? Older children realise that the entertaining choice is still available (i.e. advertisements are still funny and amusing), but with the entertaining choice alternative there is a serious breach of the promotional rule as the product is shown in a negative light. The older child is 'pushed' to the other two alternatives. Is there a corresponding 'pull' to one or the other (neutral or promotional)? I would argue that the recognition of a breach of a communicative rule is the main process in the developmental change and this is in accord with theoretical principles in that these rules are recognised more in the breach than in the observance.

In addition, rules are introduced into the child's life by strictures and prohibitions. »Don't do this!« Understanding that you just *can't* do that in advertisements (but you still can in comics or cartoons where promotion is not a necessary part of the genre) is, I would argue, a major cognitive achievement in the child's understanding of advertising. It forms the roots of an understanding that advertising is different and obeys different rules from other kinds of communication such as programmes. We have detected the beginnings of this ability by age 5-6 years with an increasing number of children rejecting the entertaining choice with age with less than 10% making this choice by 7-8 years of age.

Advertising literacy, and the particular part of it that deals with understanding of the intent behind advertising, is a complex pattern of development with many different developmental sequences operative. It has interested me for many years and has spawned this experiment, the results of which I have presented here. No doubt the odyssey has not yet finished and there are several other lines of investigation to pursue which will generate more theory and more research. There are so many different forms of media, both interactive and carrying commercial communications, and the media landscape is changing so rapidly that I will be in business I hope for quite a few years to come!

NOTES

1   This chapter is based on a presentation I gave at the Copenhagen Business School on 26 June 2001.
2   Note the careful wording here. I did learn something about nutrition on the odyssey and one of the principles is 'there's no such thing as junk *food* – only poor *diets* are (potentially) unhealthy'.
3   I'm not in any sense suggesting that any of the funding agencies involved in the research I have done have *prescribed* or even hinted that one way of approaching the subject is to be preferred to another. It does seem, though, that there is a social dynamic operating so that the factions in the debate are not just equipped with their arguments but that their arguments are conceptually underpinned in different ways.
4   'Attack and defence' frames so many public debates and the media reinforces this way of thinking about relations between those who hold differing views.
5   This alludes to a famous (or infamous) book published by Vance Packard in 1957 called The Hidden Persuaders in which advertising was portrayed as akin to the black arts with psychologists acting as the priests of darkness. I have suggested elsewhere (Young, 1990) that the title of chapter 15 'the psycho-seduction of children' invokes an image of the child as innocent and the advertiser as seducer – an image that has clouded the discussion of advertising and its relationship to children for almost half a century.
6   Many critics of advertising create the distinction between 'the consumer' and advertising and conveniently change sides and place themselves as champions of the consumer. This tactical shift

achieves the dual goal of acting positively as advocate (rather than negatively as critic) and as being on the side of David rather than Goliath. The comments about the vast amounts of money
'the other side' spends and how frugal and economical *we* are ensure that the transformation is
complete and 'we' are now firmly on the side of the angels.

7   One of the consequences of the 'publish and perish' ethos that now dominates UK research is
the need young researchers have to cite to excess. Although citation abuse can be cured with a
good supervisor, it is still sadly all too prevalent. I would diagnose insecurity early in one's career,
a tendency for reviewers to assume quality is in direct proportion to the length of one's reference list, and the easy availability of databases and e-journals. It does have serious consequences
for the spread of psychological knowledge though – many colleagues will share the experience
of being cited as saying the exact opposite of what was meant! But as the frequency of citation
(especially in high impact journals) increases one's rating … well, we're back on the treadmill of
publish or perish.

8   'Patch' here is a computer based metaphor I believe, based on software that can be downloaded
from the Net at a supplier's site to 'patch up' a glitch in the commercial software. Often this original software is so complex that errors and paradoxes cannot be predicted and will only emerge
from the trial and error of many thousands of customers.

9   I say 'most advertising' as advertising is an organic and changing institutional arrangement that is
designed ultimately to influence sales of a particular brand. I say 'influence' because although advertising should have that ultimate goal, there are plenty intermediate stages in strategies of brand
development such as repositioning, maintaining sales, special offers etc. Also within a campaign
there are different goals such as getting attention, creating a positive mood, affective and attitudinal aspects of creative techniques, etc.

10 There is no reason to suppose Searle's approach is the only way of carving language up into its
various jobs and there are other ways that are perhaps better or at least different from Searle's.
For a psychologist, though, it is what he is trying to do that is important and I would not wish
to claim that one mind (i.e. Searle's or any other author for that matter) can establish the anatomy of communicative functions. Indeed observation and empirical investigation could keep the
answers coming indefinitely depending on which communicative genre is being explored since
new ones are being invented all the time!

11 Pragmatics (see Levinson, 1983) has been defined rather cynically as the rest of language when
semantics, syntax, and phonology have been removed. I would prefer the rather more transpar-
ent gloss that pragmatics deals with how language is understood taking into account various features of the communicative situation such as the intent of the communicator and the setting
within which the communication is found.

12 The criticism against Grice – that most communication just does not adhere to the principle and
the maxims – can be countered by saying that Grice's approach was simply to present the reader with a 'reasonable' principle that governs canonical communicative conduct. There is no reason to suppose actual conversations are like this. But it provides a suitable standard against which
to flag breaches which in many cases are symptomatic of attempts to use figurative language such
as metaphor, sarcasm, irony, hyperbole and so on. Linguistic accounts of figurative language are
quite difficult and a Gricean approach provides a more elegant and simpler account.

13 The example of a new genre that comes to mind is e-mail and it might be worthwhile to establish just what local rules would be appropriate here?

14 More recently, based on the work of Sperber and Wilson (1986) who adopted a Gricean approach, there have been attempts to apply this kind of theory to advertising. Keiko Tanaka (1994)
wrote about Japanese and British advertising from a pragmatic perspective and Charles Forceville

(1996) has provided and extensive theory of pictorial metaphor in advertising relying a lot on Sperber and Wilson's theory and supplying (for the interested reader) an excellent summary of the relevance of this book (which coincidentally is called Relevance) to advertising!

15 At that time, in the 1980s, there was a group at the Psychology Department at the University of Manchester who used to meet occasionally and discuss aspects of discourse and discourse analysis. I am indebted to Ivan Leudar, a member of that group, who told me about the paper by May.

16 As I understand May's definition of 'interested' the communication should be intentional and in the communicator's interest. The former would necessarily exclude communicative accidents where e.g. some unintended communication causes behaviour that is in the communicator's interest such as 'accidentally' telling a story so that the tearful and grateful recipient who has 'seen the light' rewards the communicator. The preferences of the communicator can be altruistic so that the therapist communicates some information to the neurotic that is in the recipient's ultimate interests (some self-revelatory information) but has rather negative interpersonal effects (the neurotic starts to hate the therapist).

17 Of all the hundreds of channels available to me at home with my digital, satellite television, the only one I would argue is 'disinterested' is BBC Parliament. The paradox is that the *genre* (parliamentary debate in both Houses and various committees) is supposed to be interested but the *style* is disinterested – discussing at length, changing one's position, etc. I should add that readers who have only been exposed to Prime Minister's Questions would not recognise this, the real stuff of democracy at work.

18 There is a standard defensive move here that is usually played so I might as well pre-empt it now. The fact that many if not most conversations breach the Gricean rules in practice (i.e. people do bring up irrelevancies and talk round a topic) would be countered by Gricean linguists as follows. Linguists approach their subject by laying out ideal conditions and they are no different in that sense from mathematicians who assume perfect spheres and frictionless planes when dealing with the physical world. The power of a theory should be judged in terms of how well it accounts for basic problems in linguistics such as deixis, anaphora and of course figurative use of language in metaphor, for example, as well as providing an account of discourse at a level above the sentence. Pragmatics, and a Gricean approach in particular, is rather good at this. I agree. But why choose the canonical model of disinterested, non-figurative language in the first place? Surely that tells us something about the unconscious assumptions by Grice and others of the 'real' nature of language and what it is for?

19 I have always felt uneasy when theories based on 'the grammar' of language (which would extend to semantics, syntax and phonology) are extended to other areas in communication that are more continuous than discrete. There is a good case that linguistic units in grammar are both discrete and organised systematically in a hierarchy as Chomsky claimed. It is difficult to see what the grammar of a picture would be – what the discrete set of constituent parts would look like as well as the rules for acceptable, anomalous and unacceptable combinations. A pragmatic approach to visual communication would not have such a problem (see Forceville, op cit.).

20 Of course in textbook scientific research that is the way to do science – set up hypotheses based on general theory and then design experiments to challenge the hypotheses and try and falsify them. I get the strong impression, though, that in much of the research one does the experiment and then, as an afterthought a developmental psychologist like Piaget is brought in to support the results. 'That is what we expect from children because Piaget said this or that.'

21 These skills can be part of development through stages as suggested by Piaget and others or they can be acquired in a continuous or incremental way by learning what is appropriate.

22 Although I had met Mark Ritson and Richard Elliott before at conferences, it is fortunate that Richard now has a chair in marketing at the University of Exeter.

23 I had thought to cite Young (in preparation) Advertising Literacy but on second thoughts a set of chapter headings and a few notes on content is perhaps premature. But watch this space!

24 These ages are enshrined in legislative codes for all sorts of behaviour and differ from nation to nation. So children can drink alcohol in the UK from 18 years of age, but in most US states the age is 21 years. Similar artificial and variable boundaries exist with respect to attributing criminal intent to minors, being eligible for the death penalty, being able to vote, smoke or join the army.

25 Mean ages are meaningless without standard deviations – would median age be any better?

26 This argument comes up many times in psychology – knowing the facts does not mean that one will use the facts sensibly in practice. Providing parents with learning difficulties knowledge of 'parentcraft' does not mean they can use this knowledge in bringing up their own children. Teaching children how to cross the road safely in traffic does not mean they do this on the way home from school.

27 One could argue that it never stops and the various theses, Ph.D.s, research papers on 'decoding advertising' (which often are more complex than the advertisement itself) bear mute testimony to this. A complete understanding of advertising requires a Ph.D. and a lifetime of study!

28 I am indebted to Ricardo van der Valk, Department of Psychology (Economic Psychology), University of Tilburg, The Netherlands and Virginie Prat, Departement de Psychologie Sociale, Universite de Paris V for their ideas and work.

29 I have deliberately identified only some of the results and readers are advised to consult the original paper for more detail.

REFERENCES

Aloise-Young, P. A. (1993). »The development of self-presentation: self-promotion in 6 to 10-year-old children«, *Social Cognition*, 11(2), 201-222.

Bennett, M. and Yeeles, C. (1990). »Children's understanding of showing off«, *The Journal of Social Psychology*, 130(5), 591-596.

Belk, R. W., Wallendorf, M., and Sherry, J. F. Jr. (1989). »The sacred and the profane in consumer behavior: theodicy on the odyssey«, *Journal of Consumer Research*, 16, 1-38.

Berger, A. A. (1974). »Drug advertising and the pain, pill, pleasure model«, *Journal of Drug Issues*, 4, 208-212.

Bjurström, E. (1994). *Children and Television Advertising: A Critical Study of International Research Concerning the Effects of TV-Commercials on Children*. Stockholm: The National Swedish Board for Consumer Policies.

Bruner, J. S. *et al.* (1966). *Studies in Cognitive Growth: A Collaboration at the Center for Cognitive Studies*. New York: Wiley.

Donaldson, M. (1978). *Children's Minds*. London: Fontana.

Forceville, C. (1996). *Pictorial Metaphor in Advertising*. London: Routledge.

Gabriel, Y. and Lang, T. (1995). *The Unmanageable Consumer*. London: Sage.

Grice, H. P. (1975). »Logic and conversation«, P. Cole and J. L. Morgan (Eds.), *Syntax and Semantics 3: Speech Acts*. 41-58. New York NY: Academic Press.

Grice, H. P. (1978). »Further notes on logic and conversation«, P. Cole (Ed.), *Syntax and Semantics 9: Pragmatics*. 113-128. New York NY: Academic Press.

John, D. R. (1999). »Consumer socialization of children: a retrospective look at twenty-five years of research«, *Journal of Consumer Research*, 26(3), 183-213.

Keenan, E. O. (1976). »The universality of conversational implicature«, *Language In Society*, 5, 67-80.

Levinson, S. C. (1983). *Pragmatics*. Cambridge: Cambridge University Press.

Leymore, V. L. (1975). *Hidden Myth: Structure and Symbolism in Advertising*. London: Heinemann.

May, J. D. (1981). »Practical reasoning: extracting useful information from partial informants«, *Journal of Pragmatics*, 5, 45-59.

Packard, V. (1957). *The Hidden Persuaders*. London: Longmans Green.

Pateman, T. (1980). »How to do things with images: an essay on the pragmatics of advertising«, *Theory and Society*, 9, 603-622.

Ritson, M. and Elliott, R. (1995). »Advertising literacy and the social signification of cultural meaning«, *European Advances in Consumer Research*, 2, 1-5.

Ritson, M. and Elliott, R. (forthcoming). »A model of advertising literacy: the praxiology and co-creation of advertising meaning«, *International Journal of Research in Marketing*.

Selman, R. L. (1980). *The Growth of Interpersonal Understanding*. New York: Academic Press.

Sperber, D. and Wilson, D. (1986). *Relevance: Communication and Cognition*. Oxford: Blackwell.

Tanaka, K. (1994). *Advertising Language: A Pragmatic Approach to Advertisements in Britain and Japan*. London: Routledge.

Tannen D. (1984). *Conversational Style*. Norwood NJ: Ablex.

Vygotsky, L.S. (1962). *Thought and Language*. New York: Wiley.

Young, B. M. (1986). »New approaches to old problems: the growth of advertising literacy«, S. Ward and R. Brown (Eds.), *Commercial Television and European Children: An International Research Digest*. Aldershot, Hants.: Gower. 67-77 and 82-83.

Young, B. M. (1990). *Television Advertising and Children*. Oxford: Oxford University Press.

Young, B. M. (2000). »The child's understanding of promotional communication«, *International Journal of Advertising and Marketing to Children*, 2 (3), 191-203.

8

THE IMPACT OF CHILDREN'S AFFECTIVE REACTIONS
– ELICTED BY COMMERCIALS ON ATTITUDES TOWARD THE ADVERTISMENT AND THE BRAND

By Christian Derbaix and Joël Bree

INTRODUCTION[1+2]

This research investigates the impact of children's affective reactions elicited by TV advertisements on two essential indicators of advertising effectiveness: the attitude toward the advertisement (Aad) and post exposure brand attitude (A_{bp}).

Working with children as subjects, minimizing forced exposure and using a real program in which real commercials were embedded, were the authors' methodological choices. This offered a setting as naturalistic as possible to assess the impact of verbal as well as nonverbal affective reactions, the latter being measured through facial expressions.

It was clearly found that the evaluative judgments of the advertisement elements of execution – but not of the advertisement arguments – are instrumental in shaping children's Aad and A_{bp}. Verbal affective reactions, especially the positive ones, are important predictors of Aad and A_{bp}. The link between Aad and A_{bp} is significant both for known and unknown brands. The contribution of facial expressions is limited. Aad does not mediate the impact of affective reactions on A_{bp}. Finally, limitations of this study are pinpointed and issues for further research are offered.

Until the end of the 70's, research on the mechanisms of advertising influence on consumers essentially concentrated on the attitude toward the brand (A_b). The uppermost concern was the evaluative confrontation between the benefits the consumer was expecting and the perception he had of the brand's attributes. An advertisement was therefore essentially considered as acting on beliefs relative to brands.

It was not until the beginning of the 80's that a well-founded argument questioned this too rational approach (Mitchell and Olson 1981, Shimp 1981). The idea was based on two postulates. On the one hand, a consumer exposed to an advertisement will develop a specific reaction toward this advertisement. On the other hand, this particular response will influence the consumers' attitude toward the brand. In the following years, many studies validated this approach. They showed that the attitude toward the advertisement (Aad) played a mediating role between exposure to the advertisement and attitude toward the brand, even for highly involved individuals (Batra 1986, Batra and Ray 1986, Gardner 1985, Lutz 1985, Lutz et al. 1983, MacKenzie et al. 1986, Mitchell 1986, Park and Young 1986).

As far as children are concerned, studies concentrating on this connection are missing. The main contribution of the current study is a theoretical one, as it helps validate the existence of a link between Aad and A_b among children and first of all brings out the best predictors of both Aad and A_b. The second point is a methodological one. Emotional reactions upon exposure to the advertisement are measured in two ways: firstly through a classic verbal approach, and secondly through an observation of facial reactions. The conditions recreated in our laboratory were as close as possible to the exposure to advertisements in real life: we minimized forced exposure, the children were not aware they would see advertisements and not aware of being filmed while watching these advertisements which were embedded in a program especially conceived for them.

BACKGROUND

COGNITIVE AND AFFECTIVE REACTIONS ELICITED BY THE AD

The first studies on Aad concentrated on belief formation vis à vis the elements (hedonic or rational) that make up the advertisement (Belch 1982, Lutz 1985, Shimp 1981). Besides, the first paradigms proposed to elucidate the relationship between Aad and A_b consider advertisement cognitions (C_{ad}) as the only predictor of Aad (Lutz et al. 1983, MacKenzie et al. 1986). In parallel, and consistent with the ELM model of Petty and Cacioppo (1986), Lutz (1985) proposed four models of persuasion by connecting two levels of involvement concerning the execution with two levels of involvement concerning the message. In three out of these four cases, the only determinant of Aad is C_{ad}. In the fourth case (Pure Transfer), where the two types of involvement are low, it is the general attitude toward advertising.

Even authors who suggest that peripheral elements can influence both the formation of an attitude toward the advertisement and the Aad $- A_b$ relationship, do not escape from a predominant emphasis on evaluative predictors. For example, Park and Young (1986) demonstrated that music, while causing interference with message processing for those who were highly involved, facilitated the forming of an opinion of low involved individuals.

On the other hand, considering Aad as merely the consequence of an evaluation does not seem to be satisfactory for many researchers (Batra and Holbrook 1990, Batra and Ray 1986, Burke and Edell 1989, Edell and Burke 1987, Olney et al. 1991) who stressed the necessity of taking into account a more personal variable, encompassing all the Affective Reactions Elicited by the ad (AREAD) during the exposure.

To conclude, it seems that the attitude toward the advertisement can come from three main predictors (see figure 1), the respective weight of which seems relevant to evaluate: the central elements of the message, the peripheral elements of the message and the affective response elicited by the advertisement.

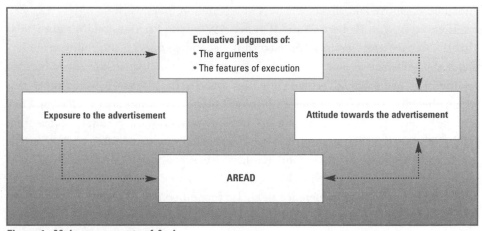

Figure 1. Main components of Aad

AFFECTIVE RESPONSES OF CHILDREN AS CONSUMERS

The idea that children's responses toward an advertisement may be organized around affective dimensions is not new. Observational studies and casual examination of children watching commercials revealed very often responses such as »that bores me« or »looking at it makes me feel good«. Even if the brand is presented very attractively, i.e. in such a way that it kindles the viewers' desires, the proposed benefit may often be considered of secondary importance.

What children seem to look for in an advertisement is a state of mind where special elements can be strong enough to generate a feeling of pleasure. For commercials as for other TV programs, positive or negative reactions will essentially depend on details such as the tone of voice, the presence of a small animal, an onomatopoeia that makes them laugh, … (Cullingford 1984). When the message interests them, their emotional reactions will immediately become intense: laughter, annoyance, mimicry, pleasure, … (Kapferer 1985).

Although many researchers underline the importance of children's affective reactions, a synthesis of thirty years of research (Brée 1993), revealed that the main conceptual frameworks have been theories of cognitive development and of social learning. The most contributive studies conducted during the 80s dealt indeed with cognitive abilities, information processing capacities and children's decision-making (Bahn 1986, Brucks et al. 1988, Macklin 1983, 1985, 1987a, 1994, Perrachio 1992, Poiesz 1986, Roedder 1982, Roedder et al. 1986, Roedder-John and Cole 1986, Roedder-John and Lakshmi-Rahan 1992, Roedder-John and Sujan 1990, Roedder-John and Withney Jr 1986, Soldow 1985, Ward 1986). Only van Raaij (1986) tried to integrate cognitive and affective factors in a common framework.

If we agree with Robertson and Rossiter (1976a) and Friedstad and Wright (1994) that the first defense against a commercial is a cognitive one, i.e. the ability to understand the informative and persuasive intents, we cannot reduce the (desirable) response of a child to an advertisement at this capacity. In this case, it would mean that when the affective response prevails it is because he/she is not able to develop consistent beliefs or counter-arguments. Children's reactions may simply differ from adults' reactions because their goals are different. Adults look at commercials – partially – for information purposes. Children have fewer reasons to do so. Finally a lot of differences in cues that are typically used by children and adults might as well be due to differences in style or preference than due to a difference in ability.

As underlined by Wartella (1984), both emotions and feelings will play a major role in explaining how persuasion works, especially with children. So, when an affective dimension is strongly linked to a given task, it will act as a catalyst which will reinforce the motivation to complete the task. By means of conjoint analysis, Brée (1987) showed that on an equivalent difficulty level, the child managed a higher degree of coherence in the trade-off between the different prices, brands and bonus proposed when he/she could get some benefit from it.

Also, Derbaix (1982) tested in the »hierarchy of effects« followed by the child after exposure to TV advertisements, that the affective factor was the dominant one. His model, called »the Emotional Reaction Hierarchy«, led him to successfully carry out experiments showing the following sequence till the third exposure: Affective → Conative → Cognitive on a sample of seven year old children. These results corroborate those of other studies demonstrating an increase of positive attitude toward the brand until the third contact and a levelling off or even a slight decrease thereafter (Goldberg and Gorn 1978, Gorn and Goldberg 1977).

As Roedder, Sternthal and Calder (1986) have shown, the strength of the last response serves to adequately explain some apparently »incoherent« reactions of the child. Indeed, these authors rightly put forward that coherent behavior occurs when the attitude associated with each alternative is mainly the result of an evaluative process. The incoherent children are those who will be mainly influenced by the last advertisement they have seen (even if by another way they have much more positive attitudes toward several other choices and even if they are aware of the selling intents of the commercials).

As far as children are concerned, there is a problem we do not have with adults: a possible confusion between Aad and A_b. According to Robertson and Rossiter (1976b), not before the age of 9 does a distinction appear between the attitude toward the brand itself, the attitude toward the brand as depicted in the commercial and the attitude toward the advertisement itself. This can lead to two opposite hypotheses for younger children: either there exists a natural strong correlation between the valences and intensities of these variables or the relationship appears by pure coincidence.

Although Goldberg and Gorn (1978) advocate that a negative attitude toward an advertisement could be associated with a similar attitude toward the product itself, the knowledge of the link between Aad and A_b for children remains more hypothetical than validated by empirical research. Some studies have concentrated on the influence of advertising versus non-commercial TV programs on children's requests (Resnik and Stern 1977, Ward et al. 1977). They showed the superiority of the former over the latter but without integrating important latent variables such as attitudes. Indeed a lot of intermediate variables can be put forward for explaining the results of these studies: the level of credibility associated to television, the fact that the brand is salient in the children's mind, cognitive dimensions like not mastering advertising language ... (Young 1986). However, things are perhaps changing.

THE MEASUREMENT OF AFFECTIVE REACTIONS

Several techniques allow the measurement of affective reactions in general and of emotional reactions in particular. The most common technique in marketing is the use of attitude scales. However there are other methods, such as the observation of facial reactions or even the measurement of physiological responses (sweating, heartbeat, pupil dilation, etc.).

Attitude scales are frequently used to collect information from children. Nevertheless, the absence of validated constructs, a lack of coherence in the number of points of the scales used and undependable methods of data collection can cast doubt on the results (Brée 1991; Macklin 1987b, Macklin and Machleit 1990, Mangleburg and Tech 1990, Rossiter 1977, 1978).

Nevertheless, this classical approach has numerous advantages. It offers the possibility of stressing the polarity, the intensity and the content of emotions. This is particularly true if one helps the respondent (by providing an explicit list of affective reactions) and if he/she does not use »display rules«, thereby voluntarily altering affective reactions. In addition, this method does not require sophisticated logistics and the format of the data makes their analysis much easier. But with this approach there is a lack of consideration given to impulse measurement as advocated by Kroeber-Riel (1979). When asked to verbalize an emotion, there is always the risk of rationalizing, interpreting or even modifying the real reaction. As underlined by Cohen (1991), subsequent responses are necessarily a mixture of affective and cognitive elements.

Among the most promising tools in the verbal approach is the one developed by Rossiter and Percy (1991). They proposed the use of 2×2 matrix combining an individual variable (high/low involvement with respect to the product) and a variable linked to the type of advertisement (aiming mainly to reduce a negative motivation or mainly to increase a positive motivation). Kover and Abruzzo (1993) applied this method and seemed to confirm its predictive validity.

The second and quite different approach is that of coding facial expressions. It has now been accepted that the face is home to a system of rapid, emotion-revealing signals (Ekman 1972, 1993; Ekman and Friesen 1978). As Derbaix wrote (1993, p.25): »The disguised observation of a motor behavior (facial expressions) offers the possibility of identifying affective reactions elicited by the advertisement (AREAD) in real time and in a non-reactive manner«.

The approach has also numerous advantages. It needs no retrospection, nor introspection, nor any other particular comprehension problem on the part of respondents. It also allows recording us the chronological appearance of emotions. As for the inconveniences, three seem important: the necessity to possess costly equipment to be able to film precisely and without being seen, complex decoding which entails long and difficult training and a low probability of being able to observe weak affective reactions.

Derbaix (1995) has compared the measurement of adults' emotional reactions to advertisements using this method of facial observations with the measurement of the same reactions using verbal measurement scales. The addition of these affective facial measurements to those obtained on evaluative responses (prior A_b, evaluative judgements on the elements of argument and on the elements of execution) did not improve the quality of the explanation of Aad, contrary to what happened when affective verbal measurements were added.

As for the third type of methods, psychophysiological measurements, Bagozzi (1991) pointed out their limits and deficiencies and the inability of most of them to gauge all the fundamental characteristics of affective reactions (intensity, polarity and content). In fact, reliable measurements have been obtained thanks to complex medical equipment, but this author clearly stressed that some are limited to intensity (psycho-galvanometer and electrical conductibility of the skin); others cannot reject alternative explanations (pupil reactions), or are focused on information processing methods (electro-oculography), or have many methodological deficiencies (voice loudness analysis), or are confined to demonstrating cognitive elaboration (electroencepha-lograph), or cannot measure affective reactions (cardio-vascular reactions), or finally need highly technical equipment to specify polarity and intensity (electromyographic activity). To the best of our knowledge, the only marketing research on children using this technique is that of Vitouch (1986).

Some methods can be considered as part of this category even though they only need very simple material (i.e. paper and pencil) such as the »Warmth Monitor« developed by Aaker, Stayman and Hagerty (1986). Vanden Abeele and MacLahan (1994) made measurements with this technique, but expressed doubts as to its efficiency.

As can be seen from the preceding arguments, none of the three approaches examined is devoid of deficiencies. As underlined by several authors (a.o. Derbaix 1993), the simultaneous use of verbal and non-verbal measurements serves to lessen their respective drawbacks. They are highly complementary to overcome at least partially their inherent bias. What is more, obtaining convergence between results from different methods strengthens the validity[3] and helps »to understand discrepancies among the different emotional responses« (Ekman 1993, p.386).

THE OBSERVATION OF FACIAL REACTIONS IN CHILDREN

The first condition to use a method based on facial expressions of emotions postulated to be universal is to admit that this thesis is one of the best plausible alternative. Since Darwin (1872) this idea was proposed by many researchers, but it was not until the work of Izard (1971), Ekman (1972) and Ekman, Sorenson and Friesen (1969) that the hypothesis of universality was adopted by numerous scientists.[4] However for Russell (1994) and others (including Klineberg (1940), Leach (1972) and Mead (1975)), the Universality thesis has not been definitely proven. In its most restrictive form, this thesis means the existence of separate specific facial configurations corresponding to the same number of separate specific emotions, easily recognized by all humans. In an insightful discussion of the extant literature, Russell (op.cit.) underlined methodological problems found in studies leading to the conclusion of the Universality thesis (pre-selected and posed facial expressions, forced-choice response format, previewing, within subject design, lack of contextual information, essentially western or westernized samples of respondents, …). Although we acknowledge that there are likely to be more than two alternatives (randomness and universality), we found the universality thesis a plausible alternative, available right now. Moreover we tried to minimize the above underlined deficiencies. We worked indeed with spontaneous and dynamic facial expression; we knew the expresser's context; the judges did not give a code to every facial expressions. Moreover partial coding of secretly videotaped faces illustrates the fact that our judges did not interpret facial expressions dichotomously[5]. Our coders were not found to be swayed by suggested labels. Our respondents and our judges were French speaking Europeans, i.e. peoples for which a »westernality« thesis applies. Finally working a child at a time and knowing the setting make it possible to disentangle face-emotion knowledge from face-situation knowledge.

Several methods for measuring facial expressions have been developed. The most complete is Ekman and Friesen's FACS (1978). Three others (much simpler to use) concentrate more specifically on the processing of emotions: Ekman, Friesen and Thomkins' FAST (1971), and Izard's MAX (1979) and Izard and Dougherty's AFFEX (1980). Can such methods based on coding facial expressions be used on children? The answer is definitively positive. Firstly, because facial musculature is completely formed at birth. And secondly, because at 18 months a child has acquired all basic emotions, with the possible exceptions of shyness and contempt which can only emerge much later (Lewis and Michalson 1983). There was therefore no problem concerning the children we were interested in (7-10 year old). This was all the more so as MAX and AFFEX are particularly suited for children as the support material, composed of photos, drawings or videos of children experiencing emotional reactions, illustrate. MAX is characterized more particularly by separate examination of three zones on the face: the forehead and eyebrows (zone 1); the eyes, eyelashes and the bridge of the nose (zone 2); the bottom of the nose, the mouth and the chin (zone 3). A code is given to each of these three areas, and from the combination of these codes an emotion or not is inferred. AFFEX, on the other hand, is more holistic and consists of examining simultaneously the three zones of the face and in seeking a correspondence (photograph) which represents an emotion.

In order to be able to code our children's facial expressions using Izard's methods, we implicitly adopt the »classical view« of emotions. Working within this »discrete view«, in which there are a finite number of fundamental affective states [Darwin (1872), Izard (1977) and others referenced by Lang (1994)], we have to realize that some facial expressions, for which there was no counterpart in Izard's material, were in fact not coded, or produced quite different coding from our judges. These facial reactions were thus not retained to be fed into our models. It is also possible that the manipulations (here the advertisements) to induce (pure) emotions produced, in fact, mixed emotions, decreasing the clarity of the signal. In contrast, Russell's prototype perspective presents the classical view as but an approximation to the inclusion relationships that hold within the emotion domain. His more »continuous view« states that »at the middle level, prototypical emotions shade into less prototypical emotions, which shade into non-emotions with no sharp boundary to be found. This level therefore contains an indeterminate number of categories from anger to zest. For the same reason, the number of subcategories into which middle-level categories can be divided is indeterminate. At a given level, categories are not mutually exclusive but overlapping« (Russell, 1991, p.38). Finally, it is quite possible that under some circumstances observers cannot go beyond a distinction between pleasant and unpleasant (Russell 1994, Woodworth and Schlosberg 1954).

TESTED MODEL AND HYPOTHESES

GENERAL DESCRIPTION

This research aims to replicate for children the work done by Derbaix (1995) for adults. The methodology followed is therefore similar. However, some of the measurements have been modified and strongly adapted to children. Involvement has been replaced by interest for the category of products since the concept of involvement has never been defined for children nor operationalized.

It is useful to recall that the general aim of the research was to validate a significant relationship between Aad and A_b for children and first of all to determine the explanatory power of each predictor of Aad and of a posteriori attitude toward the brand (A_{bp}). There was also a particular focus on the respective impact of verbal affective and facial affective variables.

Figure 2 illustrates the general model retained where NVAREAD means non verbal (facial) affective reactions elicited by the advertisement. Moreover, we also postulated the existence of a direct relation between the affective reactions elicited by the advertisement« and the attitude toward the brand. Considering the »hierarchy« identified by Derbaix (1982) and the possible confusion between Aad and A_b (Robertson and Rossiter 1976b), an affective halo could make AREAD a predictor of A_b, just like Aad or specific beliefs about the brand (see figure 2).

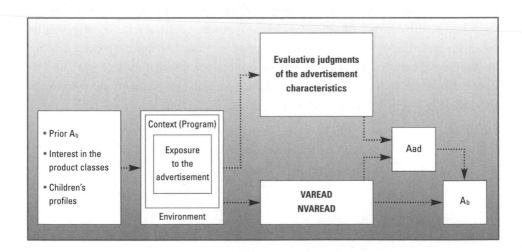

Figure 2. General framework of our research

HYPOTHESES

In order to study the relationships of our general framework, the following hypotheses were tested:

➤ **HYPOTHESIS 1:**

In the evaluation of advertisement characteristics by 7-10 year-old children, the elements of execution predict Aad better than the elements of argument do.

Considering commercials mainly as a show, even when he/she is aware of its informative and persuasive aims, does the child base his/her evaluative reactions on the message's elements of execution (story, music, characters, action, …) or on more rational elements of arguments? We postulate that Aad and persuasion mechanisms will essentially be based on peripheral processing.

➤ **HYPOTHESIS 2:**

The addition of affective reactions – verbal as well as facial – to the a priori attitude toward the brand and to the evaluation of the advertisement characteristics improves significantly the explanation of the attitudes toward the advertisement and the brand.

From what precedes, we do believe that affective reactions matter in explaining Aad and A_{bp}. Moreover, as stressed above, verbal affective reactions and non-verbal expressions of affective reactions do not tap – particularly with children – exactly the same aspects of common underlying constructs.

Finally in our quasi-naturalistic context and with our type of respondents we are convinced that affective reactions elicited by the advertisement are not overridden by attentive processing of advertisement characteristics as it may be in pre-test settings with adults as respondents.

➤ **HYPOTHESIS 3:**

The contribution of affective reactions, verbal as well as facial, to the explanation of Aad and A_{bp} is superior or equal to that provided by a priori attitude toward the brand and the judgments on the advertisement characteristics.

$H3_{bis}$. Moreover, with 7-10 year-old children, facial measurements of emotions, outperform verbal measurements of these emotions in predicting Aad and A_{bp}.

We postulate that facial observations give richer measurements than those obtained in adults by Derbaix (1995). The natural spontaneity of children, allied with weaker social checks when it comes to expressing an emotion (especially when they are not aware of being filmed), results in emotions triggered by stimuli such as commercials. From Izard (1977),[6] it could be anticipated that children show the pure facial expressions more often than adults. However, it seems more so for some emotions (joy, surprise, ...) than for others (fear) since it is rare that the minimum intensity threshold necessary to provoke such a (negative) reaction is reached with commercials.

Let us also stress that audio-visual material contains different dimensions able to evoke affective reactions and that most of the advertisements used in our research were unknown, so their ability to elicit varied affective reactions is greater than regularly aired advertisements. At this level, the researcher is facing a conundrum: natural and highly intense emotional elicitors are not feasible in the laboratory, for ethical and practical reasons, whereas recording close-ups of participants' facial expressions is a task that involves formidable practical problems outside a laboratory (Fernandez-Dols and Ruiz-Belda 1995, p.1114).

> ## HYPOTHESIS 4:
> Aad is a significant predictor of A_{bp}, especially in the case of unknown brands.

In accordance with Goldberg and Gorn (1978) and like Macklin (1988), we postulate the existence, in children, of a very strong relationship between the attitude toward the advertisement and the attitude toward the brand. Moreover, we agree with Robertson and Rossiter (1976b) concerning the confusion, which may arise between these two constructs for children, and we believe that the effects would be a reinforcement of the A_{ad}–A_{bp} relationship.

METHOD

Although we are dealing with affective reactions, our discourse will not be lyrical or poetic (Holbrook 1990) because our goal was not to thoroughly describe emotions in a study from an ethnographic type. As explained above our goal is to highlight the best predictors of Aad and A_b as well as the relationship between these two constructs. Therefore, the most suitable approach to achieve this goal is the experimental one.

SUBJECTS

Seven hundred and seventy children from 7 to 10 years were approached in class by four collaborators. From these 770 children, 152, whose parents agreed to come with them in our research center, participated in a lab-session a few days after having filled out a first questionnaire in class. They were evenly split as sex (74 boys and 78 girls) and age (age 7: 37; age 8: 34; age 9: 38; age 10: 43) are concerned.

STIMULI

We selected eight 30" commercials. Two were known advertisements for familiar brands (Contés' pencils and a video-game: Super Mario), three were unknown advertisements for familiar brands (Nesquik, Kitkat and Suchard) and three were unknown advertisements for novel brands (a parlour game, a candy and a more or less scientific magazine for children). From these eight commercials, two strings – differing in the fifth and sixth advertisements – were built on the following pattern: [X, G, H, I, A, B] with X and I as known advertisements for known brands; G and A unknown advertisements for known brands; H and B unknown advertisements for unknown brands. About 76 subjects were assigned to this string and 76 to a string differing only on the fifth and sixth advertisements which were also respectively an unknown advertisement for a familiar brand and an unknown advertisement for a novel brand. Half of the subjects in each of these groups (i.e. 38 subjects) were assigned to these strings presenting the advertisements in these orders and the 38 other children in each group were assigned to a string differing on the order of the last two advertisements. All this was achieved after the pre-test of our design, which led us to realize that questioning our young respondents thoroughly was possible only for the last advertisement they saw.

The advertisements were selected to cover a range of products particularly suited to our young respondents. Moreover, they had provoked among children during the exploratory research phase and among the eight people having collaborated in the building of the design relatively low variance in ratings of affective responses to the same advertisement (to »ensure« that the stimulus generated fairly homogeneous affective responses) and high variance across the different advertisements. The unknown advertisements (in France and in Belgium) came from Quebec and Switzerland where they were regularly aired. These unknown commercials were selected in order to be able to elicit the whole spectrum of affective reactions and were targeted at boys as well as at girls.

TV was selected on the basis that children when speaking of advertising spontaneously evoke this medium. It is also more adapted to the study of affective reactions (the subjects being in a situation where the likelihood of cognitive elaboration seems low due to the lack of control of the pace of diffusion). Finally, this medium is appropriate for the recording of facial expressions. These advertisements were preceded by a film (program).

PROCEDURE

When contacted (in class), our respondents were told that the study concerned their preferred TV shows, comic strips and a new type of program especially designed for them. Three or four days later, the child – generally accompanied by his/her mother – came to our research center. Our lab was designed to maximize a natural environment for children with posters of pets, various habitual objects, ... Each child saw, on TV, a film about a magician and then a string of six commercials similar to strings he could see while watching TV at home.

It should be noted that irrespective of the group to which the child was assigned (four groups of 38 children), the last two advertisements (on which they would be thoroughly questioned) are always preceded by the same four advertisements, thus minimizing the risk of a different »impact« of the first advertisements on the affective reactions elicited by the last two commercials.

We conducted a pre-test of our design to examine if it was realistic, if there were important problems of comprehension and if it was possible to work with two children at a time. This last option was disregarded on the basis that it is almost impossible to rule out the possibility that facial expressions of children viewing commercials in couples are at least partially elicited by the other child. So in our study, displays (of facial expressions) were recorded when the expressor (the child) was alone. These are the »least social« expressions,[7] leading to a spontaneous (as opposed to a voluntary) expression of genuine emotions. Otherwise stated, facial expressions can thus here be viewed as readouts or symptoms of underlying affective states (Hess et al. 1995, p.285). Of course working with a child at a time we are losing information about social factors as essential determinants of facial expressions (Hess et al. 1995). But otherwise it would have been impossible to disentangle the mere impact of commercials from that generated by the other child's reactions (as far as the origin of affective reactions is concerned). Moreover it was much more difficult to film very precisely their face when they were not alone. At a more technical level the film was slightly reduced in order to avoid a decrease in attention due to a too long program. During this film a collaborator (a girl) stayed and talked with the child to make him/her as comfortable as possible. She left the lab a few seconds before the commercials. After the pre-test, a few questions were reformulated and the one on beliefs was eliminated because it was clear that beliefs were created more by the questions than by the advertisement or any other sources. This pre-test was achieved with 25 children.

T1 In class	• Measurement of their interest in various product classes, of their general attitude toward TV advertising and of their a priori attitude toward various brands[24]
	• Socio-demographical profiles
	• Letter to the parents + reply coupon for an appointment in the Lab
	• Call for an appointment in the Lab
T2 Lab session	• Film, $[X, G, H, I, A, B]$ O_1 $[X]$ O_2 $[G]$ O_3 $[H]$ O_4 $[I]$ O_5 $[A]$ O_6[25]
	• O_1 = measurement of:
	– Aad 1 and Aad 2 for B;
	– their verbal affective reactions elicited by B;
	– their evaluative judgments of the arguments and of the elements of execution of B;
	– their attitude toward the film (several questions);
	– their posterior attitude toward brand B
	O_2 = Aad 1 and Aad 2 for X
	O_3 = Aad 1 and Aad 2 for G
	O_4 = Aad 1 and Aad 2 for H
	O_5 = Aad 1 and Aad 2 for I, bogus questions, posterior attitudes toward brands X, G, H and I
	O_6 = same as O_1 but for A (with questions about magy, tricks, ... before A_{bp} for A)
	• Permission asked to the parents to decode their child's recorded facial expressions
	• Gift: a comic strip

Figure 3, Final Design

With this kind of procedure, we are convinced that the treatment was »lived« in a natural way. Indeed the children did not know they would see TV advertisements at the end of the film. During the commercials, the respondents were not aware of being filmed[8] (by a camera behind a one-way mirror). At the end of the lab session, parent's permission to use their child's videotaped face was required in writing (in general the mother was with us in an adjoining production room where we saw the child on various screens and remote-controlled the camera). After the string of commercials (so after 10 minutes = 7 minutes of film and six 30" commercials), the collaborator came back in the lab for the first interview. At this moment, the respondent was asked about his/her Aad concerning the last advertisement he/she saw. After that, he/she completed the verbal affective reactions inventory followed by his/her evaluative judgments of the advertisement characteristics (arguments and executional features). Then they were asked several questions about the film and had to rate their post exposure attitude toward the brand advertised in the last advertisement. After that he/she was left alone to see a second time the first advertisement and was asked immediately after this second viewing his/her Aad for this advertisement. This procedure was repeated for the second, third and fourth advertisements of the string. For the fifth ad, after a second viewing, the procedure applied to the sixth advertisement was repeated (O_6 similar to O_1, see final design).

MEASURES

In T_1 (in class), besides the respondents' profile, we measured: the child's general attitude toward TV advertising (using the Rossiter scale), his/her (prior) attitude toward various brands (among which those that would be used in our lab session) and his/her interest in the product classes selected for our research (candies, video-games, …). This last variable was measured by the following questions: »If you have enough pocket money and can only buy one thing with it, which one would you choose«, »If you now have enough money to buy a second product, which one would you choose« and finally »If you have enough money to buy all these products, are there any you wouldn't buy? Which ones?«

The verbal affective reactions scale (hereafter VAR scale) was developed in the pilot study described above. Instructions for completing the inventory were as follows: »Here is a list of questions about the last advertisement you just saw. Please indicate how much you felt each of these affective reactions you have perhaps experienced while watching the ad«. Their answers to 13 verbal affective reactions[9] were recorded on a 4-point scale anchored by »Not at all« and by »A lot«. Before answering the VAR scale (in the laboratory), the child indicated his/her Aad in two different ways. Aad 1 was measured on a 4-point scale anchored by »I like this advertisement very much« vs. »I don't like this advertisement at all«. Aad 2 took into account a non-weariness dimension: »I would really like to see this advertisement again« vs. »I don't feel like seeing this advertisement again«. The instructions for completing evaluative judgments of the arguments were: »Now, I will ask you some questions about what you saw or heard in the last ad«. Three evaluations of the arguments (how informative, believable and helpful to understand the product they were) were measured along 4-point bi-polar scales. Using similar scales, the evaluations of the executional features were re-corded for the characters, the music, the colours, the story, the action and the level of complexity. A few questions were then asked about the film. Afterwards, their post ex-posure attitude toward the brand was measured in a classical way on a 4-point scale (I like Nesquik »not at all« … »a lot«).[10] As already said, this procedure was repeated for the fifth ad, after its second viewing. For the other advertisements in the string, the children only indicated their Aad – after a necessary second viewing – using our two scales as well as their A_{bp}.

The simplicity (number of points on each scale) and the number of items for each scale were based on the literature and on previous research with this type of young respondent.

CODING FACIAL EXPRESSIONS

Among others, Izard (1982), Ekman (1972, 1993) and Smith (1989) report support for the ability of distinct facial expressions to convey emotions. Considered as an organism's overt expressive behaviors, facial expressions tap purer affective reactions than verbal measures which are a mix of cognitive and affective reactions.

In our laboratory, filming facial expressions took the form of an unobtrusive im-pulse measurement, i.e. a continuous one-line monitoring technique not disruptive of cognitive and/or affective processes. Indeed, as opposed to verbal instruments, filming facial expressions allows for diagnosticity about how changes in message content and executional features affect facial expressions, e.g. emotional reactions. Moreover, we do not have with facial expressions some of the classical recall problems induced by ver-bal measurements: omitting (leaving things out), averaging (the tendency to normal-ize things and not to report extreme cases) and telescoping (inaccurate recall of time, problems related to the reporting of the sequence of experienced affective reactions).

More than a decade ago, Izard (1983) designed two complementary systems (MAX and AFFEX) for measuring facial expressions in infants and children. The eight primary emotions included in MAX are: interest, joy, surprise, sadness, anger, disgust, contempt and fear.

In our study, we used the precision of the MAX coding system while working with AFFEX a more holistic system. In fact, using MAX would have been much too long. We had to code eleven sequences of thirty seconds of facial expressions[11] for each of our 152 children, i.e. 836 minutes. Therefore, we advised our coders to look at the entire face and to code simultaneously two areas: the forehead, the eyebrows, the eyes and the nose on the one hand, the mouth and the chin on the other hand. During the coding sessions, all the codes and their corresponding faces (coming from Izard's material) were displayed on large boards in front of the coders to assist them. A specialist conducted six 2–hour training sessions before starting to code our material.

A classical coding session was as follows:

- the three coders[12] saw in »real time« the sequence and looked for changes in the child's face
- the patterns of change being identified, the coders decided in common about the start and the end of each pattern of change in the sequence
- then, taking a pattern of facial change at a time, they

  • stopped the tape at the place where the pattern of change was clearly apparent
  • identified the codes corresponding to the pattern and from these codes identified the corresponding affect
  • computed an interjudge reliability coefficient and to the extent that this coefficient was at least .66, computed a score for each identified emotion taking into account the duration of the pattern.

This way of working led to twenty-eight coding sessions of five hours. The technical details of this lengthy procedure – which was a mix of MAX and AFFEX – could be found in Izard (1983) and a complete description of these two complementary systems in Izard and Dougherty (1980).

RESULTS

DESCRIPTIVE RESULTS

We performed two principal component analyses in order to portray the structure of our fourteen[13] verbal affective variables: one in the case of known brands and one in the case of novel brands. Fifty percent of the variance was recovered with three factors for the known brands and 52 per cent for the novel brands. To construct our verbal affective scales, we took essentially into account the loadings on the axes. Disgust, anger, sadness, fear and positive surprise did not »load« at least .5 on any factor and were therefore eliminated in the case of known (familiar) brands. So was the case for disgust, anger and sadness for the novel brands.

Two clusters that could easily be interpreted as positive affective reactions (factor 1) and as negative affective reactions (factor 2) appeared in the two principal component analyses. Two isolated variables (boredom and non positive surprise) for the known brands and three isolated variables (boredom, non positive and positive surprise) for novel brands were kept, due to very important loading on a factor. The affective scales we formed are displayed in Table 1 along with their Cronbach α.

POSVR$_k$	Positive verbal reactions (amused, joyful, interested, happy and pleased) in the case of known brands (α = .84)
POSVR$_u$	Positive verbal reactions (amused, joyful, interested, happy and pleased) in the case of novel brands (α = .86)
NEGVR$_k$	Negative verbal reactions (nervous and anxious) in the case of known brands (α = .56)
NEGVR$_u$	Negative verbal reactions (nervous, anxious and fearful) in the case of novel brands (α = .61)
VRBO$_{k\ or\ u}$	Verbal reaction of boredom
VRNS$_{k\ or\ u}$	Verbal reaction of non positive surprise
VRPS$_u$	Verbal reaction of positive surprise

Table 1. Verbal Affective Scales

Our other independent variables are presented in table 2 along with our four dependent variables. The scale for arguments was formed by summing up the ratings of the three evaluative-items of message elements relevant to forming a »reasoned« opinion (appreciation of the claims). The same procedure was carried out for the elements of execution.

	Judgment scales		Dependent variables
AVARGEL$_k$	Average of the evaluative judgments concerning the arguments in the case of familiar brands (α = .67)[14]	Aad$_k$	Average of Aad 1 and 2 (α = .76)
AVARGEL$_u$	Average of the evaluative judgments concerning the arguments in the case of novel brands (α = .57)[14]	Aad$_u$	Average of Aad 1 and 2 (α = .82)
AVEXEL$_k$	Average of the evaluative judgments concerning the first 5[15] elements of execution in the case of familiar brands (α = .76)	A$_{bp_{k\ or\ u}}$	A posteriori attitude toward the brand
AVEXEL$_u$	Average of the evaluative judgments concerning the first 5[15] elements of execution in the case of novel brands (α = .79)		
EXEG$_{k\ or\ u}$	the sixth element of execution		

Table 2

As far as »Facial« variables are concerned, about 70% of the possible facial expressions were not displayed by more than one child and were thus eliminated. Facial expressions of joy, interest and to a lesser extend of fear, surprise and anger were the most frequently coded for the last two advertisements.

TEST OF THE HYPOTHESES

The primary purpose of our research is to test our hypotheses in a kind of setting, rarely used in studies reported in extant literature and for the first time with children for whom we had facial expressions. This was achieved through an analytical approach comprising the following models for Aad:

(1) Aad = constant + A_{ba} + the judgment scales *(evaluative model)*
(2) Aad = (1) + the verbal affective scales *(verbal affective and evaluative model)*
(3) Aad = (2) + the non-verbal (facial) affective reactions *(total model)*
(4) Aad = (1) + the non-verbal (facial) affective reactions *(facial and evaluative model)*
(5) Aad = constant + the verbal affective scales *(verbal affective model)*
(6) Aad = constant + the non-verbal affective reactions *(facial affective model)*
(7) Aad = constant + the verbal affective scales + the non-verbal affective reactions
       (total affective model)

In model (1) there is of course no A_{ba} for novel brands. Models (1) through (7) were also tested with A_{bp} as the dependent variable with the following theoretically-driven adaptation. In a second phase of analysis, we substituted Aad for the evaluative judgments of the advertisement elements in the equations explaining A_{bp} in order to test if the impact of affective reactions on A_{bp} was mediated by Aad.

Before estimating our models for known *vs.* unknown brands separately, we checked the relevance of this distinction. This was achieved by testing for the significance of interaction terms involving the known/unknown dummy variable (see details in appendix A). We first applied this procedure to a simplified version (for the known brands), i.e. dropping A_{ba}, of the evaluative model (1) explaining Aad[16]. The estimation of the *pooled* regression equation explaining Aad was achieved with AVAR GEL, AVEXEL and EXEG and as interaction terms these 3 predictors times D_i. The results showed that the evaluation of the elements of execution was highly and similarly significant in explaining Aad. We did the same for the explanation of A_{bp}, discovering a very slight difference: AVEXEL was highly significant in both cases but even more so for unknown brands.

Adding to this simplified evaluative model the verbal affective variables highlighted a significant difference for A_{bp}: verbal reaction of boredom was only significant in the case of unknown brands. One more time AVEXEL was more significant in the case of unknown brands in explaining A_{bp}. No difference emerged for Aad. Adding the non-verbal variables showed that the facial expression of interest at the first viewing was only slightly significant for Aad in the case of unknown brands whereas facial expression of joy at the first viewing was only significant for known brands. So on the basis of these results and also on the fact that the negative verbal reactions did not encompass the same variables for the advertisements of known brands (nervous and anxious) as for the advertisements of unknown brands (nervous, anxious and *fearful*)[17], it seemed advisable to test our models for known and unknown brands separately.

The first model estimated in the case of known brands was model (1). The R^2 was .403. The results of this very first estimation are reproduced hereafter.

TEST OF H1

Aad$_k$ = constant + A$_{ba}$ + AVARGEL$_k$ + AVEXEL$_k$ + EXEG$_k$						
10 cases deleted due to missing data.						
DEP VAR: Aad$_k$ N: 142 Multiple R: 635 Squared Multiple R: 403						
Adjusted Squared Multiple R: .386 Standard Error of Estimation: .569						
VARIABLE	COEFFICIENT	STD ERROR	STD COEF	TOLERANCE[18]	T	P(2 TAIL)
CONSTANT	0.596	0.395	0.000	.	1.512	0.133
A$_{ba}$	0.045	0.043	0.072	0.957	1.064	0.289
AVARGEL$_k$	0.009	0.061	0.010	0.878	0.146	0.884
AVEXEL$_k$	0.798	0.093	0.615	0.856	8.616	0.000
EXEG$_k$	-0.028	0.072	-0.025	0.995	-0.384	0.702

To the extent that, in the domain of affective reactions, predicting a sign of influence is somewhat hazardous, we worked with P(2 tail) in all our analyses. AVARGEL$_k$, A$_{ba}$ and EXEG$_k$ were not statistically significant but AVEXEL$_k$ was highly significant. The R^2 of the model: Aad$_k$ = constant + AVEXEL$_k$ was .398. In order to pinpoint the significant variables in all our estimated models (7 models × 2 types of brands × 2 dependent variables) a screening procedure was applied. This procedure based on three criteria (value of the t-test; ratio std/mean of each variable and tolerance) is detailed in appendix B and was applied to all our estimated models.[19] Applying this procedure *here* led to an equation where Aad$_k$ was explained by the sole AVEXEL$_k$ (R^2 = .398 and t-test = 9.729).

The ELM (Petty and Cacioppo, 1986) – which strictly applies to A$_b$ – contends that central processing is likely to occur only when advertisement receivers have the motivation and ability to process advertisement claims. Applying this model to the children's attitude toward the ad, it seems that our young respondents clearly followed a peripheral route.

For novel brands, the estimation of model (1) (Aad$_u$ = constant + AVARGEL$_u$ + AVEXEL$_u$ + EXEG$_u$) followed by the screening process, detailed above, led to a very similar result: AVEXEL$_u$ was the only significant variable (R^2 = .419, t = 10.256).

TEST OF H2

To test our second hypothesis, we estimated model (2) by adding the verbal affective reactions to model (1). For known brands, the squared multiple R jumped from .403 to .502. To test H2, first with model (2) (i.e. to see if adding verbal affective reactions led to a significant improvement of the explanation of Aad_k), we used the F_{ADD} (Kerlinger and Pedhazur 1973). This statistic tests whether the increase in R^2 from adding variables to a model is statistically significant. This first test was highly significant ($F_{ADD} = 6.56, p < .001$).

This procedure was applied – using models (1) through (4) – for familiar and novel brands and for our two dependent variables (Aad and A_{bp}). In three cases out of four, H2 was supported for verbal affective reactions. In fact, model (2) was a real improvement with respect to model (1), but model (3) was never a significant improvement with respect to model (2). Neither was the case for model (4) with respect to model (1). Table 3 summarizes the results of the test of H2.

Regression Results for H2				
R² comparison				
Dependent variables	Evaluative model (1)	Verbal affective and Evaluative model (2)	Total model (3)	Facial affective and Evaluative model (4)
Known brands				
Aad_k	.403(.403)	.502[b]	.520	.423
A_{bp_k}	.298	.330	.342	.302
Unknown brands				
Aad_u	.426(.423)	.546[b]	.554	.430
A_{bp_u}	.254	.324[a]	.327	.255

N.B. The significance of the increase of the R^2 of models (2) and (4) with respect to model (1) and of model (3) with respect to model (2) is reported at two levels: a p < .01 and b p < .001.

Table 3

For Aad_k and Aad_u we have in brackets the results without the evaluative judgments concerning the arguments among the explanatory variables.[20] For the total model (and for our whole sample of respondents) we add the facial expressions displayed during the first viewing[21] to the independent variables of model (2).

The screening processes applied to our different models highlighted $AVEXEL_k$ and Positive Verbal Reactions ($POSVR_k$) as the strongest predictors of Aad_k; a priori attitude toward the brand (A_{ba}) and $POSVR_k$ as the main determinants of A_{bp_k}. $AVEXEL_u$, Positive Verbal Reactions ($POSVR_u$) and the verbal reaction of positive surprise ($VRPS_u$) were the most significant predictors of Aad_u. For A_{bp_u} the screening processes essentially showed that $AVEXEL_u$, $POSVR_u$ and $VRBO_u$ (verbal reaction of boredom) were the most significant explanatory variables. Non-verbal reactions were almost never significant in explaining Aad or A_{bp}. As a tentative conclusion, it seems clear that the evaluative judgments concerning the elements of execution (except the sixth one) and the positive verbal reactions (amused, joyful, interested, happy and pleased) elicited by the advertisements are the underlying factors of advertising effectiveness. Let us also stress that the influence of these variables were in the directions expected, i.e. positive.

TEST OF H3

For H3, we used the J-test (Davidson and McKinnon 1981, see also Kennedy 1992, p.87). This test is designed to compare two non-nested alternative models. The J-test embeds the alternative models, i.e. the evaluative model (1) and the total affective model (7), into a general model. This test involves a two-stage estimation procedure. First the evaluative model is estimated and the predicted dependent variable from that model is inserted – with for example the total affective model – into a general model, which is in turn estimated. Then, this procedure is inverted[22], reversing the role of H0 and H1. When this is done, it is conceivable that both models (hypotheses) may be rejected or that neither of them be rejected. This procedure was applied to the comparison of the evaluative model (1) with the three affective models [(5), (6) and (7)] which of course share no independent variables with it.

As far as the attitude toward the advertisement is concerned, the J-test indicates that the evaluative and the verbal affective models were equivalent. For A_{bp_k}, presumably due to the weight of previous experiences (A_{ba}), the evaluative model outperforms the three affective models in explaining the post exposure attitudes toward known brands. For A_{bp_u}, the evaluative model was statistically slightly better than the verbal one when the format of the evaluative model was that of model (1). In an alternative formulation (A_{bp_u} = constant + Aad_u), we got the opposite result: the affective models (verbal and total) were better.

Summary of the results for H3				
R² of the models				
Dependent variables	Evaluative model (1)	Verbal affective model (5)	Facial affective model (6)	Total affective model (7)
Known brands				
Aad_k	.403(.403)	.419^e	.025	.427^e
Abp_k	.298(.302)	.146	.015	.159
Unknown brands				
Aad_u	.426(.423)	.505^e	.021	.520^e
Abp_u	.254(.175)	.230	.005	.236

N.B. The equality or superiority of models (5) to (7) with respect to model (1) (J-tests) is reported by e or s. e means equivalence of the model with respect to model (1).

Table 4

For Aad, in brackets, we have the results of the evaluative model without the arguments among the explanatory variables. For A_{bp}, in brackets we have the results of an alternative formulation of the evaluative model of known brands, $A_{bp_k} = $ constant + $Aad_k + A_{ba}$ and for novel brands, $A_{bp_u} = $ constant + Aad_u.

The results reproduced in Table 4 clearly illustrate that the facial affective model was the weakest. Let us stress one more time that we have here the facial expressions experienced during the first viewing of the last two advertisements, in order to get results based on the same number of respondents, i.e. 152, as those reported for the other models. So, $H3_{bis}$ was clearly not supported by our data.

Applying the screening procedure to the affective models led to show that:

- Positive Verbal Reactions and to a lesser extent Verbal Reaction of boredom were the best predictors of Aad_k. The first variable was also statistically significant in explaining A_{bp_k}.
- Positive Verbal Reactions and Verbal Reaction of Positive Surprise were highly significant in explaining Aad_u, the first variable being also a very good predictor of A_{bp_u}.

For model (6), facial reaction of joy (at the first viewing) was significant in explaining Aad_k. For Aad_u, facial reaction of interest was significant in model (6).

ADDITIONAL RESULTS

In this section, we will first detail the results of facial expressions displayed during the first *and* second viewing of the last two advertisements. Let us recall that the sixth advertisement (an unknown advertisement for a novel brand) was inverted with the fifth one (an unknown advertisement for a known brand) for half our subjects. Therefore, we had for each of the last two advertisements facial expressions displayed during a first *and* during a second viewing for 76 respondents.[23]

For the known and unknown brands, three facial expressions were coded at the second viewing: joy, positive surprise and interest. These variables were added to the independent variables of models (3), (4), (6) and (7). Applying the screening procedure, detailed above, led to the following results. With A_{bp_u} as dependent variable, the screening of model (4) left facial expression of interest (FEI2) among the highly significant variables. It seems thus that interest displayed at the second viewing of the advertisements for the unknown brands explained the a posteriori attitude toward these brands. In other words a second viewing seems necessary to elicit facial expression of interest, among our young respondents, that led to an impact on A_{bp_u}. This is reminiscent of the »what of it« question assigned to the second exposure by Krugman (1972).

Working with models (3), (4), (6) and (7) of Aad_u and with all our respondents (n = 152) displaying facial expressions at the first viewing, showed that FEI1 (facial expressions of interest) was among the significant explanatory variables of models (6) and (7). So the first viewing seemed to elicit facial expressions of interest explaining – *partially* – Aad_u and the second viewing elicited facial expression of interest explaining – *partially* – A_{bp_u}.

For the known brands, perhaps due to familiarization, facial expressions were never among the significant explanatory variables of A_{bp_k}. For Aad_k, facial expression of joy at the first viewing (FEJ1) was significant in a total model (7) with facial expressions displayed on both viewings and thus for half our sample (n = 76). This non-verbal variable was also significant in model (6) (the facial affective model) applied to our 152 respondents and in the same model with facial expressions displayed on both viewings (n = 76).

As a second point of this section, we will report the results obtained for the first four advertisements of the string. Let us remember that for these advertisements, we had as independent variables only facial expressions displayed at the two viewings plus prior A_b for the two known brands.

For the novel brand (an unknown brand of candies) the R^2 between Aad and the a posteriori brand attitude was .252, for the known brand of pencil .225, for

Nesquick .199 and for the video-game (very well known by our respondents) .539. This set of R^2 is not in line with what is found in the extant literature *for adults* where the link between Aad and A_b is greater for novel brands than for familiar brands. For these three known brands, prior A_b was a very good predictor of A_{bp} in the absence of verbal affective reactions elicited by the advertisements. If these results, as well as those reported above for our last two advertisements illustrate significant relationships between Aad and A_{bp}, *they do not support H4.*

Moreover, it appeared in regression analyses evoked in the previous section that when the VAREAD are with Aad in the models explaining A_{bp}, these verbal affective reactions remain significant. In order to assess that Aad does not mediate the effects of the affective reaction explaining A_{bp} and according to the method of Baron and Kenny (1986) a set of three regressions were used. First, for the known brands, the (supposed) mediator (Aad) was regressed on the independent variables (VAREAD). This model is the verbal affective model explaining Aad_k. Then the dependent variable (A_{bp_k}) was regressed on the independent variables (VAREAD) with also significant results and finally the dependent variable (A_{bp_k}) was regressed on both the independent variable (VAREAD) and the mediator (Aad). In this last regression the effect of the independent variables on the dependent variable was not significantly less than in the second equation (especially $POSVR_k$) and the supposed mediator was not significant. We did exactly the same for unknown brands with similar results except for the fact that Aad remained also significant. We also tried these regressions with only the significant verbal affective reactions explaining Aad and obtained the same results.

DISCUSSION

This study, conducted in as naturalistic a »setting« as possible, shows that affective reactions of children matter in assessing the effectiveness of advertising. Like previous studies (Edell and Burke (1987), Derbaix (1995)) adding verbal affective variables to evaluative models improves the explanatory capability of these models, though more so for Aad than for A_{bp}. Not surprisingly, positive verbal affective reactions elicited by the advertisements seem instrumental – with the evaluative judgments of the elements of execution – in shaping children's Aad and A_{bp}. So, as expected with such young respondents, persuasion is not strongly mediated by message – related thinking but by peripheral mechanisms, here from an affective type. In other words, elaboration – i.e. the extent to which children think about issue-relevant arguments contained in the advertisements – seems low. Moreover, the power of prior A_b to predict Aad for familiar brands is limited. This peripheral route to persuasion is regarded as more ephemeral than central route to persuasion (Petty and Cacioppo 1986). Previous researches (Rossiter 1977) indeed indicate that children's attitudes are not that stable or are not the main base of their choices (Roedder et al. 1986; Roedder-John and Lakhsmi-Rahan 1992).

As far as the impact and the use of facial expressions are concerned important things have to be underlined. Firstly, using Izard's material (especially suited to code children's facial displays) led us to implicitly adopt the categorical or classical view of emotions. This induces an underestimation of the impact of facial expressions by only coding the ones clearly corresponding to publish facial counterparts of a finite number of well-separated emotions. Facial expressions vary in their degree of exemplariness. Some expressions are prototypical examples, others are intermediate examples and still others are poor examples (Russell and Bullock 1986). So the task of the judges became increasingly complex as we move from clear signals to borderline cases, the first ones being the only ones included in our models.

Secondly, the approaches of Denzin (1984) or even the more radical behavioral ecology view of Fridlund (1994) were addressed in the design of the study, concretely leading to work one child at time. This choice has probably produced less facial displays. In a recent review Wagner and Smith (1991) showed that emotional facial expressions are facilitated by the presence of friends. As predicted by behavioral ecological theories of facial behavior (Fridlund op.cit.), some emotions are sometimes not sufficient alone for having a clear expression. They need »the help of« interactions with others. Further research will have to examine this issue by replicating a study like ours with at least a couple of children watching TV. However, in that case it will be impossible to attribute (only) to the advertisements the cause of the facial expressions.

Third, the limited impact of facial expressions can be due to inter-individual variability in the »expressiveness« of emotion, which by itself does not correlate with the intensity of »felt emotion«. It is admitted that temperamental factors contribute to the formation of unique individual response patterns. Even if children are more spontaneous than adults, they are different in their ability to suppress, exaggerate or distort their facial expressions. In addition each child has a unique history in relation to commercials and TV watching. *The* child watching TV does not exist. To attenuate this limitation, the use of unknown advertisements – to test our basic hypotheses – minimizes the possibility of children entering the experimental situation with varying levels of prior exposure to the stimulus commercials.

Moreover affective reactions can be shaped by a variety of environmental events, changing contextual demands, repeated exposures and settings. An experimental situation could not be an exact analogue to a real-life situation. We believe that our laboratory setting – which enables recording close-ups of facial expressions – was closer to a movie theatre than to natural in-home viewing. For children the difference between movie theatre and in home-TV viewing is perhaps not that great to the extent that TV is, for them, mainly a show to which they devote real attention. So the artificiality of our setting seems limited. The situation we tried to put our young respondents in was so interesting, involving and believable, i.e. one of experimental realism. However our elicitors (the advertisements) were not as highly intense as others encountered in everyday settings. Whereas other fields of research are perhaps able to reproduce easily their basic processes and variables in the laboratory, it is difficult to do so for »hot« psychological processes causing emotions equivalent to the ones experienced in natural settings. As far as limited exposure is concerned, it is quite possible that, at high exposure level, tedium or reactance is likely to develop, leading to an attack against the message and/or a decline in affect. Nevertheless, simultaneously we think that, in general, habituation is essentially positive for children (for a review see Brée, 1993). But more research is needed on the wear out pattern of children's affective reactions.

Finally, to the extent that the possibility of a shared method variance between *verbal* affective reactions and measures of Aad and of A_{bp} cannot be ruled out, the limited impact of on-line emotions measured by facial expressions can be explained. So, in future research, designing non-verbal measures of *dependent* variables should be a priority.

The variety (essentially joy, interest and to a lesser extent surprise, fear, anger and disgust) and particularly the number of decoded facial expressions were less than expected with such respondents for whom few display rules should soften facial expressions. But we have to stress that our respondents have perhaps more expertise, more »commercials' background« than their parents! In fact they spent numerous hours watching TV and commercials. Therefore it is not that easy to surprise them and/or to elicit strong affective reactions.

Additionally, an unexpected finding emerges from our research. Aad does not mediate the impact of verbal affective reactions on A_{bp}. Our respondents and our pseudo-naturalistic setting offer perhaps the conditions for the manifestation of a »superior order affect mechanism« to take place. In that case, verbal affective predictors are the dominant ones.

Finally, the results concerning facial expressions are not as disappointing as they appear at first sight. Assessment of emotions through coding facial expressions is of course demanding for the researchers but not at all for the consumers. This procedure might be taken into account when pre-testing advertisements, especially with children whose cognitive capacities are more limited. Three examples illustrate this suggestion. Facial expressions of joy (for KitKat), of interest (for Nesquik), of fear and disgust (for a parlour game: »the night of the vampires«) gave measurements revealing attractive (the first two) and repulsive (the third one) advertisements.

LIMITATIONS

The above detailed findings must be tempered by a few limitations.

Our setting was designed to get uninhibited and unmodulated facial expressions. Nevertheless our coding procedure rests on the Universality thesis, which has not been definitely proven. Working with one child at a time we missed the opportunity to work in a context where emotions and facial expressions are mainly determined by social factors. Third, children don't often watch television alone in a non-home location. Fourth, single exposure is not the normal form of children's commercial experience. Finally and at a more peripheral level, all our results were achieved with the variables of tables 1 and 2, among which some are associated with alphas, which are not as high as desired.

CONCLUSION

This research shows that when children are exposed to commercials, the way they evaluate the elements of execution is a better predictor of their Aad than their evaluation of the elements of argument. However, considering only this evaluative dimension was not enough to obtain a good explanation of Aad and it was necessary to include affective reactions elicited by the advertisement. Finally, a significant relationship was found for the child between Aad and A_b. So, our basic hypothetical model (see figure 2) is globally validated.

The other aim of the study was a methodological one, i.e. to discover the most relevant way to measure affective reactions elicited by the advertisement. We clearly showed that, even if not free from biases, verbal measurement outperforms the coding of facial expressions in explaining the attitudes of children toward the advertisement and the brand. Despite this result, it is surely premature to conclude that facial measurement comes to a deadlock. Moreover it is perhaps a conceptual confusion to consider at the same level verbal and non verbal (facial) measurements. In fact in this study, facial emotional expressions only concern strong (prototypical) reactions at clearly definite moments during exposure whereas verbal affective responses constitute an a posteriori global response. So these two types of measurement do not tap exactly the same construct and are not made at the same moment: one is intermittent and the other not. By estimating the emotional reactions with facial expressions we probably do not directly consider one component of the attitude toward the ad, but at best one component of the total affective reactions elicited by the advertisement. In that case, our facial measures would be predictors of our verbal measures, as well as our verbal measures are predictors of the children's Aad. The other predictors of the global affective reactions would be milder (less prototypical) reactions (than the observed emotions) which could perhaps be measured during the exposure through physiological devices. Consequently it seems that the next step to understand the child's attitude toward the advertisement should be the test of the following conceptual model (see figure 4).

Figure 4. Proposed Conceptual Model of the Forming of Children's Aad

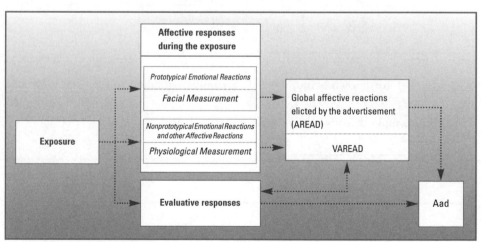

APPENDIX A

TESTING FOR THE SIGNIFICANCE OF INTERACTION TERMS INVOLVING THE KNOWN/UNKNOWN DUMMY VARIABLE

The model with the dummy and with one predictor can be formulated as:

$$\tilde{y}_i = (\beta_0 + \gamma_0 . D_i) + \beta_1 . x_i + \gamma_1 (x_i . D_i) + \tilde{u}_i$$

with: $D_i = 1$ for known brand; $D_i = 0$ for unknown brand.

If $\gamma_0 = 0$ and $\gamma_1 \neq 0$, we have a difference in slope[26].
If $\gamma_0 \neq 0$ and $\gamma_1 = 0$, we have a difference in intercept.
If $\gamma_0 \neq 0$ and $\gamma_1 \neq 0$, we have a difference both in slope and intercept.

In the general case for k independent variables the model with the Dummy (D) is:

$$\tilde{y}_i = \sum_{j=0}^{k} \beta_j . x_{ij} + \sum_{j=0}^{k} \gamma_j (x_{ij} . D_i) + \tilde{u}_i$$

with: $D_i = 1$ for known brand; $D_i = 0$ for unknown brand and $x_{i,o} = 1$, for all i.

For the subsample of known brands ($D_i = 1$), we have:

$$\tilde{y}_i = \sum_{j=0}^{k} (\beta_j + \gamma_j) . x_{ij} + \tilde{u}_i$$

For the subsample of unknown brands ($D_i = 0$), we have:

$$\tilde{y}_i = \sum_{j=0}^{k} \beta_j . x_{ij} + \tilde{u}_i$$

APPENDIX B

KEEPING OR ELIMINATING EXPLANATORY VARIABLES

Rule	Value of the t-test	Ratio: standard deviation/Mean (of the variable)	Tolerance	Decision
n° 1	Low	Low	• never mind • if high it is really »one of the worst« variables	To rule out this variable (without consequence on the other paramaters to be estimated)
n° 2	Low	High	High (no collinearity)	To rule out (this variable is an outsider; extraneous to the topic; nothing to do with the dependent and the other independents)
n° 3	Low	High	Low (collinearity)	Do no rule out in the first phases of the screening process
n° 4	High	High (or rather low)	High (no collinearity)	To be kept; most accurate estimations in this case
n° 5	High	High or low	Low (collinearity)	To be kept; less accurate estimations

Source: Bultez and Derbaix in C. Derbaix (1993)

NOTES

1   Reprinted from *International Journal of Research in Marketing*,Vol 14, No 3, Christian Derbaix and Joël Bree,The impact of children's affective reactions elicited by commercials on attitudes toward the advertisement and the brand, Page 207-229, Copyright (1997), with permission from Elsevier Science.

2   The authors are indebted to Christine Plasschaert, Catherine Chéné and Olivier Marlot for their invaluable assistance during data collection and analysis and to Luk Warlop for insightful comments on an earlier draft.

3   Vitouch (1986) had also completed his physiological measurements with verbal data.

4   For a complete review on the universality of facial expressions, see Ekman (1989, 1993) and Russell (1994).

5   Our coders did not interpret the whole facial expression (see hereunder) but its component actions.

6   See Oster et al (1989) and Camras (1992) for another point of view.

7   For Denzin (1984, p.407) »Emotions are interactive processes best studied as social acts involving self and other interactions«.

8   To the extent that children are able of suppressing, falsifying and distorting their facial expression.

9   Amused, nervous, anxious, joyful, interested, happy, disgusted, angry, annoyed, sad, fearful, pleased and surprised.

10 As their a priori attitude toward the brand (A_{ba}) measured 3 or 4 days before participating in the lab session in order to minimize an interaction with the treatment.

11 The six advertisements + the first five seen a second time.

12 These persons and one of the authors spent more than a week with Izard's training tapes concerning the Maximally Discriminative Facial Movement Coding System (MAX) under the guidance of a specialist.

13 Surprise was polarised by the respondent himself (herself) or more exactly precised as being positive, neutral or negative. Very few respondents used this third option. In our final analysis achieved with respondents for whom we had almost all the data, we used the label non positive surprise for neutral and negative surprise.

14 Principal component analyses on the three elements of arguments clearly showed the unidimensionnality of this new construct.

15 Principal component analyses on the elements of execution clearly showed that the first five elements load on the first factor and the sixth one on a second axis.

16 In order to use the standard way in which a moderator variable is tested for (e.g. Baron and Kenny 1986), we have to work with predictors that are simultaneously present for known and unknown brands.

17 See descriptive results.

18 Tolerance is one minus the squared multiple correlation between each predictor and the remaining predictors in the equation. Low values of tolerance indicate that some of the predictors are highly intercorrelated.

19 This led to eliminating one variable at a time and re-estimating (each time) the equation until all the predictors were significant ($P(2$ tail$) \leq .10$).

20 So these models are: Aadk = constant + AVEXELk + EXEGk + A_{ba} and Aad$_u$ = constant + AVEXELu + EXEGu.

21 Only half the sample (those who saw an unknown advertisement for a known brand or for an unknown brand in the fifth place in the string) displayed twice facial expressions for the fifth advertisement.

22 On the basis that a t-statistic which is valid for testing the truth of a model is not valid for testing the truth of the alternative model.

23 In fact, as stated above, there were for advertisement A two unknown advertisements for two known brands, each of these advertisements seen respectively by half the subjects. So was the case for advertisement B (i.e. there were two unknown advertisements, each for two unknown brands).

24 The ones they will see in the lab session (if they come) plus several others.

25 During the string and a second time for X, G, H, I and A the children's facial expressions were recorded.

26 Note that observing a difference in slope would necessarily lead to observing a difference in the intercept.

REFERENCES

Aaker, Davis A., Douglas M. Stayman and Michael R. Hagerty (1986). »Warmth in Advertising: Measurement, Impact, and Sequence Effects«, *Journal of Consumer Research*, 12, March, 365-381.

Bagozzi, Richard P. (1991). »The role of Psychophysiology in Consumer Research«, in *Handbook of Consumer Behavior*, ed. Thomas S. Robertson and Harold H. Kassarjian, Englewood Cliff, NJ: Prentice Hall, 124-161.

Bahn, Kenneth D. (1986). »How and When Do Brand Perceptions and Preferences First Form? A Cognitive Developmental Investigation«, *Journal of Consumer Research*, 13, December, 382-393.

Baron Reuben M. and David A. Kenny (1986). »The moderator-mediator variable distinction in Social Psychological Research: Conceptual, Strategic and Statistical Considerations«, *Journal of Personality and Social Psychology*, 51 (6), 1173-1182.

Batra, Rajeev (1986). »Affective Advertising: Role, Processes, and Measurement«, in *The Role of Affect in Consumer Behavior*, ed. Robert A. Peterson et al., Lexington, MA: Heath, 53-85.

Batra, Rajeev and Michael L. Ray (1986). »Affective Response Mediating Acceptance of Advertising«, *Journal of Consumer Research*, 12, June, 234-249.

Batra, Rajeev and Morris B. Holbrook (1990). »Developing a Typology of Affective Responses to Advertising«, *Psychology and Marketing*, 7, 11-25.

Belch, George E. (1982). »The Effects of Television Commercial Repetition on Cognitive Response and Message Acceptance«, *Journal of Consumer Research*, 13, September, 234-249.

Brée, Joël (1987). »L'Enfant et le Processus de Consommation: l'Utilisation des Attributs »Marque, Prix et Prime« dans l'Acte d'Achat«, *Recherche et Applications en Marketing*, 2 (2), 1-29.

Brée, Joël (1991). »Quelques Problèmes de Choix d'Echelles pour Mesurer les Attitudes Chez les Enfants«, *Recherche et Applications en Marketing*, 6 (4), 27-58.

Brée, Joël (1993). *Les Enfants, la Consommation et le Marketing*, Paris: Presses Universitaires de France.

Brucks, Merrie, Gary M. Armstrong and Marvin E. Goldberg (1988). »Children's Use of Cognitive Defenses Against Television Advertising: a Cognitive Response Approach«, *Journal of Consumer Research*, 14, March, 471-482.

Burke, Marian C. and Julie A. Edell (1989). »The Impact of Feelings on Ad-Based Affect and Cognition«, *Journal of Marketing Research*, 26, February, 69-83.

Camras, L. (1992). »A dynamic systems perspective on expressive development«, in K. Strongman (Ed.), *International Review of Studies on Emotion*, New York: Wiley, 16-28.

Cohen, Joel B. (1991). in »Tears, Cheers and Fears: The Role of Emotions in Advertising«, Conference Summary prepared by Carolyn Yoon, Duke University, May.

Cullingford, Cedric (1984). *Children and Television*, Avebury: Gower Publishing Company.

Darwin, Charles (1965). *The Expression of Emotions in Men and Animals*, Chicago: University of Chicago Press (original edition, 1872).

Davidson, R. and J.G. MacKinnon (1981). »Several Tests for Model Specification in the Presence of Alternative Hypotheses«, *Econometrica*, 49, 781-793.

Denzin, Norman K. (1984). »Reply to Baldwin«, *American Journal of Sociology*, September, 90, 2, pp. 423-427.

Derbaix, Christian (1982). »L'Enfant, la Communication Publicitaire et la Hiérarchie des Effets«, *Revue Française du Marketing*, Cahier 89, 31-47.

Derbaix, Christian (1993). *La Mesure de l'Emotionnel et de l'Affectif dans la réception des Messages Publicitaires*, Paris: IREP.

Derbaix, Christian (1995). »The Impact of Affective Reactions on Attitudes toward the advertisement and the brand: A step toward ecologicial validity«, *Journal of Marketing Research*, 32, November, 470-479.

Edell, Julie A. and Marian C. Burke (1987). »The Power of Feelings in Understanding Advertising Effects«, *Journal of Consumer Research*, 14, December, 421-433.

Ekman, P., Sorenson, E.R. and Friesen, W.V. (1969). »Pan-cultural elements in the facial displays of emotions, *Science*, 164, 86-88.

Ekman, Paul (1972). »Universal and Cultural Differences in Facial Expressions of Emotions«, in *Nebraska Symposium on Motivation*, n° 19, ed. J.K. Cole, Lincoln: University of Nebraska Press, 207-228.

Ekman, Paul (1989). »The Argument and Evidence About Universals in Facial Expressions of Emotion«, in *Handbook of Social Psychophysiology*, ed. H. Wagner and A. Manstead, Chichester, England: Wiley, 143-164.

Ekman, Paul (1993). »Facial Expression and Emotion«, *American Psychologist*, April, 384-392.

Ekman, Paul and Wallace V. Friesen (1978). *Facial Action Coding System*, Palo Alto, The Consulting Psychologists Press.

Ekman, Paul, Wallace V. Friesen and S.S. Thomkins (1971). »Facial Affect Scoring Technique: A First Validity Study«, *Semiotica*, 3 (1), 37-58.

Fernández-Dols, José-Miguel and María-Angeles Ruiz-Belda (1995). »Are Smiles a Sign of Happiness? Gold Medal Winners at the Olympic Games«, *Journal of Personality and Social Psychology*, 69, 6, 1113-1119.

Fridlund, A.J. (1994). *Human Facial Expression: An Evolutionary View*, San Diego, CA: Academic Press.

Friedstad Marian and P. Wright (1994). »The Persuasion Knowledge Model: How People Cope with Persuasion Attempts«, *Journal of Consumer Research*, 21, June, 1-31.

Gardner, Meryl P. (1985). »Does Attitude Toward the Advertisement Affect Brand Attitude under a Brand Evaluation Set?«, *Journal of Marketing Research*, 22, May, 192-198.

Goldberg, Marvin E. and Gerald J. Gorn (1978). »Some Unintended Consequences of TV Advertising to Children«, *Journal of Consumer Research*, 5, June, 22-29.

Gorn, Gerald J. and Goldberg Marvin E. (1977). »The Impact of Television Advertising on Children from Low Income Families«, *Journal of Consumer Research*, 4, September, 86-88.

Hess Ursula, Rainer Banse and Arvid Kappas (1995). »The Intensity of Facial Expression is determined by Underlying Affective State and Social Situation«, *Journal of Personality and Social Psychology*, 69, 2, 280-288.

Holbrook, Morris B. (1990). »The Role of Lyricism in Research on Consumers Emotions: Sky-
  lark, Have You Anything to Say to Me«, *Advances in Consumer Research*, Vol. 17, in M. Goldberg,
  G. Gorn and R. W Pollay Ed., New Orleans, Louisiana, 1-18.
Izard, Caroll E. (1971). *The Face of Emotion*, New York, Appleton Century Crofts.
Izard, Caroll E. (1977). *Human Emotions*, New York: Plenum Press.
Izard, Caroll E. (1979). *The Maximally Discriminative Facial Movement Coding System (MAX)*, Un-
  published Manuscript (Available from Instructional Resource Center, University of Delaware,
  Newark, DE).
Izard, C. and L. M. Dougherty (1980). *A System for Identifying Affect Expressions by Holistic Judgments
  (Affex)*, Newark: Instructional Resources Center, University of Delaware.
Izard, Caroll E. (1982). *Measuring Emotions in Infants and Children*, Cambridge: Cambridge Univer-
  sity Press.
Izard, Caroll E. (1983). *The Maximally Discriminative Facial Movement Coding System* (Rev.ed.),
  Newark, DE: Instructional Resources Center.
Kapferer, Jean-Noël (1985). *L'Enfant et la Publicité*, Paris: Dunod.
Kennedy, Peter (1992). *A Guide to Econometrics*, 3rd ed., The MIT Press, Massachussets.
Kerlinger Fred N. and Elazar J. Pedhazur (1973). *Multiple Regression in Behavioral Research*, New
  York: Holt Rinehart and Winston.
Klineberg, O. (1940). *Social Psychology*, New York: Holt.
Kover, Arthur J. and Joseph Abruzzo (1993). »The Rossiter-Percy Grid and Emotional Response
  to Advertising: an Initial Evaluation«, *Journal of Advertising Research*, 33, November-December,
  21-27.
Kroeber-Riel, Werner (1979). »Activation Research: Psychobiological Approaches in Consumer
  Research«, *Journal of Consumer Research*, 5, March, 240-250.
Krugman, Herbert E. (1972). »Why three Exposures may be Enough«, *Journal of Advertising Re-
  search*«, 12, 6, December, 11-14.
Lang, Peter J. (1994). »The Varieties of Emotional Experience: A Meditation on James-Lange The-
  ory«, *Psychology Review*, 1101, 2, 210-221.
Leach, E. (1972). »The influence of cultural context on nonverbal communication in man«, in R.
  Hinde (Ed.), *Nonverbal communication*, Cambridge, England: Cambridge University Press, 212-
  227.
Lewis, Michael and L. Michalson (1983). *Children's Emotions and Moods: Developmental Theory and
  Measurement*, New York, Plenum Press.
Lutz, Richard J. (1985). »Affective and Cognitive Antecedents of Attitude Toward the Ad: a Con-
  ceptual Framework«, in *Psychological Processes and Advertising Effects: Theory, Research and Applica-
  tion*, ed. Linda F. Alwitt and Andrew A. Mitchell, Hillsdale, NJ: Lawrence Erlbaum Associates
  Publishers, 45-63.
Lutz, Richard J., Scott B. MacKenzie and George Belch (1983). »Attitude Toward the Advertise-
  ment as a Mediator of Advertising Effectiveness: Determinants and Consequences«, *Advances in
  Consumer Research*, vol.10, ed. Richard P. Bagozzi, Ann Arbor, MI: Association for Consumer
  Research, 532-539.
MacKenzie, Scott B., Richard J. Lutz and George E. Belch (1986). »The Role of Attitude Toward
  the Advertisement as a Mediator of Advertising Effectiveness: A Test of Competing Explana-
  tions«, *Journal of Marketing Research*, 23, May, 130-143
Macklin, Carole M. (1983). »Do Children Understand TV Advertisements?«; *Journal of Advertising
  Research*, 23 (1), 63-70.
Macklin, Carole M. (1985). »Do Young Children Understand the Selling Intent of Commercials?«,
  Journal of Consumer Affairs, 19 (2), 293-304.

Macklin, Carole M. (1987a). »Preschoolers' Understanding of the Informational Function of Television«, *Journal of Consumer Research*, 14, September, 229-239.

Macklin, Carole M. (1987b). »The Effects of Question Form and Format on Children's Responses to Television Advertising«, *Advances in Consumer Research*, vol.14, ed. Melanie Wallendorf and Paul Anderson, Provo, UT: Association for Consumer Research, 293-297.

Macklin, Carole M. (1988). »The Relationship Between Music in Advertising and Children's Responses: an Experimental Investigation«, in *Nonverbal Communication in Advertising*, ed. David W. Stewart and Sydney Hecker, Lexington, Mass.: Lexington Books, 225-252.

Macklin, Carole M. (1994). »The Impact of Audiovisual Information on Children's Product-Related Recall«, *Journal of Consumer Research*, 21, June, 154-164.

Macklin, Carole M. and Karen A. Machleit (1990), »Measuring Preschool Children's Attitude«, *Marketing Letters*, 1-3, 253-265.

Mangleburg, Tamara F. and Virginia Tech (1990). »Children's Influence in Purchase Decisions: A Review and Critique«, *Advances in Consumer Research*, vol.17, ed. Marvin Goldberg, Gerald Gorn and Marvin Goldberg, Provo, UT: Association for Consumer Research, 813-825.

Mead, M. (1975). Review of »Darwin and facial expression«, *Journal of Communication*, 25, 209-213.

Mitchell, Andrew A. (1986). »The Effects of Visual and Verbal Components of Advertisements on Brand Attitudes and Attitudes Toward the Advertisement«, *Journal of Consumer Research*, 13, June, 12-24.

Mitchell, Andrew A. and Jerry C. Olson (1981). »Are Product Attribute Beliefs the Only Mediator of Advertising Effects on Brand Attitudes?«, *Journal of Marketing Research*, 18, August, 318-322.

Olney, Thomas J., Morris B. Holbrook and Rajeev Batra (1991). »Consumer Responses to Advertising: The Effects of Advertisement Content, Emotions, and Attitude Toward the Advertisement on Viewing Time«, *Journal of Consumer Research*, 17, March, 440-453.

Oster, H., L. Daily and P. Goldenthal (1989). »Processing facial affect«, in A. W. Young & H.D. Ellis (Eds.), *Handbook of research on face processing*, Amsterdam: Elsevier, 107-161.

Park, C. Whan and S. Mark Young (1986). »Consumer Response to Television Commercials: the Impact of Involvement and Background Music on Brand Attitude Formation«, *Journal of Marketing Research*, 23, February, 11-24.

Peracchio, Laura A. (1992). »How Do Young Children Learn To Be Consumers?: A Script Processing Perspective«, *Journal of Consumer Research*, 16, March, 425-440.

Petty, Richard E. and John T. Cacioppo (1986). *Communication and Persuasion: Central and Peripheral Routes to Attitude Change*, New York: Springer-Verlag.

Poiesz, Théo B. (1986). »Children's Relationships Between Repetition and Affect: Theory, Research and Policy Implications«, in *Commercial Television and European Children*, ed. Scott Ward, Thomas S. Robertson and Ray Brown, Avebury: Gower Publishing Company, 55-66.

Resnik, Alan and Bruce L. Stern (1977). »Children's Television Advertising and Brand Choice: A Laboratory Experiment«, *Journal of Advertising*, 6, Summer, 11-17.

Robertson, Thomas S. and John R. Rossiter (1976a). »Short Run Advertising Effects on Children: a Field Study«, *Journal of Marketing Research*, 13, February, 68-70.

Robertson, Thomas S. and John R. Rossiter (1976b). *Attitude Theory and Children's Consumer Behavior*, Draft for AMA Attitude Research Conference, Hilton Head, South Carolina.

Roedder, Deborah L. (1982). »Understanding and Overcoming Children's Processing Deficits«, *Advances in Consumer Research*, vol.9, ed. Andrew Mitchell, Ann Arbor, MI: Association for Consumer Research, 148-152.

Roedder, Deborah L., Brian Sternthal and Bobby J. Calder (1986). »Attitude Behavior Consistency in Children's Response to Television Advertising«, *Journal of Marketing Research*, 20, November, 337-349.

Roedder-John, Deborah and Catherine A. Cole (1986). »Age Differences in Information Processing: Understanding Deficits in Young and Elderly Consumers«, *Journal of Consumer Research*, 13,
December, 297-315.

Roedder-John, Deborah and John C. Withney Jr (1986). »The Development of Consumer
Knowledge in Children: a Cognitive Structure Approach«, *Journal of Consumer Research*, 12,
March, 406-417.

Roedder-John, Deborah and Mita Sujan (1990). »Age Differences in Product Categorization«,
Journal of Consumer Research, 16, March, 452-460.

Roedder-John, Deborah and Ramnath Lakshmi-Rahan (1992). »Age Differences in Children's
Choice Behavior: the Impact of Available Alternatives«, *Journal of Marketing Research*, 29, May,
216-226.

Rossiter, John R. (1977). »Reliability of a Short Test Measuring Children's Attitudes Toward TV
Commercials«, *Journal of Consumer Research*, 3, September, 179-184.

Rossiter, John R. (1978). »Children's Consumer Research: A Call for Rigor«, *Advances in Consumer
Research*, vol.6, ed. William L. Wilkie, Ann Arbor, MI: Association for Consumer Research, 424-
426.

Rossiter, John R. and Larry Percy (1991). »Emotions and Motivations in Advertising«, *Advances in
Consumer Research*, vol.18, ed. Rebecca H. Holman and Michael R. Solomon, Provo, UT: Association for Consumer Research, 100-110.

Russell, J.A. and M. Bullock (1986). »Fuzzy concepts and the perception of emotion in facial expressions«, *Social Cognition*, 4, 309-341.

Russell, James A. (1991). »In Defense of a Prototype Approach to Emotion Concepts«, *Journal of
Personality and Social Psychology*, 60, 1, 37-47.

Russell, James A. (1994). »Is there Universal Recognition of Emotion from Facial Expression? A
Review of the Cross-Cultural Studies«, *Psychological Bulletin*, Vol. 115, n° 1, 102-141.

Shimp, Terence A. (1981). »Attitude Toward the Advertisement as a Mediator of Consumer Brand
Choice«, *Journal of Advertising*, 10 (2), 9-15.

Smith, C.A. (1989). »Dimensions of Appraisal and Physiological Response in Emotion«, *Journal of
Personality and Social Psychology*, 56, 339-353.

Soldow, Gary F. (1985). »The Ability of Children to Understand the Product Package: a Study of
Limitations Imposed by Cognitive Developmental Stages«, *Journal of Public Policy and Marketing*,
4, 55-68.

Vanden Abeele, Piet and Douglas L. MacLahan (1994). »Process Tracing of Emotional Responses
to TV Advertisements: Revisiting the Warmth Monitor«, *Journal of Consumer Research*, 20 (-
March), 586-600.

van Raaij, W. Fred (1986). »Cognitive and Affective Effects of TV Advertising on Children«, in
Commercial Television and European Children, ed. Scott Ward, Thomas S. Robertson and Ray
Brown, Avebury: Gower Publishing Company, 99-109.

Vitouch, Peter (1986). »The Influence of Word-Picture Relationships of TV Films on the Emotional Reactions and Retention Performance of Children«, in *Commercial Television and European Children*, ed. Scott Ward, Thomas S. Robertson and Ray Brown, Avebury: Gower Publishing
Company, 110-112.

Wagner, H.L. and J. Smith (1991). »Social Influence and Expressiveness«, *Journal of Nonverbal Behavior*, 15, 201-214.

Ward, Scott (1986). »How Children Understand With Age«, in *Commercial Television and European
Children*, ed. Scott Ward, Thomas S. Robertson and Ray Brown, Avebury: Gower Publishing
Company, 33-53.

Ward, Scott, Daniel D. Wackman and Ellen Wartella (1977). *How Children Learn to Buy*, Beverly
Hills, Sage Publications.

Wartella, Ellen (1984). »Cognitive and Affective Factors of TV Advertising's Influence on Children«, *The Western Journal of Speech Communication Research*, 48, 171-183.

Woodworth, R.S. and Schlosberg, H. (1954). *Experimental Psychology*, New York: Holt.

Young, Brian M. (1986). »New Approaches to Old Problems: The Growth of Advertising Literacy«, in *Commercial Television and European Children*, ed. Scott Ward, Thomas S. Robertson and Ray Brown, Avebury: Gower Publishing Company.

9

DRUG, ALCOHOL, AND TOBACCO USE PREVENTION EFFORTS

— BENEFITS AND CHALLENGES OF TARGETING YOUNG CHILDREN

By Dan Freeman and Merrie Brucks

INTRODUCTION[1]

Drug, alcohol and tobacco use prevention programs have traditionally focused on proximal (i.e., immediate) factors related to the likelihood of experimentation by teenagers. In contrast, this paper explores the potential of prevention efforts focusing on temporally distal (i.e., much earlier) factors relating to use initiation. Specifically, this paper highlights how social marketers can maximize the benefits and overcome the challenges of targeting young children with drug, alcohol, and tobacco use prevention efforts.

Borrowing from Goldberg (1995), we adopt the metaphor of a river to describe the socialization process leading from childhood naiveté to drug, alcohol and/or tobacco abuse or addiction (see also Wallack, Dorfman, Jernigan & Themba 1993). Upstream, near the headwaters, numerous socialization agents work to entice or repel children from the stream. In the earliest years of childhood, family and mass media provide most of the implicit and explicit messages that children receive about the use of controlled substances. These messages lead to young children's early beliefs and lifestyle associations with use (users) of these substances. To the extent that positive, prosubstance use imagery is being created in the minds of children, the stream may look cool and inviting, enticingly dangerous, or at least evoke curiosity and interest. As children develop into teenagers, they may gather in groups around the banks of the river, adding peer influences to the major socialization factors. Teenagers may be drawn to the river to test the water or to accept their peers' invitations to join them for an unauthorized swim. By that time, the mutual and synergistic effects of positive (i.e., pro-use) socialization agents have created raging currents. This is the point that most tobacco prevention efforts target – teens on the banks of a quick flowing river. Unfortunately, the allure of the river is now strong, and nothing can prevent many from falling or jumping in. Those who can be quickly pulled from the river will be placed on the road to better health, while the remainder will enter the powerful rapids of addiction (Goldberg 1995). This process is diagrammed in Figure 1.

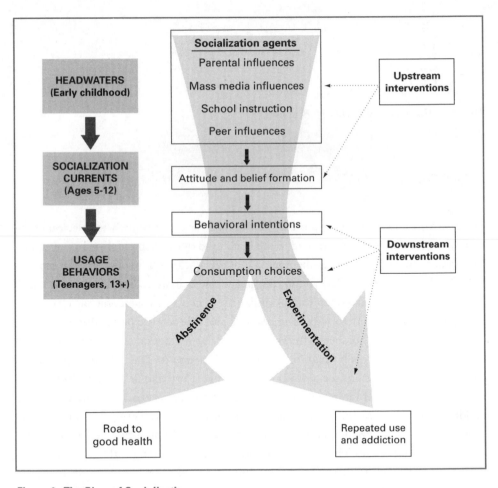

Figure 1. The River of Socialization

This analogy puts prevention efforts in perspective. The downstream focus of most prevention efforts is laudable, but leaves much room for more proactive efforts. From a practical standpoint, the downstream interventions are attractive to researchers and funding agencies because they can produce measurable, behavioral outcomes over a short time horizon. From a theoretical standpoint, however, it may be more efficient and effective in the long run to shift some of the focus to upstream socialization. To the extent that prevention programs can shape young children's beliefs, lifestyle associations and emerging predispositions toward substance abuse, fewer teens will be open to experimentation later.

Early prevention programs have one clear goal: create and maintain deeply held attitudes that will predispose the child against controlled substance use initiation. To achieve this goal, social marketing programs must create appropriate messages and deliver them at an effective level of frequency through the most compelling and efficient media to the correct target markets. Thus, the emphasis for *early* prevention programs focuses directly on the promotion element of the marketing mix. In contrast, social marketing programs targeted at more *immediate* prevention should involve product, price and distribution, in addition to communication, as suggested by leading social marketers (for example, Rothschild 1998 and Smith 1998).

BENEFITS OF EARLY PREVENTION

Although the observed behavioral response is many years downstream and perhaps difficult to trace to early prevention efforts, several factors suggest that targeting communication campaigns to young children is likely to be an efficacious use of prevention resources. (1) Communication aims at building rather than changing attitudes; (2) Children are more susceptible to persuasion than are teens; (3) Children are less likely than teens to respond with psychological reactance; and (4) Children have high potential to become cessation advocates.

BUILDING RATHER THAN CHANGING ATTITUDES

By targeting young children, who have yet to form strong perceptions, beliefs and attitudes towards controlled substances, social marketing strategies can be proactive rather than reactive. As suggested by numerous theories in social psychology (see Eagly & Chaiken 1993 for an excellent review and discussion), well-developed attitudes based on complex cognitive and affective structure are more resistant to change than are attitudes newly being formed. When exposed to persuasive messages promoting healthy behaviors, children with highly developed attitude structures, including beliefs, imagery and associated positive affect towards the undesirable behavior(s), have greater ability and motivation to counter-argue the messages than those who have not yet been exposed to pro-substance-use socializing influences. Therefore, young children, who will have had much less cumulative exposure than teens to the glamorizing and normalizing images promoted by some socialization agents, are in the best position to accept the social marketers' messages.

To build pro-health attitudes that will one day produce resistance to any temptations to engage in substance use, we invoke cultivation theory (see Gerbner, Gross, Morgan, & Signorielli 1986). Unlike the »one-shot« approach implied by most theories of attitude change (c.f., inoculation theory, McGuire 1964; the elaboration-likelihood model, Petty & Cacioppo 1986), cultivation theory involves continuous nurturing to create and maintain an environment that encourages healthy growth. A social marketing program based on cultivation theory would aim to create and steadily reinforce strong negative associations with the enactment of detrimental behaviors and/or positive associations with the enactment of healthy behaviors. This strategy mirrors that of the leading cigarette and beer brands, which have consistently used appealing imagery presented over long time intervals to nurture positive associations with the use of these products (see Schooler, Basil, & Altman 1996; for a review see USDHHS 1994). Thus, utilizing a proactive early prevention strategy will allow social marketers to beat alcohol and tobacco marketers at their own game.

Clearly, the components of such programs will need to address constraints related to social and cognitive development of young children (see the discussion of challenges below). Cultivation programs will also require coordination among social marketing agents to ensure that children and youths are receiving frequent, consistent and appealing prevention messages. These messages should be channeled through school, community and mass media-based vehicles for maximum effectiveness (Pechmann, 1997).

CHILDREN'S SUSCEPTIBILITY TO PERSUASION

Not only are young children relatively unaware of the issues pertaining to substance abuse, they are also notably susceptible to persuasive appeals because of their cognitive limitations (Armstrong & Brucks 1988; Roedder, Sternthal, & Calder 1983). To date, the most compelling explanation for these findings is that young children under age eight generally fail to account for the inherently biased nature of persuasive co٢... munications (Rossitor & Robertson 1974; Ward, Wackman, & Wartella 1977), while children aged 8–12 are unlikely to spontaneously engage in counter-arguing or source derogation (Brucks, Goldberg, & Armstrong 1988). Consequently, young children can be more easily persuaded than teenagers and young adults to hold negative attitudes toward substance use. Thus, social marketing programs that target pre-teen children will benefit from their greater susceptibility to persuasive appeals.

REDUCED LIKELIHOOD OF PSYCHOLOGICAL REACTANCE

Although teenagers have been noted to become more attracted to prohibited behaviors as a form of reactance, pre-teen children are unlikely to do so. According to Brehm (1966), such reactance is likely to occur when an individual perceives an attempt to curtail his or her freedom to engage in a given behavior. Since young children have generally not developed the notion of individual freedom as a component of their self-identities (Erikson 1968), they are very unlikely to perceive prevention messages as threatening. In contrast, most teenagers' self-schemas include an emerging sense of independence (Erikson 1968), which increases the likelihood that they will perceive prevention messages as attempting to constrain their freedom. When this occurs, teenagers will often react by judging the prohibited behavior as more desirable. Thus, social marketing programs targeting young children have less potential to backfire.

HIGH POTENTIAL TO BECOME ADVOCATES

Targeting young children with social marketing programs increases the likelihood that they will become advocates for cessation. Teaching children the health consequences of drug, alcohol and tobacco use, heightens the salience of these behaviors. In other words, prevention messages can lead children to notice substance use (abuse) and think about the consequences for the user (addict). As a result, children may ask family members, and perhaps even strangers, why they do drugs (drink or smoke), or children may state outright that doing drugs (drinking or smoking) is very bad.

When children persistently comment about the substance use of adults and older siblings they have the potential to produce three positive outcomes. First, children's advocacy may exert sufficient pressure on the substance user that s/he attempts cessation. Second, children may exert enough pressure to modify the behaviors of the sub-

reduce their exposure to second-hand smoke and/or negative so-
…ndura 1989). And finally, a child may come to see themselves as the
…who opposes substance use, thereby reducing the probability of future
…as per self-perception theory, see Bem 1972).

CHALLENGES OF EARLY PREVENTION

To reap the benefits stemming from upstream social marketing programs, several difficult challenges must be overcome. These challenges include: (1) developing effective,
age-appropriate messages; (2) educating children about the risks of drug, alcohol and
tobacco use without arousing their curiosity; (3) avoiding unintended consequences
on non-targeted groups of youth; and (4) initiating new prevention programs without adverse effects on current substance users (abusers).

DEVELOPING EFFECTIVE, AGE-APPROPRIATE MESSAGES

From birth through age 13+, children rapidly develop the mental skills and knowledge structures necessary to understand increasingly complex information (e.g.,
Bjorklund 1995). Such rapid changes imply the need for comprehensive, generaliz-
able, empirical investigations of children's responses to substance use prevention messages. These investigations should be guided by developmental theory and persuasion
theory to ensure that important constructs (e.g., message concreteness vs. abstractness)
are not inadvertently confounded with message content manipulations. Buoyed by
the knowledge produced through such rigorous investigations, social marketers will
have a useful foundation to begin designing specific campaigns.

No amount of theory can predict how individual children might interpret a specific message, however. Thus, it is necessary to pre-test advertisement concepts, rough
production executions and finished advertisements to determine the comprehensibil-
ity and appeal of various message themes and executions for children at different levels
of social and cognitive development. For example, generalized theory may not indicate the potential for children to miscomprehend the simple directive »don't drink
and drive«. But young children may interpret this statement to mean that you
shouldn't hold a can of soda in your hand while you drive (as did some children who
were interviewed as part of this project).

EDUCATING CHILDREN WITHOUT AROUSING THEIR CURIOSITY

Drawing attention to the dangers of smoking, drinking alcohol or taking drugs may also have the undesirable effect of arousing children's curiosity about these things. Not only do prevention messages make these behaviors more salient, they may provoke the child to wonder about the benefits of substance use, especially when they see appealing images of use (users) in the media, and encounter use (users) at home and in public. Inoculation theory, however, suggests that weak exposures to pro-substance messages will lead to internal build up of cognitive defenses if the target market has been given the information needed to counter-argue this influence (McGuire 1964). This perspective suggests that prevention messages can be designed for young children to arm them with the information needed to reduce the appeal of the many glamorizing or normalizing images they will encounter without giving explicit attention to any »perceived benefits« of substance use.

Once children have reached the age where they are receiving direct inducements to accept or experiment with controlled substances, it may be more effective to adopt a more explicit »two-sided« message strategy. In the context of substance use prevention, two-sided messages present both reasons to initiate use and reasons to avoid use before explaining why avoidance is better. Messages of this type are most effective when recipients know the issue is controversial (Baumgardner, Leippe, Ronis, & Greenwald 1983) and are fully attentive to the message. Using a two-sided message tends to provoke more elaborative processing of the message, and seems more credible by acknowledging the opposing viewpoint. Unfortunately, however, two-sided messages often include previously unknown information with the potential to evoke curiosity and lead to an increase in children's likelihood of experimentation.

Some critics argue that targeting prevention messages for young children raises these issues prematurely, but empirical research suggests that elementary school age children as young as five have already begun to associate psychosocial benefits with alcohol and tobacco use (Brucks & Wallendorf 1995; Brucks, Wallendorf & Freeman 1998). Thus, at least for these substances, early prevention programs aimed at elementary school children address attitudes that are already beginning to form rather than arousing curiosity about something previously unknown.

AVOIDING UNINTENDED CONSEQUENCES AMONG NON-TARGETED GROUPS

It is practically impossible to use mass media to reach members of any targeted group without also reaching substantial numbers of children, teenagers and/or adults from non-targeted groups because of commonalities in media exposure. With marketing to children and teens, it is important to note that message strategies that are effective in one age group may have the reverse effect in other age groups. For example, as suggested above, two-sided messages may be most appropriate for teenagers, but could foster positive associations with drug, alcohol and tobacco use among younger children. In a similar vein, directive advertisements that present a clear, concrete message to younger children (e.g., »Don't do drugs«) may provoke psychological reactance among teens because the message represents a blatant attempt to curtail their individual freedom. And advertisements that depict smokers as hopelessly addicted to an expensive habit may help prevent teen experimentation, but may hinder cessation efforts by lowering the self-esteem and perceived self-control of current teen smokers.

To overcome the challenge of multiple relevant markets being exposed to public health messages, social marketers will need to utilize much broader pretesting procedures than is usually done in for-profit contexts. Drawing from the business model, state-of-the-art social marketing programs usually test messages with a sample from the target market to gauge effectiveness prior to releasing a new campaign. For example, every advertisement in the Office of National Drug Control Policy's (ONDCP) drug use prevention campaign must pass a certain pre-test standard with members of the target audience before it will be implemented in the media (C. Pechmann, personal communication, January 15, 1999). While this practice works well for commercial marketing practitioners who are generally unconcerned about potential unintended consequences for people outside their target markets, it does not go far enough in the context of social marketing. Social marketing messages need to be pre-tested across a wider range of audiences to ensure that the messages are not adversely affecting non-targeted groups.

INITIATING NEW PREVENTION PROGRAMS WITHOUT ADVERSE EFFECTS ON CURRENT SUBSTANCE ABUSERS

Perhaps the single common denominator for all social marketing programs is that they exist in resource-constrained environments. Therefore, moving social marketing programs upstream, which implies new expenditures on early prevention programs targeting children and youths, will require either increased funding for social marketing initiatives, or reductions in programs geared toward drug, alcohol and tobacco cessation.

SUMMARY AND CONCLUSION

Social marketing practice stands at an important crossroad. Fueled by windfall tobacco settlements and increased public concern over substance use by children and youth, hundreds of millions of dollars will be spent on drug, alcohol and tobacco use prevention programs over the next decade. We hope that our discussion of benefits and challenges stemming from moving prevention programs upstream will lead social marketers to consider the formulation of innovative programs targeting young children. Rather than attempting to »counter« what has already been learned, such programs can, and should, be designed to proactively shape children's associations with substance use. By cultivating negative associations throughout childhood and reinforcing these associations when children reach the age when they will decide whether to initiate substance use, upstream prevention programs promise to substantially reduce the likelihood of experimentation and addiction. The synergistic effects of upstream cultivation followed by downstream reinforcement should prove to be a powerful force in reducing drug, alcohol and tobacco use initiation.

NOTE

1. The Marketing Science and the Arizona Disease Control Research Commission provided financial support for this project. Professor Melanie Wallendorf was instrumental in obtaining that funding. In addition the authors thank Professor Aric Rindfleisch for his helpful comments on an earlier draft of this manuscript.

REFERENCES

Armstrong, G. & Brucks, M. (1988). »Dealing with children's advertising: Public policy issues and alternatives«, *Journal of Public Policy and Marketing*, 7, 98-113.

Bandura, A. (1989). »Social cognitive theory«, *Annals of Child Development*, 6, 1-60.

Baumgartner, M.H., Leippe, M.R., Ronis, D.L. & Greenwald, A.G. (1983). »In Search of reliable persuasion effects II: Associative interference and persistence of persuasion in a message-dense environment«, *Journal of Personality and Social Psychology*, 45, 524-537.

Bem, D. (1972). »Self-perception theory«, in L. Berkowitz (ed.). *Advances in Experimental and Social Psychology*. New York: Academic Press.

Bjorklund, D. F. (1995). *Children's Thinking: Developmental Function and Individual Differences*. Pacific Grove, CA: Brooks/Cole Publishing Company.

Brehm, J. W. (1966). *A Theory of Psychological Reactance*. New York: Academic Press.

Brucks, M., Goldberg, M.E., & Armstrong, G.M. (1988). »Children's use of cognitive defenses against television advertising: A cognitive response approach«, *Journal of Consumer Research, 14,* 471-482.

Brucks, M. & Wallendorf, M. (1995). »Children's perceptions of billboard advertisements for alcoholic beverages«, presented at the Marketing and Public Policy Conference, Atlanta, Georgia, May.

Brucks, M., Wallendorf, M. & Freeman, D. (1998). »The Impact of advertising on young children's beliefs about alcohol and tobacco use/users: What's lurking at the headwaters?«, presented at Association for Consumer Research Conference, Montreal, Quebec, October 1-4.

Eagly, A.H. & Chaiken, S. (1993). *The Psychology of Attitudes*. Fort Worth, TX: Harcourt, Brace Jovanovich.

Erikson, E.H. (1968). *Identity: Youth in Crisis*. New York: W. W. Norton.

Gerbner, G., Gross, L., Morgan, M., & Signorielli, N. (1986). »Living with television: The dynamics of cultivation process«, in J. Bryant and D. Zillman (eds.). *Perspectives on Media Effects*. Hillsdale, NJ: Erlbaum, 17-48.

Goldberg, M.E. (1995). »Social marketing: Are we fiddling while Rome burns?«, *Journal of Consumer Psychology*, 4, 347-370.

McGuire, W. J. (1964). »Inducing resistance to persuasion: Some contemporary approaches«, in L. Berkowitz (ed.). *Advances in Experimental Social Psychology*. San Diego, CA: Academic Press, 191-229.

Pechmann, C. (1997). »Does antismoking advertising combat underage smoking? A review of past practices and research«, in M.E. Goldberg, M. Fishbein, and S.E. Middlestadt (eds.). *Social Marketing*. Mahwah, NJ: Lawrence Erlbaum, 189-216.

Petty, R.E., & Cacioppo, J.T. (1986). *Communication and Persuasion: Central and Peripheral Routes to Attitude Change*. New York: Spinger-Verlag.

Roedder, D.L., Sternthal, B., & Calder, B.J. (1983). »Attitude-behavior consistency in children's responses to television advertising«, *Journal of Marketing Research, 20,* 337-349.

Rossitor, J.R. & Robertson, T.S. (1974). »Children's TV commercials: Testing the defenses«, *Journal of Communication*, 24 (Autumn), 137-144.

Rothschild, M.L. (1998). »Closing comments«, *Social Marketing Quarterly*, 4 (4), 72-75.

Schooler, C., Basil, M.D. & Altman, D.G. (1996). »Alcohol and cigarette advertising on billboards: Targeting with social cues«, *Health Communication*, 8, 109-129.

Smith, W. (1998). »Forget messages … think about structural change first«, *Social Marketing Quarterly*, 4(3), 13-19.

U.S. Department of Health and Human Services (1994). *Preventing Tobacco Use Among Young People: A Report of the Surgeon General*. Rockville, MD: Centers for Disease Control.

Wallack, L., Dorfman, L., Jernigan, D. & Themba, M. (1993). *Media Advocacy and Public Health*. Newbury Park, CA: Sage.

Ward, S., Wackman, D., & Wartella, E. (1977). *How Children Learn to Buy: The Development of Consumer Information Processing*. Beverly Hills, CA: Sage.

10

SOME ETHICAL IMPLICATIONS OF CONSUMER BEHAVIOR

– PRINCIPLES WHEN KIDS ARE INVOLVED

By Whiton S. Paine

INTRODUCTION

The role marketing plays in the transmission of cultural norms and values is obvious-ly complex (John 1999). In general, the ethical implications of the utilization of con-sumer behavior (CB) principles in this process are diverse, inadequately defined, and increasingly controversial. These principles clearly inform the major recent books for practitioners (Guber and Berry 1993, Del Vecchio 1997, McNeal 1998, 1999, Zollo 1999, Siegel, Coffey and Livingston 2001) as well as the academic literature (McNeal 1991, Chandler and Heinzerling 1999). Particularly in the United States, companies using these principles to market to children and youth and their relatives are increas-ingly under attack by regulatory agencies, politicians, professionals working with chil-dren, advocacy groups and the media (Paine, Stewart and Kruger 2001).

In particular, as Heckman (1999) recently noted:

> »Children always are a hot-button issue, so anything from sales appeals directed to children to obtaining marketing information from children is vulnerable (to regulation and attack). Health-care, such as regulating herbals or HMOs, also is an emotional issue along with vanity issues such as virility or weight control.«

Both vanity-related and health care-related marketing also have the potential to generate increasing levels of controversy over how children are being socialized. However, because these areas are so large, the following discussion will focus on two partial case studies of highly successful marketing. These illustrate some of the ethical issues that can arise when some of the more potent consumer behavior principles are employed to influence tweens and their parents in the marketplace.

The two cases are »Barbie®« and »Ritalin®« – a doll of primary interest to 6-9 year old girls (Siegel, Coffee and Livingston 2001) and a drug treatment most commonly prescribed for similarly aged boys (Schachter, Pham, King, Langford and Moher 2001). While at first glance these cases appear to have little in common, both used a variety of marketing techniques to successfully create ongoing »communities« of loyalists. Such communities can be an important goal in marketing to younger consumers. They are summarized in a recent article as »a well-defined customer segment united by an emotional, often intense interest« (Butscher and Luby 2002). Like other communities, these creations have the potential to significantly impact on the values of children. Unfortunately this is a possibility that has not been empirically validated to date and this paper may be one of the first analyses to begin to look at some of the issues.

The Barbie community of girls and their mothers has been built over a forty-year period and feminists and others have raised multiple concerns about the long-term impacts the marketing of this doll has had. Particularly in recent years, Mattel has become more effective in dealing with many of these issues. In contrast, the growing controversies surrounding the promotion of ethical pharmaceuticals have generally been handled less well by marketers. This is illustrated in the discussion of concerns related to how Ceiba-Geigy (now Novartis) constructed the Ritalin community of physicians, parents and educators between 1975 and 1995. Neither of these analyses is intended to be comprehensive but rather they exemplify issues that are of wider interest to those marketing to children and youth (also referred to here as »minors« and »kids«).

SOME CAVEATS

Before proceeding it is important to note some of the major limitations of this type of analysis. A focus on evolving issues invariably creates problems particularly when it involves a consideration of academic and other bodies of information that have relatively little in common. Conceptual analyses and research findings in the consumer behavior, medicine, marketing, philosophy, business ethics, and developmental psychology literatures are all potentially relevant but reflect quite different philosophical and historical biases. In addition, each of these literatures is limited in scope and depth with respect to children and youth in the marketplace.

As a result, attempting to link them together to fill in the present gaps is inherently speculative. More specifically, studies of the consumer behavior of children represent a relatively small proportion of the entire CB literature and have dealt mainly with advertising and media issues (Chandler and Heinzerling 1999). Developmental psychologists have primarily focused on theoretical and research issues outside the marketplace (Parke, Ornstein, Rieser, and Zahn-Waxler 1994, Bornstein and Lamb 1999). Only recently have modern marketing practices become prominent in health-care categories and their impact on kids has just begun to be studied. Outside the area of moral education, philosophers have seldom been interested in ethical issues involving minors (Jackson and Paine 2001). Similarly, business ethicists concerned with marketing have focused their attention mainly on adults (Murphy 2001).

Many of the issues being raised herein also reflect relatively recent and rapidly evolving technological, intellectual or social trends. As a result, any analysis must rely heavily on non-academic sources including media reports, surveys, the Internet, and the often-biased efforts of advocacy and other organizations. These too are limited in scope. They also typically lack intellectual rigor and frequently reflect different political, personal, or social agendas. The literature review for this chapter is also selective and biased toward recent sources and work done in the United States since many of the issues being raised are presently most prominent in that country. However, these same issues are beginning to have impacts in other countries, particularly Canada and Great Britain.

Finally, any discussion of ethics is inherently controversial and marketers have good cause to be confused by what information does exist. In particular, the often-fine line between ethical and unethical target marketing is important here (Sims 1997). At one extreme, Brenkert (1998, p 16) expresses a common assumption of the marketing ethics literature that »because children are cognitively vulnerable due to their un-developed abilities, any marketing done to children must be done in ways that do not presuppose those vulnerabilities.« Today, few marketers would defend such recent abuses as Joe Camel, marketing 900-numbers to minors (Laczniak, Muehling and Carlson 1995), or the promotion of other clearly undesirable products to kids (Rotfeld 1998). However, many products are less obviously dangerous and most have received too little attention in the marketing literature.

In a careful analysis of the general issue, Smith and Cooper-Martin (1997) documented some of the potential general links between ethical controversy and perceptions of potential harm and of target segment vulnerability. However, with kids, there

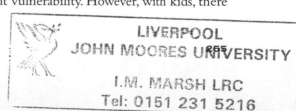

is increasing confusion about both potential harm and vulnerability in many product categories. For example, several recent efforts take the position that, at least for advertising, children relatively rapidly pass through a vulnerable stage and become hardened realists well able to protect themselves (Gunter and Furnham 1998, Wright-Isak 1999, Stoltman 1999). In direct contrast is the blunt statement in an *Adweek* article that »Marketers covet young customers for the same reason child advocates want to protect them: the belief that the young are vulnerable to marketing in a way that adult consumers are not (Goldman 1999, p 20).« Considerable research on all aspects of the marketing mix in different categories will be required to begin to resolve this confusion. As part of that resolution, marketers and managers will have to deal with the multiple issues related to dangerous personal attitudes and the often-inadequate organizational policies and practices related to marketing to minors (Paine, Stewart and Kruger 2001).

These factors make much of the following discussion rather speculative and any conclusions should be treated with skepticism and the recognition that they may fall in the face of later research. However, Barbie and Ritalin do illustrate the ethical controversies that may arise when companies successfully create communities that may impact on the continuing socialization of minors as consumers.

THE MARKETING OF BARBIE

Gender is a fundamental categorical variable in marketing and has been a particular focus of marketing to children and youth (Acuff with Reiher 1997). Developmentally, the core gender identity is typically established between the second and third years of life (Stoller 1980) and is elaborated throughout childhood in response to a variety of influences. From an ethics perspective, a key issue here is the ways in which marketing and experiences with products influence this process (Monczunski 1999).

Barbie is clearly one of the most successful toy marketing efforts in an industry where product introductions typically fail. This is a product primarily of interest to younger tween girls (Siegel, Coffey and Livingston 2001). The brand entered the market in 1958 and quickly created an enduring link between TV and toys (Alexander, Benjamin, Hoearner and Roe 1999). Barbie's market penetration has grown to over 90 percent, most girls have multiple branded products, sales exceed $1.5 billion a year, and over one billion dolls have been produced for a worldwide market (Stevens 1997, Goldstein 1998). The brand meets Del Vecchio's (1997) criteria for creating an ever-cool toy and within the industry is perceived as »evergreen« because of sales successes over almost 40 years (Gruber and Berry 1994). However, over time Mattel has had to address a wide variety of ethical issues.

From the beginning this brand has leveraged a variety of consumer behavior principles to create this success. Marketing and the product have evoked a young girl's needs to feel glamorous; to fantasize about being older or like mom; to transform into another, more beautiful and competent, person; to operate effectively in the future world of a teen; to emulate beautiful and professional role models; to move away from being a »little girl«, and to play more creatively and competitively alone and with peers (Guber and Berry 1994, Del Vecchio 1997, Acuff, with Reiher 1997). Many of these dynamics have the potential to appropriately socialize young girls in terms of their later role in a modern society. They may also influence the formation of an unattainable personal identity based on a personal identification with a physically overdeveloped image of womanhood. This has led to an enduring controversy about Barbie and eating disorders. These are discussed below as »Eating Disorders and Barbie«. That analysis is followed by a more general discussion of »High Involvement and Barbie« based on the model developed by Charles L. Martin for the analysis of high-involvement/relationship prone brands (Martin 1998, Morris and Martin 2000).

EATING DISORDERS AND BARBIE

The incidence and prevalence of eating disorders, particularly in women, appears to be increasing and has become a significant public health problem in both North America and Europe (Whitaker 1992, Jones, Bennett, Olmsted, Lawson and Rodin 2001, Ghaderi and Scott 2001). Dissatisfaction with weight and perceived body image are complex phenomena with multiple determinants (Kearney-Cooke and Striegel-Moore 1997). In some cases negative self-perceptions can lead to potentially dangerous patterns of eating or dieting and these may motivate self-destructive behaviors in as many as a quarter of pathological dieters (Shisslak and Crago 1995).

There is growing evidence that many children and youth internalize unrealistically thin beauty ideals and this can lead to potentially life threatening eating disorders including obesity, anorexia nervosa, and bulimia (Striegel-Moore 2001). Typically, problem behaviors start to become apparent in mid-adolescence and progress over time to full-blown syndromes (Fairburn, Welch, Doll, Davies and O'Connor 1997). However problems with body image have been documented as early as age 5 (Davison, Markey and Birch 2000), and by the third grade one study found them occurring across the major ethnic groups in the US (Robinson, Chang, Haydel and Killen 2001).

The possible role of Barbie in this process became an issue among feminists in the 1980's and their concerns were summarized in detail by Lord (1994) and more recently by Wanlass (2001). She concluded that »Fashion models, movie stars, and a host of other mediated images link thinness with social desirability and achievement. And I believe it begins with Barbie dolls (Wanlass 2001, p 127).« This belief appears to be widespread at least within the feminist community (Edut 1998, McDonough 1999) but it is based far more on face validity than on empirical research (Lord 1994).

Early in Barbie's history this was not a major area of concern. Back in 1965 Mattel even had a »Slumber Party« doll with accessories that included a bathroom scale pre-set at a weight of 110 pounds and a book on »How To Lose Weight« (Lord 1994). Since then the marketing environment has changed and there is a greater recognition that companies need to change their marketing to respond more appropriately to the social issues being raised by feminists and other critics (Macchiette and Roy 1994). And so, thirty years later, Barbie received a new image – smaller breasts, wider waist, and a closed mouth (Borger 1997). She also became surrounded by non-blond, and in some cases international, peers that tweens could relate to as they play. Girls were also given such options as creating their own, less sexy, clothing via a computer program and there even was a companion exercise video.

What is surprising about Mattel's recent actions is that there is no broad consensus about the negative role Barbie may play in children's developing an inappropriate idealized body image (Lord 1994). In addition, as Dubin (1999) pointed out, Barbie is a cultural icon that both reflects and influences the culture. Even though the doll itself, and many of the outfits sold by Mattel, reflect an exaggerated, sexualized, body shape, that highly visual fact is inadequate support for the presumed negative influences on·young girls. While there is growing evidence for a link between media content, body image dissatisfaction, poor self concept, and psychiatric problems (Stephens, Hill and Hanson 1994, Becker and Hamburg 1996), the relevance of this literature to controversies surrounding Barbie is unclear. Here Grow (1996) provided an interesting model linking idealized, hypernormal images of beautiful women to a wide range of negative outcomes but a key missing element in any discussion of the doll is that playing with Barbie creates the same types of self-learning as may observing living models in advertising. This is not a trivial issue given the evidence that the influence of »highly attractive models« appears to vary by category (Bower and Landreth 2001).

However, Mattel's recent actions do represent a potentially effective response to an increasingly negative public relations situation. Radical feminists had identified the doll as a target and their widely publicized actions included the Barbie Liberation Organization countering gender stereotypes by swapping voice boxes so that GI Joe could suggest »Let's go shopping. Will we ever have enough clothes?« Barbie's new persona was now able to respond »Eat lead, Cobra. Vengeance is mine! (Lord 1994).« Later the Barbie Disinformation Organization carefully counterfeited Mattel package stickers to transform »Barbie's Stylin' Salon« into the »Barbie Lesbian Barber Shop« and Barbie the cheerleader into »Theme Hooker Barbie« (Marguiles, No date).

In addition, the increasing social concern about potentially life-threatening eating patterns in children also has had an impact. This issue is unlikely to recede as US children continue to gain weight and react by dieting in inappropriate ways. In addition, body image has been nominated as a rallying focus for the third wave of feminism (Richards 1998). Concerns are also being raised about the negative impacts of action figures on the development of boys (Pope, Olivardia, Gruber et al 1999). These events suggest that Mattel was facing even more public acrimony based on Barbie's exaggerated measurements and that their decision to physically change the doll was an appropriate one.

HIGH INVOLVEMENT AND BARBIE

Some additional ethical issues arise when Barbie is analyzed as a high-involvement brand (Martin 1998, Morris and Martin 2000). In their detailed analysis of Beanie Babies Morris and Martin (2000) identified ten traits of a successful high-involvement product with kids. Their research should be duplicated for Barbie since the doll appears to exhibit many of the aspects found in the analysis of Beanie Babies. In particular, the brand seems to evoke nostalgia in mothers, can be identified with as a person, is unique in that each year brings new dolls and accessories, helps girls attain social goals and key personal roles, strongly engages the owner in play activities, is aesthetically appealing and of good quality, links girls to other people and places, and supports social visibility and congruence with a desired set of self-images. However, unlike the relatively inexpensive stuffed Beanie Babies, the dolls do reflect a higher degree of price risk.

Many of these brand »traits« may create additional ethical controversies. Some of the possible issues related to the traits of Personification, Facilitation of role play, Engagement to support use, Aesthetic Appeal, Social visibility and Image Congruence are suggested above in the discussion of »Eating Disorders and Barbie.« The traits of Nostalgia value, Association, and Quality/excellence also raise some interesting issues.

NOSTALGIC VALUE

With adults, Mattel has done an excellent job of linking the doll with a mother's childhood and a child's need to collect. Children are natural accumulators of sets of objects and many move on after age 8 to become a more careful and discriminating collector (Acuff with Reiher 1997, Norton 2000, Stauffacher 2000, Siegel, Coffey and Livingston 2001). The yearly flood of Barbies, and associated goods take advantage of this dynamic in some children. Margo Moschel, senior vice president-preliminary visual design for the Barbie group explained their overall product development strategy as »The design challenge was to create a new Barbie toy line that stimulated little girls to buy more Barbies to meet specific play needs« (Stevens 1997, p 24). This successful strategy results in the average owner having between five and ten Barbies. However, collecting can have a quite neurotic side (Muensterberger 1993) particularly when the accumulation of valuable objects is used to bolster low self-esteem or other inadequacies of childhood. The extent to which Mattel plays into these processes is unclear.

In addition, a pricing decision made by Mattel in 1995 raised concerns about fairness. Nostalgia is a particularly strong motivator in Baby Boomers attempting to evoke their childhood by collecting classic Barbies (The Washington Times 2001). Mattel attempted to leverage these dynamics by producing a Barbie Collectibles® line for mothers with some priced at $500 and over. Their marketing strategy infuriated collectors and those involved in the secondary market (Millican, no date). It also had the potential to create an unfortunate competitive dynamic between mothers and daughters who felt it was unfair that they could not play with Mommy's Barbies. From a child's viewpoint, this raises the ethical issue of fairness.

QUALITY / EXCELLENCE

Mattel has always been zealous in creating and maintaining a quality image for the product. An aspect of quality of particular importance to parents is safety because of their strong desire to protect children from harm. Mattel recently showed respect for this concern by quickly withdrawing from the market some Barbie sun glasses which, if broken, could leak a toxic and corrosive chemical (Associated Press 2001). A more interesting situation arose because part of the initial success of the doll was that it used a new plastic, polyviolchloride (PVC), to create movable extremities. Years later Green Peace initiated a movement in Europe to ban the use of PVC in toys because of the possibility that it could leak potential carcinogens (phthalates). Phthlates were the very additives that made PVC flexible (The Economist 1998, Bodytalk Magazine No date).

Despite a lack of scientific evidence, PVC was banned for some toys in both the US and Europe. This escalating controversy led Mattel to publicly break with the Toy Manufactures Association and to agree to substitute other materials (Noble 1999). What is particularly interesting here is that, after an initial resistance, the company decided to work closely with advocacy organizations on the problem (Environment News Service 1999)

ASSOCIATION

An important issue is how a product is linked to other people or places. Mattel, for example, has tied Barbie to a very wide range of occupations and to an increasing number of cultures. However, in a global economy, fairness and justice are continuing concerns of both business ethicists and young children (Shaw and Barry 1998, Church 2001). From both a branding and a PR perspective, it is often damaging when a company is perceived as unfair or unjust. Initially, Barbie was manufactured in the United States but by 1995 half of the production was moved elsewhere. However, from Mattel's point of view, an unfortunate association was created by some scathing articles, which linked Barbie to the growing issue of labor exploitation in the Third World (Press 1996, Foek 1997). As NIKE discovered, this is a potentially explosive issue with young and idealistic consumers concerned about fairness.

However, again after some initial resistance, Mattel moved relatively quickly to address problems in this area (Bernstein 1999, The Economist 1999, Bernstein with Shari and Malkin 2000) and seems to have limited any damage. In particular, the company avoided any possibility of a boycott that could have seriously damaged sales during a key Christmas season. There still is the related issue of the gap between Third World production costs and sales prices. According to one analysis (Cote 1997) the least expensive Barbie at $16.99 contains under one dollar's worth of material, costs 50 cents to manufacture and by time it arrives on the shelves has cost Mattel only $4.80. Idealistic children are unlikely to be interested in Cote's detailed analysis of other costs. Instead they, and some parents, may wonder why they are paying so much when a young employee half-way around the world is paid so little that they cannot afford the same doll.

The issue of environmentalism is also an growing force in many markets and consumers (including children) seem increasingly willing to reward environmentally conscious companies (Laroche, Bergeron and Barbaro-Forleo 2001). Mattel has had some problems in this area but they recently joined in a consent decree to clean up a Superfund hazardous waste site in New Jersey (Regulatory Intelligence Data 1999).

UNIQUENESS

Finally, one of the ways that Barbie has been kept evergreen is through providing product variety. Basically, Mattel uses extensive marketing research to identify what lifestyles young girls see as »hip and cool« and as a result change 80 percent or more of the product line each year (Stevens 1997). Along with the over 500 Barbies to date, there are companion dolls including Ken and an amazing variety of accessories and line extensions include trading cards, Pogs (when those were popular), stickers, Christmas tree ornaments and clothing for children. (Mattel 2000).

This strategy guarantees uniqueness and rarity but also plays into increasing concerns about the possible undesirable outcomes recently summarized by John (1999) as conspicuous consumption, materialistic attitudes, and nonrational impulse-oriented consumption. Belk identified the importance of materialism as a potentially important consumer variable in 1985 and the more recent work in this area has been summarized by John (1999). As a social phenomenon it seems to be increasing as societies become more affluent and influenced by what has been called »Affluenza« in the United States (de Graaf, Wann and Naylor 2001). Affluenza is conceptualized as the socially transmitted tendency to sacrifice family life, personal health, and the environment in the dogged pursuit of material goods. However, the problem extends well beyond the United States and is certainly not a new concern. For example, in 1957 Pope Pius XII denounced the »terrible temptation to materialism« (Paragraph 45). An even stronger attack was made by Pope John Paul when he used an Encyclical Letter to analyze the destructive impacts of excessive consumption on both spiritual and physical health (John Paul II 1991).

Parents too are beginning to see problems in this area. In one recent major survey, adult consumers felt that materialism and the related motivation of greed, particularly in children, were increasingly distorting social values and family life in the US (Harwood Group 1995). For example, 86 percent of the adult respondents in 1995 agreed with the statement that »Today's youth are too focused on buying and consuming things« and 73 percent were »very concerned« about the values their children were learning (Harwood Group 1995). A separate study of a national sample of youth aged 9-14 found that highly materialistic kids shopped more often, had a higher interest in new products, attended more to, and were more responsive to, advertising and promotions, and did slightly less well in school. (Goldberg et al. 2002). While this may be good news to marketers, youth materialism can have negative consequences from a social perspective (Goldberg, et al. 2002).

One particularly negative possible outcome is the development of later compulsive buying patterns. This is chronic, repetitive purchasing as a primary response to negative events or feelings. For example, today's college students in the US are the first generation to have been directly marketed to throughout most of their lives, and one recent study of this group indicated that 6 percent may be compulsive buyers with 90 percent of that group being female (Roberts 1998). Over time, compulsive buying and the need for instant gratification can exacerbate lower self-esteem and lead to poorer emotional functioning (Kasser and Ryan 1993).

To summarize, both of these discussions of Barbie raise the basic issue of the extent to which the experience of playing with the doll socializes children in ways which may predispose them to behavior that is damaging to them later in life. Poor body image, eating disorders, materialism, and compulsive buying are particular problems in the United States but may also increase elsewhere as a global consumer culture continues to mature. However, without empirical research that links the experience of playing with the doll to these conditions, the discussion of these linkages will remain largely speculative. It is to Mattel's credit that, despite a lack of evidence, it has in recent years been sensitive to many of these issues in part because they have sparked public controversy. They are a good example of an experienced children's marketer who realizes the importance of rapidly responding to the perceptions of diverse stakeholders – parents, children's advocates, and regulators. The same cannot yet be said of the pharmaceutical industry and health-related marketing.

THE MARKETING OF RITALIN AND OF COMPETITORS

With respect to physical health, an increasing number of companies are marketing a wide variety of products and services directly to minors and/or indirectly through their parents or other adults. Some of the key product categories involve ethical pharmaceuticals, over-the-counter medications, and a variety of dietary supplements including fortified foods, herbal preparations, and vitamins. Compared to the Barbie example above, much less is known here about possible linkages between consumer behavior principles, the socialization of consumers, health-related marketing, and ethics. However, it is already clear that this is an area creating serious and growing ethical challenges.

The marketing of Ritalin illustrates how one company (Ciba-Geigy) now Novartis was able to create a community of parents, experts, teachers and doctors that were united in their approval of this drug as the main treatment of Attention Deficit Hyperactivity Disorder (ADHD). One consequence of this process is that there is now a billion dollar market for stimulant drugs in the United States. The usual consequence of such success is that it attracts competitors and now Ritalin competes with an increasing number of alternative stimulants.

SOME GENERAL CONSUMER BEHAVIOR DYNAMICS

Several dynamics are potentially salient with respect to the promotion of ethical pharmaceuticals like Ritalin. In parents, a major motivation is to see themselves and be seen by others as »good« – as maximizing their children's physical and emotional health, protecting them from illness, and minimizing the consequences of any health problems that may occur. Other dynamics may come into play when children and youth are perceived as »bad«. Parental guilt, frustration, desire for control, the need to publicly and privately take pride in the accomplishments of a child, and the often negative impacts of such children on a parent's family and work life also can play a role here. In addition, teachers have a high need to limit the impact of disruptive children on the learning environment and in some cases a similar need to control the behavior of children. Finally, harried physicians dealing with anguished parents are motivated to prescribe solutions to medical problems that appear to have the support of scientific studies.

Pharmaceutical and over-the-counter marketers, responding to the desire of parents and other adults to »do the best« and »avoid the worst« for kids routinely leverage these feelings to increase the sales of products to children. While appropriate in many areas, this may be less so with respect to mind-altering pharmaceuticals, which are promoted to modify moods, attitudes, or behaviors in kids that their parents or other adults find objectionable. The longest running controversy in this area involves Ritalin and the treatment of Attention Deficit Hyperactive Disorders. In addition to the continuing controversies surrounding this drug, the recent trend to market drugs directly to parents will add additional ethical complexity.

ATTENTION DEFICIT HYPERACTIVITY DISORDER

According to the American Academy of Pediatrics (2000), in the United States, ADHD, and the related Attention Deficit Disorder (ADD), are the most commonly treated neurobehavioral disorders of childhood. The major symptoms include inattention, impulsivity, and hyperactivity which can lead to behavior which creates significant and chronic difficulties in school, with peers, at home, and on into adulthood. Community prevalence studies report widely varying rates with one summary of recent studies reporting a median of 5.8 percent (Brown et al 2001). There also appear to be widespread rate variations across geographic areas and across individual physicians (American Academy of Pediatrics 2000).

This is not the place to map out the multiple controversies surrounding treatment of ADHD. The most comprehensive relatively long-term study of stimulants indicates that they do appear to have positive effects on symptoms (MTA Cooperative Group, 1999a, b). Additional analyses of this study have provided some support for the idea that treatment regimens which combine stimulants with other interventions may also have desirable impacts on the behaviors of most concern to teachers and parents (Jensen et al 2001). Despite this and other evidence, the rise of Ritalin and similar drugs has raised a wide variety of controversies including the use of any drug to control unwanted behavior, misdiagnoses by adults (physicians, teachers and parents), the neglect of alternative treatments, and drug abuse by children (Goldman, et al. 1998).

THE MARKETING OF RITALIN

Ritalin (methylphenidate hydrochloride or MPH) was patented in 1950 and originally promoted by Ciba-Geigy as a mild central nervous system stimulant. In the 1970's such stimulants began to be used as a treatment for ADHD (Farley 1997). Ciba-Geigy was able to create a »Ritalin Nation« community through an integrated marketing campaign that was directed at physicians (particularly primary care physicians and psychiatrists) and pharmacists while also targeting educators and parents (Diller 1998, Degrandpre 1999, Breggin 2001). The success of these promotions was extraordinary and Ritalin rapidly became the treatment of choice when parents complained about their children's behavior in school.

Between 1990 and 1995, sales of the drug increased markedly (Morrow, Morrow and Haislip 1998). This increase was so large that it raised concerns in the Austria-based International Narcotics Control Board about the overuse of an addictive Schedule II drug in the US (Alcoholism and Drug Abuse Weekly 1996). According to a 1997 report, at any one time up to 3 million American schoolchildren were on amphetamines to control attention deficit/hyperactivity disorder and over half a million more were on drugs like Prozac (available in a mint-flavored liquid for children), lithium or other psychiatric drugs (Allen 1997). This market continues to grow with one estimate being over six million children taking the drug (Sax 2000). According to Sax (2000) »No other medication in American history has had this kind of success in achieving and maintaining such a grip on its market: not Valium, not Prozac, not Viagra. The United States, with less than 5 percent of the world's population, now accounts for 85 percent of the world's consumption of Ritalin« (p. 286). Other countries are beginning to follow the US lead.

Initially the drug was aggressively promoted to physicians and pharmacists through the use of traditional marketing tools (detailing by sales representative, brochures, research reports, etc.) in order to influence prescribing patterns and recommendations to parents (Diller 1998). In general, there is little doubt that the marketing activitities of pharmaceutical companies (particularly personal selling) directly influence the prescribing patterns of physicians (Chren 1999). Abuses of this process have declined somewhat in recent years but the primary mechanism remains the presentation of effectiveness and safety evidence from, in particular, published and unpublished studies and clinical trials. Unfortunately there is increasing concern about the general quality of that evidence. In general, such reports reflect a publication bias strongly favoring positive results (Dickersin, Chan, Chalmers, Sacks and Smith 1987, Esterbrook, Berlin, Gopalan and Matthews 1991). A recent meta-analysis of the research literature published in the Canadian Medical Association Journal was quite critical of the quality of the studies done to date (Schachter, Pham, King, Langford and Moher 2001).

Also there are multiple conflicts of interest issues due to the close ties between pharmaceutical companies, academic researchers studying ADHD, presenters at professional meetings, and schools of medicine (Korn 2000, Diller 1998). The relevance of many of these studies to community-based treatment may also be limited because the studies are mainly done in academic medical centers using samples of patients that are often unrepresentative of the national population. Finally sales presentations to physicians often contain inaccuracies and tend to be strongly biased toward the promotion of one treatment alternative (Zeigler and Singer 1995, Shaughnessy and Slawson 1996). Breggin (2001) in particular provides evidence that all of these controversial issues directly apply to the detailing of Ritalin.

An important element in this promotion was to reassure physicians that Ritalin is effective with relatively few side effects, a conclusion strongly condemned by psychiatrist Peter R. Breggin who has summarized evidence to the contrary (Breggin 1995, 2001). The US Drug Enforcement Administration and National Institute of Drug Abuse also have serious concerns about Ritalin use and abuse (Drug Enforcement Administration 1995, Haslip 1996, National Institute of Drug Abuse 2000). In particular, the DEA pointed out that all of the available indicators including scientific abuse liability studies, statistics on actual abuse, the limited number of scientific studies on possible adverse effects associated with long-term use of stimulants, the varying prescribing practices of U.S. physicians, and lack of concurrent treatment and follow-up, support much greater caution on the use of MPH.

A separate major element of the marketing strategy was to support the activities of Children and Adults with Attention-Deficit/Hyperactivity Disorder (CHADD). This was an advocacy group formed in 1987 to deal with widespread parental frustration and the general lack of information on ADD and ADHD (Anonymous 1997). However, the US Public Broadcast System aired an expose in 1995 which revealed that Ciba had contributed over one million dollars to CHADD starting in the early 1990's (http://www.pbs.org /merrow/tv/transcripts/add.pdf.). This contribution was not made public nor did CHADD members know of it.

This aspect of community building raised the serious ethical issue of whether or not CHADD, which at the time was a firm supporter of Ritalin treatment, was acting independently of the manufacturer. Indeed, Ciba identified CHADD on the PBS broadcast as a »conduit« for passing information on to the public at large. In that process, CHADD prepared a variety of materials including public service announcements and grew to become the largest advocacy and lobbying organization of its type and played a major role in the protection of ADHD through the Disabilities Education Act. According to Eberstadt (1999) they also mounted an extraordinary campaign to lift the regulation of Ritalin and make it easier to obtain. This effort was supported by the American Academy of Neurology, the American Academy of Pediatrics, the American Psychological Association, and the American Academy of Child and Adolescent Psychiatry (Diller 1999). Above all CHADD provided parents with a face-saving rationale for drug use in that ADHD was seen as a neurobiological disorder caused by a chemical imbalance in the brain that could be corrected by another chemical, Ritalin. Whether or not this is ultimately proven to be scientifically correct, it was a brilliant and continuing marketing tool.

An additional conduit for information was a variety of positive descriptions of the treatment in books in the 1980s and early 1990s which were aimed at parents but which were probably also read by teachers (Eberstadt 1999). More recent volumes have been far less certain about safety and efficacy (Diller 1998: Degradpre 1999, Breggin 2001). Teachers and school systems have also played a particularly important role in the success of Ritalin (Diller 1998, Breggin 2001). Unfortunately, no detailed analysis of this aspect of the successful Ciba-Geigy marketing program has been done to date. The impact of this effort is suggested by an early survey of teachers in Grand Rapids Michigan which indicated that awareness of the drug was widespread in that city early in the 1970's (Robin and Bosco 1972). At that time there also apparently was considerable debate about the use of Ritalin to treat ADHD (Bosco 1972). It is not clear how teachers were learning about the drug but it is unlikely that advertisements were being placed in their professional periodicals in the 1970's and 80's.

In part this success may be an early example of »buzz« or »word-of-mouth« marketing within the educational community (Rosen 2000, Khermouch with Green

2001). Breggin (2001) indicates that teachers were heavily propagandized particularly by workshops led by »professional advocates of ADHD/Ritalin (p. 239).« In addition, teachers had access to positive company and US Department of Education materials (Breggin 2001) and DOE videotape which was quite laudatory about Ritalinn and did not stress other alternatives (Portner 1995). As it turned out, much of the tape involves testimonials by CHADD Board Members and, when that was brought to the attention of the government, the tape was withdrawn.

Whatever marketing mechanisms were used, by the end of the century teacher and school system pressure on parents had become increasingly intrusive. As a result, in 2001 Connecticut became the first state to pass a law prohibiting any school staff from suggesting or recommending psychotropic drugs to parents. Similar legislation is under consideration in Arizona, Illinois, New York, New Jersey and Utah (Edwards 2001). The general assumption behind these efforts is that teachers have no right to recommend chemical treatments nor school systems any right to sanction parents who do not want their children put on prescribed drugs.

Despite this setback, by the late 1990s the attempts to promote the chemical treatment of ADHD using Ritalin had been highly successful in creating a community. This outcome is indicated by a Harris Interactive survey that was commissioned by one of the main marketers in the category. In this survey, nine in 10 physicians, teachers, and parents of children with ADHD believed that if the disorder is left untreated, it would seriously effect performance in school and in relationships. The success of the treatment, and of industry's efforts to inform the public, is also suggested by the finding that over 90 percent of the parents of children with ADHD, teachers, adults with the condition, and physicians surveyed agreed that medication is a successful treatment for children with ADHD (Shire Richwood 2000).

Thus ADHD became the most commonly diagnosed psychiatric disorder among children and Ritalin, through aggressive marketing, became the treatment of choice. However, the use of pharmaceuticals to treat the condition raises a wide variety of ethical issues (Diller 1996, Perring 1997, Goldman, et al 1998). They include basic questions of efficacy and safety, diagnostic inaccuracy, the impacts on the brain of treatment over long periods of time, the potential for abuse of stimulants, and concerns about the use of drugs to »control« children against their best interests.

A paper focused on marketing is not the place to analyze the large and confused literature on these issues. A recent article by the prestigious Council on Scientific Affairs of the American Medical Association largely dismissed many of these concerns (Goldman et al 1998) as did the most comprehensive ethical analysis of Ritalin (Perring 2000). These are rational discussions closely based on their analysis of the available evidence and they discount the power of the irrational fears evoked by

ADHD drug treatments. Marketers do not have the same luxury particularly with respect to control-related fears, variance in prescribing patterns across the country, and the extent to which Ciba-Geigy actually created, rather than served, this market.

CONTROL-RELATED FEARS

An unusually balanced view of the ethical issues can be found in a brief paper prepared by the Institute for Philosophy and Public Policy (1998). It correctly identifies the overall fear, that is, as a society, the US is increasingly relying on pharmaceuticals to force children to conform to adult expectations. This includes drugs like Ritalin for the hyperactive and disruptive and Prozac to energize introverts (Allen 1997). If valid, the inappropriate use of pharmaceuticals for social control is a clear violation of the rights of children and also contradicts the message from adults and the school system that kids should »Say No« to drugs. A basic ethical issue here is that Ritalin may primarily benefit others – non-ADHD students in the same classroom and overworked parents and teachers – at the long-term expense of those taking the pills. Ritalin, a drug used to reduce the disruptive behavior which characterizes Attention Deficit Disorders may ultimately become the poster boy for this increasing concern (Novak 2001). Perring's conclusion that control is largely a »stipulative matter« is absolutely correct and raises the issue of who (parents, advocates, regulators, politicians, professionals, etc.) will ultimately win the right to stipulate what is, and is not, the acceptable control of behavior through chemicals.

PRESCRIBING PATTERNS

The most recent analysis of Ritalin in the United States revealed extreme variation across the country (Marchak and Eaton 2001). When the data are mapped geographically, less than 25 counties nationally reported rates over 5 percent (http//: www.cleveland.com/indexssf?/news/pd/ritalin.html), rates of 2.6-4.9 percent tended to occur in a band stretching from the upper Midwest to New England, and much of the country reported rates under 1.4 percent. Given prevalence estimates of 3-5 percent, and the fact that 10-30 percent do not respond to stimulants, this data does provide some limited evidence of overprescription of the drug in 1999 in some counties. However, there are reports of rates as high as 20 percent in some suburban schools (Leibson 2001). These data suggest both a marketing opportunity in the underprescribing counties and a strong educational/public relations need in school districts where the rates grossly exceed expected prevalence. The pharmaceutical industry could, and probably should, play a strong role here.

A CREATED MARKET?

Finally, a fascinating consequence of the success of Ritalin is that it has generated multiple, class action, law suits which include some of the lawyers who were involved in successful past asbestos and tobacco litigation efforts (Public Broadcasting System 1999, Pharmaceutical Law And Policy Report 2001). The basic allegation of these actions is that that pharmaceutical companies (Particularly Ciba-Geigy/Novartis) conspired with the American Psychiatric Association and advocacy groups including CHADD to fraudulently promote the expansion of the ADD/ADHD diagnosis as a way of increasing Ritalin sales (Public Broadcasting System 1999, Pharmaceutical Law And Policy Report 2001). So far none of the suits have been successful but this is an interesting example of how a public controversy over marketing can lead to unexpected and costly legal consequences when children are involved. Also potentially relevant here is the history of Big Tobacco – multiple failures in the courts over a period of years and, ultimately, a very expensive national settlement.

Partially in response to these controversies, in 1995, Ritalin's manufacturer mounted a national campaign to reduce the risks associated with Ritalin. The target was doctors and pharmacists but the mailing included handouts for patients, parents and school nurses. (Farley 1997). However, by that time competitors were beginning to woo the community essentially created by Ciba-Geigy. In particular, other manufacturers have taken advantage of the new opportunities inherent in direct-to-consumer (DTC) to advertise alternative stimulants and in once-a-day formulations. But the actions of competitors meant that ADHD now became part of the larger problem of DTC promotion.

DIRECT-TO-CONSUMER ADVERTISING

Expenditures for direct-to-consumer (DTC) campaigns reached almost 2.5 billion dollars a year in 2000 and accounted for 15.7% of total drug marketing costs of almost 16 billion dollars (The Henry J. Kaiser Family Foundation 2001a). The area now represents half the expenditures involved in detailing doctors, five times professional journal outlays and almost a third of the total costs of sampling programs. In the same year, the division between TV and print advertising was 63.6 percent to 36.4 percent which is a reversal of the 13.4/86.6 percent split found in 1994. Studies indicate that

the most common messages were related to efficacy, control of symptoms, convenience, and innovativeness (Bell, Kravitz and Wilks 2000). In magazine advertisements,
emotional appeals, vague benefit claims, and statements about the physical causes of
illnesses predominated (Woloshin, Schwartz, Tremmel and Welch 2001).

The present level of DTC promotions is expected to increase rapidly and is estimated to reach $7.5 billion by 2005 (Kravitz 2001). To put that number in perspec-
tive, the entire US toy industry's advertising expenditures were only $837,102,500 in
2000 (http://www.toy-tma.com/industry/statistics/advertising.html), the four largest
media budgets in the tobacco industry barely exceeded $350 million in 1999 (Turner-
Bowker and Hamilton 2000), and total advertising expenditures for the entire beer
industry were $3,739,43,900 (http://www.cspinet.org/booze/A-B_Campaign.html).
If the pharmaceutical industry follows the path of consumer goods companies, as it is
doing with adults, the result will be an increased emphasis on directly promoting
drugs to minors. In the past, two experiments on exposure to medical advertising and
children's attitudes found little effect but this research predates the more sophisticated
marketing of recent years (Rossano and Butter 1987).

As the above figures indicate, pharmaceutical companies are moving their promotional dollars to TV advertising. As a result, children and youth will increasingly be
exposed to advertisements that are allegedly primarily intended for adults. In 2000,
fully half of the ten drugs with the largest advertising budgets were potentially of
interest to children or youth: Flonase for asthma, two antihistamines (Claritin and Al-
legra), Paxil – An increasingly controversial anti-depressant also used to treat social and
other anxiety, and the Meridia weight-loss formulation. (The Henry J. Kaiser Family
Foundation 2001a). Even if a drug like Meridia is not recommended for those under
16 years of age, the advertising has the potential to educate minors that a general solution to many of their problems can be found in an ethical pharmaceutical. In addition, promotions attempting to sway children to request specific drugs from physicians, either directly or through their parents, are likely to increase. This could be a
particularly dangerous situation with a anti-acne drug like Accutane which can both
damage fetuses and induce a suicidal depression (Stewart and Paine 2001).

COMPETITORS TO RITALIN

New competitors promoting Adderall, Concerta, and Metadate have quickly grasped
the opportunities inherent in DTC advertising.

ADDERALL

In 1996, Richwood Pharmaceutical Company, Inc (Now Shire Pharmaceuticals Group, PLC) entered the market with Adderall, an existing longer-acting amphetamine, as a direct competitor to Ritalin. In October of 2001 they became the first to launch a sustained release pill Adderall XR. The basic cognitive positioning was »ADDERALL XR is convenient for children suffering from ADHD because they can take it at home rather than at school. It has a rapid onset of action, its once a day delivery system is what patients and doctors want and ADDERALL XR is shown to be well tolerated, with few side effects.« (http://www.shire.com/shire/press/AdderallXRlaunchFinal.doc, Paragraph 4)

The line experienced rapid sales growth and by January 16, 2002 Adderall and ADDERALL XR had a combined share of 36.1 percent of the market with the XR version accounting for almost a third of that number (http://www.shire.com/shire/custom/2weeklydata22.ppt). Their CEO has announced that »This is a major product launch for Shire. We shall dedicate maximum sales and marketing effort to this launch through further increasing the effectiveness of our sales force, the share of voice in the market and our direct and indirect marketing support for the ADDERALL XR brand.« (Pharmalicensing 2001)

Shire has indeed followed the traditional marketing strategy for the category by paying physicians to conduct, and publish, research on their drugs (Public Broadcasting System 2000). Dr. Lawrence Diller author of *Running on Ritalin* has been particularly concerned about the aggressive marketing of Adderall. He comments that:

> »Adderall represents a triumph of American marketing know-how. The only remarkable thing about Adderall is the amount of promotion and advertising directed at physicians. It has reached new levels of hype activity in terms of its assault on doctors.« (Diller 1999, Paragraph 15)

As one example, he cites being offered $100 to sit and listen to someone talk about ADHD and Adderall for 15 minutes on the telephone and to fill out a five-minute questionnaire (Diller 1999). This strategy was quite successful and in a later article he cites IMS National Prescription Audit data indicating that Adderall supplanted Ritalin as the most widely prescribed ADHD medication in 1999 (Diller 2000). Both Adderall and the competing drug Metadate have come under fire for the ways in which they are being aggressively promoted to physicians (Thomas 2001).

With respect to parents Adderall developed a strategy of directly promoting the drug as the medical management solution to ADHD that assured parents their children could »Soar confidently into summer and the new school year.« (http://www.amphetamines.com /adderall/adderallad.html) They also jointed competitors in directly advertising to mothers in a variety of women's magazines starting in September of 2001.

Concerta

McNeil Consumer and Specialty Pharmaceuticals and ALZA obtained US Federal Drug Administration approval of once-a-day Concerta on August 1, 2000. Their marketing slogan was »One dose lasts from home to homework« because it was the first to last a full 12 hours. The launch slogan for doctors was »It's about time« (http://www.onsetdesign.com/port-alza.html) and within six months of FDA approval Concerta reached almost a 15 percent US market share (http://www.currentdrugdiscovery.com /CDDPDF/Issue%202/BUSINESS-NOVEN.pdf).

McNeal's stated mission is »To be the largest U.S. consumer healthcare company offering products which provide professionally endorsed benefits for healthcare.« (http://www.mcneilcampusrecruiting.com/mission.htm) which is a bit frightening in the context of ADHD treatment. They joined Adderall and Metadent in women's magazines but also began airing 60 second commercials on some of the more intellectual cable TV channels including Discovery and A & E (Thomas 2001).

Metadate

Finally, United Kingdom-based Celltech Pharma, Ltd. introduced Metadate CD in late May of 2001 and expanded its sales force from 250 to 400 sales representatives as part of this process. (http://www.medeva.co.uk/pharmaceuticals/) They achieved a share of approximately 8 percent of the market for once-daily methylphenidate by August, which was before an accelerated promotion to target parents during the early months of the school year. The Metadate CD magazine advertisements directly linked the brand to a smiling mother and son and to the slogan »One dose covers his ADHD for the whole school day.« The campaign included pamphlets for doctor's offices even featuring a blue-suited cartoon superhero Shades of Joe Camel (Thomas 2001).

However, a major ethical controversy arose when they added network television advertising to their promotional mix. That advertisement generated a cease-and-desist order from the Federal Drug Administration and concerns that such advertising is inconsistent with a 30-year-old international agreement in which the industry agreed that it would not advertise controlled substances with a high potential for abuse such as these drugs.

These new entries into the category raise very basic issues. The first is whether stimulants should ever be advertised to consumers. Diller (2001) argues strongly that even non-brand promotions of stimulants are fundamentally unethical because they represent an attempt to avoid present regulations and international agreements. A second concern involves the difference between the two major types of DTC advertisements. The »help-seeking« advertisements for Ritalin, Adderall and Concerta recommend that parents seek information and advice from a physician without highlighting a specific brand. The DTC messages from Metadate's are brand-specific. As such they may increase the possibility that consumers will demand specific prescriptions, a demand which can include the implicit possibility of an angry parent going elsewhere if a physician demurs. In this situation, physicians may prescribe Metadate even if they would prefer a competitor or no stimulant at all.

This marketing fray is likely to continue as Novartis promotes its new sustained release tablet (Ritalin-SR ®). These ADHD drugs, and other about to enter the market, may also become a major topic within the growing debate about the direct-to-consumer promotions for ethical pharmaceuticals. In addition, the discussion above only hints at some of the problems in the many other health-related categories.

SUMMARY

These two examples illustrate the range of ethical controversies that can occur when a brand effectively uses some of the more potent consumer behavior principles to create communities of children and adults, communities which have the potential to influence the socialization of minors as consumers. Too little is known about how this process operates but both the Barbie and Ritalin examples suggest that this type of success in the marketplace can be troubling to multiple stakeholders. Here companies should consider adopting a model like integrated social contracts theory which stresses the importance of understanding and appropriately responding to the concerns of all legitimate stakeholders including advocacy groups (Donaldson and Preston 1995, Donaldson and Dunphy 1999). Working effectively with, but not co-opting, the wide range of stakeholders interested in a given marketing issue is one way to limit ethical controversies.

Steps also need to be taken to increase the limited amount of valid information on the perceptions and reactions of minors. Barbie, by evoking the needs of children as emulate, to become older and more glamorous, to collect, and to evolve physically and mentally through play may also put some vulnerable individuals at risk of eating disorders and destructive materialism. Much more empirical research is needed to document whether or not playing with this doll provides benefits that exceed these risks particularly for vulnerable children. Consideration should also be given to how these same kids can be better protected from other factors that may act to increase their risks. Similarly, absent from most discussions of ADD are the voices of children. A striking element of the PBS Frontline special was those on Ritalin discussing their discontents (http://www.pbs.org/wgbh/pages /frontline/shows/medicating/four/). Not only did they feel stigmatized by the diagnosis and the treatment but the drug itself caused uncomfortable side effects.

Above all, companies must also constantly reexamine their role in the marketplace. The members of these brand-oriented communities have the potential to reinforce appropriate, or inappropriate, cultural values and marketers can influence this process. For example, Mattel's recent redesign of the physical attributes of the doll may have created a more achievable ideal for young girls. However, their profitable blizzard of new products could be feeding into the increased materialism of children. Given the actions of competitors and the pervasiveness of all types of toy promotion, particularly at Christmas, it is unlikely that Mattel will halt the yearly flood of line extensions. However, they might consider other actions that would act to counter the development of undesirable attitudes. This would be consistent with the other company actions, which seem to reflect a heightened sensitivity to ethical issues when marketing to children.

Treating ADHD chemically will also continue to be controversial. The above analysis suggests that the actions of Novartis have been less than optimal in terms of protecting children and the recent marketing approaches of their once-a-day competitors approach the deplorable. Ironically, the case of Ritalin may also illustrate how easily competitors can take advantage of the communication links within a community created through marketing. Ethically, the most important issue here is a greater focus on the utility of a multifaceted approach to the treatment of the condition. Pharmaceutical companies need to move beyond paying lip service to this concept and more aggressively promote drugs as part of a larger set of treatment options, which might be considered by parents, teachers and physicians.

Unfortunately, as health care-related products for kids continue to proliferate, the ethical inexperience of the companies involved are likely to create increasing problems. These will occur not only for pharmaceuticals but also for over-the-counter preparations, food supplements, and neutraceuticals. These problems will become even more serious as advertisers mount an increasing variety of promotions directly or indirectly targeting minors.

Finally, as a recent paper suggests, it is particularly important to incorporate increased ethical sensitivity into the culture, policies, supervision, personnel training, procedures, and marketing practices of any company marketing to children and youth (- Paine, Stewart and Kruger 2001). Mattel, an experienced children's marketer, appears to be doing this while Novartis and their competitors, all of whom are relatively new to this area, may need to reevaluate their efforts. As may many other companies whose use of the latest marketing tools to create communities around a brand may unethically influence the socialization of children and youth as consumers.

REFERENCES

Alcoholism and Drug Abuse Weekly (1996). »Agency Survey Reports Overuse Of Ritalin Among U.S. Children«, *Author 8*, no. 12:6-11.

Acuff, D. S. with Reiher, R. H. (1997). *What Kids Buy and Why*. New York, NY: The Free Press.

Alexander, Alison, Benjamin, Louise M, Hoearner, Keisha L. and Roe, Darrel (1999). »We'll Be Back In A Moment«, In Macklin, M. Carole and Carlson, Les. *Advertising To Children: Concepts and Controversies*, Thousand Oaks, CA: Sage Publications, 97-115.

Allen, Arthur (1997). »Readin', Ritin' And Ritalin«, *Salon Magazine*, July. Accessed 12/20/01 at http://www.salon.com/july97/mothers/ritalin970716.html.

American Academy Of Pediatrics (2000). »Diagnosis And Evaluation Of The Child With Attention-Deficit/Hyperactivity Disorder«, *Pediatrics*, 105, no. 5:1158-1170.

Anonymous (1997). »Druglord Ciba-Geigy Pushes Ritalin On Kids«, *The Gainesville Iguana*, May/June 1997. Accessed 1/8/02 at
http://www.afn.org/~iguana/archives /1997_05/19970503.html

Associated Press (2001). »Barbie Sunglasses Recalled For Toxic Chemicals«, *Author,* 2/21. Accessed 12/29/01 at http://archive.nandotimes.com/noframes/story/ 0,2107,500312200-500502557-503549483-0,00.html

Becker AE and Hamburg P. (1996). »Culture, The Media, And Eating Disorders«, *Harvard Review of Psychiatry* 4, no.3:163-7.

Belk, Russell W. (1985). »Materialism: Trait Aspects of Living in the Material World«, *Journal of Consumer Research*, 12, December, 265-280.

Bell RA, Kravitz RL and Wilkes MS. (2000). »Direct-To-Consumer Prescription Drug Advertising, 1989-1998«, A Content Analysis Of Conditions, Targets, Inducements, And Appeals. *Journal of Family Practice*, 49, no. 4:329-35.

Bernstein, Aaron (1999). »Sweatshops: No More Excuses«, *Business Week*, 3654, (11-08): 104.

Bernstein, Aaron, with Shari, Michael and Malkin, Elisabeth (2000). »Special Report: Global Labor: A World Of Sweatshops«, *Business Week*, 3706, (11-06): 84.

Bodytalk Magazine (No date). »Toxic Barbie«, Accessed 1/3/02 at
http://www.bodytalkmagazine.com/toxic%20barbie.htm

Borger, Gloria (1997). »Barbie's Newest Values«, *U.S. News and World Report* 23, (12-01): 40.

Bornstein, M. H. and Lamb, M.E. (1999). *Developmental Psychology: An Advanced Textbook*. Mahwah, NJ: Lawrence Erlbaum Associates.

Bosco, James (1972). »The Use of Ritalin for Treatment of Minimal Brain Dysfunction and Hyperkinesis in Children«, August 1, *Teacher Education Clearinghouse*: (SP006450)

Bower, Amanda B. and Landreth, Stacy (2001). »Is Beauty Best? High Versus Normally Attractive Models In Advertising«, *Journal of Advertising*, 30, no.1:1-8.

Brown, Ronald T. et al. »Prevalence and Assessment of Attention-Deficit/Hyperactivity Disorder in Primary Care Settings«, *Pediatrics* 107, no. 3:E43-54.

Brenkert, George G.(1998). »Marketing And The Vulnerable.« *Business Ethics Quarterly*, Ruffin Series, Special Issue 1, 7-20. Reprinted (pp 515-526) in Hartman, L. P. (1998): *Perspectives in Business Ethics*. Chicago, Irwin McGraw-Hill.

Breggin, Peter R. (1995, 2001). *Talking Back to Ritalin*. Monroe, MA: Common Courage Press. Paperback is by Perseus Books.

Butscher, Stephan A. & Luby, Frank (2002). »The Real Toy Story«, *Wall Street Journal*, January 28. Accessed 1/28/02 at http://online.wsj.com/article/0,,SB1012161753241194960.djm,00.html.

Chandler, T. M. and Heinzerling, B.M. (1999). *Children And Adolescents In The Market Place: Twenty-Five Years Of Academic Research,* Ann Arbor, MI: Pierian Press.

Church, Ellen B. (2001). »A Sense Of Justice«, *Scholastic Parent and Child* 8, no.5: 55.

Chren MM. (1999). »Interactions Between Physicians And Drug Company Representatives«, *American Journal of Medicine* 107, no. 2:182-3. No abstract available.

Cote, Marcel (1997). »A lesson on Barbie«, *CA Magazine, 130,* no. 1:56. Accessed 1/2/01 at http://www.camagazine.com/cica/camagazine.nsf/e1997-Jan/TOC/$file/e_eco.pdf

Davison, K.K., Markey, C. N. and Birch, L. L. (2000). »Etiology Of Body Dissatisfaction And Weight Concerns Among Five-Year-Old Girls«, *Appetite, 35,* 143-151.

de Graaf, John; Wann, David and Naylor, Thomas (2001). *Affluenza: The All Consuming Epidemic.* San Francisco: Berrett-Koehler

Degrandpre, Richard. (1999). *Ritalin Nation Rapid-Fire Culture and the Transformation of Human Consciousness*. New York, New York, NY: Norton.

Del Vecchio, G. (1997). *Creating Ever-Cool: A Marketer's Guide To A Kid's Heart*. Gretna, LA: Pelican.

Dickersin K, Chan S, Chalmers TC, Sacks HS, and Smith H Jr. (1987). »Publication bias and clinical trials«, *Controlled Clinical Trials* 8, no.4:343-53.

Diller, Lawrence H. (1998). *Running On Ritalin: A Physician Reflects On Children, Society, And Performance In A Pill*. New York, NY: Bantam

Diller Lawrence H. (2001). »An End Run To Marketing Victory«, *Salon Magazine*, Oct. 18. Accessed 1/16/02 at http://www.salon.com/mwt/feature/2001/10/18/drug_advertisements/

Donaldson, Thomas and Dunfee Thomas W. (1999). *Ties That Bind: A Social Contracts Approach to Business Ethics*. Boston, MA: Harvard Business School Publishing.

Donaldson, Thomas and Preston, Lee E. (1995). »The Stakeholder Theory Of The Corporation: Concepts, Evidence, And Implications«, *Academy of Management Review* 20, no.1: 65-92.

Drug Enforcement Administration (1995). »Methylphenidate«, Press Release, October 20 accessed 12/28/01 at http://web1.caryacademy.org/chemistry/rushin/StudentProjects /Compound-WebSites/2000/Ritalin/deapress.html

Dubin, Steven C. (1999). In McDonough, Yona Zeldis (1999). *The Barbie Chronicles: A Living Doll Turns Forty*. New York, NY: Touchstone, 19-38.

The Economist (1998). »The Environment: Chewing On The Issue«, *Author* 348, (07-11).

The Economist (1999). »Business Ethics: Sweatshop Wars«, *Author* 350, (2/27).

Eberstadt, Mary (1999). »Why Ritalin Rules«, *Policy Review* 94, Apr/May: 24-46.

Edut, Ophiria (Editor) (1998). *Adios Barbie: Young Women Write About Body Image And Identity*. Seattle, WA: Seal Press.

Edwards, Bob (2001). »Analysis: Connecticut Passes Law Prohibiting School Staff From Suggesting Psychotropic Drugs For Disruptive Children«, *National Public Radio, Morning Edition*, 12-17-2001.

Environment News Service (1999). Tide turns against chemical softeners in plastic toys. Author, (12/9): Accessed 1/5/02 at http://ens.lycos.com/ens/dec99/1999L-12-09-02.htmlLycos.com

Easterbrook PJ, Berlin JA, Gopalan R. and Matthews DR (1991). »Publication Bias In Clinical Research«, *Lancet* 13, no. 337(8746):867-72.

Environment News Service (1999). »Tide Turns Against Chemical Softeners In Plastic Toys«, *Author, 12/9*. Accessed 1/5/02 at http://ens.lycos.com/ens/dec99/1999L-12-09-02.htmlLycos.com.

Fairburn CG, Welch SL, Doll HA, Davies BA and O'Connor ME. (1997). »Risk Factors For Bulimia Nervosa: A Community-Based Case Control Study«, *Archives of General Psychiatry* 54: 509-517.

Farley, Dixie (1997). »Attention Disorder: Overcoming the Deficit«, *FDA Consumer Magazine* July-August Accessed 1/ 21/02 at http://www.fda.gov/fdac/features/1997/597_adhd.html

Foek, Anton (1997). »Sweatshop Barbie«, *The Humanitarist* January/February: 5-6.

Ghaderi A. and Scott B. (2001). »Prevalence, Incidence And Prospective Risk Factors For Eating Disorders«, *Acta Psychiatrica Scandinavica* 104, no. 2:122-30.

Goldberg, Marvin E. et al. (2002). »Understanding Materialism Among Youth«, *Journal of Consumer Psychology*, in press.

Goldman, Debra (1999). »Consumer Republic«, *Adweek* 40, no. 25:20.

Goldman, Larry S. et al., for the Council on Scientific Affairs, American Medical Association (1998). »Diagnosis And Treatment Of Attention-Deficit/Hyperactivity Disorder In Children And Adolescents«, *Journal of the American Medical Assocation* 279, no. 14:1100-1107.

Goldstein, Lauren (1998). »First: The Fashion-Industrial Complex: Barbie's Secret Plan For World Domination«, *Fortune*, 11-23-1998: 38-40.

Grow, Gerald O. (1996). »Dont Hate Me Because I'm Beautiful – A Commercial In Context«, Accessed 1/11/02 at http:www.longleaf.net/ggrow. An earlier version of this paper appears in Fox, Roy (1994): *Images in Language, Media, and Mind*. Urbana, IL: NCTE Press.

Guber, S. S. and Berry, J. (1994). *Marketing To And Through Kids*. New York: McGraw-Hill.

Gunter, Barrie and Furnham, Adrian (1998). *Children as Consumers: A Psychological Analysis of the Young People's Market*. London, UK:Routledge.

The Harwood Group (1995). »Yearning For Balance: Views On Consumption, Materialism And The Environment«, Report commissioned by the Merck Family Fund. Accessed 11/27/01 at http://www.newdream.org/yearning/yearn_full.html

Haislip, Gene R. (1996). »Attention Deficit Disorder ADD/ADHD: Statement of Drug Enforcement Administration«, Accessed 1 21 02 at http://www.add-adhd.org/ritalin.html

Heckman, James (1999) »Don't Shoot The Messenger«, *Marketing News* 33, no. 11: 1,9.

Institute for Philosophy And Public Policy (1998). »One Pill Makes You Smarter: An Ethical Appraisal of the Rise of Ritalin«, Author. Accessed 1/15/02 at http://www.puaf.umd.edu/IPPP/fall98 /one_pill_makes_you_smarter.htm

Jackson, Rodger L. and Paine, Whiton S. (2001). »Salvaging Kids and Ethical Principles at the Same Time«, *Proceedings of the Sixteenth Annual Conference of the Atlantic Marketing Association*, Portland, Maine, September 26-29. [page #]

Jensen P. S. et al. (2001). »Findings From The NIMH Multimodal Treatment Study Of ADHD (MTA): Implications And Applications For Primary Care Providers«, *Journal of Developmental Behavioral Pediatrics* 22, no.1:60-73.

John; Deborah R. (1999). »Consumer Socialization Of Children: A Retrospective Look At Twenty-Five Years Of Research«, *Journal of Consumer Research* 26, no. 3: 183-213.

John Paul II, Pope (1991). »Encyclical Letter Centesimus Annus Addressed By The Supreme Pontiff John Paul II To His Venerable Brothers In The Episcopate The Priests And Deacons Families Of Men And Women Religious All The Christian Faithful And To All Men And Women

Of Good Will On The Hundredth Anniversary Of Rerum Novarum«, Accessed 12/28/01 at ttp://www.vatican.va/holy_father/john_paul_ii/encyclicals/documents/hf_jp-ii_enc_01051991_centesimus-annus_en.html

Jones, Jennifer M. et al. (2001). »Disordered Eating Attitudes And Behaviours In Teenaged Girls: A School-Based Study«, *Canadian Medical Association Journal*165, no. 5:547-52. Accessed 1/16/02 at http://www.cma.ca/cmaj/vol-165/issue-5/0547.asp

The Henry J. Kaiser Family Foundation (2001). Prescription Drug Trends: A Chartbook Update, November 2001. Menlo Park, CA. The Henry J. Kaiser Family Foundation. Accessed 12/13/01 at http://www.kff.org/content/2001/3112/RxChartbook.pdf.

Kasser, Tim and Ryan, Richard M (1993). »A Dark Side Of The American Dream: Correlation Of Financial Success As A Central Life Aspiration«, *Journal of Personality and Social Psychology* 65:410-422.

Kearney-Cooke A, Striegel-Moore R. (1997). »The Etiology And Treatment Of Body Image Disturbance«, In: Garner D. M. and Garfinkel P.D., eds. *Handbook of Treatment for Eating Disorders.* 2nd ed. New York, NY: The Guilford Press, 295-306.

Korn D. (2000). »Conflicts of interest in biomedical research«, *Journal of the American Medical Association* 284, no. 17:2234-7.

Khermouch, Gerry with Green, Jeff (2001). »Buzz Marketing«, *Business Week*, July 30. Accessed 1/8/02 at http://www.businessweek.com:/print/magazine/content _31/b3743001.htmlmain-window)

Kravitz Richard L. (2000). »Direct-To-Consumer Advertising Of Prescription Drugs.« *Western Journal of Medicine* 173:221-222. Accessed 1/18/02 at http://www.ewjm.com/cgi/content/full/173/4/221

Laczniak, Russell N. et al. (1995). »Mothers' Attitudes Toward 900-Number Advertising Directed At Children«, *Journal of Public Policy and Marketing* 14 (Spring), 108-16.

Laroche, Michel; Bergeron, Jasmin and Barbaro-Forleo, Guido (2001). »Targeting Consumers Who Are Willing To Pay More For Environmentally Friendly Products«, *Journal of Consumer Marketing* 18, no. 6:520-538.

Leibson, Cynthia L. et al. (2001). »Use and Costs of Medical Care for Children and Adolescents With and Without Attention-Deficit/Hyperactivity Disorder«, *Journal of the American Medical Association* 285, no. 1:60-66.

Lord, M.G (1994). *Forever Barbie: The Unauthorized Biography of a Real Doll.* New York: William Morrow.

Macklin, M. Carole and Carlson, Les (1999). *Advertising To Children: Concepts and Controversies.* Thousand Oaks, CA: Sage Publications.

Macchiette, Bart and Roy, Abhijit (1994). »Sensitive Groups and Social Issues: Are You Marketing Correct?«, *Journal of Consumer Marketing*11, no. 4: 55-64.

Marchak, Beth and Eaton, Sabrina (2001). »Ritalin prescribed unevenly in U.S.«, *The Plain Dealer* 05/06/01.

Marguiles, Peggy (No Date). »The Barbie Disinformation Organization.« Accessed 1/10/02 at http://www-2.cs.cmu.edu/afs/cs/user/jthomas/SurReview/reviews-html/bdo.html

Martin, C. L. (1998). »Engineering High-Meaning, High-Involvement Brands As A Relationship Marketing Strategy«, *Journal of Product and Brand Management* 7, no. 1: 6-26.

Mattel (2000). *Barbie: A Visual Guide To The Ultimate Fashion Doll.* London, UK: DK Publishing

McDonough, Yona Zeldis (1999). *The Barbie Chronicles: A Living Doll Turns Forty.* New York, NY: Touchstone.

McNeal, J. U (1999). *The Kids Market. 'Myths and Realities'.* Ithaca, NY: Paramount Market Publishing.

McNeal, J. U. (1998). »Tapping The Three Kids Markets«, *American Demographics*, April. Accessed 11/11/01 at http://www.demographics.com/

McNeal, J. U. (1992). *Kids As Customers: A Handbook Of Marketing To Children*. New York: Jossey-Bass.

McNeal, J. U. (1991*). A Bibliography Of Research And Writings On Marketing And Advertising To Children*. NY: Lexington Books.

Monczunski, John (1999). »The Meaning of Things«, *Notre Dame Magazine* Summer Accessed 1/16/02 at http://www.nd.edu/~ndmag/stuf2s99.htm

Millican, April (No date). »Editorial: The Soapbox – The Rise and Fall of the Barbie Doll«, http://www-2.cs.cmu.edu/afs/cs/user/jthomas/SurReview/reviews-html/bdo.html Accessed 12/22/01 at http://www.dollzine.com/soapbox4.asp

Morris, Rebecca J. and Martin, Charles L (2000). »Beanie Babies: A Case Study In The Engineering Of A High-Involvement/Relationship-Prone Brand«, *Journal of Product and Brand Management 9*, no.2: 78-98.

Morrow, Robert C; Morrow Ardythe L and Haislip, Gene (1998). »Methylphenidate In The United States, 1990 Through 1995«, *American Journal of Public Health* 88, no.7: 1121-2.

Muensterberger, Werner L. (1993). *Collecting*. Princeton, NJ: Princeton University Press.

MTA Cooperative Group (1999a). »A 14–Month Randomized Clinical Trial Of Treatment Strategies For Attention-Deficit/Hyperactivity Disorder. The MTA Cooperative Group. Multimodal Treatment Study Of Children With ADHD«, *Archives of General Psychiatry* 56, no.12:1073-86.

MTA Cooperative Group (1999b). »Moderators And Mediators Of Treatment Response For Children With Attention-Deficit/Hyperactivity Disorder: The Multimodal Treatment Study Of Children With Attention-Deficit/Hyperactivity Disorder«, *Archives of General Psychiatry* 56, no.12:1088-96.

Murphy, Patrick E. (2001). »Marketing Ethics At The Millenium: Review, Reflections And Recommendtions«, *Society for Business Ethics*, Washington, DC, August.

Noble, Holcomb B. (1999). »Barbie and Other Toys to Go on an Oil-Free Diet«, *New York Times*, 12/21 Accessed 1/5/02 at http://www.nytimes.com/learning/teachers/featured_articles/19991221tuesday.html

Norton, Mike (2000). »These Kids Perfected Art Of Collecting Early«, *Marketing News* 34, no. 19: 29.

Novak V. (2001). »New Ritalin Advertisement Blitz Makes Parents Jumpy«, *Time* 158, no.10:62-3.

Paine, Whiton S. (1994). »Reducing Barriers In Focus Groups With Kids«, American Marketing Association's »Bridging The Gap« Marketing Research Conference. San Francisco. September 20.

Paine, Whiton S. et al. (2001). »Preventing Ethical Problems When Marketing To Minors«, *International Journal of Advertising and Marketing to Children* 3, no. 2:69-80.

Palmes GK. (2001). »Some reflections on the origins of biological psychiatry«, *North Carolina Medical Journal,* 2001 Jul-Aug; 62(4):224-8.

Parke, R.D. et al. (1994). *A Century of Developmental Psychology*. Washington, D. C.: American Psychological Association.

Perring, Christian (1997). »Medicating Children: The Case of Ritalin«, *Bioethics*, Vol. 11, No. 3&4, 1997, pp. 228-240.

Pharmaceutical Law And Policy Report (2001). »Plaintiffs Drop Federal Ritalin Class Action Against Novartis, Psychiatric Organization«, *Author*, Volume 1 Number 5. Accessed 12/18/01 at http://subscript.bna.com/SAMPLES/plp.nsf/85256269004a9921852562540065050d/a8fee329cd31991785256aa30008483c?OpenDocument

Pharmalicensing (2001). »INTERVIEW – Rolf Stahel, Chief Executive of Shire Pharmaceuticals Group plc.«, *Drug and Market Development, 28 March*. Accessed 1/16/02 at http://pharmalicensing.com/features/disp/985783686_3ac1dd86a02b4

Pius XII, Pope (1957). »Le Pelerinage De Lourdes (Warning Against Materialism On The Centenary Of The Apparitions At Lourdes)«, Encyclical Promulgated on 2 July 1957. Accessed 1/3/02 at http://www.ewtn.com/library/ENCYC/P12PELER.HTM

Pope HG Jr. et al. (1999). »Evolving Ideals Of Male Body Image As Seen Through Action Toys«, *International Journal of Eating Disorders*, 26, no.1:65-72

Portner, Jessica (1995). »Worried About Message, E.D. Halts Video Distribution«, *Education Week 15,* Nov. 8: p. 20.

Press, Eyal (1996). »Barbie's Betrayal: The Toy Industry's Broken Workers«, *The Nation*, 12/30. Accessed 12/18/01 at http://past.thenation.com/issue /961230/1230pres.htm

Public Broadcasting System (1999). »Frontline, ADHD Lawsuits«, Accessed 1/16/02 at http://www.pbs.org/wgbh/pages/frontline/shows/medicating/backlash/lawsuits.html

Regulatory Intelligence Data (1999). Responsible parties agree to clean up contaminated soil and roundwater at the chemsol, inc. Superfund site in Piscataway, New Jersey. *Author,* (08-19): Available through Electric Library http://ask.elibrary.com/printdoc.asp?querydocid= 29336842@urn: bigchalk:US;Lib&dtype=0~0&dinst=0&title=RESPONSIBLE+PARTIES+ AGREE+TO+CLEAN+UP+CONTAMINATED+SOIL+AND+ROUNDWATER+ AT+THE+CHEMSOL%2C+INC%2E+SUPERFUND+SITE+IN+PISCATAWAY%2C+ NEW++

Richards, Amelia (Amy) (1998). »Body Image: Third Wave Feminism's Issue?« In Edut, Ophiria (Editor) (1998): *Adios Barbie: Young Women Write About Body Image And Identity.* Seattle, WA: Seal Press. 196-2000.

Richins, Marsha L. (1994a). »Valuing Things: The Public and Private Meanings of Possessions«, *Journal of Consumer Research*, 21 (December), 504-521.

Richins, Marsha L. (1994b). »Special Possessions and the Expression of Material Values«, *Journal of Consumer Research*, 21 (December), 522-533.

Roberts, James A. (1998). »Compulsive Buying Among College Students: An Investigation Of Its Antecedents, Consequences, And Implications For Public Policy«, *The Journal of Consumer Affairs* 32, no.2:295-319.

Robinson T. N. et al. (2001). »Overweight Concerns And Body Dissatisfaction Among Third-Grade Children: The Impacts Of Ethnicity And Socioeconomic Status«, *Journal of Pediatrics* 138:181-7.

Rosen, Emanuel (2000). *The Anatomy of Buzz: How to Create Word-Of-Mouth Marketing.* New York, NY: Doubleday.

Rossano, Matt J. and Butter, Eliot J. (1987). »Television Advertising And Childrens' Attitudes Toward Proprietary Medicine«, *Psychology and Marketing* 4, no.3: 213-24.

Rotfeld, Herb (1998). »Marketing Is Target When Product 'Undesirable«, *Marketing News* 32, no. 8, 8.

Rutter T. (1997). Drugs must be tested for use in children. British Medical Journal Aug 23;315(7106):445

Sax, Leonard (2000). »Ritalin: Better Living Through Chemistry?«, *The World and I* 15, 11-01:286.

Schachter H. M. et al. (2001). »How Efficacious And Safe Is Short-Acting Methylphenidate For The Treatment Of Attention-Deficit Disorder In Children And Adolescents? A Meta-Analysis«, *Canadian Medical Association Journal* 165, no. 11:1475-88

Shaw, W. H. and Barry, V. (1998). *Moral issues in business (7th ed.):* Belmont, CA: Wadsworth.

Shaughnessy AF and Slawson DC. (1996). »Pharmaceutical Representatives«, *British Medical Journal* 312, no. 7045:1494.

Shire Richwood (2000, September 11). »New Survey Shows Fear of Medication, Confusing Information Keep Children With Attention Deficit/Hyperactivity Disorder from Getting Treatment«, Accessed 1/16/02 at http://www.kidsource.com/ld/adhd.survey.html

Shisslak CM, Crago M, and Estes LS (1995). »The Spectrum Of Eating Disturbances«, *International Journal of Eating Disorders* 18:209-219.

Siegel, Dave et al. (2001). *The Great Tween Buying Machine: Marketing to Today's Tweens,* Ithaca, NY: Paramount Market Publishing.

Sims, Rodman (1997). »When Does Target Marketing Become Exploitation?«, *Marketing News,* 31 (November 24), 10.

Smith, N. C. and Cooper-Martin, E. (1997). »Ethics And Target Marketing: The Role Of Product Harm And Consumer Vulnerability«, *Journal of Marketing* 61, July:1-20.

Stauffacher, Sue (2000). »Magnificent Obsessions. (Children As Collectors)«, *Better Homes And Gardens, June, 01.* Accessed 1/13/01 at www.findarticles.com/cf_dls/m1041/6_78/62161897/p1/article.jhtml

Stephens, Debra Lynn et al. »The Beauty Myth And Female Consumers: The Controversial Role Of Advertising«, *Journal of Consumer Affairs* 28:137-154.

Stevens, Tim (1997). »Playing to win. (Mattel Inc.) (includes related articles on the 'Barbie' doll, and on company brainstorming«, *Industry Week* 246,11-03-1997:18-24.

Stewart, Karen L. & Paine, Whiton S.(2001). »Marketing to Children over the Internet: Some Ethical Issues and Concerns«, *Proceedings of the Sixteenth Annual Conference of the Atlantic Marketing Association*, Portland, Maine, September 26-29.

Stoller, R. J. (1980). »A Different View Of Oedipal Conflict«, In S. I. Greenspan and G. H. Pollock (Eds.), *The course of life,* Vol. 1, Infancy and early childhood. Adelphi, MD: Mental Health Study Center, 589-602.

Stoltman, J. J. »The Context Of Advertising And Children«, In Macklin, M. C. and Carlson, L. (Eds.): *Advertising to Children: Concepts and Controversies.* Thousand Oaks, CA: Sage Publishing, 291-98.

Striegel-Moore, Ruth H (2001). »Editorial: Body Image Concerns Among Children«, *Journal of Pediatrics* 138, no. 2, 158-160.

Stevens, Tim, (1997). »Playing To Win (Includes Related Articles On The 'Barbie' Doll, And On Company Brainstorming)«, *Industry Week, 246,* 11-03: 18-24.

Surgeon General of the United States (2002). »Mental Health: A report of the Surgeon General«, Washington, DC: Government Printing Office. Available at http://www.surgeongeneral.gov/library/mentalhealth/home.html

Thomas, Karen (2001). »Back To School For ADHD Drugs«, *USA Today* 10/31. Accessed 12/16/02 at http://www.usatoday.com/life/2001-08-28-adhd.htm

Wanless, Mary D. (2001). »Barbie's Body Images«, *Feminist Media Studies, 1,* no. 1:126-7.

The Washington Times (2001). »Barbie Boomers, Women Rekindle Childhood With Past Playthings«, *Author,* 10-25. Available at http://www.washtimes.com/archives.htm, Article ID: U00733060097.

Whitaker AH. (1992). »An Epidemiological Study Of Anorectic And Bulimic Symptoms In Adolescent Girls: Implications For Pediatricians«, *Pediatric Annals* 21:752-9.

Woloshin S, Schwartz LM, Tremmel J. and Welch HG.(2001). »Direct-To-Consumer Advertisements For Prescription Drugs: What Are Americans Being Sold?«, *Lancet* 358, no. 9288:1141-6.

Wright-Isak, C. (1999). »Advertising To Children In The Twenty-First Century«, In Macklin, M. C. and Carlson, L. (Eds.): *Advertising to Children: Concepts and Controversies.* Thousand Oaks, CA: Sage Publishing, 275-80.

Ziegler MG, Lew P and Singer BC.(1995). »The Accuracy Of Drug Information From Pharmaceutical Sales Representatives«, *Journal of the American Medical Association* 995, no. 273:1296-8.

Zollo, P. (1999). *Wise Up To Teens: Insights Into Marketing And Advertising To Teenagers (2nd Ed.).* Ithaca, NY: New Strategist Publications.

11

ADVERTISING, BRANDING, AND CONSUMING

– THE ABCS OF MARKETING IN AMERICAN SCHOOLS

By Nancy Jennings

INTRODUCTION

Over the past several decades, children have become an increasingly important consumer market. James McNeal (1987), a leading scholar in children's consumer behavior, suggests that marketers have realized that children are three markets in one – they spend their own money (current market), they influence their family's purchases (influence market), and through their own consumer experiences as children, they can become brand loyal into adulthood (future market). As such, children between the ages of 4 and 12 spent almost $29 billion of their own money and had a direct influence on $290 billion in family spending in 2000 (McDonald and Lavelle 2001). Furthermore, Teenage Research Unlimited estimates that teens between the ages of 12 and 19 spent $155 billion of their own money in 2000, an increase of $2 billion from 1999 (Poe 2001).

As a result of children's spending power and influence, American business has shown an increased interest in reaching these young consumers. Marketing efforts to children have expanded beyond television advertising to include such venues as in-store displays, direct mail, kids clubs, and product placement in movies, and video games. One of the more controversial marketing strategies has been the growing commercialization of schools. Alex Molnar, director of the Commercialism in Education

Research Unit at Arizona State University, indicates that the number of references in the press that discuss commercial activities in schools has increased 395 percent between 1990 and 2000 (Molnar and Morales 2000). This chapter will explore different marketing activities within the school system, drawing upon specific case studies, and discuss public policies regarding these practices, including the rise of advocacy groups against in-school commercialism.

GAO Report (2000)	Consumers Union (1995)	Communication Scholars (1998)	Education Scholars (2000)
Direct Advertising	• In-school advertisements • Advertisements in classroom materials and programs	• Direct advertising • Free products in schools (cross-listed under Indirect Advertising)	• Appropriation of space (cross-listed under Market Research and Product Sales) • Electronic marketing (cross-listed under Indirect Advertising)
Indirect Advertising	• Corporate-sponsored educational materials and programs • Corporate-sponsored contests and incentive programs	• Curricular involvement • Free products in schools (cross-listed under Direct Advertising)	• Sponsored-educational materials • Incentive programs • Sponsorship of programs and activities • Electronic marketing (cross-listed under Direct Advertising)
Product Sales		• Fund raising activities • Selling of products in schools	• Fund raising • Exclusive agreements • Appropriation of space (cross-listed under Direct Advertising and Market Research)
Market Research			• Appropriation of space (cross-listed under Direct Advertising and Product Sales)
			• Privatization

Table 1. Four categorizations of marketing activities in schools

CURRENT MARKETING PRACTICES IN SCHOOLS

Commercialism in schools includes a variety of marketing strategies. In order to discuss these strategies, researchers have sorted these activities into a number of categories. Four categorization structures have been proposed by different researchers. The Consumers Union Education Services (1995) identifies four categories of marketing strategies including in-school advertisements, advertisements in classroom materials and programs, corporate-sponsored educational materials and programs, and corporate-sponsored contests and incentive programs. Communication scholars describe five categories which include direct advertising, free product give-aways, the sale of products in schools, fundraising activities, and curricular involvement (Richards, Wartella, Morton, & Thompson 1998). A recent federal study of in-school commercialism categorizes these activities into four groups including product sales, direct advertising, indirect advertising, and market research (United States General Accounting Office 2000). Finally, education scholars group commercial activities into eight different categories including sponsorship of program and activities, exclusive agreements, incentive programs, appropriation of space, sponsored-educational materials, electronic marketing, privatization, and fund raising (Molnar and Morales 2000). While most of these categories are similar, others offer a unique perspective regarding marketing strategies. Thus far, the report which offers the most comprehensive categorization strategy has been produced by the federal government. Therefore, marketing strategies across these four structures will be synthesized under the headings put forth by that report (See Table 1).

DIRECT ADVERTISING

The most obvious marketing practice is the advertising of products and services to students in school buildings and school settings such as sports fields, buses, or yearbooks. The Consumers Union report defines in-school advertisements as »advertising that is displayed in the school itself or on property closely related to the school« (Consumers Union 1995, p. 3) and would include such things as advertising on school buses, scoreboards, and billboards and wallboards in school hallways. All four sets of researchers include this practice in their categorization structure. For example, a school district near the Dallas-Fort Worth International Airport is receiving $3.45 million over a 10-year period to place advertisements for Dr Pepper in their gyms, stadiums and atop two schools' roofs (»This school« 1998). School buses in Colorado Springs and New York City sport advertising for Burger King and 7-Up across the sides of the buses (Wells 1996). Sycamore High School in Cincinnati has a $200,000 high-tech scoreboard with space for 17 advertisements on turning panels in its gymnasium (Wolff 1996), and some schools are now selling advertising space on their athlete's warm-up suits (Winters 1995).

According to the GAO report, direct advertising would also include such activities as media-based advertising (USGAO 2000). These activities would be classified as »electronic marketing« by education scholars (Molnar and Morales 2000), »advertise-ments in classroom materials and programs« by Consumers Union (1995), and »direct advertising« by communication scholars (Richards, Wartella, Morton, and Thompson 1998). This would include advertisements in classroom magazines and television pro-grams. An example of this would include Channel One, a 12-minute news program created by Whittle Communication in 1990 and acquired by Primedia in 1994 which includes two minutes of advertising in each daily newscast (Primedia web site). As part of the Channel One package, Primedia provides $25,000 worth of equipment includ-ing a fixed KU-based satellite dish, two video cassette recorders, 19-inch color tele-vision monitors mounted in the classrooms and internal wiring along with free service maintenance of the equipment (Primedia website). In exchange for the equip-ment and service, the schools are required to air the 12-minute news program with the commercials in tact every school day. According to Primedia, Channel One reach-es 400,000 educators and more than 8 million teenagers through 12,000 public, pri-vate, and parochial schools (Primedia web site).

Other media-based advertising companies have followed in the footsteps of Pri-media. Star Broadcasting, a small company in St. Paul, Minnesota, proposed to provide schools across the country with music which is interspersed with advertising. The company planned to provide a minimum of 8 minutes of national advertiser's com-mercials for every 52 minutes of music, and the schools could get two more minutes of advertisements if they solicited local business to advertise as well (Walsh 1993). Schools would broadcast the music and commercials in the school hallways, cafeterias and courtyards for a minimum of 3 hours per day (Walsh 1993). Similarly, ZapMe! had been offering computer equipment and Internet access in exchange for a captive audience and market research. ZapMe!'s offer included creating a computer lab of computers, a laser printer, a roof-mounted satellite dish for Internet connection to a collection of 13,000 child-safe web sites, free computer training for teachers, and free technical support to schools (Schwartz 2000). As part of the contract with ZapMe!, schools must agree to use the computers at least 4 hours a day, and the computers come pre-loaded with a permanent interface known as »netspace« which features a 2-inch border around the screen where advertisements appear in a box in the lower

left-hand (Bazeley 1999). A further discussion of a variety of other electronic marketing practices will be addressed in the case studies.

According to the GAO report, another form of direct advertising in schools involves the distribution of free sample products. While the GAO report would consider this practice direct advertising, communication scholars (Richards et al 1998)
separated this activity from direct advertising practices and include corporate-sponsored contests and incentives with free give-aways. Corporate-sponsored contests and
incentives are listed as »indirect advertising« according to the GAO report (USGAO
2000), and have a separate category according to the Consumers Union report (1995)
and education scholars (Molnar and Morales 2000). For purposes of this chapter, free
samples will be discussed as direct advertising, and corporate-sponsored contests and
incentives will be reviewed under indirect advertising practices. Examples of free
product distribution include such activities as Nike's annual dispersal of new athletic
shoes for sports teams in over a hundred schools (Glamser 1997) and packages of
hygiene products with items like deodorant and toothpaste by such companies as
Procter and Gamble (Jimenez 1997). Each semester, Cover Concepts distributes free
book covers which contain company logos among public service messages from celebrities such as Michael Jordan or Spike Lee to 31,000 schools and almost 25 million students across the country (Stead 1997).

INDIRECT ADVERTISING

Indirect advertising covers a wide variety of marketing practices from the distribution
of curricular materials and supplies to corporate-sponsored events and incentive programs. These practices often ride the fence between blatant advertising and public service. Furthermore, in some cases, such as product placement in textbooks, there are
no commercial or promotional arrangements between commercial businesses and
textbook publishers regarding use of products or logos in schoolbooks (Hays 1999).
Yet the presence of corporate logos still appear in the schools which would be considered commercial activity.

One practice that seems to cross the line between indirect and direct advertising
is the appearance of commercial products and brand names in textbooks. According
to education scholars, this activity would be categorized under »appropriation of
space« (Molnar and Morales 2000); however, communication scholars would label
such activities as »curricular involvement« (Wartella and Jennings 2001). Corporate
logos and products have appeared in textbooks in 15 states across the country including California, Texas, and New York. A textbook series called *Mathematics: Applications*

and Connections first appeared in 1995 and was followed by a revised version in 1999, both published by McGraw-Hill Inc. and both containing pictures of corporate logos and using corporate products as examples in various mathematics problems. Examples of products used in the series include Barbie dolls, Cocoa Frosted Flakes, Sony Play Stations, Spalding basketballs, characters and sites owned by Disney and Warner Brothers and fast food from Burger King & McDonald's (Hays 1999). In this series, students learn percentages by calculating the percent of the discount received on a $94 pair of Reebok Intimidator shoes that were on sale for $76 (Hegarty 1999), and they learn symmetry by studying the design of the Chevrolet and Hallmark logos (Gaines 2000). One of the book's authors claims that the products were mentioned to make the problems more relevant to today's youth (Hays 1999). According to McGraw-Hill's director of media relations, Bill Jordan, companies did not request or pay for their presence in the textbooks, although permission was obtained to use their logos (Gaines 2000).

One step beyond product placement has been the creation and distribution of corporate-sponsored educational materials and programs. Education scholars describe this practice as »materials supplied to schools by corporations or trade associations that claim to have an instructional content« (Molnar and Morales 2000) and, according to Consumers Union (1995), may include such things as multimedia teaching kits, videos, software, books, posters, reproducible activity sheets, workbooks, or other teaching aids. Communication scholars (Richards et al 1998) would label this practice as »curricular involvement« and indicate public concern over the objectivity of these materials. For example, Kellogg's has published nutrition posters with pictures of Rice Krispies cereal boxes on them, and General Mills has sent teachers »Gushers: Wonders of the Earth« a science lesson about volcanoes that uses the company's Fruit Gushers candy as part of the lesson plan (Stead 1997). Other examples include Exxon distributing free booklets that teach children to protect the environment, and the manufacturer of Prozac, an anti-depressant, sending speakers to schools to discuss mental health issues, according to the Center for Commercial Free Public Education (Maller 2000).

Similarly, corporations often sponsor contests or events and offer incentives for academic achievement within the school system. While communication scholars include these incentives and contests as »free products« (Richards et al 1998), Consumers Union (1995) considers these activities as »corporate-sponsored contests and incentive programs« and education scholars separate these activities in two categories, »sponsorship of programs and activities« and »incentive programs« (Molnar and Morales 2000). Incentive programs involve providing discounted or free products at local businesses for meeting certain educational goals. For instance, children in the Washington, DC area with good grades receive discounts or free products at several businesses including Athlete's Foot, Blockbuster, Chuck E. Cheese, Athletic USA, Chesapeake Bagel Bakery, Village Eye Center, and even Wintergreen Resort where honor roll students receive half-price ski lift tickets (Kelleher 2000). Pizza Hut provides coupons redeemable for a free personal pan pizza for students who reach their teacher's reading goals (Dodge 1998), and children with at least a »B« average in the Atlanta area are rewarded with an Eagle Card which is good for discounts at 13 local businesses including Burger King, Chick-fil-A, Smoothie King, Wendy's, and Subway (Dickerson 2001).

Related to incentive programs, corporations also offer contests and sponsor events for students and teachers. Contests often encourage participants to get involved with products and to use their skills to create award-winning essays, recipes, and the like. According to McNeal (1992), through these activities, corporations benefit in several ways including stronger band/seller identity by requiring children to concentrate on the brand or logo as well as positive image-building of businesses with parents, teachers, and school officials as a result of the company's »interest« in children. Contests include the »teacher of the year« sponsored by Walt Disney Co. in which local winners are greeted by Mickey Mouse and other Disney characters at their hometown Disney Store, and the »Block the sun, not the fun« poster contest sponsored by Coppertone sun-tan lotion (Bowler 1998). Some contests involve more direct ties to the product such as Chips Ahoy! which had student confirm that there really were 1,000 chocolate chips in every bag of cookies or Kellogg's which had students create sculptures from Rice Krispies and melted butter (Labi 1999).

Some schools have built corporate relationships with different companies in exchange for equipment and training. These activities would be considered »indirect advertising« by the GAO report (2000) and a form of »electronic marketing« by education scholars (Molnar and Morales 2000). Major computer companies have donated computer equipment and advice to schools across the country; Apple Computer donated more the $8 million in equipment and advice in 1990 alone (Larson 1991). In 1996, Sun Microsystems coordinated »Net Day« in California where about 200 companies and 20,000 volunteers worked together to wire public schools in California for Internet access (Stead 1997). More recently, corporations such as Hewlett-Packard, Gateway, American Online, and Cisco Systems committed donations of Internet access, hardware and construction of computer labs in schools with low-income children in response to the digital divide. While this gesture builds goodwill for these companies, the underlying reasons for such corporate involvement is called into question when children are dressed in T-shirts reading »Cicso Systems and Costao School« and sing a song praising its corporate sponsor at a media event (Colie 2000 as cited in Molnar and Morales 2000).

PRODUCTS SALES

From candy sales in school bookstores and vending machines to fundraising for the school band, students have purchased and sold products on school property or for school activities. The sale of commercial products has become standard practice in many schools across the country and has lead to the privatization of school lunch-rooms and exclusive contracts with soft drink manufacturers. While Consumers Union did not consider this as a part of commercial activities in schools, researchers in education, communication and authors of the GAO report identify product sales and fundraising activities as examples of the growing commercialization of schools.

One practice that is recognized by the GAO report (2000) and communication scholars (Richards et al 1998) is the practice of the privatization of school lunch-rooms. This involves allowing fast food vendors to provide food service within the school cafeteria. For example, Taco Bell sells in or delivers to 3,000 schools nation-wide. Pizza Hut's products are sold in more than 4,500 schools (Jacobson 1995). A recent survey of California schools indicated that more than half of the 345 schools that responded had brand-name fast food in their cafeteria including Taco Bell, Subway and Domino's Pizza (Magge 2000). With the increase in childhood obesity, concerns about the availability of fast food in schools has been called into question.

Privatization and exclusive contracts extend beyond the cafeteria. A number of school districts have signed exclusive contracts with soft drink vendors to allow only one vendor on school property. This practice is labeled as »exclusive agreements« by education scholars (Molnar and Morales 2000) and is incorporated into product sales by communication scholars (Wartella and Jennings 2001). A school district in Seattle signed an exclusive, five-year contract with Coca-cola which generated $330,000 in revenue for student activities among 20 schools in 2000 (Ervin 2001). Another school district in Colorado Springs signed a 10-year, $8 million contract with Coca-cola in August of 1997 with an additional $3 million guaranteed if the district sold 70,000 cases of Coke products during one of the first three years (White, Ruskin, Mokhiber, & Weissman 1999). The contract calls for a yearly consumption of 1.68 million bot-tles of Coke products (Labi 1999). After one year into the contract, the District had consumed only 21,000 cases, falling short of expected sales (White, Ruskin, Mokhi-ber, & Weissman 1999). In order to meet consumption demands of the contract, a dis-trict administrator wrote a memo to area principals advising them to allow Coke products in the classroom, and to place vending machines in easily accessible areas (Labi 1999). Other suggestions by the district administrator include circumventing school rules that prohibit carbonated vending machines to be on during lunchtime by moving such machines »outside the meal service area« (White, Ruskin, Mokhiber,

& Weissman 1999). Recently, however, Coca-cola announced a change in their policies towards schools. These changes include encouraging local bottlers to no longer require exclusive beverage contracts with school districts, offering more juices, water and sugar-free, caffeine-free and calcium-rich beverages, installing vending machines without as much commercial signage, and urging bottlers to »unconditionally honor« the wishes of schools to refrain from beverage sales at certain times during the day or in certain locations (Unger and Paul 2001).

A variation on direct product sales is the growth of school fundraising activities by which children serve as a sales force to generate revenue for school bands, sports groups and technology. While the GAO report categorizes this activity under a general heading of »product sales«, education scholars (Molnar and Morales 2000) and communication scholars (Richards et al 1998) alike separate this activity into its own category. Students sell candy, frozen pizzas, magazine subscriptions, and gift wrap to help raise funds for school activities (Bower 1996). According to Vickie Mabry, an official with the Association of Fund Raisers and Direct Sellers, US K-12 schools raise about $1.5 billion through fund raising activities (Kittredge 2000). Class time was interrupted in a Missouri elementary school to teach children how to sell frozen pizzas for a fund raising activity (Bower 1996). Not only are students selling products, but they are also engaging in a variety of other fund raising events such as raffles and auctions. For example, an elementary school in California hosts a silent auction where local businesses and artisans donate goods and services to raise funds for the technology and enrichment program. Each classroom of children made items for the auction including stained-glass sun catchers, bedroom furniture that was sanded and decorated by first and second graders, and handmade quilts with squares that were made by kindergartners (McKinley 2001). One high school in Missouri had a raffle for a 1963 Corvette (Gerry 1998). One school even rented its softball field to a production company to shoot an episode of »Melrose Place« (USGAO 2000). The rental of school property would be considered an »appropriation of space« by education scholars (Molnar and Morales 2000).

MARKET RESEARCH

Recently, schools have been getting involved in market research as a source of income. The GAO report (2000) considers market research a separate category including activities as student questionnaires, taste tests, and tracking students' Internet behavior, whereas education scholars consider this practice an »appropriation of space« since school facilities are used for commercial activities (Molnar and Morales 2000).

Students engage in product testing and survey research for companies such as McDonald's and Toys R Us. Schools can earn anywhere from $800 to a few thousand dollars for each market research project (Farber 1999). ZapMe! engaged in market research by collecting demographic information on the student users and tracking their Internet use. Each student completed a user profile including the student's age, sex, and zip code. When the students used the computers, they would have logged-in with their password and the tracking began. Although this data was collected and shared with advertisers as an aggregate, ZapMe! did offer a program called ZapPoints in which students could acquire points toward prizes while the company gathered personally identifiable information about them (Schwartz 2000).

UNIQUE CATEGORIES: PRIVATIZATION

One practice that has a specialized category by education scholars is the privatization of schools. According to Molnar and Morales (2000), privatization involves the »management of public schools, especially charter schools, by private for-profit corporations or other nonpublic entities« (p. 2). One example of this is Chris Whittle's Edison Project. As an extension of Channel One, Whittle Communications entered the business of school administration with the establishment of for-profit schools. With the promise of improving the country's educational system while cutting costs, Chris Whittle developed and implemented a plan to run schools like a business. The results of the Edison Project are mixed. Whittle reported that students in Edison schools show measurable improvements in reading and math when compared to their scores on earlier tests and with the scores of students with similar backgrounds within the same school districts (Steinberg 1997). A later report indicated that students in Edison schools outperform students in other schools on state and national tests with an average gain of 5 percentage points (Lewin 1999). Yet, controversy has surrounded the studies of Edison school performance with charges of odd reporting procedures of academic achievement (Lewin 1999) and questionable practices in some schools including physical restraint of young children (Farber 1998).

CASE STUDIES

ELECTRONIC MARKETING PRACTICES

Commercial practices have begun to turn high-tech in the Information Age. Door-to-door fund raising sales have been replaced with Internet shopping. For instance, one school district in Canada had accepted money from Pepsi with the understanding that computer screen savers in the lab would carry the Pepsi logo with the message: »develop a thirst for knowledge« (Jenkins 1999). School computer screens display advertisements and a software company that is supposed to screen Internet sites for schools is tracking the Internet use of the children it is supposed to protect. This section will focus on some of the most recent uses of technology to engage in practices of commercialization in education.

The first practice discussed previously involves the exchange of equipment for a captive audience. ZapMe! had followed in the footsteps of Channel One, extending the offer of access to educational material for eyeballs and mouse trails. Over a three-year period from 1998 to 2000, nearly 2,000 schools had received nearly 25,000 computers (Bell 2000). However, as a result of negative attention to their practices, Zap-Me! announced that it would no longer provide free computers and Internet access to schools. ZapMe!'s stock price fell from a high of $12.50 per share to a low of 96 cents in just one year (Bell 2000). The majority of the company's shares were purchased by Gilate Satellite Networks, and the company has decided to focus on fee-based services to businesses rather than schools. Founder and CEO Lance Mortensen said it was too risky for shareholders to continue to serve schools, especially in light of proposed legislation regarding commercial practices in schools (Bell 2000).

Similar market research practices have been found with a company that provides filtering software for schools. N2H2, a Seattle-based company, contracts with schools to block unwanted material from the district's Internet connections and partners with the New York market research firm of Roper Starch to sell aggregate information of children's online habits (Brown 2001). According to the company's reports, N2H2 provides filtering for more than 11 million students across the country (Brown 2001). Material deemed inappropriate includes web sites that provide pornographic images, profanity, chatrooms and gambling (»Net Filter« 1999). Additionally, N2H2 had been offering the filtering for free to schools who would allow banner advertisements on the bottom of the computer screens; however, according to N2H2, that had not been profitable and was planned to be phased out by the end of 2001 (Brown 2001).

Fundraising has gone high-tech with Internet-based purchasing schemes where schools get a portion of online purchases made by family and friends. After logging on at Schoolpop.com, schools can earn money with every parent's purchase from some of the Internet's most frequented stores, including Amazon.com and eToys.com. At Electronic scrip (escripinc.com), parents and other web-users make donations to schools by registering their credit card numbers with the company; every time a purchase is made with the registered card, a percentage of the purchase price goes to the designated school (Wykes 1999). Another web site, kickstart.com, offers revenue for groups when site visitors click merchant or advertising links, use the search engine or buy online (Everitt 1999).

PUBLIC POLICY AND COMMERCIAL PRACTICES IN SCHOOLS

Despite the growing concerns regarding commercialism in the schools, public policy often falls behind public practice. Very little legislation exists concerning marketing practices and advertising in schools. At the national level, U.S. Representative George Miller introduced a bill in 1999 to ban the collection of any information in school from any student under the age of 18 for commercial purposes without the written consent from parents (Pollak 1999). This bill, known as the Student Privacy Protection Act, was established to protect children from commercial exploitation as market research subjects, but does not impinge on corporate donations to schools or fundraising activities. Marketing firms and associations indicated their objections to such legislation stating that many firms already require parental consent for surveys of children. The Marketing Research Association, an organization representing more than 3,000 opinion and marketing research firms worldwide, has a membership code that says children under 12 should not be surveyed without the documented consent of parents (Frahm 2001).

Although this bill failed, it did result in a national study of commercial activities in school and public policies regarding these activities conducted by the U.S. General Accounting Office. Results of this study indicate that decisions regarding commercial practices in schools are often left in the hands of local school officials since no national laws and only a few state laws specifically address these activities. Nationwide, only general laws and regulations that apply to all businesses or that govern school finance cover school-based commercial activities, and very few states have any regulations regarding specific commercial activities in schools (USGAO 2000). At the state-level, only 19 states have statues or regulations that specifically address school-related commercial activities, but that these laws are not comprehensive. Of these 19 states, 18 states have regulations covering direct advertising, 7 states cover product sales, and only 2 states address indirect advertising in schools such as curricular involvement (USGAO 2000). State educational codes do not specifically address school-based market research, but student privacy laws prohibit many of these activities, such as the selling of student personal information (name, address, and phone number). Furthermore, while it is true that some states have regulated how advertising is conducted in schools, such efforts have hardly been uniform. For instance, New Mexico law allows advertising in and on school busses whereas Virginia regulation prohibits such practices. Florida law permits school boards to establish policies regarding fundraising in schools, whereas New York regulations prohibit commercial activities on school grounds (USGAO 2000).

With the disparity in state regulations of commercial activities and the lack of federal regulation, a second push for federal laws regarding commercial activities in school has been broached in Congress again this year. Senators Patrick Leahy (D – Vt.) and Tom Harkin (D – Iowa) plan to introduce legislation that would give the Agriculture Department authority to restrict beverage and snack sales before and during lunch periods (Unger and Paul 2001). This bill would apply to any schools that participate in the National School Lunch Program (McKay 2001). Furthermore, U.S. Senator Christopher Dodd (D – Conn.) and Senator Richard Shelby (R – Ala.) have announced plans to reintroduce the Student Privacy Protection Act as an attachment to changes in federal education laws being sought by President George W. Bush (Teinowitz 2001). Marketing groups are concerned that this legislation may pass given the President's interest in educational policy. However, the results of these efforts and potential policies are yet to be seen.

CONCLUSION

American children live in a commercial society. Commercial strategies have focused on youth as their importance as a current, future, and influence market has grown. Marketing practices now cross many boundaries, even into children's educational experiences. Through direct advertising, indirect advertising, product sales, market research, and privatization, corporate involvement in America's public schools has been on the rise. American schools often face a shortage of funds to provide educational materials and technology for their students. In the face of ever-shrinking school budgets, schools must turn to outside funding for support; however, this support often comes with a price. The commercialization of schools is a double-edged sword, providing materials and technology to schools while exposing them to more advertising and corporate sponsorship. There is no easy solution. However, parents, teachers, administrators, legislators and the industry must work together to address these concerns and create a legitimate response to this growing phenomenon.

REFERENCES

Bazeley, M. (1999). »ZapMe! school role debated: Students get computers; advertisers get a market!«, [Online] In *Silicon Valley News,* 21 March, Available: http://www.mercurycenter.com/svtech/news/indepth/docs/zapme032299.htm (1999-March-23).

Bell, Elizabeth (2000). »Schools lament loss of PCs; Politics persuade firm to pull out«, *The San Francisco Chronicle,* 7 December, p. A19.

Bower, Carolyn (1996). »Higher math: Student fund raising aids school budgets«, *St. Louis Post-Dispatch,* 23 September, p. 1A.

Bowler, Mike (1998). »Firms leave brand on schools; Children's vast spending power attracts«, *Austin American-Statesman,* 28 June, p. A26.

Brown, Marilyn (2001). »Schools' net nanny mines student data for profit«, *The Tampa Tribune,* 15 January, p. 1.

Colie, Z. (2000). »Clinton: Fight poverty with tech«, *San Francisco Examiner,* 18 April, p. A1.

Consumers Union (1995). *Captive Kids: Commercial pressures on kids at school.* Yonkers, NY: Consumers Union Education Services.

Dickerson, Ann (2001). »Students reaping academic rewards«, *The Atlanta Journal and Constitution,* 3 May, p. 1JQ.

Dodge, Susan (1998). »Advertisements adding up in local schools«, *Chicago Sun Times,* 27 December, p. 1.

Ervin, Keith (2001). »Schools expel Channel One. New policy also limits advertisements, logos«, *The Seattle Times,* 22 November, p. B1.

Everitt, Lisa Greim (1999). »Web site helps kids raise funds for school; company provides online alternative to car washes, candy sales«, *Denver Rocky Mountain News,* 4 September, p. 2B.

Farber, Peggy J. (1998, March). »The Edison Project scores – in Boston«, *Phi Delta Kappan,* Vol. 79, No. 7, pp. 506-511.

Frahm, Robert A. (2001). »Dodd bill would limit market research on kids«, *The Hartford Courant,* 9 February, p. A13.

Gaines, Judith (2000). »Oreos and M&M's? Learning tools«, *The Boston Globe,* 23 January, p. B1.

Gerry, Sarah (1998). »Red corvette convertible is grand prize in raffle to raise funds for school field«, *St. Louis Post-Dispatch,* 16 November, p. 8.

Glasmer, Deeann (1997). »This class is brought to you by …«, *USA Today,* 3 January, p. 3A.

Hays, Constance L. (1999). »Math book salted with brand names raises new alarm«, *New York Times,* 21 March, pp. 1 and 28.

Hegarty, Stephen (1999). »Brand names crop up in texts«, *St. Petersburg Times,* 5 April, p. 1B.

Jacobson, Michael F. (1995). »Now there's a fourth R: Retailing«, *New York Times,* 29 January, p. F9.

Jenkins, L. (1999). »Advertisers use schools to Zap! Kids«, *San Diego Union-Tribune,* 8 January, pp. B-3:1,6,7, and 8.

Jimenez, Ralph (1997). »Freebies in schools get mixed reaction«, *The Boston Globe,* 19 October, p. 1.

Kelleher, Elizabeth (2000). »Good deals as Easy as A-B-C; Some stores will let you cash in on your report card«, *The Washington Post,* 3 November, p. C13.

Kittredge, Clare (2000). »New Hampshire weekly; Alarms sounded on commercials in schools«, *The Boston Globe,* 8 October, p. 1.

Labi, Nadya (1999). »Classrooms for Sale«, *Time,* 19 April, Vol. 153, No. 15, pp. 44–45.

Larson, Jan (1991). »Computers in school can be habit forming«, *American Demographics,* October, Vol. 13, No. 10, p. 12.

Lewin, Tamar (1999). »Edison schools say students gain«, *The New York Times,* 7 April, p. B9.

Magee, Maureen (2000). »More schools ask students: 'Want fries with that?'«, *The San Diego Union-Tribune,* 17 February, p. A-1.

Maller, Peter (2000). »Advertising to young minds; Schools accepting more business ties, but some worry«, *Milwaukee Journal Sentinel,* 14 August, p. 01A.

McDonald, Marci, and Marianne Lavelle (2001). »Call it 'kid-fluence'« *U.S. News and World Report,* 30 July, Vol. 131, No. 4, p. 32.

McKay, Gretchen (2001). »Not too sweet coca-cola's decision to back off exclusive school pacts could crimp cash-starved districts' hopes of cashing in« *Pittsburgh Post-Gazette,* 7 April, p. C1.

McKinley, Shay K. (2001). »An art odyssey; School's auction items to raise funds for technology«, *The San Diego Union-Tribune,* 19 April, pp. NC-10; NI-4.

McNeal, James U. (1992). *Kids as customers: A handbook of marketing to children.* New York, NY: Lexington Books.

Molnar, Alex and Jennifer Morales (2000). »Commercialism@school«, *Educational Leadership,* October, Vol. 58, No. 2, available online: http://www.ascd.org/readingroom/edlead/0010/molnar.html

»Net filter N2H2 files with SEC for IPO«, *The Seattle Times,* p. E2.

Poe, Janita (2001). »Helping teens saving early; First jobs inspire some«, *The Atlanta Journal and Constitution,* 5 August, p. 5.

Pollak, M. (1999). »Notebook; Marketing in schools«, *The New York Times,* 29 September, p. 9B.

Primedia website. Available: http://www.primedia.com/html2/products.html.

Richards, Jef I. et al. (1998). »The Growing Commercialization of Schools: Issues and Practices«, *The Annals of the American Academy of Political and Social Science, 557,* pp. 148–163.

Schwartz, John (2000). »Offer of free computers for schools is withdrawn«, *The New York Times,* 2 November, p. 1C.

Stead, Deborah (1997). »Corporations, classrooms, and commercialism: Some say business has gone too far«, *The New York Times,* 5 January, Section 4A, pp. 30–33+.

Steinberg, Jacques (1997). »Edison project reports measurable progress in reading and math at its schools«, *The New York Times,* 17 December, p. B8.

Teinowitz, I. (2001). »Senators seek bill to protect privacy of kids; Marketers would need permission from parents to conduct surveys«, *Advertising Age,* 19 February, p. 35.

»This school is brought to you by: Cola? Sneakers?« (1998). *USA Today,* 27 March, p. 12A.

Unger, Henry and Peralte C. Paul (2001). »Coca-cola learns a lesson in schools; Nutrition is in, exclusivity is out in strategy shift«, *The Atlanta Journal and Constitution,* 14 March, p. 1A.

United States General Accounting Office (2000). *Commercial activities in schools (GAO Publication No. GAO/HEHS-00-156),* September. Washington, DC: Author.

Walsh, James (1993). »Radio music – and advertisements – at school; Hallways here and across U.S. will get satellite signal«, *Star Tribune,* 29 July, p. 1B.

Walters, Joan (1998). »ZapMe! stirs up educators: Controversial program supplies cash-strapped school boards with free computers in return for running advertisements and monitoring students«, *The Gazette (Montreal),* 30 December, p. D3.

Wartella, Ellen and Nancy Jennings (2001). »Hazards and Possibilities of Commercial TV in the Schools«, in eds. Dorothy G. Singer and Jerome L. Singer, *Handbook of Children and the Media.* Thousand Oaks, CA: Sage Publications.

Wells, Melanie (1996). »Advertisement pitches target teen consumers«, *USA Today,* 9 May, p. 1B.

White, Anna et al. (1999). »The Cola-ized classroom«, *Multinational Monitor,* Vol. 20, pp. 16-23.

Winters, Patricia (1995). »School Bells Ring for Advertisers«, *New York Daily News,* 1 June, p. 61.

Wolff, Christine (1996). »Schools know the score: Advertisers providing sports equipment, Money«, *Cincinnati Enquirer,* 1 December, p. B01.

Wykes, S.L. (1999). »Schools turn to Internet«, [Online] In *Silicon Valley News,* 27 June. Available: http://www.mercurycenter.com/svtech/news/ (1999-June28).

ABOUT THE AUTHORS

JOËL BRÉE is professor at the University of Caen and Head of the Marketing Department at Rouen Graduate School of Management, France. He is a board member of the French Marketing Association (AFM), the Editorial Board of *Recherche et Applications en Marketing*, of the Editorial Advisory Board of *International Journal of Advertising and Marketing to Children*, and the Academic Advisory Board of the Advertising Education Forum (AEF). He has published several articles about children as consumers and is the author of the book *Les enfants, la consommation et le marketing* published in 1993.

MERRIE BRUCKS is Eller Professor of Marketing with a joint appointment in the Department of Psychology at the University of Arizona, USA. Dr. Brucks teaches undergraduate, graduate and postgraduate courses with teaching specialties in advertising, consumer behavior and research methods. Her research explores consumer information search, learning, evaluation, and consumer choises for both children and adults. She has published her research in the field's top journals, including the *Journal of Consumer Research, Journal of Marketing Research, Journal of Consumer Psychology* and *Journal of Public Policy*. She currently serves on the Editorial Board of the Journal of Consumer Research, after recently completing her term as Associate Editor of the journal. She is very active in the Association of Consumer Research, where her contributions have included co-chairing the major conference, editing the proceedings, and serving on the Board of Directors of Treasurer.

CHRISTIAN DERBAIX is professor and Head of the marketing department at the Catholic University of Mons (FUCaM), Belgium. His research interests focus on the measurement of affective reactions elicited by commercials, the study of children's consumer behavior, the symbolic consumption of Material Possessions by Soccer Fans, and the effectiveness of sponsorship. Dr. Derbaix's work has been published in the *Journal of Marketing Research*, the *International Journal of Research in Marketing*, the *Journal of Economic Psychology*, the *Scandinavian Journal of Psychology*, *Recherche et Applications en Marketing* and elsewhere. From 2002 until 2004, he is also President of the French Marketing Association (Association Française du Marketing).

CECILIA VON FEILITZEN, Ph.D., is Senior Researcher in Media and Communication Science at University College of Södertörn, Sweden. She is also Scientific Coordinator of The UNESCO International Clearinghouse on Children and Violence on the Screen, at Nordicom, Goteborg University, Sweden. As a media researcher since 1964, Cecilia von Feilitzen has published more than 150 research reports, articles, and books – of which many are international publications. A great deal of her research has been devoted to children and media.

DAN FREEMAN is Assistant Professor of Marketing and Information Technology at the University of Delaware, USA. He teaches a variety of courses at the graduate and undergraduate levels, including Principles of Marketing, Information Technology Applications in Marketing, and Marketing Issues for New Ventures. Dr. Freeman's primary research focus involves investigating the impact of the social information contained in media imagery on consumers' socio-cultural brand associations.

ADRIAN FURNHAM is Professor of Psychology at University College London where he has taught for 22 years. He is a graduate of four universities and holds three doctorates and three masters degrees. Author of 36 books and 500 peer reviewed papers he has wide interests in applied psychology. He is a chartered Health and Occupational Psychologist and does many consultancy assignments. He has just finished a book on management incompetence and is writing another on lying, stealing and cheating in the workplace. He has also just written a book on alcohol advertising to young people. He rides to work on a bicycle and thinks of himself as a well adjusted workaholic.

JENS HALLING, M.Sc. is research assistant at Forum for Advertising Research, Department of Marketing, Copenhagen Business School, Denmark. He has written several papers in areas ranging from children as consumers to sponsoring and effects of advertising. He is co-author of the book *Danish Children's Upbringing as Consumers* (Samfundslitteratur, 2002).

FLEMMING HANSEN, Ekon.dr. is professor at the Department of Marketing and Forum for Advertising Research, Copenhagen Business School, Denmark. He is also the Director of Development, Gallup A/S (part of Taylor Nelson Sofres) and is on the Editorial Board for several international journals. He has written more than 80 articles in international journals, published several books on consumer behavior, marketing research and communication and is co-author of the book *Danish Children's Upbringing as Consumers* (Samfundslitteratur, 2002).

NANCY JENNINGS, Ph.D., is a post-doctoral research associate and lecturer at the University of Texas at Austin, College of Communication, USA, and has recently taken a position as a Visiting Assistant Professor at the University of Michigan, Department of Communication Studies, Ann Arbor, Michigan, USA. Her research focuses on the impact of media on children and in particular how computers and the Internet impact on the lives of children and families. She has served as a Graduate Research Assistant for the National Television Violence Study, which monitored violence on American television for three years, has co-authored six book chapters and journal articles, and has presented at 5 academic conferences.

DEBORAH ROEDDER JOHN is professor and Curtis L. Carlson Chair in Marketing at the Carlson School of Management, University of Minnesota, USA. She is an expert in consumer behavior, with an emphasis on children's consumer behavior and consumer branding. She has published extensively in marketing journals, including the *Journal of Consumer Research*, the *Journal of Marketing Research*, and *Journal of Marketing*. She has served on the editorial boards of these journals as well as the *Journal of Consumer Psychology* and the *Journal of Public Policy & Marketing*. She is a past-president of the Association for Consumer Research, past associate-editor of the *Journal of Consumer Research*, and founding editor of the Monographs of the *Journal of Consumer Research*.

ANNE MARTENSEN, Ph.D. is associate professor at the Department of Marketing and is associated with Forum for Advertising Research, Copenhagen Business School, Denmark. Her main areas of research are advertising and consumer behaviour, and particularly children and advertising, modeling and measuring customer and employee satisfaction and loyalty, innovation management and new product development. She is also co-author of the book *Danish Children's Upbringing as Consumers* (Samfundslitteratur, 2002).

JENS CARSTEN NIELSEN, M.Sc. is director of Forum for Advertising Research, Department of Marketing, Copenhagen Business School, Denmark. He is engaged in several projects involving the media-, advertising-, entertainment and consumer goods industries. His main areas of interest are advertising effectiveness, branding and consumer research. He is also co-author of the book *Danish Children's Upbringing as Consumers* (Samfundslitteratur, 2002).

WHITON S. PAINE, Ph.D. is Associate Professor of Business Studies at the Richard Stockton College of New Jersey, USA. He teaches consumer behavior, electronic marketing, and market research at the graduate and undergraduate levels as well as business ethics to undergraduates. Whiton also trains medical and surgical residents in research methods and is a Principal in KID2KID, a marketing research firm specializing in the qualitative analysis of the consumer behavior of minors. His primary research interests include the study of ethical issues raised by marketing to children and youth and the influence of oriental celadon on modern pottery and porcelain.

BIRGITTE TUFTE, Dr. (Media Literacy), is associate professor and director of Secretariat of Children's Culture Network at the Danish University of Education, Copenhagen, Denmark. She is head of a research project, financed by the Danish Research Council: »Girl's and boy's everyday life and media culture«. She is a member of various boards and commissions regarding media policy and children and has been working with research regarding children, adolescents and media for more than 20 years. She has published a great number of books and articles – of which many are international publications.

BRIAN YOUNG, Ph.D is lecturer in the School of Psychology at the University of Exeter in England. His main areas of research are in children and advertising. Young has written several books and academic papers and is the author of *Television Advertising and Children* published by Oxford University Press in 1990. He is currently co-editing *Faces of Televisual Media: Teaching, Violence, Selling to Children* with Professor Ed Palmer which will be published by Erlbaum in 2002. Brian is chair of the Academic Advisory Board of the Advertising Education Forum (www.aeforum.org) and sits on the Advertising Advisory Committee of the Independent Television Commission (ITC) in the UK.

* * * * * * * * * * * * * * *